Perspectives: From Adult Literacy to Continuing Education

Perspectives: From Adult Literacy to Continuing Education

Alice M. Scales, Senior Editor, University of Pittsburgh
Joanne E. Burley, Editor, Chatham College

 Wm. C. Brown Publishers

Book Team

Editor *Paul Tavenner*
Developmental Editor *Ann Shaffer*
Production Coordinator *Deborah Donner*

 Wm. C. Brown Publishers

President *G. Franklin Lewis*
Vice President, Publisher *George Wm. Bergquist*
Vice President, Publisher *Thomas E. Doran*
Vice President, Operations and Production *Beverly Kolz*
National Sales Manager *Virginia S. Moffat*
Advertising Manager *Ann M. Knepper*
Marketing Manager *Craig S. Marty*
Editor-in-Chief *Edward G. Jaffe*
Managing Editor, Production *Colleen A. Yonda*
Production Editorial Manager *Julie A. Kennedy*
Production Editorial Manager *Ann Fuerste*
Publishing Services Manager *Karen J. Slaght*
Manager of Visuals and Design *Faye M. Schilling*

Cover design by Dale Rosenbach.

Printed in the United States of America by Wm. C. Brown Publishers,
2460 Kerper Boulevard, Dubuque, IA 52001

10 9 8 7 6 5 4 3 2 1

dedication

To those who believe that achievement of literacy will make a difference in the lives of people throughout the world.

To the Scales family: Eller—Lorenzo, Zeela, Cerone; Gracie—George, Gerald; Verlenia—John, Michael, William, John Jr., Robert; Goldie—Octavia, Kelly; Joe Jr.—Sean; and my parents, Lennie and Joe.

To the Burley family: Jack Sr., Diana, Jack Jr., and my parents, Elmer and Josephine Cobb.

table of contents

foreword

In 1990 the United Nations launched International Literacy Year. With walls coming down all over the world, educators are challenged to empower all people with the basic skills they need to function effectively in their environs. To meet the challenge, Scales and Burley have provided us with a broad range of philosophical, psychological, sociological, and economical perspectives that address literacy and continuing education. Such is evidenced by the contributors who have rich backgrounds in many arenas (e.g., colleges, universities, military, industry, communities) where literacy is being addressed today.

Literacy is a global concern. Clearly, illiteracy presents every country with tremendous human and social problems. To solve these problems, "literacy providers" must acknowledge that literacy is more than the ability of individuals to read and write. Literacy sets the stage for empowerment and opens the door to further opportunities for education and training. I am pleased to see chapters from leaders whose international experience can help readers understand how educators in other countries and other contexts are addressing issues that affect all people.

During my twenty years of involvement with literacy education, I have learned the importance of being sensitive to perspectives from academia, government, nongovernment, and business. This volume captures that sensitivity. Likewise, I believe it will make readers more aware of the issues under discussion. Specifically, I believe readers will benefit from this well-balanced exposure to literacy education as well as to the problems and solutions currently under discussion among educators, administrators, researchers, practitioners, and others. Alice M. Scales and JoAnne E. Burley have given us a book that will be helpful to anyone who is involved in the literacy movement today. I am pleased to add it to my collection and I look forward to sharing it with my adult literacy and continuing education colleagues throughout the world.

Jane L. Evanson, President (1989–1990)
American Association for Adult and Continuing Education

preface

This volume is based on the premise that adults (urban and rural dwellers, rich and poor, employed, underemployed, and unemployed) want to remain productive their entire lives. It has been designed for college students and instructors; educators, researchers, and administrators of adult education programs; personnel in adult education programs; and others worldwide who are interested in adult literacy and continuing education. As this anthology is read, the reader will learn what experts from various disciplines have to say about challenges, beliefs, endeavors, accomplishments, and outlooks for adult literacy and continuing education.

Herein literacy has been examined from philosophical, psychological, sociological, and economical perspectives. Philosophy, in this volume, has reference to the underlying developments of literacy in that it is inherent in the total educational milieu. Psychology has reference to the influence of human behaviors upon selected populations in literacy education. Sociology has reference to how literacy programs, in part, have changed the lives of adults who are in transition. Economics has reference to the funding aspects and costs of adult literacy programs. The four perspectives are to be viewed as aspects of life. Each suggests parameters whereby issues of literacy education have been examined from various countries in the world. Each chapter is meant to be one of provocation rather than of resolve. Challenges are to consider the perspectives and to relate content from the chapters contained therein to a more immediate environment.

Alice M. Scales
JoAnne E. Burley

list of contributors

Senior Editor

Alice M. Scales, Ed.D., Associate Professor & Coordinator of Reading Education, University of Pittsburgh

Editor

JoAnne E. Burley, Ph.D., Associate Professor of Education, Assistant Vice-President of Academic Affairs & Director of Adult Literacy Program, Chatham College

Foreword

Jane L. Evanson, Ph.D., Professor of Education, Alaska Pacific University and Past President of the American Association for Adult and Continuing Education

Authors of Chapters

Donna D. Amstutz, Ed.D., Assistant Professor & Director of the Adult Education Research-to-Practice Office, Northern Illinois University

Clinton L. Anderson, Ed.D., Lieutenant Colonel, United States Army (retired) & Senior consultant for the American Association for State Colleges and Universities

Vincenne Revilla Beltran, Ph.D., Associate Professor in Human Resources, Assistant to the President for Special Projects & Associate Dean of Student Development, Point Park College

Shirley A. Biggs, Ed.D, Associate Professor of Reading Education, University of Pittsburgh

H. S. Bhola, Ph.D., Professor of Education, Indiana University & Consultant to UNESCO and the German Foundation for International Development

Robert K. Branson, Ph.D., Professor & Director of the Center for Educational Technology, Florida State University

Mary Newton Bruder, Ph.D., ESL/Linguistics Specialist, Chatham College

Joanne E. Burley, Ph.D., Associate Professor of Education, Assistant Vice-President of Academic Affairs, & Director of Adult Literacy Program, Chatham College

James F. Condell, Ed.D., Professor of Psychology, Moorehead State University

Theresa Cronan, Ed.D., Instructor of Reading & Administrative Assistant in the College of Education, University of Arkansas

William E. Gardner, Jr., Ph.D., President, Savannah State College

Laura Ginyard, Reading Specialist, Youth Development Center in East Palo Alto, CA

James C. Hall, Jr., Ed.D., Vice-President for Special Programs and External Affairs, York College/City University of New York

Dolores M. Harris, Ed.D., Acting Associate Vice-President for Academic Affairs, Glassboro State College

Rhonda L. Harvey, Ph.D., Associate Professor of Reading and Adult Education, University of Arkansas

Asa G. Hilliard, III, Ed.D., Fuller E. Callaway Professor of Urban Education, Georgia State University

Mary Rhodes Hoover, Ph.D., Professor of Black Studies/Black Literature and Language Skills, San Francisco State University

Debra A. Kilmek-Suchla, Fiscal Manager, Western Wisconsin Private Industry Council

William E. Kofmehl, Jr., Ph.D., Executive Director, Christian Literacy Associates/Allegheny County Literacy Council, Pittsburgh, PA

R. Grann Lloyd, Ph.D., Research Professor & Chairman of the Division of Studies in Economics and Business, University of North Florida

Emma T. Lucas, Ph.D., Adjunct Assistant Professor of Human Service Administration & Associate Vice-President for Academic Affairs, Chatham College

Irving J. McPhail, Ed.D., President, LeMoyne-Owen College

Larry Milulecky, Ph.D., Professor of Education & Director of Learning Skills Center, Indiana University

Karen R. Norton, Development Consultant, Laubach Literacy International

Rosemarie J. Park, Ed.D., Associate Professor of Education, University of Minnesota

F. C. Richardson, Ph.D., President, State University College at Buffalo

Hope B. Richardson, Ed.D., Associate Professor of Education and Reading, Bronx Community College of the City University of New York

Amy D. Rose, Ed.D., Assistant Professor of Adult and Continuing Education, Northern Illinois University

Jovita M. Ross-Gordon, Ed.D., Assistant Professor of Education, The Pennsylvania State University

T. A. Ryan, Ph.D., Professor & Director of Criminal Justice Planning, Implementation, and Evaluation, University of South Carolina

Alice M. Scales, Ed.D., Associate Professor & Coordinator of Reading Education, University of Pittsburgh

Claire V. Sibold, Ph.D., Associate Professor & Chair Education Department, Biola University

Susana M. Sotillo, Assistant Professor of Linguistics, Montclair State College

Cecile M. Springer, President of Westinghouse Foundation and Director of Community Affairs for Westinghouse Electric Corporation (retired)

Lawrence B. Zikri, Ph.D., Assistant Professor, Education Department, Bahrain University, State of Bahrain, Egypt

Philosophical Perspectives

Philosophy is inherent in all that people do. It influences beginnings or initiatives, understandings, personality developments, belief systems, relationships, and so forth. Philosophy is not an isolated field; it merges easily with other academic areas of study. Moreover, philosophers have merged with psychologists to explore and explain phenomena as they relate to educating adults and children. That educating has been examined through such philosophical viewpoints as (*a*) a *liberalist* whose view is that good comes from within oneself and education is the tool to release it; (*b*) a *humanist* whose view is that people are inherently good and with an education, albeit not a formal education, each has the power for obtaining a good life; (*c*) a *behaviorist* whose view is that an individual's personality and character are the product of his/her total experience, which includes education; and (*d*) a *pragmatist* whose view is that one's education is a means of freedom from confusion and ignorance.

The viewpoints presented in the previous paragraph describe a frame of reference that suggests that literacy education causes good in the lives of people. Education that has advanced such goodness has been advanced through adult literacy efforts. To learn about this education and goodness in adult literacy, we asked the question, How can students of adult literacy learn about such education for goodness in the lives of people? Our answer is to study the chapters that focus on how UNESCO's global commitment has advanced literacy (see Bhola); how literacy began (see Hilliard); how countries have campaigned against illiteracy (see Amstutz); how literacy education has become more evident in selected African countries (see Lucas); how literacy is perceived in Senegal and Egypt (see Scales & Zikri); how literacy evolved in the U.S. (see Rose); how intergenerational relationships can teach the importance of an education (see Sibold); and how industry has involved itself in efforts to improve literacy (see Klimek-Suchla).

Initiatives of UNESCO in Adult Literacy Education

H. S. Bhola

United Nations Educational, Scientific and Cultural Organization (UNESCO), today, is the world's conscience keeper as the nations around the world move haltingly toward implementing the ideal of universal literacy. UNESCO adopted literacy as the central theme of its programming from its very inception in 1946 when hardly a country had put adult literacy on its educational agenda. Some forty-five years later, UNESCO led in the commemoration of International Literacy Year, 1990 (*World Charter on Education . . .* 1989). Jointly with the United Nations Development Programme (UNDP), the United Nations Children's Fund (UNICEF), and The World Bank, UNESCO cosponsored the World Conference on Education for All (WC-EFA) held in Jomtien, Thailand, during March 5–9, 1990. This conference had hoped that all the world's nations that came to gather in Thailand would agree upon the following planning targets for the year 2000.

Primary Education: Each country would strive to ensure that at least 80 percent of all fourteen-year-old boys and girls attain a common level of learning achievement for primary education, set by the respective national authorities.

Adult Education: Access to basic skills and knowledge for all.

Literacy: Massive reduction of illiteracy with targets to be set by each country prioritized by age and sex (Inter-agency Commission 1989).

These are certainly bold initiatives in behalf of truly great ideals. However, to put things in a proper perspective, both the limitations and the possibilities of UNESCO's role in being an educational leader to the world must be stated before proceeding any further. UNESCO's limitations lie in the fact that it is an international organization, and not an instrument of a world government. None of UNESCO's resolutions are binding on its member states. All of UNESCO's policy initiatives must indeed be submitted anew to the political processes of each country. There they must be approved by policy-making organs of each member state before they become official policy, often in some adapted form.

In terms of resources, UNESCO is greatly limited. Its annual budget in a normal year would be no more than half the annual budget of a typical midwestern university in the U.S. Yet, exciting possibilities remain. UNESCO is indeed one of the most important policy makers that influences education, science, and culture on the world scene. Through dialogue and discussion, and sometimes by providing seed money for pilot projects, UNESCO has disseminated new theories and conceptualizations, new policy directions, and new methodologies of planning and research.

In this chapter the reader can explore literacy theories that have contributed to UNESCO's focus, polities and projects that have been supported by UNESCO, and various consequences of literacy. One hope is that the reader will generate questions as she/he reads this chapter and that the questions will serve as the bases for further in-depth study of UNESCO's literacy initiatives.

The Birth of a Commitment for Literacy

UNESCO is an international institution born of practical idealism. Having seen unnecessary death and destruction and senseless sufferings of millions during World War II, there was the need to mobilize the intellectual resources of the world in behalf of world peace. The governments of the states that were parties to the UNESCO constitution adopted in London on November 16, 1945, the following: "That since wars begin in the minds of men, it is in the minds of men that the defenses of peace must be constructed."

The battle, thus, was for the minds of men! In other words, UNESCO's strategy for peace was an educational-psychological strategy. It was by educating the minds of men that peace was to be defended and assured in perpetuity and the horrors of war avoided. Individual psyche was to be the theatre of peace. School children had to learn about peace, but adults had to learn about peace with an even greater urgency, for it was they who allowed wars to happen and they who went to fight the wars. That would mean *adult* education for those now out of school or bypassed by the school in the first place.

In the Third World, then and now, adult education could be equated with *adult literacy*. Illiteracy rates in the Third World have always been high, and even today 98 percent of the world's illiterates live in the Third World. The first director-general of UNESCO, Julian Huxley, had made the right connection between literacy and peace when he said that

> . . . where half the people of the world are denied the elementary freedom which consists in the ability to read and write, there lacks something of the basic unity and basic justice which the United Nations are pledged together to further. (cited in Hamadache 1989, 3 & 4)

Since then, the struggle against illiteracy has been on the agenda of UNESCO. Over the years, literacy has found many more justifications in UNESCO programming: as an instrument of mass education, social progress, and international understanding; and as a human right needing no outside justification (Jones 1988).

UNESCO's Theory of Literacy: Tension Between Psychological and Structural

The theory of literacy implied in UNESCO discussions and actions can be characterized as being essentially *psychological*. UNESCO documents do not, of course, directly argue about Goody's (1968) *technology of intellect* hypothesis that asserts that literacy (particularly writing) changes human intellect so much so that the new literates change their mentalities in regard to their modes of logic, abstraction, memory, and communication. Nor does one find in UNESCO's materials systematic theoretical discussions of Scribner and Cole's (1981) cautions about the Goody hypothesis, asserting that consequences of literacy may not be as general as earlier claimed but rather limited and contextual to social uses of literacy. It could be surmised, however, that UNESCO does not consider Scribner and Cole as serious challengers to Goody but merely as offering a sensible modification of his position. Literacy per se may not change the mentalities of people, but it does, nonetheless, significantly affect the habits of the mind in the specific social contexts of the uses of literacy.

Thus, UNESCO's theory of literacy could be seen as accepting the notion of literacy leading to some sort of individual modernity in the new learner (Inkeles & Smith 1974). It accepts that the new literate does become relatively more objective, more independent, and even more individualistic. This position is quite reasonable. Indeed, it is impossible to deny that literacy is "potential added" to the new literate so that the new literate is able to make more effective transactions within the *totality* of his or her environment—economic, social, political, informational, educational, and cultural (Bhola 1984b). But UNESCO cannot be satisfied with only a psychological theory of literacy. It has to have a complementary *structural* theory of literacy as well. In this policy-oriented world, literacy cannot be justified in terms of individual growth alone. It must be justified as a function of development. Development, in turn, is not just more wealth but more distribution of the wealth. Both modernization and democratization are considered equally important. This means that existing economic, social, and political structures must often be renovated, if not drastically changed.

This is where the tension between the psychological and the structural appears in UNESCO's theory of literacy. UNESCO must take the economic, social, and political structures of its member states as given. It cannot question existing political arrangements within its member states. It cannot preach that the oppressed overthrow the structures that oppress them. Irrespective of the institutional values of universalism to which UNESCO subscribes, it must serve both the U.S. and the USSR, Israel and Syria, Iran and Iraq, India and Pakistan, North Korea and South Korea, Libya and Chad, and everyone in between. Naturally, UNESCO has to define development in apolitical terms, hinting, but not stating. It must remain general and ambiguous, using economic, social, and cultural discourse that accommodates the relatives of socialism, capitalism, fascism, and plain barbarism. When the individual purposes and the purposes of the state are congruent in a nation, the tension between the psychological and the structural does not become apparent. However, when the state is not propeople or is insensitive to their immediate needs, the tension between the two levels of theory creates serious contradictions.

UNESCO's Policy on Literacy: 1946–1990

The tension inherent in UNESCO's theory of literacy reappears, understandably, in the policy initiatives that UNESCO promotes (Bhola 1984a, 1989). The language of literacy promotion may sound quite radical, but in implementation, most UNESCO-sponsored campaigns, programs, and projects have to be acceptable to the governors of the member states. International institutional arrangements being what they are, UNESCO is obliged to deal only with governments, and therefore, its projects do often end up serving state purposes more effectively than peoples' interests. Yet over the years 1946–1990, one can see that the language of UNESCO's policy discourse has moved from literacy as charity to literacy as the professionalization of labor, to literacy for the liberation of the human being. UNESCO does dare set objectives that seek to serve the interests of the disadvantaged, the marginalized, and the excluded.

While literacy had been embraced by UNESCO at its very inception in 1946, the love affair with literacy took time to heat up (Bhola 1989). The First International Conference on Adult Education held in Elsinore, Denmark, in 1949, was much allured by the new electronic media and thought that while literacy would be nice to have, literacy was not indispensable. Media, it was thought, could reach the illiterate in the meantime. By the time the Second International Conference on Adult Education met in Montreal in 1960, literacy had moved center stage, and the Montreal conference was asking for the establishment of a special fund for adult literacy promotion in the Third World. What the Third World got, however, was no special fund for a world campaign but the Experimental World Literacy Programme (EWLP) (UNESCO 1976). During the years 1966–1974, UNESCO with support from UNDP sponsored functional literacy projects in eleven countries: Algeria, Ecuador, Ethiopia, Guinea, India, Iran, Madagascar, Mali, Sudan, Syrian Arab Republic, and United Republic of Tanzania. The total expenditure was around U.S. $27,184,973; 40.6 percent of this was provided by UNDP and the rest by host governments. Some 1,028,381 adults (45 percent male, 55 percent female), whose average age was twenty-five years, were taught in 20,000 classes by 24,000 teachers. On average, 24 percent completed the final stage. Most classes had agricultural content.

In the Third International Conference on Adult Education in Tokyo in 1972, while delegates were impressed with the high-tech gadgets that had become available, they were also expressing discontent with the rather narrow work-oriented conception of literacy. The International Symposium for Literacy held in Persepolis, Iran, during 1975 heartily rejected the work-oriented conception of literacy. Instead of technical literacy, it proposed humanist literacy that would contribute to the liberation of individuals and to their full development (Bataille 1976).

In the most recent Fourth International Conference on Adult Education in Paris (*Final Report: . . .* 1985), the world adult educators had an even broader conception of literacy that included basic literacy, cultural literacy, and technological literacy. The Paris declaration that embodies these "literacies" is worth quoting in full:

The right to learn is:
> —the right to read and write;
> —the right to question and analyze;
> —the right to imagine and create;
> —the right to read one's own world and to write history;

—the right to have access to educational resources;

—the right to develop individual and collective skills . . .

The right to learn is an indispensable tool for the survival of humanity.

If we want the peoples of the world to be self-sufficient in food production and other essential human needs, they must have the right to learn.

If women and men are to enjoy better health, they must have the right to learn.

If we are to avoid war, we must learn to live in peace, and learn to understand one another.

"Learn" is the key word . . .

It is a fundamental human right whose legitimacy is universal . . . . (*Final Report: . . .* 1985, 67)

UNESCO's Field Projects Since EWLP

Since the EWLP of 1966–1974, that covered eleven countries, there has been a rather small activity on the part of UNESCO in regard to literacy promotion. Donor support for literacy has been small; withdrawal from UNESCO by the U.S. and the U.K. has not helped matters. A recent UNESCO report suggested that a dozen countries were receiving some UNESCO assistance, but those countries had not been listed. For these dozen countries receiving assistance, the scale and the nature of UNESCO's contribution varied in dollar amounts as well as in its nature from material assistance to expert assistance. El Salvador was quoted as one example where an unusual campaign was being waged. The report said: "It breaks fresh ground in two respects: the diversity of the parties involved and the duality of the literacy methods employed" (UNESCO 1989, 2). A whole range of public and semipublic bodies have been involved, and they cover sectors ranging from education to agriculture. Both traditional and modern methods of delivering instruction were being employed, accommodating, on the one hand, the traditional primer based on the alphabetical method, and on the other hand, an innovative radio program teaching literacy to learners at a distance.

Consequences of Literacy on the Lives of People

Development workers sometimes seem to be looking for the consequences of literacy in the wrong places. Too often they have looked for the effects of literacy within the formal structures of the economy and polity. Thereby, they have missed the most important results that are appearing in the informal structures of subsistence economies where most farmers of the world live. Statistical operations, cost-benefit analyses, and rate-of-return analyses have missed the meanings available only to the ethnographers.

Indeed, it is in the daily lives of common people that real effects of literacy are emerging. Whether it is Africa or Asia, New Zealand or Latin America, whether people are living under socialism or capitalism, the new literates are *all* using the same metaphors of freedom and light in describing their experiences with becoming literate.

Here are some voices of new literates.

"Literacy education has radically changed my way of thinking and I want my children to get proper education."

"Education is improvement in life. It is the path from darkness to light."

"The basic health education we received has completely changed our life. After completing basic health education, I have completely abolished the old ways of keeping home."

"A literate peasant becomes a citizen who knows too much and can't be ordered around so easily."

"It was like emerging from the shadows. (UNESCO 1989, 1–4)

All of the previous words are quoted from nonprofessional men and women and farmers and housewives.

After reviewing my field notes recorded in rural Zimbabwe, during 1989, I wrote:

The consequences of literacy have been remarkable. Without a single exception, the 146 adult learners, both men and women, the quite young and the very old, claimed that literacy had improved their lives, irrespective of the level of literacy attained and the subsequent contexture of its use. Learners' "minds opened up" and they could "do things without help." "Everything improved"; "everything became up-to-date."

A surge of confidence somehow seemed universal and intoxicating. Learners had indeed emerged from **a culture of silence.** They had found their voices, and their voices were often poignant. The learners said they felt free, unafraid, not shy, not inferior. They felt transformed. If not a new *technology of intellect,* there certainly was a new *social reinvention of oneself.* Literacy had become the great equalizer of men and women.

Conclusion

Despite tensions in UNESCO's theory of literacy and some contradictions in the execution of UNESCO's policies on literacy, UNESCO has had a significant and far-reaching influence on literacy promotion in the world during the last half century. There is, indeed, one important factor at work here in favor of UNESCO. UNESCO could do no wrong! One can do no wrong by doing literacy work. Even when literacy is serving the immediate purposes of exploitative and oppressive structures, it is at the same time building understanding and solidarity among the people and adding potential to their lives that they may make more effective transactions with their environment—material and social. The world of men and women who become literate opens up unto them. They become informed. Their horizons expand. They find their voices. They feel empowered in the psychological sense and will perhaps be able to become empowered in the social sense as well. In the long run, literacy will win over illiteracy.

References

Bataille, L., ed. 1976. *A turning point in literacy.* Oxford: Pergamon Press.

Bhola, H. S. 1984a. *Campaigning for literacy: Eight national experiences of the twentieth century, with a memorandum to decision-makers.* Paris: UNESCO.

Bhola, H. S. 1984b. A policy analysis of adult literacy promotion in the Third World: An accounting of promises made and promises fulfilled. *International Review of Education* 30: 249–64.

Bhola, H. S. 1989. *World trends and issues in adult education.* Paris/London: UNESCO/Jessica Kingsley Publishers.

Final report: Fourth international conference on adult education. 1985. Paris: UNESCO, 19–29, March.

Goody, J., ed. 1968. *Literacy in traditional societies.* NY: Cambridge University Press.

Hamadache, A. 1989. *Literacy, human rights and peace.* Geneva: International Bureau of Education.

Inkeles, A., and D. H. Smith. 1974. *Becoming modern.* Cambridge, MA: Harvard University Press.

Inter-agency Commission. 1989. *World conference of education for all—meeting basic learning needs—March 5–9, 1990, Thailand.* NY: The Interagency Commission.

Jones, P. W. 1988. *International policies for Third World education: UNESCO, literacy and development.* London: Routledge.

Scribner, S., and M. Cole. 1981. *The psychology of literacy.* Cambridge, MA: Harvard University Press.

UNESCO. 1976. *The experimental world literacy programme: A critical assessment.* Paris/NY: UNESCO/UNDP.

UNESCO. 1989. *UNESCO Sources.* No. 2, March.

World Charter on Education for All and Framework for Action to Meet Basic Needs. 1989. Working documents for World Conference on Education for All: Meeting Basic Learning Needs. NY: Inter-agency Commission.

Literacy Education: Origin and Developments

Asa G. Hilliard, III

> . . . [In 1826] Claperton . . . decided that he would go alone to Sokoto, leaving Lander behind with their house's servant Pasko. Claperton reached Sokoto on 20 October and occupied the same house as on his first visit. He was cordially received by the Sultan, whom he found reading an Arabic copy of Euclid's Elements. (De Gramont 1976, 167)

Hugh Claperton was an English explorer. Sokoto was a large city encompassing a large geographic area within the Hausa nation in Nigeria, West Africa. Sultan Bello was a literate, bilingual, and highly educated African man. Even though this event occurred in Africa as the slave trade was in progress, it illustrates the continuance of literacy from antiquity.

Literacy's origin, like the origin of civilization (Van Sertima & Williams 1986; Hilliard, Williams, & Damali 1987; Van Sertima 1989), began in Africa. To that end I will provide a brief historical overview of the origin of civilization that shows how Africans have developed literacy's initiatives, and how such influenced education in the United States. Next, based on ancient records, I will discuss a beginning for literacy. Finally, my conclusion will show how African's literacy initiatives can relate to today's adult literacy instruction. Overall, such is meant to show how, as a result of literacy's origin in Africa, humanity has been able to advance through written and spoken communication.

For a more in-depth understanding of this chapter, the reader must keep in mind that the educational estimates of the mental abilities of African and African American people are linked to images of Africa's past. Unfortunately, virtually all of the images of Africa's past, especially its ancient past, are usually grossly misrepresented.

Historical Overview
African

Adult literacy programs, as they are known today, were not among the research—dealing with ancient African literacy initiatives—that I have conducted nor the literature that I have studied. On the other hand, I found university systems of ancient Africa to be well documented. Therefore, my discussion will be centered more on higher education as I discuss contributions of the oldest civilization (African) to literacy education.

African people are ancient people (Van Sertima & Williams 1986; Van Sertima 1989). African civilization is also ancient. In fact, it is the most ancient in the world. The earliest development of higher education in the world is the independent product of African genius (Hilliard 1985, 1988, 1990; Bernal 1987). The most ancient university system yet recorded in the world was the University of Ipet Isut (today called Karnak Temple in Egypt) located in Waset (today called Luxor, previously called Thebes by the Greeks), Kemet (today called Egypt from the Greek). This was the university system that produced the arts and sciences curriculum that was to have a profound and defining impact on the foundation of Western European civilization (James 1976; Diop 1978). It was a university system that had its roots in the parent civilization of Africa, south of Egypt (i.e., ancient Nubia and Cush). It was, therefore, truly the cultural product of Africa.

It was the late Cheikh Anta Diop, of Senegal, who taught and provided the impressive documentation for the concept of cultural unity on the African continent. Within the climate of political scholarship in Europe during the slavery, colonial, and apartheid periods, emphasis was placed on the cultural and physical diversities that have been observed across the continent, while ignoring the commonalities. Such a view distorted the true cultural reality of African people. It was such views that caused the contributions to literacy by African people to be overlooked. Instead, the concept of the *savage* or *primitive* peoples emerged (Montague 1968).

Further documentation of this view can be observed in the design of higher education for African people by European people during the slavery, colonial, and apartheid periods. That design for miseducation, unfortunately, was rooted in the assumption of diversities among African people (Woodson 1933; Spivey 1978; Rodney 1974; Bullock 1970; Ross, Ross, & Power 1969). Such ideas about African diversity served to divide and conquer African people and to allow for the elevation of European people. Why was such necessary? Politically, throughout history, groups of people have tried to dominate other groups. Domination, then, must be through. That is, all that suggest superior performance and creativity by the dominated group must be destroyed. So, African people were dominated. Their ancient higher educational system was imitated by Europeans and claimed by them to be the product of Europe. In short, the African's potential was tied to the political decisions regarding the place of Africans as a group in the general society. Concurrently, politically inspired scholarship was used to create false views of the African's potential.

Even so, the record shows that in such places as West Africa, there was a vast elementary and secondary education system in place to support African's higher educational systems. The best-recorded manifestation of highly developed African higher education systems was in the Ghana/Mali/Songhay areas of West Africa. Gao, Jenne, and Timbucktu in the Ghana/Mali/Songhay areas and Sokoto (the city of vision) in Nigeria were university cities long before the beginning of the seventeenth century (Dubois 1969; Saad 1983; Austin 1984; Keita 1989; Hull 1976; Davidson 1974; De Gramont 1977; Griaule 1965). At their peak, they had a worldwide reputation and were influential in other parts of Africa. Even today, remnants of the purest forms of indigenous African systems of higher education are present in Mali (Griaule & Dieterlen 1986; Curtin 1964). This means that some of the Africans who were enslaved in the Western hemisphere were highly literate scholars (see also Niangoran-bouah 1984).

The image of Africans held by Europeans during the past few hundred years has been inaccurate (King 1971). Such inaccurateness has affected the estimates of the educability of Africans and influenced the type of higher education that was provided. In the absence of these inaccuracies, Africans could have been seen as a creative and an intellectual people with initiative and leadership. With the picture as such, probably, different prescriptions for higher education would have been justified.

The pattern of African independent higher education was intended to produce leaders and problem solvers for African people. However, under domination in Africa and in the Western hemisphere, two key elements operated: (*a*) the elimination of African independent control over the aims of education and (*b*) the provision of curricula that were guaranteed to channel schooled Africans into work that did not lead to wealth and leadership. These two elements were high-priority design principles and were not left to chance. A very carefully developed and sophisticated strategy to ensure that the principles were carried out was executed through government policy and through private philanthropy (Spivey 1978; Du Bois 1973; West 1972; Smith-Browning & Williams 1978). This miseducation, which failed to offer higher levels of liberal arts and sciences, served to maintain disabling conditions among African communities.

United States

> The first great mass movement for public education at the expense of the state, in the South, came from Negroes [African Americans]. Many leaders before the war had advocated general education, but few had been listened to. Schools for indigents and paupers were supported, here and there, and more or less spasmodically. Some states had elaborate plans, but they were not carried out. Public education for all at public expense, was, in the South, a Negro idea. (Du Bois 1973, 638)

Even though laws forbade the teaching of slaves to read and write, as late as 1862, their desire for an education was evident.

> Prior to the abolition of slavery, there was no general public educational system, properly speaking, in the Southern states, except perhaps, in North Carolina. In some populous centers, there were free schools; in some localities, academies and colleges, but for the most part, no adequate provision was made for the education even of the poorer whites [European Americans]. . . . Emerging from their bondage, the Negroes [African Americans] in the very beginning manifested the utmost eagerness for instruction, and their hunger was met by a corresponding readiness on the part of the people of the North to make provisions for it. (*Results of emancipation . . .* 1867, 28)

African Americans continued their tradition of becoming literate under harsh conditions in the U.S. Seemingly freed Africans, in keeping with their need for literacy, urged the development of public education. A characteristic of Africans, in Africa, was to obtain and use educational skills. As Sultan Bello, in 1826, was capable of reading Euclid's *Elements* in West Africa so were slaves and freedmen in the U.S. capable of reading and writing (Webber 1978; Austin 1984).

> . . . On one point, . . . there can be no question—no hesitation: unless . . . [people] develop . . . [their] full capabilities, . . . [they] cannot survive. If . . . [they] are to be

trained grudgingly and suspiciously: trained not with reference to what . . . [they] can be, but with sole reference to what somebody wants . . . [them] to be: if instead of following the methods pointed out by the accumulated wisdom of the world for the development of full human power, . . . [teachers] teach . . . [Africans, Americans, Europeans, and Asians] only such things and by such methods as are momentarily popular, . . . [they] are going to fail and fail ignominiously in . . . [their] attempt to raise . . . [all] race[s] to . . . full humanity and with that failure falls the fairest and fullest dream of a great united humanity. (Aptheker 1973, 9–10)

(Literacy education in the U.S. has been addressed in another chapter).

Literacy

Some of the oldest rock art in the world is located in the Sahara in northern Africa and also in areas of southern Africa. Such art is dated between 30 and 50 thousand years ago and was itself a form of literacy. Another fully developed form of literacy was the Medu Netcher system (hieroglyphic symbols). This system was in operation when Egypt, as a nation, was established (circa 3100 B.C.). That nation has the best-recorded civilization in ancient Africa or anywhere else. Egypt's civilization represents a native African contribution to the world (*The art of gold weights* . . . 1977).

Examples of literacy are evident all over the continent of Africa—north, south, east, and west. Literacy was not only the property of the elite, the priesthood, and the royalty; it was also typical among the masses, since African countries required a vast army of scribes to conduct business. Literacy was seen in many forms. Many writing systems that included writing on paper, writing on stone, and writing on the human body were developed. Architecture itself was a form of literacy, as were weaving, symbols, and braided hair. All conveyed messages to the literate observer. To outsiders the meaning was often obscure. That is true even today. For example, the gold weights of the Asante are said to be a veritable encyclopedia of Ghanaian history. Some gold weights actually expressed proverbs.

The proverb is, more or less, a fixed chain of words which is widely known and widely accepted by those who use and hear it as embodying some indisputable truth or generally held state throughout the world they inhabit and life as they know it . . . it is important to stress that the Akan knowledge of proverbs is seen as giving a man access to a vast and ever-useful store of traditional wisdom; for proverbs can be applied to almost every one of the multivarious aspects of existence within their society. Knowing proverbs and how to use them was thus a prime requirement for all who sought authority or influence within their society. The proverbs were learned and used by chiefs, both lesser and great (Odikroo, Ohene), priests (Akomfo), and elders (Mpanyimofoo, Nananom) above all that knowledge and understanding of proverbs was required of the spokesmen (Akyeme), for it was the task of these to mediate between king and people, and to act as the human channel through which all messages, from both sides were relayed. (*The art of gold weights* . . . 1977, 13–14)

An examination of the Asante tradition has shown that literacy was not only widespread but was very sophisticated and complex.

Proverbs appear almost everywhere in Asante verbal culture; they are sung in dirges or praise songs, beaten out on drums, painted all over lorries, or above the doors of shops, used as pseudonyms by entrants in competition, incorporated in prayers to God and spoken as parts of blessings and sacrifices. Formally men and youth would compete among themselves to see who could remember the most proverbs and who could top those put forth by other competitors. Men might keep near them collections of different objects to help them recall proverbs for such occasions: caries, grains of maze, feathers, husks of maze (burono), charcoal, pieces of cloth, fibers, adobe (a type of palm) strung in order to help recollect and repeat proverbs. The necessity of proverbs shows the relationship between the material object and the verbal formulae. (*The art of gold weights* . . . 1977, 14)

What is the value of the previous information for adult educators? Adult educators are responsible for teaching literacy skills to adults. Like other educators, who need to understand the history of their disciplines before they teach, adult educators also need to understand the history of literacy.

Conclusion

One way to help adult learners develop their full literacy capabilities is not only to teach them about the history of literacy, but to teach them about the ancient African people who were responsible for beginning and developing literacy initiatives. Literacy skills were taught and learned by people in schools during ancient times. Further, scribal schools were ubiquitous in ancient Egypt, and to attend them was regarded as the highest educational goal (Williams 1972). In the instruction of Dua-Khety, for his son Pepi, the work of the scribe is glorified, in ancient manuscripts that date back to Egypt's (circa 1500 to 1200 B.C.) eighteenth and nineteenth dynasties. An example follows:

I have seen many beatings—
Set your heart on books!
I watched those seized for labor—
There is nothing better than books!
It's like a boat on water.

Read the end of the *Kemit*-Book,
You'll find this saying there:
A scribe at whatever post in town,
He will not suffer in it;
As he fills another's need,
He will not lack rewards.
I don't see a calling like it
Of which this saying could be said.

I'll make you love scribedom more than your mother,
I'll make its beauties stand before you;
Its the greatest of all callings,
There's none like it in the land . . .

Low, I have set you on God's path,
A scribe's Renenet is on his shoulder
On the day he is born. (Lichtheim 1973, 185 & 191)

Educators can use ancient manuscripts, historical records, and ancient writing symbols to teach adults basic literacy skills. For example, teaching students that a form of writing (hieroglyphics) dates back to 3100 B.C. might instill in them an appreciation for the written text. An instructor could show students the hieroglyphic symbols and ask them to use the symbols to write their names. An appreciation for proverbs might help adult students try mnemonic devices as a way of increasing their memory. Beyond that are the facts that (*a*) complex elementary, secondary, and university systems were developed by Africans and copied by Europeans places history in its correct perspective, and (*b*) those educational systems are the bases for education curricula as it is known today. Such could encourage students to study ancient history.

My recommendation for educators is that they continue to study the ancient records. Those ancient records will provide important knowledge that should be passed on to students.

References

Aptheker, H. ed. 1973. *The education of black people: Ten* critiques, 1906–1960, by W. E. B. Du Bois. NY: Monthly Review Press.
The art of gold weights: Words, form, and meaning. 1977. University Museum of Philadelphia and the Anko Foundation.
Austin, A. D. 1984. *African Muslims in antebellum America: A sourcebook.* NY: Garland.
Bernal, M. 1987. *Black Athena: The Afroasiatic roots of classical civilization: Volume I The fabrication of ancient Greece 1785–1985.* London: Free Association Books.
Bullock, H. A. 1970. *A history of Negro education in the South from 1619 to the present.* NY: Praeger.
Curtin, P. D. 1964. *The image of Africa: British ideas and action, 1780–1850, Volumes 1 & 2.* Madison: University of Wisconsin Press.
Davidson, B. 1974. *Africa in history: Themes and outlines.* NY: Collier.
De Gramont, S. 1976. *The strong brown god: The story of the Niger River.* Boston: Houghton Mifflin.
De Gramont, S. 1977. *The strong brown god: The story of the Niger River.* Boston: Houghton Mifflin.
Diop, C. A. 1978. *The cultural unity of black Africa.* Chicago: Third World Press.
Dubois, F. 1969. *Timbuctoo the mysterious.* Translated by Diana White. NY: Negro Universities Press.
Du Bois, W. E. B. 1973. *Black reconstruction in America: 1860–1880.* NY: Atheneum.
Griaule, M. 1965. *Conversations with Ogotemmeli: An introduction to Dogon religious ideas.* NY: Oxford University Press.
Griaule, M., and G. Dieterlen. 1986. *The pale fox.* Chino Valley, AZ: The Continuum Foundation.
Hilliard, A. G., III. 1985. Kemetic concepts in education. In M. Karenga and J. H. Carruthers, eds. *Kemet and the African worldview.* Los Angeles: University of Sankore Press.
Hilliard, A. G., III. 1988. *Free your mind: Return to the source, African orgins.* East Point, GA: Waset Educational Productions. Videocassette.
Hilliard, A. G., III. 1990. *Master keys to ancient Kemet.* East Point, GA: Waset Educational Productions. Videocassette.
Hilliard, A. G., III, L. Williams, and N. Damali. 1987. *The teaching of Ptahhotep: The oldest book in the world.* Atlanta, GA: Blackwook Press.
Hull, R. W. 1976. *African cities and towns before the European conquest.* NY: Norton.
James, G. G. M. 1976. *Stolen legacy.* San Francisco: Julian Richardson.
Keita, M. 1989. *Scholarship as a global commodity: African intellectual communities in the medieval and renaissance periods.* Unpublished manuscript.
King, K. 1971. *Pan-Africanism and education: A study of race philanthropy and education in the southern states of America and East Africa.* London: Clarendon Press-Oxford.

Lichtheim, M. 1973. *Ancient Egyptian literature: A book of readings Volume I.* Berkeley: University of California Press.

Montague, A. 1968. *The concept of the primitive.* NY: The Free Press..

Niangoran-bouah, G. 1984. *The Akan world of gold weights. Vols. 1–2.* Abidjan: Lles Novells Africaines.

Results of emancipation in the United States of America. 1867. A Committee of the American Freedman's Union Commission. NY: American Freedman's Union Commission.

Rodney, W. 1974. *How Europe underdeveloped Africa.* Washington, DC: Howard University Press.

Ross, Sir E., D. Ross, and E. Power, eds. 1969. *Ibn Battuta: Travels in Asia and Africa 1325–1354.* NY: Augustus M. Kelley.

Saad, E. N. 1983. *Social history of Timbuktu: The role of Muslim scholars and notables 1400–1900.* Cambridge: Cambridge University Press.

Smith-Browning, J. E., and J. B. Williams. 1978. History and goals of black institutions of higher learning. In C. V. Willie and R. R. Edmonds, eds., *Black colleges in America: Challenge, development, survival.* NY: Teachers College Press.

Spivey, D. 1978. *Schooling for the new slavery: Black industrial education 1868–1915.* Westport, CT: Greenwood Press.

Van Sertima, I. ed. 1989. Egypt revisited. *Journal of African Civilizations* 10. New Brunswick: Transaction Books.

Van Sertima, I., and L. Williams, eds. 1986. Great African thinkers: Cheikh Anta Diop. *Journal of African civilizations* 8. New Brunswick: Transaction Books.

Webber, T. L. 1978. *Deep like the rivers: Education in the slave quarter community 1831–1865.* NY: W. W. Norton & Company, Inc.

West, E. 1972. *The black American and education.* Columbus, OH: Charles E. Merrill.

Williams, R. J. 1972. Scribal training in ancient Egypt. *The Journal of the American Oriental Society* 92.:214–21.

Woodson, C. G. 1933. *The Mis-education of the Negro.* Washington, DC: The Associated Publishers, Inc.

Literacy: An International Perspective

Donna D. Amstutz

Illiteracy is directly linked to poverty (UNESCO 1989, 1968; Duke 1985). Literacy, or reading and writing, is often not highly valued when the struggle for survival requires constant attention. When basic needs such as food, shelter, clothes, water, and medicine are inadequate, the energy needed for learning to read is devoted to surviving each day. As John Ryan, UNESCO's Associate Coordinator for International Literacy Year, indicates,

> People living in extreme poverty and rural environments sense that they have very little need for literacy, and until you can transform the environment and circumstances in which they live, they in fact have little need for it. (UNESCO 1989, 6)

One in every four adults in the world is unable to read or write, according to figures published by UNESCO in 1985. Asia has 666 million (75 percent of the total) people who are illiterate; Africa, 162 million (18 percent); Latin America and the Caribbean, 44 million (5 percent); and the industrialized countries, 20 million (2 percent) (UNESCO 1989). Reports of the exact number of illiterates vary according to the definition used. Within this chapter, various definitions of literacy are given and six basic literacy purposes are discussed. A summary of mass literacy campaigns in Cuba, Tanzania, and China, have been selected as representative of different areas of the world. Together they present alternative methods and processes of delivering literacy instruction. The chapter concludes with possible courses of action, drawn from the experiences in these selected countries, for literacy programs in other countries.

Definitions of Literacy

All definitions of literacy can be divided into three basic types: reading ability, problem solving, and politics. Over thirty-five years ago, UNESCO defined literacy as being able to read with understanding and write a simple statement on daily life (UNESCO 1951). Most Americans, if asked to define literacy, would paraphrase this statement as simply the ability to read and write. This definition has served to divide citizens of various countries into two classes: those who can read and those who cannot. Such a definition has been encouraged by those people who control the resources available to the working classes. Those who can read and write control the legal processes, economic situations, and media influence to their advantage. Those who cannot read or write are dependent upon the interpretations of written communications by those who are literate. Such dependency places putting the illiterate citizens at a distinct disadvantage.

In 1962, UNESCO reformulated its definition of literacy to reflect the various contexts in which it is discussed.

> A person is literate when he [or she] has acquired the essential knowledge and skills which enable him [or her] to engage in all those activities in which literacy is required for effective functioning in his [or her] group and community and whose attainment in reading, writing and arithmetic make it possible for him [or her] to continue to use these skills towards his [or her] own and the community's development. (UNESCO 1962, 3)

Literacy definitions vary according to context (Delker 1987; Arnove & Graff 1987; Kayser 1987).

> Each context demands a new literacy . . . the adult must have the competence and knowledge to deal with different sets of tasks with which he or she is confronted in these different contexts. (Delker 1987, 7)

Contextual literacy can refer to two different concepts. The first, or generic, concept of contextual literacy can be interpreted as meaning that the skills or tasks that adults need to be considered literate are not limited to reading and writing, but rather focus on being able to solve problems that occur in one's daily life. The skills may include appropriate farming techniques in one context or appropriate fishing/hunting techniques in another. This definition implies that individuals become literate to benefit their own lives, or to become empowered to manipulate circumstances in which they live to more favorable ones.

A second way of interpreting contextual literacy is as functional literacy. Functional contextual literacy refers to people being able to function within the context in which they live and work. For this reason, functional literacy has often been associated with improved work skills or, more generally, increased productivity of individuals. This form of literacy is often promoted by those who control the wealth because it is in their interest to have efficient skilled workers who can effectively produce the goods and perform the services that keep the wealthy in power.

There are political definitions of literacy. Such definitions view the acquisition of written language skills in terms of social and political empowerment. Freire's (1970) conception of literacy as *cultural action for freedom* typifies this category. Such definitions assume that individuals become literate by posing critical questions about the structures that control the lives of illiterates. These definitions also assume that literacy skills do not necessarily relate directly to increased economic or social benefits. As Fingeret (1984, 45) noted,

> education will not create additional jobs, solve the problems of crime and malnutrition, or make the world safe from terrorism. Social structures and social forces beyond the reach of literacy educators are at work maintaining the structures of social inequality.

However, literacy can provide the basis for collaboratively working with others to change the structures that can increase the equality of opportunity.

Purposes of Literacy

Literacy is not an end in itself. It is a means to other ends, such as political, economic, or social development (Street 1984; Ryan 1981; Faure 1972). Countries initiate literacy campaigns for a variety of reasons. Usually a national declaration of the need for literacy is tied to a goal that a government wants to accomplish. Governmental purposes may include integration of society, political and/or economic changes, and social class changes.

Not all literacy programs are conducted by governmental organizations, however. Religious-based agencies, concerned community activists, and non-governmental organizations initiate and maintain literacy programs for differing purposes than those purported by a government. Purposes often fostered by these groups include equality of opportunity, religious conversion or maintenance of religious beliefs, and changes in the social structures.

Regardless of the sponsoring agent, six basic purposes of literacy have emerged from the literature:

1. *To Preserve the Equality of People.* A perspective of this kind defines literacy as a basic human right. In many societies, illiterates are viewed as deficient individuals who lack skills. Literacy, then, becomes a mechanism to divide citizens into two groups: those who can manipulate their environment through power (such as written legal processes) and those who are unable to affect their environment because they do not understand the written language of those in power. This barrier reduces illiterates to marginal status and leads to inferior economic, social, and political positions. Therefore, the purpose of some literacy efforts leads to ensuring equality of all people through a common understanding of written communication.

2. *To Integrate Society.* Geographic and social divisions within a society can be reduced by increased literacy levels of all citizens (Arnove & Graff 1987). For example, literacy has been used to standardize a common language in countries that are multilingual, providing the citizens with the means to communicate with others within their national border. Although multiplicity of languages can hinder literacy efforts (Ampene 1981), the decision to utilize one local language over others can result in political upheaval within a country. However, if a commitment is made to achieve literacy, a common language is not a necessity to accomplish the objective. In some cases, literacy efforts in a multilingual country have included instruction and written materials in a number of languages or dialects.

3. *To Promote and Maintain Religious Beliefs.* Literacy was historically used as a tool for religious conversion of nonbelievers, as a mechanism for moral training, and as maintenance of religious beliefs. The U.S.-based Laubach Literacy program began as a Protestant missionary program that supported literacy as a mechanism to help individuals gain control of their environmental circumstances (Laubach 1951). The fact that newly literate adults were then encouraged to convert to Protestantism has not been widely publicized.

Other religious organizations have also viewed literacy as necessary to maintaining a belief system. According to Israeli and Klevins (1987, 95), "Judaism, as a religious doctrine and a way of life does not recognize, let alone allow, the state of being ignorant. Ignorance of the Holy Scriptures equals, for Judaism, the impossibility of properly practicing the Halacha" (the Jewish code of behavior). Literacy instruction to promote religious beliefs is still conducted by many evangelical denominations.

4. *To Promote Social Change (Individually and Collectively).* Social change has become a primary purpose of literacy. On an individual level, many international adult educators believe that men and women can change their social position in any society by increasing their literacy level. By increasing the ability to read, write, and understand the written language, people can increase social mobility and economic circumstances related to higher educational levels. Collectively, groups of people (minority communities, racial subgroups, and economic classes) can increase the relative ascribed social standing of their group as a whole as the group becomes more literate. While critics of this purpose maintain that increased literacy does not relate to increased social mobility, many proponents of literacy for social status changes still exist. Collective social change can also be positive in the sense that it can further goals identified by the communities themselves.

5. *To Promote Political Changes.* Changing the circumstances in which one lives is the impetus for using literacy to force political changes. Paulo Freire has been the leading proponent of conceptualizing literacy as *cultural action for freedom.* Reflective of this purpose, the 1975 Declaration of Persepolis (Iran) stated that,

> . . . literacy . . . [is] not just the process of learning the skills of reading, writing, and arithmetic, but a contribution to the liberation of man and to his full development. Thus conceived, literacy creates the conditions for the acquisition of a critical consciousness of the contradictions of society in which man lives and of its aims; it also stimulates [the learner's] initiative and his participation in the creation of projects capable of acting upon the world, of transforming it, and of defining the aims of an authentic human development. (United Nations Food and Agricultural Organization 1975, 43)

The political purpose has received recognition through major literacy programs implemented in Latin America (particularly Cuba, Brazil, and Nicaragua) and Tanzania.

6. *To Promote Economic Changes.* Governments that are concerned with severe economic difficulties, particularly in traditionally agricultural countries, have viewed literacy as necessary to positively impact needed economic changes. This purpose is most often translated into occupational training as increased vocational skills have been expected to affect the rate of production and, thus, the wealth of rela-

tively poor countries. As a mechanism to further national economic goals, some government officials have viewed literacy as an efficient investment in human resources.

Literacy Campaigns

Cuba. Two years after the revolution of 1959 when Fidel Castro came to power, Cuba initiated the National Literacy Campaign of 1961. Its mission was to transform the society and the economy. The campaign used the services of 250,000 literacy workers to teach 707,212 adult illiterates, 27 percent of whom were located in rural areas (Bhola 1982; Leiner 1987).

Initially, the literacy workers were adult volunteers. After the first four months, the public schools were closed and 100,000 school-aged youngsters, known as the brigatistia, were used to teach adults. After another four months, 15,000 workers were added. These literacy instructors were supervised by 35,000 teachers. The younger literacy workers training included a copy of a teacher's manual, a primer, instruction in methodology, and an orientation to the countryside (since most of the literacy workers were urban dwellers). These youngsters were then sent to live with rural families while they taught the adults how to read and write. To be considered literate, adults had to pass a final test that was composed of reading two short paragraphs, writing a brief passage that was dictated by the literacy worker, and writing a letter to Fidel Castro.

The government of Cuba made education its highest priority. Money was provided for training, production and dissemination of materials, and program development. The leaders of Cuba believed in "educacion permanente." While some critics have noted that the literacy levels achieved during the campaign were only of a first-grade level, Cuban educators say this was the foundation of a *lifelong education for all.* Within two years, the number of illiterate adults decreased from 23 percent of the total population to 4 percent.

Cuba continued its obsession with education by instituting progressively higher level programs for adults. For example, in 1975 Castro supported a proposal to achieve a sixth-grade minimum education for workers and farmers. He believed that this minimal level was necessary to effectively produce quality services and goods.

Adult basic education is now entrenched firmly in the Cuban educational system. In addition to farmer and worker education programs at the elementary and secondary levels, independent study programs and classes are delivered in alternative settings. Emphasizing science and math in the Cuban curriculum has helped train scientists and engineers who are now helping build Cuba's economic base. The literacy campaign conducted in Cuba has received global attention and has been promoted as a model for achieving literacy in other underdeveloped countries. Cuban educators, however, stress that countries must adapt the Cuban model to the specific historical, social, and political context of each nation.

Tanzania. First funded by UNESCO's Experimental World Literacy Program in 1968, Tanzania's literacy efforts were judged to be successful by reducing the official illiteracy rate from 67 percent to 39 percent over four years. President Julius Nyerere initiated a mass campaign as part of a social/political reform in 1970. In four years, over 5 million adults were enrolled in the national literacy campaign. *Education for self-reliance* is now a concept used to denote the empowerment of citizens and the potential to increase economic production.

Nyerere committed the nation to "ujamaa" socialism that, among other things, established villages of extended families. The ujamaa villages were the center of literacy activities. Nyerere believed that these villages, through literacy, agriculture, and community development strategies, could become productive economic units. An emphasis on a self-help philosophy could then make the citizens less dependent on outside resources and increase reliance on local knowledge, skills, and products.

This campaign, unlike Cuba's that focused on academic skills, integrated reading instruction with practical skills. The 13,500 trained literacy teachers used primers that focused on rural concerns (cotton, banana and rice production, cattle rearing, fishing, home economics, and political education). Rural libraries and newspapers were established and a radio education program begun. The literacy instruction was supported by weekly broadcasts, which often included *songs for literacy* (Unsicker 1987).

The library services were expanded by using vans to transport literacy materials to the villages. Eventually, these vans took tools to groups of literacy students for the purpose of vocational instruction in carpentry, sewing, and masonry. Within these projects, reading instruction was integrated with practical occupational skills.

Tanzania did not take a centralized approach to training as did Cuba. Rather, they organized the literacy instruction through a decentralized system of training of literacy teachers. Those literate citizens who were trained during the UNESCO program were paid an honorarium to train teachers in workshops organized by regional and district adult education staff. Like Cuba, Tanzania has continued its efforts to the present day.

After UNESCO's concentrated program ended, the Swedish International Development Authority provided substantial support for the continuation of Tanzania's literacy program. In 1976, postliteracy classes were initiated for graduates of the literacy classes.

One of the outcomes of Tanzania's literacy campaign was the standard use of Kiswahili as the national language. This helped unify the country through written communications and generated many publications that are now commonly read.

Since the early 1980s, the literacy campaign, while still active, has been reduced in response to other, more pressing economic concerns. A reduction in international monetary aid has jeopardized the amount of money available for literacy efforts. Tanzania remains, however, an example of a concentrated effort that linked literacy to practical concerns of the populace.

China. Literacy in China had long been reserved as a spiritual wealth for the rich and ruling classes. At the beginning of the twentieth century, intellectuals and some reformers began to tie the 90 percent illiteracy rate to political, economic, and societal problems. In 1921, Yen Yangchu introduced a textbook that used a thousand of the most common Chinese characters in connection with a rural reconstruction effort. However, by the time of Mao's founding of the new China in 1949, more than 348 million people (80 percent) were still illiterate (Li Xiao Pei 1989).

China is a centrally controlled governmental system. It has the political power to ensure the implementation of a literacy campaign. The system has worked quite well since the absolute authority of the central government has been internalized by most citizens and because the government could and would repress any opponents to its policies.

Initially, the proclaimed purpose of China's literacy efforts was to strengthen the country by uplifting the people. However, it soon became apparent that the primary purpose of literacy was to build socialism and communism. Mao Tsetung proclaimed, "The eradication of illiteracy is a necessary condition for the construction of a new China" (Mao 1957, 2).

A governor of the Shandong Province noted that as the masses became increasingly educated, the easier it was for government orders to be implemented. The political aim of making the *great leap forward* again emphasized the role literacy would have to play in order to accomplish that objective. Workers and peasants would have to become literate in order to meet the production goals set by the government.

Since such a large proportion of the Chinese population was illiterate and because the government had so few resources, literacy education in China was organized outside the formal school system (Bhola 1982). Three methods, described later, that are widely used today by varying areas and ethnic groups within China have implications for literacy instruction in other countries as well.

Method One: Ninety percent of new adult literates are graduates from *winter schools, spare-time schools,* and *intensive literacy classes.* These rather traditionally delivered programs (in the sense that they are formal classes) are offered when the work load for peasants and workers is the lowest. During winter, when little farm work can be accomplished, adults are relatively free to attend literacy classes. These schools have been criticized as being too cyclical. What adults learn one winter may be forgotten by the time the next winter season arrives. Nevertheless, winter schools have been effective in reaching the previously hard-to-reach farmers. Spare-time schools have fewer classes when it is a busy season for a production unit, and more classes when the unit is not as busy. Learning time coincides with the ebb and flow of work. The advantage to spare-time schools is that adults can actively learn year round and thus continually reinforce a new literacy. Intensive classes are programs for adults who can be released from their duties for a month's intensive study.

This allows for a more concentrated effort as opposed to a prolonged process. These types of formal class programs usually use texts that are produced by the local community. For this reason, they can use their own names and words that describe locally used tools, animals, crops, or industries. It adapts literacy instruction to the local context.

Method Two: Some Chinese communities use a *paired* approach. Since some illiterates are unable to go to classes because of housework, remote locations, or infirmity, those who can read are paired with those who cannot. All literate people in a community are mobilized to teach. Literacy is developed without textbooks, formal teachers, or schools. Success of this approach is dependent on both the teacher's and the student's commitment to the process. In most cases, the student makes a promise to become literate in a certain period of time.

Method Three: Other communities establish literacy environments. Objects throughout a village are labeled with the appropriate characters. Farmers memorize the characters for the different farming processes as they perform them. These literacy environments are occasionally compulsory. For example, literacy checkpoints are set up to test adults. Only those who can read are allowed to continue on the way to their destination. If an adult is not able to read the characters, instruction is given immediately. Before patients are allowed to see a doctor in a hospital, they must learn a few basic characters that relate to health care; before they can purchase items in a shop, they must learn the characters of what they intend to buy. While compulsory, these techniques have proved to be quite successful during campaigns with limited time frames.

Some Chinese adult educators have charged that these three methods are simply ways to deposit words to the illiterates, without any real impact on the adults' lives. The instructors who mechanically deliver literacy see literacy as the sole objective. Most instructors have not yet considered the ultimate ends, or purposes, that literacy could serve in improving the lives of the citizens. In the last analysis, however, literacy education in China has effectively utilized both governmental decrees and nongovernmental human resources.

Conclusion

An increasingly literate population does not guarantee economic advances, better living conditions, higher levels of employment, or participation in a democratic society. However, the belief that literacy can change the person, and often the community in which one lives, has inspired many countries to conduct mass literacy campaigns. A study of the campaigns provides some possible implications for increasing literacy. While the context will change with implementation, the following are some possible courses of action that may benefit citizens in various countries.

First, a national commitment with adequate resources and leadership could be established. In all three campaigns discussed in this chapter, literacy programs were a priority for the government. Citizens believed that literacy could improve their lives and ensure their participation in the circumstances that affected them. They identified with the established priority, either by making a commitment to becoming literate or by helping others learn to read and write.

A second possible course of action is to encourage, through government funding, a national literacy volunteers' association. Literacy volunteers in many established programs are making substantial contributions to the literacy efforts. However, it seems that cyclical training is more effective than a long initial training period. As volunteers and teachers gain more experience, in-service education becomes more relevant. The training given should be intensive for short periods of time and supported by a knowledgeable administration.

A final course of action is to strongly promote the integration of adult literacy curricula with the needs and interests of adult learners. Literacy efforts seem to be more effective when tied to an individual's life circumstances. Farmers learn to read those words that relate to farming, mothers learn words that relate to improving their children's lives, and so on. When materials are produced locally, they can be customized to that particular community and may be more relevant than commercially published materials. As noted by the International Development Research Centre (1979, 111), "Adult-centered methods and learner-based content are two essential elements in successful literacy programs."

References

Ampene, K. 1981. Reaching unreached adults. In A. Charters and Associates, *Comparing adult education worldwide.* San Francisco: Jossey-Bass.

Arnove, R. F., and H. J. Graff. 1987. *National Literacy Campaigns: Historical and comparative perspectives.* NY: Plenum.

Bhola, H. S. 1982. *Campaigning for Literacy: A critical analysis of some selected literacy campaigns of the 20th century, with a memorandum to decision makers.* UNESCO/ICAE. Paris: UNESCO, May.

Delker, P. V. 1987. Beyond literacy in an uncertain world. In C. Klevins, ed. *Materials and methods in adult continuing education, international—illiteracy.* Los Angeles: Klevens Publications.

Duke, C. 1985. *Combating poverty through adult education: National development strategies.* London: Croom Helm.

Faure, E., ed. 1972. *Learning to be.* Paris: UNESCO.

Fingeret, A. 1984. *Adult literacy education: Current and future directions.* Columbus, OH: ERIC Clearinghouse on Adult, Career, and Vocational Education.

Freire, P. 1970. *Pedagogy of the oppressed.* NY: Herder & Herder.

International Development Research Centre. 1979. *The world of literacy: Policy, research, and action.* Ottawa, Canada: International Council for Adult Education.

Israeli, E., and C. Klevins. 1987. Adult and continuing education in Israel. In C. Klevins, ed. *Materials and methods in adult continuing education, international—illiteracy.* Los Angeles: Klevens Publications.

Kayser, C. 1987. Adult literacy: Problems of diagnosis and evaluation. *Adult Education and Development.* Bonn: German Adult Education Association. 28:114–18.

Laubach, F. C. 1951. *Wake up or blow up.* Los Angeles, CA: Fleming H. Revelle Company.

Leiner, M. 1987. The 1961 national Cuban literacy campaign. In R. Arnove and H. Graff, eds., *National literacy campaigns: Historical and comparative perspectives.* NY: Plenum.

Li, X. P. 1989. Literacy in China: The mass campaign. *Thresholds in Education.* 5(4). DeKalb, IL: College of Education, Northern Illinois University.

Mao, T. 1957. *Socialist upsurge in China's countryside.* Beijing: Foreign Language Press.

Ryan, J. 1981. Design and development of literacy programs. In A. Charters and Associates, *Comparing adult education worldwide.* San Francisco: Jossey-Bass.

Street, B. V. 1984. *Literacy in theory and practice.* NY: Cambridge University Press.

Unsicker, J. 1987. Tanzania's literacy campaign in historical-structural perspective. In R. Arnove and H. Graff, eds., *National literacy campaign: Historical and comparative perspectives.* NY: Plenum.

UNESCO. 1951. *Measures for supressing illiteracy which could be applied in non-self-governing terrorities.* Geneva, 24 September.

UNESCO. 1962. *Statement of the international committee of experts on literacy.* Paris.

UNESCO. 1968. *Illiteracy and human rights.* Paris.

UNESCO. 1989. *Illiteracy: The alarming statistics. UNESCO Sources* 2:6–7. Paris, March.

United Nations Food and Agricultural Organization (FAO). 1975. The Declaration of Persepolis, *Ideas and Action* 10:43.

Literacy Education in Selected African Countries

Emma T. Lucas

Poverty and an underdeveloped educational system are generally viewed as fundamental causes of illiteracy. Undisputedly, economic, educational, and social factors are directly related to the disturbing rise in illiteracy rates. Africa, with her high number of underdeveloped countries, continues to face the problem of chronic illiteracy.

While the urgency to address such an educational crisis does not escape national development agendas, many underdeveloped countries are nonetheless faced with a multitude of other problems, all vying for top priority. Anyadike (1989) offers the following:

> There has been progress made by literacy programs in a number of African countries, helped by the trend towards universal primary education in the late 1970s and early 80s, but it is being swamped by rapid population growth, falling pupil enrollment, and in the era of austerity, dwindling education budgets. (P. 1040)

The United Nations Department of International Economic and Social Affairs (1986) estimated Africa's adult illiteracy rate to be approximately 54 percent. There are numerous African sub-regional variations in illiteracy rates, with the highest rate of 63 percent in West Africa. Although the largest aggregate number of illiterates is in Asia, the highest percentages are in African countries.

How have literacy education efforts become evidenced in African countries? A thorough examination of the question was not possible in this chapter, so I narrowed my answer to discuss Africa's response to illiteracy, literacy education and African women, and literacy education in two African countries. My specific intent is to provide history and development of literacy initiatives in Africa.

Africa's Response to Illiteracy

Campaigns for literacy during the twentieth century in Third World countries increased rapidly as literacy was linked to nation-building, industrialization, democratization, urbanization, and wealth. The 1961 Addis Ababa Conference of Independent African countries had education and training as its main agenda for important development strategies. At that time the education situation in Africa was catastrophic. Even so, the conference identified strategies to address educational issues. They included (a) provisions for universalization of primary education at a presupposed annual growth rate of 5.6 percent and (b) an increase, within twenty years, of the enrollment ratios in secondary education to 23 percent and in higher education to 2 percent for the whole continent (Yacine 1982). Unfortunately, after twenty years, the conference's plan was only partially fulfilled. One of the shortfalls was that the conference's plan underestimated how large the population would grow in twenty years. Particularly, not enough people were considered in that plan.

At the Conference of Heads of State and Government of the Organization of African Unity in 1979, held in Monrovia, the problem of developing education and training in relation to economic and sociocultural development was discussed. Yacine (1982) indicated that leaders at this conference perceived education as both a tool of development and a political act to further the liberation of humanity. The resulting scheme, the Monrovia Declaration, included objectives that would implement clearly defined education policies. One of these policies specifically addressed illiteracy. It stated that maximum prominence should be given to all matters affecting the development of human resources, beginning with the elimination of illiteracy.

In 1980, the Lagos Action Plan confirmed and further expanded the Monrovia Declaration for self-sustained and self-reliant development. Yacine (1982) points out that the Lagos Action Plan emphasized, in particular, the establishment and implementation of programs of large-scale development of human resources. Such programs would take note of the high population growth, the growing level of unemployment and underemployment, the shortage of different types and levels of trained manpower, the high level of adult illiteracy, the deficiencies in the educational system, and the lack of coordinated policies and programs of manpower training at both national and regional levels.

In 1982, twenty-one years after the Addis Ababa Plan, the Harare Conference of Ministers of Education and Administrators Responsible for Economic Planning in Africa was held. At that conference, African countries advocated measures to meet the challenges of educational development for the continent (Yacine 1982). Central to their deliberations was a clarification of the problems of developing education and training in relation to the economic and sociocultural development of African countries. Thus, the new perspective was that education should be perceived both as a tool of development and as a political act to further the liberation of humanity.

A final comment is that conference participants were well aware of the need to expand their educational efforts. For example, with the Monrovia Declaration and Lagos Plan, participants recognized the need to maximize human resources by adopting educational policies and systems. Likewise, with the Harare Declaration, participants moved toward a strategy of eradicating illiteracy through a sustained campaign that was designed to universalize primary schooling for children and to promote literacy among young people and older adults.

In Africa during the mid-1980s, there were only sixty-five literate females for every 100 literate males (United Nations . . . 1986). One view of the status of women in African society holds that the exploitation of women is a gender phenomenon (Aluko & Alfa 1985). The traditional roles (reproduction, cooking, cleaning, child care) identified with women have generally relegated them to a subordinate position. In issuing a call for solidarity among Nigerian women,

African Women and Literacy

Nweke (1985) reflected on the historical basis of Nigerian and other African women's subordination. She states:

> Whereas in classical colonialism the struggle is based on that of regaining the land, the people's traditions, and the old way of life, the major difference between the classical colonialist position and that of women is that the old way of life is the very thing which colonizes. (P. 204)

Because of this prevailing thinking throughout African societies today, women are faced with a situation of anomie due to the institutionalized means by which women are expected to achieve womanhood. Oloruntimehin (1985) predicted that African women of the next generation, based on the experiences of traditional and modern women, might be less able to cope with their situation, and that there is a need for societal solutions to this problem rather than solutions by a particular set of women.

Lestage (1982) states that women are the victims of out-and-out discrimination where literacy activities are concerned in least-developed countries far more than in others. He further notes that although there are instances where women receive no education, they may exercise considerable influence in the community. He continues:

> The unjustifiable dichotomy resulting from this leads to a loosening, if not a severing, of the links between educational activities, and social activities, and the child, through the mother, suffers as a result. Such circumstances are not likely to produce literate children or more generally, a literate society. Trying to eradicate illiteracy may therefore involve trying to eradicate obscurantist taboos and traditions, which is a very difficult thing to do. (P. 19)

Makinwa-Adebusoye (1985) notes that every male or female must have equal and unfettered access to knowledge and skill acquisition to enable him/her to contribute in full measure to their nation's development. Other researchers (Synder & Ju 1984; Adeyeye 1985; Okojie 1985; Kendakai 1987; Brown-Sherman 1988) note the need for increased educational opportunities in all forms for girls and women. A 1988 UNICEF report indicates that the 1985 literacy rate for women in Liberia was 23 percent and for Nigeria 31 percent. Of particular note is the fact that the proportion of illiterate women is extremely high in rural areas. The stark fact is that illiteracy is cyclical, and because of women's close contact with young family members, the literacy rate for future generations partially rests in the early educational exposure the young girls receive. The importance of female literacy is further emphasized because of its direct link to child health and survival. According to Browne (cited in Anyadike 1989), there is an extraordinarily high correlation between mothers' literacy and their children's health. Various programs have been organized to address the educational needs of women as a target group. For example, programs that provide training in agriculture, nutrition, home economics, health, child psychology, etc., have been tried in Third World countries. However, more program development is needed.

Liberia. The concept of universal education has been subscribed to by Liberia since the 1830 resolution of the Board of Managers of the American Colonization Society. An 1839 public school law (revised in 1912) promulgated compulsory education in Liberia (Republic of Liberia Ministry of Education 1984). During the nineteenth century, few Liberians had access to formal education. Through the establishment of church-sponsored schools, children of American Liberians were more likely to receive primary and secondary schooling. Indigenous children were more likely to receive training through the Poro and Sande societies or other *bush schools* (Best 1974; Brown-Sherman 1982; Nelson 1984). As late as the post-World War II era, formal schooling was still limited to American Liberians.

In 1950 President William V. Tubman declared an all-out Literacy Campaign drive and called upon all civic, educational, and religious institutions, all officials of the government, all paramount and clan chiefs, and all citizens of the Republic to cooperate in this drive so as to reduce the percentage of illiteracy in the country (Laubach 1960). In 1965 President Tubman initiated a set of principles to guide educational activities. President Tolbert, in 1974, expanded the educational agenda to emphasize development of the total individual and equal opportunity.

The problem of providing education continued to plague the Liberian government, partly due to the mounting frustrations about inadequate educational opportunities of the indigenous populace. Although there were government efforts to equalize educational opportunities, the efforts were limited. For example, the 1971 Conference on Development Objectives and Strategies addressed regional equalization of educational opportunities, and the 1976–1980 National Socioeconomic Development Plan addressed the same national objective. Even though that objective did address the regional equalization needs of Liberian children and adults, others were needed. The need becomes clearer with the recognition of a Liberian population of 2.1 million and a literacy rate of 31.4 percent for individuals ten years of age and above (Republic of Liberia Ministry of Planning and Economic Affairs 1985). Equally noticeable is the 1988 UNICEF statistics that indicate literacy rates of 47 percent and 23 percent for men and women, respectively.

Adult Education in Liberia. According to the Republic of Liberia Ministry of Education (1984),

> The Division of Adult Education should be strengthened to fulfill its role in the promotion of literacy and general education; and the Division of Continuing Education, University of Liberia, and Cuttington University College should establish programs for trainers in Adult Education and Literacy. Specific attention was recommended to the provision of trainers for programs for women. (P. 12)

In addition to the efforts of the Ministry of Education, adult literacy initiatives have been undertaken by other government ministries, religious organizations, and concessionary companies. Deemed the coordinating agency, the Division of Adult Education (DAE) of the Ministry of Education is charged with developing programs and instructional materials and coordinating and monitoring all adult education (AE) and adult literacy (AL) programs. At present, however, sparse communication exists between DAE and AE/AL program sponsors (USAID 1988).

DAE instructional programs emphasize reading, writing, and numeracy, as well as community development (nutrition, health care, and food preparation). In 1987 most of this instruction took place in adult education centers, with a student population (minimum age of fifteen) of 3,763 at 207 centers (USAID 1988). This figure is a minuscule number when compared to the previously cited literacy rates.

Nonformal education programs that reach a larger segment of the population are operated by the Ministries of Agriculture, Rural Development, Health and Social Welfare, Family Planning Association of Liberia, the Catholic Diocese, the Methodist Church, the Lutheran Church, the Baptist Seminary, and the National Association for Adult Education (a nongovernmental agency). The Liberian Rural Communications Network (LRCN) offers additional avenues for reaching communities with adult literacy programs and nonformal education. Approximately 58 percent of Liberia's rural population is within the range of LRCN. Unfortunately, due to the absence of funds to purchase broadcast time, this valuable resource has been minimally used by the Division of Adult Education (USAID 1988).

Nigeria. At independence on 1 October 1960, Nigeria faced manpower shortages in all sectors of development. In an effort to seek remedies to this situation, the Ashby Commission convened at the request of the Nigerian government to conduct an investigation of Nigeria's need in the field of postschool certificate and higher education from 1960 to 1980. The Commission recommended the Anglo-American secondary and postsecondary model of education and massive funding for those levels. However, for that twenty-year period, Nigerian's population was underestimated by several million people. So the forecasted needs, up to 1980, for Nigeria's postsecondary education were out of date by 1970 (Federal Ministry of Information and Culture 1986).

With the military control of the government in January 1966 came revolutionary practices in the management of Nigerian education. Even though the missionary stronghold on education was firm, the first attempt at total government control of education commenced in early 1968. By October 1979, with the reintroduction of civilian governments, the takeover of missionary schools was virtually complete. In an effort to comply with the 1961 UNESCO proposal, free universal primary education was nationally introduced in 1976.

Until 1977, the general structure of formal education was the 6–5–2–3 system (6 years primary, 5 years secondary, 2 years postsecondary, and 3 years university education), a system that was changed to a 6–3–3–4 (6 years primary, 3 years junior secondary, 3 years senior secondary, 4 years university) structure in 1982 (Henshaw 1988). The junior secondary program is prevocational, while the senior secondary combines liberal arts, scientific, agricultural, technical, and commercial streams that are directed partly toward employment and partly toward higher education (Federal Ministry of Information and Culture

1986). It should be noted that universal primary education was not compulsory. However, parents who had been opposed to compulsory education soon realized its value to their children. Consequently, primary enrollments increased steadily. In 1977–1978 there were 845,838; in 1978–1979 there were 11,457,772; and in 1980 there were 15 million children (Akinde 1985).

Adult Education in Nigeria. In its *Blueprint* (1978–79) report, the Implementation Committee for the National Policy on Education outlined the approaches for adult and nonformal education. Recognizing the existence of the infrastructure for other types of education, primary to university, recommendations were advanced for the expansion, modification, and transformation of existing programs and materials. However, adult and nonformal education were virtually neglected; thus there was a dearth of teaching materials and trained personnel. Owing to a national policy of lifelong learning, the *Blueprint* (1978–79) recommended that educational facilities be open to persons of all ages at any time of life suitable to them. It further recommended that educational programs be systematized into recurrent programs where older learners can go back periodically into education and where there would be reciprocal recognition of qualifications gained in the formal sector of maturity and experience in lieu of formal educational achievement. Nonformal education, or education outside the formal school system, could take place on a farm, in a workshop, in a place of work, or in any other convenient place.

The objectives of the National Policy on Education were to (*a*) provide functional literacy education for adults who have never had the advantage of any formal education; (*b*) provide functional and remedial education for those young people who prematurely dropped out of the formal school system; (*c*) provide further education for different categories of completers of the formal education system in order to improve their basic knowledge and skills; (*d*) provide in-service, on-the-job, vocational and professional training for different categories of workers and professionals in order to improve their skills; and (*e*) give the adult citizens of the country the necessary aesthetic, cultural, and civic education for public enlightenment. The 1978 Implementation Committee recommended a sixth objective. The objective was to enable adult citizens of the country to contribute as productively as possible to national social and economic development. These objectives emphasized the need to provide meaningful connectives between formal education and work for adult learners.

The Nigerian National Council for Adult Education (NNCAE), launched in 1971 (Anyanwu, cited in Akinde 1985), was charged with strengthening adult education by enhancing training programs; by producing adequate literature; by conducting adult education conferences, seminars, and workshops; and by publishing adult education journals. Further, its role was to garner national support for adult education. Additionally, NNCAE encouraged cooperation among adult education, community development, and the coordination of programs; the promotion and organization of educational tours, national and international residential seminars, workshops and conferences, and community development projects; and the publication of a newsletter, a journal, and other publications.

According to Akinde (1985), adult education was an essential part of the Nigerian educational system with every state having a department of adult education. Most states have designated responsibility for this area to the Ministry of Education. At the university level, the Institute of Education has Adult Education Departments, as do Departments of Extramural Studies, Extension, or correspondence services in others. Adult literacy programs have also been organized by voluntary agencies including church missions, youth organizations, professional and private associations, and community organizations. There has been limited use of the mass media for nonformal education and adult literacy programs. However, Akinde (1985) notes that encouraging results have been realized from programming on Radio and Television Kaduna, Anambra State Broadcasting Corporation at Enugu, broadcasting through the Division of Extramural Studies at the University of Nigeria at Nsukka, and Nigerian Television in Ibadan. The expansion of these broadcasting services would provide greater outreach opportunities for bringing education programming to a larger number of individuals, especially in rural areas.

Conclusion

National policies indicate a recognition of the need by African countries to address the critical problem of illiteracy among all segments of its population. However, the bleak economic outlook for many countries suggests a need for an increase in financial support to improve educational systems. Although such increases could enhance the educational levels of both children and adults, most of the support will probably be used to educate children. The educational opportunities, then, for these children offer a greater safeguard for decreasing high illiteracy rates among them as they become adults. Also, an increase in enrollments at the primary level dictates the need for increased educational opportunities at the secondary and postsecondary levels. Finally, better coordination of educational programs by a designated governmental department with other governmental agencies and voluntary organizations could result in better outreach and greater yields among the adult illiterate population. African countries must make the reformation of their educational systems one of their highest priorities.

References

Adeyeye, V. 1985. *Avenues for and constraints on women's involvement in agriculture and rural development process in Nigeria.* Paper presented at Seminar on Nigerian Women and Development, June, University of Ibadan, Ibadan, Nigeria.

Akinde, C. O. 1985. Post-literacy activities and continuing education of adults in Nigeria. In R. H. Dave, D. A. Perera, and A. Ouane, eds., *Learning strategies for post-literacy and continuing education in Kenya, Nigeria, Tanzania, and United Kingdom.* Federal Republic of Germany: UNESCO, Institute of Education.

Aluko, G. B., and M. Alfa. 1985. Marriage and the family. In *Women in Nigeria.* London: Zed Books.

Anyadike, O. 1989. The illiteracy cycle. *West Africa.* 26 June–2 July, 1040–1041.

Best, K. Y. 1974. *Cultural policy in Liberia.* Paris: UNESCO.

Blueprint. 1978–79. Implementation Committee for the National Policy on Eduction. Lagos: Federal Republic of Nigeria.

Brown-Sherman, M. 1982. Education in Liberia. In A. Fatunway and T. U. Aisiku, eds., *Education in Africa: A comparative survey,* 162–87. London: George Allen and Unwin.

Brown-Sherman, M. A. 1988. An interview of the Liberian Professional Exchange. *The Liberian Professional Exchange,* August, 3–10.

Federal Ministry of Information and Culture. 1986. *Education in Nigeria.* Lagos: Federal Ministry of Information and Culture.

Henshaw, E. 1988. *Profile of Nigeria: Cultural heritage and national character.* Indiana, PA: Indiana University of Pennsylvania, School of Education.

Kendakai, D. E. S. 1987. *The role of Liberian women in the development process.* Paper presented at Fulbright-Hays Seminar on History and Culture, July, Monrovia, Liberia.

Laubach, F. C. 1960. *Thirty years with the silent billion.* Westwood, NJ: Fleming H. Revell, Co.

Lestage, A. 1982. *Literacy and illiteracy.* Report no. 42. Paris: UNESCO.

Makinwa-Adebusoye, P. 1985. *The socioeconomic contribution of Nigerian women to national development.* Paper presented at the Seminar on Nigerian Women and National Development, June, University of Ibadan.

Nelson, H. D. 1985. *Liberia: A country study.* Washington, DC: American University.

Nweke, T. 1985. The role of women in Nigerian society. In *Women In Nigeria,* 201–7. London: Zed Books.

Okojie, C. 1985. *A basic needs approach to the integration of Nigerian women in national development.* Paper presented at the Seminar on Nigerian Women and Development, June, University of Ibadan.

Oloruntimehin, O. 1985. *A new orientation to the inequality of rights of women: The cultural goals, institutional means and individual adaptation approach.* Paper presented at Seminar on Nigerian Women and Development, June, University of Ibadan.

Republic of Liberia Ministry of Education. 1984. *Towards the twenty-first century: Development-oriented policies and activities in the Liberian educational system.* McLean, VA: Institute for International Research.

Republic of Liberia Ministry of Planning and Economic Affairs. 1985. *Economic Survey of Liberia.* Monrovia, Liberia.

Synder, C., and S. Ju. 1984. *Architecture for progress: Information architecture and the ministerial management of the Liberian education system.* McLean, VA: Institute for International Research, Inc.

United Nations Department of International Economic and Social Affairs. 1986. *Living conditions in developing countries in the mid-1980s: Supplement to the 1985 report on the world social situation.* NY: United Nations.

USAID. 1988. United States Agency for International Development. *Liberia: Education and Human Resources Sector Assessment.* Tallahassee, FL: Education Efficiency Clearinghouse.

Yacine, S. 1982. *Education in Africa in the light of the Harare Conference, 1982, no. 42.* Paris: UNESCO.

Adults' Perceptions of Literacy in Senegal and Egypt

Alice M. Scales and Lawrence B. Zikri

Educators must know their students' interests, habits, needs, ideas, etc., to better plan and therefore influence the learning of those students. Often, teachers in adult literacy education programs lack appropriate instructional preparation for teaching adults. Many lack the basic knowledge regarding adult habits, needs, and ideas. Particularly in North America where faculty in higher education institutions provide education programs for teachers and students from developing countries, many faculty members

> . . . however dedicated and well-intentioned, lack . . . the knowledge to provide truly relevant and useful programs. . . . those teaching should frequently and for sustained periods of time, visit countries from which they draw their students and maintain professional contacts . . . so that they are better equipped to teach . . . students . . . . (*Final report: Fourth international* . . . 1985, 35)

Adult literacy education programs

> should be designed to take into account the fact that adults enter education from very diverse backgrounds with a wide range of life experiences and learning needs and therefore should be designed specifically with adult's needs, interests and learning styles in mind. (*Final report: Fourth international* . . . 1985, 65)

This chapter is designed to provide adult educators with knowledge of the educational experiences and learning needs of adults in two developing African countries. Particularly, the reader will examine literacy educational experiences through reading habits and reading interests of adult students in Senegal, West Africa, and in Egypt, East Africa. Low literacy rates in those countries provided the impetus for exploring their reading habits and their reading interests. Estimated literacy levels for Senegal and Egypt were 10 percent and 45 percent respectively (*The World Factbook* 1988).

Whereas we summarized information regarding Senegal's literacy status (that includes an overview of its educational system and an investigation of Senegalese adult reading habits) from a previous study (Scales & Burley 1984), a presentation of Egypt's literacy status (which includes an overview of its educational system and an investigation of Egyptian adult reading habits) is the primary focus for this chapter. Lastly, the discussion and conclusion section contrasts major findings from the Senegalese and Egyptian studies.

Senegal

Scales and Burley (1984) studied the reading habits of college and adult subjects in Senegal. Included in their study was a review of Senegal's educational system. It has an elementary, two secondary, a vocational, and a university level of study. Several factors that were noted as having a negative impact on that system were (*a*) school language—children had to spend about

50 percent of their time learning the French language; (*b*) school curriculum—it was heavily influenced by the French model of education; (*c*) expatriated faculties—large numbers of faculty were Frenchmen who perpetuated France's system of education; (*d*) school availability—schools were not accessible to large numbers of children; and (*e*) insufficient finance—not enough money was available to support education for most of the people.

Fifty-nine male and female subjects whose ages ranged from sixteen to forty-five participated in the study. Their educational levels ranged from secondary school to postgraduate study. Subjects were grouped as married and single and as traditional and nontraditional students. All subjects were attending classes at the Centre Cultural Americain in Dakar, Senegal.

Subjects responded to a four-category, fifteen-item written questionnaire. The categories were "satisfaction with reading, types of material read, perceptions of reading efficiency, and ease and availability of obtaining reading materials" (Scales & Burley 1984, 123). Data from the questionnaire were subjected to chi-square analysis to determine differences between subjects (married and single, traditional and nontraditional). No differences were found. However, data inspected by categories for practical differences (3/4 or more of the subjects answered yes to an item) among responses of subjects showed preferences for their satisfaction with reading, types of material read, and reading efficiency. Specifically, results indicated that subjects would like to read better; they enjoyed reading; they read newspapers often; they enjoyed reading fiction and nonfiction; they would take a course to improve their reading; and they retained most of what they read within a reasonable period of time (Scales & Burley 1984).

A report (Specialized Committee of Adult Education . . . 1983) indicated that the latest statistics, which were 1977, estimated literacy in Egypt to be around 47 percent for those individuals between fifteen and fifty years of age. Forty-five percent was the estimated literacy level reported in *The world factbook* (1988); no age designation was given. This suggests an illiteracy level that ranges from 53 percent to 55 percent of the 50 million Egyptians. Of that 50 million, an estimated 22 million cannot read or write above a fourth-grade level.

Egypt
Educational System

In spite of the Egyptian authorities' efforts to fight illiteracy for many years, hardly any percentage decrease has occurred within the last twenty years. This very slow decrease is related to the educational system, the curricula, and some social and economic factors.

The National Egyptian System of Education (National Center for Education Research . . . 1984) has several components. First is the basic compulsory education that consists of six years of elementary school and three years of academic or vocational preparatory education. At the end of the elementary and preparatory levels, students must pass a final examination in order to proceed to the next level (Sorour 1977). Second is the secondary education stage. That stage includes three years of general secondary schooling (high academic);

three or five years of technical secondary schooling (industrial, agricultural, commercial administrative, and serviceable); and five years in teacher preparation institutions that prepare teachers to teach at the primary level. Certificates are awarded after successful completion of the secondary program and the national examination. Third, a university or college education requires four to seven years of education depending on the type of college and area of specialization. For example: the College of Arts and Science requires four years of education, the College of Engineering requires five years, and the College of Medicine requires seven years. All universities and colleges have such graduate education programs as M.A., M.S., and Ph.D. Programs are different in content and required number of years in attendance.

Parallel to the National Egyptian System of Education is the El-Azhar educational system. El-Azhar's purpose is to teach Islamic religious studies and to teach academic and vocational studies. El-Azhar's system contains six years of elementary, four years of preparatory, four years of secondary, and four to seven years of university education. El-Azhar attracts a number of foreign students from Asia and other African countries. Their primary interest is learning the Arabic language, studying Islamic subjects, and conducting research in those areas.

Examinations are the same in the two systems of education. For each student, a final examination at the end of an academic year represents 60 percent of their grade, and several periodic tests during the academic year represent 40 percent of their grade. At the end of every educational level, a final examination constitutes 100 percent of their grade, irrespective of tests taken during the year. Some colleges and universities are using two terms or two semesters per academic year. Likewise, examinations are administered per term or semester.

Apart from the traditional educational system are educational types that have been introduced for social and environmental conditions. Among them are language schools, schools for the gifted and handicapped, and specific schools.

The educational system in Egypt seems to be suffering from insufficient finances. Evidence of this may be noted from their poor physical facilities. Many teachers are poorly prepared to teach. Even though all children between the ages of five and seven must be enrolled in the first elementary grade of the basic education curriculum, a lack of enough schools prevents enrollment for many children. Among those who do enroll in elementary school, the dropout rate is high. An incentive for dropping out of school in Egypt is to become a handworker (laborer). Handworkers may have significantly higher incomes than university graduates. Knowledge of this difference in income seems to stimulate youth to want to become handworkers, so they drop out of school.

Investigation

1. *Problem.* Adults from the Cairo and El-Giza areas of northern Egypt in East Africa were the subjects in our study. Their perceptions of their own reading habits and interests were investigated. Specifically, we used five reading habits categories (satisfaction with reading, types of material read, reading efficiency, ease and availability of

obtaining reading materials, impact of environment on reading) to investigate, through six hypotheses, differences within groups of Egyptian subjects.

2. *Subjects.* Two hundred thirty-three Egyptian males and sixty-one Egyptian females, who were students at Centers for Vocational Training, College of Tourism and Hotels, and El-Azhar University participated in this study. Mean age for the males was 21, females 23.5, married males and females 30.5, and single males and females 19. When grouped as industrial subjects, their mean age was 17; as city subjects, their mean age was 25. Married males comprised 15.6 percent of the subjects, single males 63.6 percent, married females 7.2 percent, and single females 13.6 percent. Educationally, 40.5 percent were enrolled in vocational training centers, 8.8 percent had graduated from commercial secondary schools, 25.9 percent were enrolled in colleges, 10.5 percent had graduated from college and were employed in government offices, and 14.3 percent had completed postgraduate study. Geographically, 60 percent of the subjects lived in the city of Cairo where the population is over 10 million. In that city can be found various socioeconomic levels, various classes of people, and persons working at different types of jobs. Forty percent of the subjects lived in industrial areas that include Shopra, El-Khema, and Impapa, El-Giza. Large-size factories employed people in those areas. Middle class represents the socioeconomic level in that area.

3. *Questionnaire.* The twenty-nine-item Reading Habits Questionnaire (RHQ) (see Appendix) was developed by the authors for this study. Some of the items were rewritten and/or compiled from Scales and Burley (1984) and Youssef and Hamshari (1981) questionnaires. RHQ was translated into Arabic before it was administered to the Egyptian students. RHQ was untimed. Responses to the items were either yes (positive) or no (negative). One item was open-ended. All items except the open-ended one were clustered into five categories. The categories were (*a*) *satisfaction with reading* (items 1, 2, 3, 4, 28)—it revealed current reading status; (*b*) *types of material read* (items 5, 6, 7, 8, 9)—it included reading of newspapers, religious materials, etc.; (*c*) *reading efficiency* (items 10, 11, 21, 22, 23)—it included levels of competence in reading; (*d*) *ease and availability of obtaining reading materials* (items 12, 14, 16, 24, 26, 27)—it included borrowing and purchasing (Scales & Burley 1984); and (*e*) *impact of environment on reading* (items 13, 15, 17, 18, 19, 20, 25)—it included places where reading materials can be found (Youssef & Hamshari 1981). The open-ended item asked subjects to list topics that describe types of material that they preferred to read. Other items on the questionnaire requested such demographic information as gender, marital status, occupation, age, and education.

4. *Procedures.* Permission to administer RHQ to Egyptian subjects was obtained from the Ministry of Industry, the College of Tourism and Hotels, and El-Azhar University. Sites were three randomly selected Centers for Vocational Training, the College of Tourism and Hotels, and El-Azhar University. Two classes of students in each Center for Vocational Training were chosen at random as subjects for this study. Students at the College of Tourism and Hotels were selected at random. At El-Azhar University, government employees were chosen at random as subjects. At each institution, purposes of the study and the questionnaire were explained to the dean, the teachers, and the subjects by one of the authors. All selected subjects filled out the questionnaire.

Even though it took approximately twenty minutes for the Egyptian subjects to fill out the questionnaire, it took approximately three months for the authors to get permission to administer the questionnaire and to administer it to the 294 subjects.

In this study subjects were grouped by marital status (married and single), gender (male and female), and occupation (white-collar [WC], professional, WC married, WC single, WC males, WC females). Pertinent issues to the study's problem were investigated for marital status and gender, through hypotheses 1 and 2. Occupation was investigated through hypotheses 3, 4, 5, and 6. Following each hypothesis is a presentation of the analyzed data from the questionnaire. Results from item 29 have been presented in the findings section.

5. *Results.* Hypotheses 1, 3, and 5 were subjected to chi-square analysis. Significance was at the .05 level. Hypotheses 2, 4, and 6 were considered to be of practical significance by the authors when 3/4 or more of the subjects responded yes to an item. Results of subjects' responses for practical significance are presented by categories as (*a*) satisfaction with reading, (*b*) types of material read, (*c*) reading efficiency, (*d*) ease and availability of obtaining reading materials, and (*e*) impact of environment on reading.

Hypothesis 1. No statistically significant differences will be found between *married and single* and between *male and female* subjects regarding their perceptions of their reading habits.

These data for hypothesis 1 were analyzed by chi-square. Of the twenty-eight items, a statistical significant difference (X^2 = 16.198) between married and single subjects was found for only item 7 with 1 *df* at *p.* < .05 level. Significant differences with 1 *df* at *p.* < .05 level were reported between males and females for items 1, 4, 6, 9, 14, 15, 26, and 28. Significant chi-square values for the eight items were 5.468, 4.143, 19.513, 14.448, 14.657, 8.061, 14.074, and 10.648, respectively.

Hypothesis 2. Practical differences will not be found in the responses of *married, single, male,* and *female* subjects regarding perceptions of their reading habits.

These data for hypothesis 2 were analyzed and are presented by each category. *Satisfaction with reading category.* Practical differences were reported for items 2, 3, and 28. All groups reported (range was 85.9 percent to 93.7 percent) that they would like to read better and that they enjoyed reading. Only the married, single, and male groups reported (range was 77.3 percent to 80.7 percent) that they would like to take a reading course to improve their reading.

Types of material read category. Practical differences were found for items 5, 6, 7, and 9. All groups reported (range was 85.4 percent to 90.2 percent) that they read newspapers often. The female group with a percentage range from 80.2 percent to 85.3 percent reported enjoying reading magazines and works of fiction. Married (94.7 percent) and male (75 percent) groups reported enjoying reading religious materials.

Reading efficiency category. A practical difference was reported for item 22. Specifically, 75.6 percent of the married group, 81.4 percent of the single group, 80.3 percent of the male group, and 80.3 percent of the female group reported remembering most of what they read within a reasonable period of time.

Ease and availability of obtaining reading materials category. A practical difference was reported for item 24. Percentages were 84.2 for the married group, 82.7 for the single group, 81.1 for the male group, and 90.2 for the female group. Moreover, the groups reported that they have reading material in their homes.

Impact of environment on reading category. Practical differences were reported for items 18 and 25. All four groups with a percentage range from 79 percent to 90.2 percent reported that they read text on the television screen and that they read at home.

Hypothesis 3. There is no statistically significant difference between *white-collar* (office workers and secretaries) and *professional* (graduate assistants and teachers at universities) subjects regarding their perceptions of their reading habits.

These data for hypothesis 3 were analyzed by chi-square. Of the 28 items, statistically significant differences were found for items 3, 10, 11, 12, 13, 18, 22, 25, and 26 between white collar and professional groups at $p. < .05$ level. Significant chi-square values for the nine items were 4.137, 33.483, 17.079, 42.708, 10.99, 4.708, 5.00, 8.370, and 7.257, respectively.

Hypothesis 4. Practical differences will not be found in the responses of *white-collar* and *professional* subjects regarding their reading habits.

These data for hypothesis 4 were analyzed and are presented by each category. *Satisfaction with reading category.* Practical differences were found for white-collar and professional subjects. Specifically, for item 2, from 92.8 percent to 98.2 percent subjects would like to read better; for item 3, from 93 percent to 100 percent subjects like to read; and for item 28, from 77.2 percent to 88.1 percent subjects would like to take a course to improve their reading.

Types of material read category. Practical significant differences were found for items 5 and 7. Eighty-nine and one-half percent of the white-collar and 93 percent of the professional subjects indicated that they read newspapers. Ninety-one percent of the white-collar and 88 percent of the professional subjects indicated that they read religious materials.

Reading efficiency category. Practical differences were found for the professional subjects group only. For item 10, 97.6 percent and item 11, 83.3 percent indicated that their job required a lot of reading and required them to read. For item 22, 90.1 percent reported remembering most of what they read in a reasonable period of time.

Ease and availability of obtaining reading materials category. Practical differences for the professional group were reported for item 12 (83.3 percent) and item 26 (92.2 percent). That group indicated that it did find material to read at work and that it did use the library to obtain reading materials. For item 24, 86 percent of the white-collar and 95.2 percent of the professional subjects reported that they had reading materials at home.

Impact of environment on reading category. A practical difference was reported for item 18 (78.6 percent read text on the television screen) for the professional group. Item 25 showed differences for white-collar (80.7 percent) and professional (100 percent) subjects. Both groups reported that they read at home.

Hypothesis 5. No statistically significant differences will be found between *white-collar (WC)* married and *WC single* and between *WC males* and *WC females* perceptions of their reading habits.

Chi-square analysis of the data for hypothesis 5 revealed significant differences between WC married and WC single for item 9 (X^2 with 1 df = 5.326) and item 18 (X^2 with 1 df = 6.771) at the .05 level. Significant differences were also determined between WC males and WC females for items 6, 9, 13, 14, 15, 16, 17, 18, and 23. Significant chi-square values for the nine items were 5.642, 7.086, 5.605, 3.903, 5.829, 10.514, 8.132, 7.438, and 4.740, respectively.

Hypothesis 6. Practical differences will not be found in the responses of *WC married, WC single, WC males,* and *WC females* regarding their perceptions of their reading habits.

These data for hypothesis 6 were analyzed and presented by each category. Satisfaction with reading category. Practical differences were found (range 76.2 percent to 100 percent) for WC married, WC single, WC males, and WC females for items 2, 3, and 28. Specifically, subjects would like to read better; they liked to read; and excluding the males group, all would like to take a course to improve their reading.

Types of materials read category. Practical differences were found for WC married and WC males (items 5, 7), WC single and WC females (items 5, 6, 7, 9). All groups reported (range 81 percent to 97.2 percent) that they read newspapers and that they read religious materials. WC single and WC females reported that they also read magazines and that they enjoyed reading nonfiction.

Reading efficiency category. A practical difference was reported for item 22. Specifically, 78.1 percent of the WC females reported that they remembered most of what they read within a reasonable period of time.

Ease and availability of obtaining reading materials category. A practical difference was reported for item 24. Eighty-one percent of the WC married, 95.2 percent of the WC single, 84 percent of the WC males, and 87.5 percent of the WC females reported that they have reading materials in their homes.

Impact of environment on reading category. Practical differences were reported for items 18 and 25. For item 18, 88.9 percent of the WC married and 90.6 percent of the WC females reported that they read from the television screen. For item 25, 75 percent of the WC married, 90.5 percent of the WC single, 80 percent of the WC males, and 81.3 percent of the WC females reported that they read at home.

6. *Findings.* From this investigation we found the following: (*a*) *Marital and Gender Groups.* There was a reported significant difference between *married* and *single* Egyptian groups regarding the reading of religious materials. Futhermore, more married than single and more males than females indicated that they read religious materials.

Significant differences were reported between Egyptian *males* and *females* regarding their satisfaction with current reading behavior, their allotting of their time for reading, their reading of magazines, their reading of fiction, their finding reading materials at Mosques, their borrowing reading materials from libraries, and their taking a reading course to improve their reading. Additionally, at least 75 percent of the married, single, and male groups indicated that they would like to take a reading course to improve their reading.

Seventy-five percent or more of *all groups* reported that they would like to read better than they do now, they liked to read, they read newspapers, they remembered most of what they read within a reasonable period of time, they have reading materials in their homes, they read in their homes, and they read text on the television screen. Only the *female* group reported enjoying reading magazines and works of fiction. The *married* and *male* groups reported that they enjoyed reading religious materials.

(*b*) *Occupational Groups.* Significant differences were reported between *white-collar* and *professional* groups regarding their like for reading, their job demands that require a lot of reading, their reading anything for their job, their finding anything to read at work, their reading at work, their reading text on the television screen, their remembering most of what they read in a reasonable period of time, their reading at home, and their using the library to obtain reading materials. But more *white-collar* than *professional* subjects reported reading religious materials.

Seventy-five percent or more of *white-collar* and *professional* groups reported that they would: like to read better, liked to read, would like to take a course to improve their reading, read newspapers, read religious materials, and read at home. Further, the *professional group* reported that a lot of reading was required on the job, most of what was read was remembered, the library was used to obtain reading materials, and text was read from the television screen.

A reported significant difference did occur between the WC married and WC single groups regarding their enjoyment of reading nonfiction and their reading from the television screen.

Significant differences were reported between *WC males* and *WC females* regarding their reading of religious material, reading of fiction, reading at work, finding reading materials at the Mosques, reading at the Mosques, finding reading material at health centers or hospitals, reading at health centers or hospitals, reading text from the television screen, and like for reading to other people.

Seventy-five percent or more of *all groups* reported that they would like to read better, liked to read, read newspapers and religious materials, had reading materials in their homes, and read at home.

(c) *Topics that Subjects Prefer.* The Egyptian subjects reported twenty-six topics as their preferences for reading material. Of the twenty-six topics, over 50 percent of *all groups* indicated religion as a reading preference. Novels received the second highest rating with over 50 percent for all except the married, males, and professional groups. Over 50 percent of the female group reported poetry as their reading preference, and over 50 percent of the married group reported technology as their reading preference (Scales & Zikri 1988a).

Discussion and Conclusion

Common problems noted within the Senegalese and Egyptian educational systems were that there was a need for sufficient funds to finance their educational systems, the curricula did not seem to necessarily correspond to the needs and interests of the people, there were not enough schools to accommodate the populations, and many teachers seemed to have been either unprepared as teachers or nescience of the cultures where they taught.

In 1975 the school enrollment ratio for girls ages six through twenty-three in Egypt was reported as 30 percent to less than 40 percent, and in Senegal, as 10 percent to less than 20 percent. For boys of the same age group in Egypt it was 50 percent to less than 60 percent, and in Senegal, 20 percent to less than

30 percent (*Comparative analysis of male and female . . .* April 1980). Reasons for such low enrollments may be due to the lack of schools, inappropriate curricula, and underprepared teachers. An additional reason may be the shortage of books in the countries. *An international survey of book production during the last decades* (1985) indicated that Egypt published 1,037 books in 1955; 3,335 in 1965; and 1,486 in 1976 for its population. On the other hand, statistics for Senegal indicated no data for 1955; 67 books published in 1960; no data for 1965; and 47 books published in 1976 for its population. Low book production rates were attributed to the paucity of funds to finance the book industry, lack of experienced educational writers and illustrators in Africa, low purchasing power of the populations, and a multiplicity of languages in most African countries. Problems with book production has necessitated the importation of books from developed countries. Such books, written not necessarily for Senegalese and Egyptian populations, are used to educate them.

Results from the Senegalese (Scales & Burley 1984) and Egyptian studies noted that subjects from both countries would like to read better, liked to read, read newspapers often, enjoyed reading fiction, would like to take a course to improve their reading, and retained most of what they read within a reasonable period of time. Preparation to respond to their reading preferences, by educators, would necessitate that the educators become knowledgeable of the needs and interests of the people in those countries. Additionally, educators should be cognizant of literacy developments and political situations (Scales & Zikri 1988b) that may impede their intended educational endeavors. Hence, an attempt to teach them to read and write should be considered as one factor that is relevant to the improvement of their social, economic, cultural, and civic conditions. Improvement of that factor may occur within the rubric of literacy programs (*The struggle against . . .* 1983).

Youssef and Hamshari (1981) studied reading habits of young people (primary, preparatory, secondary) in the Cairo and Giza educational zones. Among the findings were that their reading preferences included reading newspapers, magazines, novels, poetry, history, biographies, riddles, and games. Percentages of the 894 subjects in the study who selected the reading preferences ranged from 20 percent to 53 percent. Negative factors that seem to have contributed to the development of such low percentages were (*a*) the concept of learning—memorization and recitation seem to have been the dominate approach, thus not allowing for inferential activities that could increase reading comprehension; (*b*) the lack in school-library services—few existed and they were generally understaffed; (*c*) the lack of suitable reading materials—beyond textbooks that respond to prescribed syllabi, little or no effort had been made to produce free reading or trade books; (*d*) the soaring prices of books—inflation had been among the factors responsible for reducing the purchasing power of the Egyptian family's income, therefore books were not considered a priority. Results from their study, like the results from the studies presented in this chapter, suggested a need for literacy programs.

Over 50 percent of all groups in the current Egyptian study reported religious material as their reading preference, seven groups reported novels, two groups reported poetry, and one group reported technology. A recommendation is that whenever adult literacy programs are planned for Senegalese and Egyptian students or whenever educators plan to prepare themselves to teach Senegalese and Egyptian learners that the previous findings be considered as a part of the plan. Our final comment is to encourage more study and research, not only of adult Senegalese and Egyptian literacy perceptions, but of adults' literacy perceptions in other developing countries. Such study and research will assist in the continued preparation of adult educators.

References

An international survey of book production during the last decades. 1985. Division of Statistics on Culture and Communication, Office of Statistics. No. 26, Statistical Reports and Studies. Distributed by NY: Unipub. Paris: UNESCO.

Comparative analysis of male and female enrollment and illiteracy. 1980. Two studies prepared by the division of statistics on education Office of Statistics, with assistance of S. Slama and C. Sauvageot, consultants. UNESCO, April.

Final report: Fourth international conference on adult education. 1985. Paris: UNESCO, 19–29, March.

National Center for Educational Research and G. Directorate for Documentation and Information. 1984. *The development of education in the Arab Republic of Egypt from 1981–1984.* Cairo, Egypt.

Scales, A. M., and J. A. Burley. 1984. Reading habits of Senegalese adult and college students. *The Negro Educational Review* XXXV(3–4):121–30.

Scales, A. M., and L. B. Zikri. 1988b. Literacy development in Egypt: Current research and practice issues. *The Negro Educational Review* XXXVIV(3–4):4–13.

Scales, A. M., and L. B. Zikri. 1988a. *Reading habits of adults in Egypt.* ERIC Document Reproduction Service no. CS 009–141.

Sorour, A. H. 1977. Arab Republic of Egypt. In A. S. Knowles, ed. in chief, *The international encyclopedia of higher education,* 1411. San Francisco: Jossey-Bass Publishers.

The Specialized Committee of Adult Education and the Academy of Scientific and Technological Research of Egypt. 1983. *The report of fighting literacy in Egypt in 1983.* Special unpublished report. Cairo, Egypt.

The struggle against Illiteracy throughout the world: Some successful experiments between 1971 and 1981 and future prospects. 1983. UNESCO.

The world factbook. 1988. Produced by the Central Intelligence Agency. USA.

Youssef, Y. K., and M. A. E. Hamshari. 1981 January. *Required reading levels for post literacy needs and contributions of educational institutions to the spread of the reading habit among young people: A field study.* National Center for Educational Research in collaboration with UNESCO. Egypt.

**APPENDIX
READING HABITS
QUESTIONNAIRE**

DIRECTIONS: Fill in the appropriate spaces for items A through F.

A. _____ or _____
     (city)   (industrial area)

B. Sex: Male ____ Female ____   C. Married ____ Single ____

D. Your occupation is _____   E. Your age is _____

F. EDUCATION: Check the highest level attained.

Elementary school: enrolled ____, completed ____

Vocational preparatory: enrolled ____, completed ____

Secondary: enrolled ___, completed ____

Technical: enrolled ____, completed ____

Teacher training: enrolled ____, completed ____

College: enrolled ____, completed ____

Postgraduate: enrolled ____, completed ____

G. DIRECTIONS: Please circle *Y* for yes or circle *N* for no.

Y – N   1.   Are you satisfied with the way you read now?

Y – N   2.   Would you like to read better than you do now?

Y – N   3.   Do you like to read?

Y – N   4.   Do you ever stop to read when you are busy?

Y – N   5.   Do you read newspapers?

Y – N   6.   Do you read magazines?

Y – N   7.   Do you read religious materials?

Y – N   8.   Do you enjoy reading nonfiction such as diaries, essays, and biographies?

Y – N   9.   Do you enjoy reading works of fiction such as short stories, novels, and poetry?

Y – N   10.   Does your job require a lot of reading?

Y – N   11.   Does your job require you to read anything?

Y – N   12.   Do you find anything to read where you work?

Y – N   13.   Do you read at work?

Y – N   14.   Do you find anything to read at the Mosque?

Y – N   15.   Do you read at the Mosque?

Y – N   16.   Do you find anything to read at the health centers or hospitals?

Y – N   17.   Do you read at the health centers or hospitals?

Y – N   18.   Do you read anything on the television screen?

Y – N   19.   Do television programs make you read anything afterwards?

Y – N   20.   Does the radio make you read anything afterwards?

Y – N   21.   Do you use much of what you read?

Y – N   22.   Do you remember most of what you read in a reasonable period of time?

Y – N   23.   Do you like to read to other people?

Y – N   24.   Do you have any reading materials at home?

Y – N   25.   Do you read at home?

Y – N   26.   Do you use the library to obtain reading materials?

Y – N   27.   Do you buy most of your reading materials?

Y – N   28.   If possible, would you take a reading course to improve your reading?

        29.   List topics of material that you would prefer to read.

Literacy Education in the U.S.
Amy D. Rose

Evidence shows that there has always been a need for adults to demonstrate some form of literacy in the U.S. For example, adults have the need to read religious documents, cultural items, and local, federal, and other public records. When they are unable to read such documents and records, they must depend on others. Literacy assures freedom from dependency. It has become an instrument to independence. My purpose in this chapter is to explore how such independence emerged through the U.S. history of adult literacy education. Moreover, how has literacy supported religion; how has it influenced U.S. culture; how has it assisted movement into modern times; and how have U.S. federal policies influenced it? Even though a thorough examination of my previously stated concerns are not possible in this chapter, my following discussion will show literacy as a religious instrument, literacy as a cultural imperative, literacy's link to modern society, and other dimensions of literacy.

Literacy as Religious Instrumentality

The development of literacy education cannot be understood without some mention of the estimates of national literacy rates. During the colonial period, especially the eighteenth century, literacy rates steadily rose. By 1789, 90 percent of the European American males had some form of crude literacy as indicated by their ability to sign legal documents. The latest evidence seems to indicate that European American women's literacy was also rising during this period, but did not reach the same level (Kaestle 1985; Lockridge 1974).

Historians differ in their interpretations of the reasons for this increase. While some ascribe it to a religious impulse, which occurred primarily through the development of schools, others saw it as more of a social phenomenon with family instruction playing a key role (Kaestle 1985; Lockridge 1974). In any event, increasing literacy rates are ascribed to better education for children with almost no mention being made of efforts to educate adults. There is good reason for this. The education of adults was never a priority and, in fact, was usually an afterthought. Whatever formal literacy education took place was to be found in evening schools.

Initially, these evening schools were restricted to the winter, but by the mid-eighteenth century, there is evidence of evening school classes being held in the summer as well. While the hours varied, most instruction seems to have taken place between six and eight in the evening, every night of the week.

Different types of individuals attended the classes. For example, there were classes for women, African Americans, and Native Americans. In all cases, the classes were offshoots of schools for children. Some were operated by schoolmasters offering classes for pay; others were subsidized by philanthropic associations. Little distinction was made between children and adults in terms of curriculum. There is some indication of feeling that young children should not attend the evening schools because they would take up too much of the teacher's time. Other than this, however, many different classes and types of individuals could be found attending these schools. By the end of the eighteenth century, indenture agreement sometimes indicated that the master was to allow the servant to attend evening or winter schools. These agreements stipulated that the servant would attend school to learn reading, writing, and mathematics, "so far as will be sufficient to manage his trade" (Seybolt 1925, 21). As the curriculum became more complex and the teachers more qualified, some of the emphasis on basic education shifted. Yet many schools still concentrated on basic reading and writing.

Beyond mere description, however, it is difficult to arrive at the meaning of these schools or of their literacy efforts. The initial impetus behind the schools seems to have been for religious advancement. The schools were part of a general Protestant belief that each individual should be able to read the Bible in order to achieve salvation. Thus, while literacy was not a social good by itself, it was an instrument for salvation. By the eighteenth century, when evening school education was introduced into indenture contracts in urban areas, basic literacy was considered an important aspect of commerce, essential enough for it to be considered the master's responsibility to provide.

Teaching and learning basic reading and writing was embedded in both religious and economic motives. By the eighteenth century, in urban areas, basic literacy had become a key to economic survival. Literacy was not seen in and of itself as a value, rather it was deemed important in helping the individual improve materially as well as gain salvation. While schooling for children was growing in importance, basic education for adults was not emphasized (although it was provided). Literacy would help form a truly Christian character as well as encourage the poor to help themselves (Soltow & Stevens 1981).

By the nineteenth century, literacy had become a "favored vehicle for cultural and political integration" (Soltow & Stevens 1981, 19). That is, no longer was literacy a means to achieving an end, but an end in itself, which would signify greater consensus within the community. Basic literacy had become a cultural imperative by midcentury. It was necessary for socialization at a time of increasing diversity. Literacy was thus a virtue in and of itself. The methods and materials used to teach adults reading and writing varied little from previous formats. Even though this focus could be seen in the education of adults, it was more forcefully exhibited in the public school movement of this period.

Literacy as a Cultural Imperative: 1780–1880

By 1790, 90 percent of adult European American males were literate. Thus, efforts at promoting adult literacy were primarily focused on African Americans and immigrants (Kaestle 1985). Some of the most prominent schools for African Americans were in Philadelphia. In 1789, the Quakers established the Association for the Free Instruction of Adult Colored Persons. This group sponsored classes for men and women, which were held in three locations in the evenings and on Sundays. The impetus for such classes came from both

African American and European American leaders. Many of the African American leaders ascribed their own success to their ability to read and write and, hence, saw literacy as a key to social mobility. Within the African American community in Philadelphia, there was a high rate of illiteracy among former slaves. Education was viewed as the ingredient that could make citizens out of slaves. Yet, due to a lack of money and a tradition of early indenture, children were rarely sent to school. Thus, despite the efforts of leaders, illiteracy remained high among the ex-slaves. Nash (1988) postulates that for ex-slaves, brought up in an oral culture, the investment of time necessary to attend school was just not worth it. Thus, while the elite was calling for a community based on a common education, the African American community in Philadelphia was using its religious and fraternal organizations to educate its people.

The first time that the federal government became directly involved in education was when a series of schools were set up under the auspices of the Freedmen's Bureau. The schools represented the merging of religious, economic, and communal aspirations. Freedmen's schools, originally begun by philanthropic religious organizations, were expanded in 1865 with the passage of the Freedmen's Bureau Law. Although federal government funding was at first nonexistent and then minimal, it did provide the impetus for the establishment of public schools throughout the South.

The schools were designed with children in mind, but Sunday and evening schools were opened in order to attract adults. By all reports, the adults were particularly eager to learn and flocked to the new schools. Yet, they quickly dropped out, as energy levels flagged. If a choice had to be made, then clearly the children would stay in school at the expense of the parent (Morris 1981).

The reason behind the movement to educate the freed men was complex. Motivated by missionary groups, the educational effort was led by European American abolitionists who were determined to prove that the people freed from slavery were educable. Through education, the people would prove their character and assume their rightful place as valuable community members and citizens. Additionally, there were many instances of southern African Americans who, on their own, set up schools for children and adults before the evangelical groups arrived. For African Americans, education represented the possibility of mobility as well as full participation in a democratic society (Morris 1981).

As literacy among European American males became almost universal, literacy came to be seen not only as an instrument for mobility and salvation, but a virtue in and of itself. Merely the acquisition of literacy would change the individual. It would in effect socialize people who were not part of the mainstream culture. The transformation of literacy during this period placed a stigma on illiterates. Not only were they unable to compete in the marketplace, but they were viewed as lacking in the prerequisites for social intercourse. Literacy was a "favored vehicle for cultural and political integration." Thus, literacy came to be a means for developing community and moral consensus. In an increasingly diverse population, literacy provided access to common views and mores (Soltow & Stevens 1981, 19).

The late nineteenth and early twentieth centuries saw another shift in perceptions of literacy. In addition to being a social virtue, literacy was viewed as imperative for proper functioning in modern life. In this sense, literacy proponents maintained an individualistic orientation, while placing literacy as a prerequisite to the economic and social well-being of the entire community. Thus, the necessity of integration and consensus was merged with the perception that the new economic order required literacy. No longer was literacy deemed important for advancement, rather the lack of it was a disability that needed to be remedied. Thus, literacy became a symbol of acceptability into modern American society. Talbot (1916) wrote:

Literacy and Modernization

> Literacy is the first requisite for democracy. Unless means are provided for reaching the illiterate and the near-illiterate, every social problem must remain needlessly complex and slow of solution, because social and representative government rests upon an implied basis of universal ability to read and write. (P. 5)

The period before World War I saw a dramatic change in public perceptions about illiteracy. In 1910, few had seen illiteracy as a major social problem, but by 1920 its eradication had become an accepted idea. By 1920, the war had clearly indicated that illiteracy interfered with national defense, subverted voting, led to misinformation and susceptibility to propaganda, and hindered religion. Most importantly it hindered economic growth and industrial productivity (Stewart 1922).

Several notable attempts to teach adults basic literacy were inaugurated during this period. One of the most prominent was the Moonlight Schools movement, which began in Kentucky and eventually led to state and national campaigns against illiteracy. The first Moonlight School was established in Kentucky in 1911, arising out of the human need "to emancipate from illiteracy all those enslaved in its bondage" (Stewart 1922, 9).

Begun as a countywide effort to teach adults how to read and write, the Moonlight Schools were held on evenings when there was a moon, so that the students would be able to find their way in the dark. Initially, the structure of the schools was similar to that found elsewhere. Regular school buildings were used, and classes were staffed by volunteer teachers who taught the classes and also recruited the students. The importance of the effort lay in the founder's (Cora Wilson Stewart) ability to propagandize about the effort, thereby gaining statewide support and spawning many imitators. In addition, an early emphasis on teacher training and materials development made the program noteworthy.

From the beginning, it was deemed important to have materials developed for adults. Since readers for adults were not available, a weekly newspaper was started. Using simple words, repetition, "and a content that related to the activity of the reader," the newspaper was a tool that attempted to link the student's experience with classroom activity (Stewart 1922, 21). In addition, the sentences used were designed to motivate the student and provoke discussion.

Thus Stewart uses the example of the sentence, "The Man who does not learn to read and write is not a good citizen and would not fight for his country if it needed him" (p. 22). Although she admits that this statement was ultimately proven to be incorrect, in 1911 and the years preceding the First World War, the statement stimulated lively discussions and great motivation among the learners. According to Stewart, the newspaper had four primary purposes: to teach adults to read without the humiliation of using children's texts, to give the students a sense of dignity by reading something with value, to stimulate curiosity about local events, and to provide information about improvements in other districts.

The idea of Moonlight Schools quickly spread to other counties and regions. In 1914, Kentucky established a Commission on Illiteracy, which launched a statewide literacy campaign. A primer was developed as more individuals became involved in the effort. In 1915 the first county illiteracy agents were hired. These were county agents who both taught illiterate adults and enforced attendance laws. The idea spread to other states. The period between 1911 and 1918 saw the beginning of statewide campaigns throughout the country. Many times such campaigns were combined with programs for immigrants. State funding was, however, minimal, and most of the efforts were subsidized through private philanthropic efforts and staffed by volunteers.

For Stewart, the whole movement to eradicate illiteracy was inextricably linked to a vision of the New South. Illiteracy not only hindered individual prosperity and social integration, but it also held back the entire region. By adopting a progressive stance, many saw education as the key to modernizing the New South. To that end, they focused primarily on expanding children's education and on enforcing compulsory school laws. One outcome of the Moonlight Schools was the greater support gained for day schools (Stewart 1922).

While the Moonlight Schools exemplify a regional effort to modernize, Americanization programs were concerned with what was perceived to be a threat to the "American" way of life. While programs that taught the foreign-born were certainly not new, the period before World War I with its rising xenophobia contributed to a push to Americanize the immigrants. This involved the teaching of language and basic skills, homemaking and childrearing, and classes in citizenship and culture. Programs were offered in a wide variety of locales. Some were sponsored by the local schools or industry, while others were supported by the different ethnic organizations within cities.

Even though programs offered by neighborhood and ethnic organizations were often successful, the government-sponsored programs were abysmal failures. For example, one survey of all aspects of education in Cleveland in 1916 found that the Americanization program was strikingly ineffective. With a high rate of dropouts, poor teachers, and inadequate teaching materials, the conclusion was that little was being accomplished (Miller 1916).

Another study tried to ascertain why the majority of immigrants were not participating in these programs. It found that contrary to popular opinion, most immigrants were quite interested in learning English and that they did not attend the public program because they were already involved in English classes in their local ethnic organizations or labor unions. Those who were not attending any class indicated that they could not because they lacked time, had varying schedules, or had to share family responsibilities. Some said they had tried and failed. Others said they had tried classes but found the teachers were too young or inexperienced or the course materials were too childish. The researchers found that the immigrants enthusiastically supported having someone from their own ethnic group teach the class (Department of Interior, Bureau of Education 1920).

The whole experience of both the Americanization movement and the Moonlight Schools served to emphasize the importance of developing basic materials that would be appropriate for use with adults. Both urged the development of new materials and methods that would go beyond the juvenile texts and rote learning used with children. In addition, both stressed the poor teaching that was available to adults. Unfortunately, teachers were not prepared; they relied on rote learning; and in general, they were condescending to adult students who could not relate classroom experiences to their daily lives.

Thus, both movements were part of a more general rethinking of the way adults were taught. Emerging concerns dealt with the development of appropriate materials and methods for adults as well as the training of teachers to work with adults. As a result, literacy education for adults entered a new phase that was more professionalized in its approach, although still primarily volunteer in terms of who was involved. This coincided with the development of the broader adult education movement that drew closer together, in the 1920s, under the auspices of the Carnegie Corporation. The initiative behind the founding of the American Association of Adult Education (AAAE) was influenced by the experiences of these groups.

Both of these examples (and there are others) illustrate the new concerns and goals of the literacy education movement during the first part of the twentieth century. Literacy had taken on a new meaning. It included not only learning to read and write, but information on work in the U.S., social customs, and ethical values as well. Those who lacked it were seen as outsiders and noncontributors to modern society. The opposite was true for those who were literate.

By and large the teaching of literacy to adults has been a voluntary effort. Closely allied with the public school movement, early efforts in this century tied it in with other educational efforts that were primarily state and local issues. Teachers were usually volunteers, often public school teachers who had teaching experience but not expertise in working with adults. Yet this was considered a major improvement over a period when the teachers were primarily untrained volunteers. In the 1920s the nascent adult education movement, especially that part affiliated with the National Education

Dimensions of Literacy

Association (NEA), was concerned with the different ways adults learned and how such knowledge might be applied to basic education.

The federal relief efforts during the Great Depression of the 1930s unexpectedly provided a laboratory for testing new materials and approaches. One of the broadest federal efforts in literacy education took place when the Works Progress Administration (WPA) initiated programs as a way of hiring unemployed teachers. As Tyack, Lowe, and Hansot (1984) illustrate, adult education was one area with which the federal government could become involved without treading on the turf of local schools. According to some estimates, 1.3 million adults became literate through such programs. The WPA programs were experimental; they attempted to use new techniques and methods to reach previously excluded populations. In the South and in northern cities, programs were offered to African Americans, and indeed, half a million African Americans learned to read and write in WPA programs (Tyack, Lowe, & Hansot 1984).

In addition, the Civilian Conservation Corps (CCC) offered literacy programs for young adult men. While primarily a work program for young men between the ages of eighteen and twenty-five, the CCC as a military branch offered educational courses as a leisure-time activity. Literacy education, while never predominant, became an important part of the program as it became clear that a significant number of the participants could not read and write.

The federal and state goals for these programs were short-term. Of primary importance, the WPA programs were meant to provide work opportunities for unemployed teachers. Additionally, this work, subsidized with nonlocal funds, was not to infringe on the local prerogative to make decisions about education. The education of adults and other excluded populations did not encroach on the turf of established educational agencies and groups and was, therefore, a way for the government to become involved in education through a side door. Finally, programs such as the CCC included literacy education as a healthy use of leisure time.

While literacy had become the focus of academic interest during the 1920s (as a result of experiences of the First World War), little had been done other than to formulate the problem. In addition, the beginnings of the debate over the dimensions of literacy came with the introduction of the notion of *functional literacy*. While some have seen this as the beginning of a movement toward paid professional literacy work instead of volunteer, it is important to keep in mind that the work was temporary. Federal and state programs set up to deal with literacy were concerned primarily with relief. Illiteracy was part of a larger economic disease, although no one thought that economic problems could be alleviated through the eradication of illiteracy.

For many, the levels of illiteracy that surfaced during World War I raised a profound moral problem that needed a solution. Perhaps the clearest idea of how illiteracy was viewed can be seen in the national reaction to the disclosure that 25 percent of those tested for the draft at the beginning of World War I were found to be illiterate. Others who scored low on intelligence testing were also probably illiterate. A large percentage of these were native-born and European Americans. This situation was viewed as a national scandal, with widespread implications for the fighting of the war. Thus, basic literacy was considered essential to the success of the war effort as well as an important aspect of morale building (Cook 1977).

Because U.S. participation in World War I was brief and demobilization was rapid, the government never fully dealt with the issues raised by widespread illiteracy. It was not until the eve of World War II that the armed services really dealt with the question of illiteracy. Initially, there had been no literacy requirement for service, and by one estimate, before Pearl Harbor, 347,000 men were unable to write their names for draft registration. Because of concerns over the ability of illiterates to follow written orders, a directive was issued in May 1941 limiting draft registration to those who had reached at least the fourth grade in school. This resulted in a massive number of deferrals, particularly in the South. Since only the most educated were being drafted, there was growing national concern about manpower shortages in key areas. By May 1942, Roosevelt reported that 433,000 men had been deferred for reasons of illiteracy alone. This was roughly the size of fifteen army divisions (Cook 1977).

As a result of concern over a shortage of draftable men, a new directive was issued stating that men who could understand English and were intelligent enough to absorb military training could be inducted into the service. Once the decision was made to accept illiterates, it became necessary to train them. Special Training Units (STUs) were set up to help illiterates gain the necessary skills. They were given thirteen weeks to reach a level that would enable them to begin regular training. If they did not reach this level, they were discharged (Cook 1977).

Within the STUs, a specialized approach to teaching literacy was developed. This involved a functional approach focusing on the teaching of reading within the context of adjustment to U.S. Army life. Efforts were made to relate the materials and instruction to different aspects of service life. Studies found that this effort was generally quite successful. One report indicated a success rate of between 60 and 95 percent. However, these numbers are somewhat suspect, due to administrative pressure to report success.

There was general agreement that the literacy program was successful. One study on the effectiveness of the program ascribed its success to five factors: high motivation among the participants; the program was under the total control of the U.S. Army; the personnel were highly qualified; there was unlimited funding; and the staff was free to develop innovative and experimental techniques without answering to a conservative civilian population. Even though some of the factors would be desirable under civilian circumstances, others, including the total control over a civilian population, were undesirable and impossible (Goldberg 1951).

The postwar period was marked by a desire to translate the experience of the wartime educational programs to peacetime institutions. These efforts focused on the development of appropriate techniques and materials and on trying to adapt U.S. Army materials for civilian use. As before the war, the target group was often African Americans. Such extended federal interest was fueled by both the war experience and the recognition that valuable manpower resources were being wasted because of the inability to attain literacy. This lost manpower meant that valuable resources were not being properly utilized and that productivity was thereby lessened (Ginzberg & Bray 1953).

The new drive to focus on literacy was accompanied by a greater sense of professionalization within adult education and, hence, more of a reliance on specialized teacher training. This was translated into training programs for literacy teachers and volunteers. Also, it was accompanied by a continued search for acceptable teaching methods or systems. The Laubach system (Laubach 1947; Laubach & Laubach 1960), utilizing phonetic spelling and pictures, became popular. Originally used by missionaries in Third World countries, many groups adapted the method for use in the U.S. Although limited in its resources, the success of Laubach materials indicated that there was a need for such specialized materials.

Widespread efforts at literacy education took place in the 1960s, funded through President Lyndon Johnson's Great Society programs. These programs were meant to allocate funds directly to literacy education and research. Literacy was viewed as essential for minimal participation in modern society. As such, it was found that job training and other economic and social welfare programs could not succeed before individuals had gained functional literacy (eighth-grade education). The Manpower Development and Training Act of 1962, the Economic Opportunity Act of 1964, and the Adult Education Act of 1966 all designated federal funds for literacy programs. Money went to both program development and implementation and to teacher training. Many of the methods initially used by volunteer groups such as Laubach Literacy and Literacy Volunteers of America were adapted for broader use. Special programs for adults were developed. Some utilized new technology, particularly television, others developed new materials. All tried to make the learning experience more relevant and appropriate to the adult experience. There was an explosion of new reading materials prepared specifically for adults. Even the U.S. Armed Forces experimented with "a War on Poverty program" (Sticht, Armstrong, Hickey, & Caylor 1987, 9).

The 1970s and the 1980s saw continued experimentation in the development of better teaching methods, curricula, materials, and diagnostic and evaluation tools. Among the most controversial was the nationally funded movement away from evaluation by grade level to measure of competency—Adult Performance Levels (APL). This was combined with a revival of the term *functional literacy* and was part of an effort to operationalize this term precisely. With the increased research and growing professional involvement in literacy, the field of literacy education for adults has grown rapidly. Today, literacy education in the U.S. draws on literacy work initiated in other countries. Certainly the renewed emphasis on literacy at the end of the 1980s, particularly Workplace Literacy, continues the debate about the role and purpose of literacy in the modern world.

Understanding the historical development of literacy education for adults involves tracing the complex interaction between social, economic, and political factors that have led to different views of the nature of literacy and its importance to society. In the U.S., literacy education has gone from an informal, volunteer effort that made little distinction between children and adults to one that is multifaceted, adult oriented, and a mixture of professionals and volunteers. Literacy is not a value-neutral term. Rather it has come to mean a variety of skills that can be used to social integration or exclusion. Initially it was considered a cultural value that defined the individual as part of the broader community. In the twentieth century literacy has become increasingly essential for what has been considered minimal participation in an industrial society. The need for it will certainly span future centuries.

Conclusion

References

Cook, W. D. 1977. *Adult literacy education in the United States.* Newark, DE: International Reading Association.

Department of the Interior, Bureau of Education. 1920. *The problem of adult education in Passaic, New Jersey.* Bulletin no. 4. Washington, DC: Government Printing Office.

Ginzberg, E., and D. W. Bray. 1953. *The uneducated.* NY: Columbia University Press.

Goldberg, S. 1951. *Army training of illiterates in World War II.* Contributions to education no. 966. NY: Bureau of Publication, Teachers College, Columbia University.

Kaestle C. E. 1985. The history of literacy and the history of readers. *Review of Research in Education* 12:11–54.

Laubach, F. C. 1947. *Teaching the world to read.* NY: Friendship Press.

Laubach, F. C., and R. Laubach. 1960. *Toward world literacy.* Syracuse, NY: Syracuse University Press.

Lockridge, K. A. 1974. *Literacy in Colonial New England: An inquiry into the social context of literacy in the early modern west.* NY: W. W. North & Company, Inc.

Miller, H. A., ed. 1916, 1970. *The school and the immigrant.* Cleveland: The Survey Committee of the Cleveland Foundation. Reprinted NY: Arno Press and the New York Times.

Morris, R. C. 1981. *Reading, 'riting, and reconstruction: The education of freedmen in the South 1861–1870.* Chicago and London: University of Chicago Press.

Nash, G. B. 1988. *Forging Freedom.* Cambridge, MA: Harvard University Press.

Seybolt, R. F., ed. 1925, 1971. *The evening school in colonial America.* Urbana, IL.: Bureau of Educational Research, College of Education, Bulletin no. 24. Reprinted *American education: Its men, ideas, and institutions—Series II.*

Soltow, L., and E. Stevens. 1981. *The rise of literacy and the common school in the U.S.: A socioeconomic analysis to 1870.* Chicago: The University of Chicago Press.

Stewart, C. W. 1922. *Moonlight schools for the emancipation of adult illiterates.* NY: E.P. Dutton & Co.

Sticht, T. G., W. B. Armstrong, D. T. Hickey, and J. S. Caylor. 1987. *Cast-off youth policy and training methods from the military experience.* NY, Westport, London: Praeger.

Talbot, W. 1916. *Adult illiteracy.* Department of the Interior, Bureau of Education, Bulletin no. 35. Washington DC: Government Printing Office.

Tyack, D., R. Lowe, and E. Hansot. 1984. *Public schools in hard times: The great depression and recent years.* Cambridge, MA: Harvard University Press.

Intergenerational Literacy

Claire V. Sibold

Throughout history, man has endeavored to pass along much to his children. In ancient times, wise men would recount stories detailing the history of families' births, deaths, and major events. At death, major artifacts, property, money, or family heirlooms would be passed along to family members, oftentimes to the eldest son. Native Americans had elders who filled the role of re-creating the history of tribes and individuals for coming generations. Today, many traditions still exist. Intergenerationally, families pass along their genealogy, antiques, specific religious and moral values, and health traits.

Studies show that various phenomena are passed from one generation to another. Certain diseases such as diabetes, multiple sclerosis, and retinitis pigmentosa are all passed from one generation to another. Chemical addiction, including alcoholism and drug abuse, is much more prevalent in families where parents have been subjected to the same addictions. Physical abuse, both child and spouse, are linked to families with previous histories of the problem. Frequently, illiteracy, a form of ignorance, is intergenerationally passed within families. In homes where parents do not possess adequate reading or writing skills, it is almost certain that their children will not possess the skills.

Epstein (1986) revealed in his study that parent involvement programs "mitigated the disadvantages typically associated with race, social class, and level of education" (p. 279). Other studies suggested that parental involvement promotes student achievement (Finn 1986; Handel & Goldsmith 1988; Strickland & Morrow 1989), thereby supporting the notion that home environments play an important role in children's early literacy development.

At times some illiterate parents in the U.S. rely on the schools, hoping that their children will become literate as they attend. Some parents believe that the award of a twelfth-grade diploma ensures literacy, and also that that diploma will enable their children to become independent productive members of their community. This diploma would presumably represent the ability to read at the twelfth-grade level, understand concepts presented at that level, and write coherent sentences and paragraphs. However, the possession of that diploma does not necessarily mean that a child is literate. One only has to examine the headlines depicting the lack of skills of many students to see that some have been passed through the U.S. educational system without acquiring necessary reading and writing skills. Reasons why they did not acquire the skills may be due to their parents illiteracy and/or lack of interest and encouragement. Why are they illiterate, and how can they be helped? Answers to these and other questions will be examined as I explore some current facts about illiteracy, examine the parent/child literacy connection, review some intergenerational programs, and highlight some efforts executed by businesses to increase literacy in the home and school.

Today adults in the U.S. who lack sufficient literacy skills to function effectively are found in various segments of that society. Many tend to congregate together as poor and racial and ethnic minority groups. Often they reside in inner cities, prisons, and rural communities (Kunisawa 1988a).

Current statistics in the U.S. show that an estimated 25 percent of high school students dropped out in 1988; an estimated 13 percent of 17-year-olds are functionally illiterate; only 46 percent of adults living in rural communities have completed high school; and approximately 87 percent of the teens who become pregnant each year drop out of high school. According to Kunisawa (1988b), the U.S. is not *at risk,* but with an overall 25 percent of students dropping out of school each year, the country is *in crisis.* Among the eighteen to twenty-one year olds, 13.6 percent of European Americans, 17.5 percent of African Americans, and 29.3 percent of Hispanic Americans drop out of school each year (*Business Week* 1988). Approximately 60 percent of prison inmates are high school dropouts. Further, 52 percent of the dropouts in America are unemployed or they receive welfare assistance (Kunisawa 1988b). Often these individuals cannot read newspapers, understand a driver's license manual, complete simple forms for employment or taxes, nor help their children with schoolwork. A related concern is the number of accidents caused by those who are unable to read safety instructions, such as ''Do not Enter,'' ''High Voltage,'' and instructions on various kinds of machinery. Their lack of literacy skills have cost the public billions of dollars (Berney 1988). Such costs will continue to escalate from generation to generation unless literacy skills are mastered by those who are illiterate.

> Literacy, an essential aim of education in the modern world, is not [an] autonomous empty skill, but depends upon a literate culture. Like any other aspect of acculturation, literacy requires the early and continued transmission of specific information. (Hirsch 1987, xvii)

An estimated 23 million adults in the U.S. (U.S. Department of Education n.d.) lack the basic literacy skills they need to understand and transmit information. Parents, themselves, who do not have basic literacy skills often handicap their children. Unfortunately, such parents cannot read school notices, cannot prepare written responses to teachers, cannot help their children with homework, and often will not participate in school activities. Their lack of basic literacy skills often serves to impair the development of their children's basic skills. Children who have been deprived of, or who have not attained, basic literacy skills are at a disadvantage. The opposite is true of children who have been exposed to such continuous literacy skills as oral language, writing, and reading; they are at a distinct advantage.

Studies have demonstrated that early readers come from homes where diverse oral language is used and the importance of reading has been established by the parents (Snow 1983; Snow & Goldfield 1983; Teale 1978; Teale & Sulzby 1986). Parents and other family members have served to instill a lifelong activity of reading by their own example as well as by involving their children in conversations relative to printed text. Just as a child learns to swim by having direct instruction and follow-up practice, the child can learn to read with instruction and practice. If the interest in either of these activities is maintained, the child is more likely to continue the activity after formal instruction has ceased, and the probability of continuous engagement in reading or swimming as a leisure activity is greater for that child than a nonparticipating child throughout his/her life.

According to Finn (1986), "parents are their children's first and most influential teacher" (p. 7). The parents provide children with multiple experiences. Such experiences help children develop their attitudes, interests, and foundations for learning. For example, a child's parent is usually the first one to expose him/her to water. That initial contact helps the child feel more secure in water. The parent who enjoys swimming and communicates this through his actions—going into the water with the child and being seen swimming—acts as a model for the child. Similarly, parents who enjoy reading demonstrate this by reading in front of their children and serve as models for reading.

Anderson, Heibert, Scott, and Wilkinson (1985) indicated that reading to children at home is generally considered the best way to prepare them for attaining skill in reading at school. Thus, a parent's literacy skills can have a major impact on the literacy attainment of their children, especially when they model reading or engage their children in reading activities. Research shows that home efforts such as parents reading to their children, being a good literate model, providing reading materials, talking about books, and providing opportunities for children to read, write, and talk can greatly improve children's literacy skills.

Parents who are unable to read can engage their children in such literacy-related activities as playing a word game, viewing a TV program together and discussing it, visiting a library with the child, giving the child a book as a present, listening to the child read, and asking about the child's homework (Nickse, Speicher, & Buchek 1988).

Reading and other literacy skills are not perfected through a set of sequential steps, but through on-going participation and practice. For example, Scales (1978) suggested family reading squads (a selected group of family members) as a way of getting all members of a family involved in reading. Squads could be organized so that there would always be a leader to initiate reading activities in the home. Whereas an activity for one day might focus on reading the newspaper and discussing its contents, another day's activity could focus on reading, discussing, illustrating, and dramatizing certain parts of a book. The objective is to ensure that family members read in the home.

Intergenerational Programs

Intergenerational literacy can be used to describe the impact one generation has on the literacy level of the next generation. It links older family members' levels of literacy with younger family members' levels of literacy. Such intergenerationalness often causes children of literate families to become literate and children of illiterate families to become illiterate.

Family literacy programs have been designed to treat intergenerational families as a learning unit. Their designs have encouraged partnerships between the school and the family. For example, the Kenan Family Trust and Literacy Project and Program Model brings together at-risk parents with their preschool children in a school three days a week to engage both in learning opportunities. Specifically, this program, and its parent program PACE, teaches within the context of the family. Its primary focus is to strengthen *learning for children* and *teaching for parents* together in the same atmosphere. Additionally, the program addresses such family needs as vocation, parenting, and education (Darling 1989).

Even Start (Chisman 1989) is a quasi-experimental program that was established by Congress and administered by the U.S. Department of Education.

> Its goal is to promote "family literacy" through programs that provide training both to parents who have deficient basic skills and to their children. The assumption behind the program is that children reared in a home where reading and other basic skills are taken seriously will have a better chance of keeping up with their peers and that parents and children joined in a common learning experience will reinforce each other. This approach has proved extremely promising in small-scale experiments. (P. 32)

New Educational Options for Grandmothers (NEOG) was a university-based experiential project initiated by Blevins (1986). Intergenerational consequences for mothers of adolescent parents and their infants that included high-risk health factors of infants, economic factors, occupational and employability options, and quality of parenting among care-giving helpmates living in the same household were a major reason for this project. It consisted of a twelve-month, comprehensive instructional program directed primarily toward enhancing the grandmothers' general literacy, occupational training, and employment search skills. The age range of the grandmothers was twenty-five to sixty years. Conception among their "children-parents" occurred between ages ten and seventeen. A major criterion for participation in the project was that the grandmothers had their own education interrupted by early adolescent parenthood. Also, project participants were the primary caregivers for themselves as well as their two-generation household members. Results from the project show that the grandmothers were the most reliable helpmates to their children and grandchildren, that their general literacy skills improved, and that they were able to use their literacy skills to assist their "children-parents" (Blevins 1986).

Project BOND (Bristow 1989) is a family literacy program created to help parents improve their reading skills and assist them in working with their children. Parents whose children participate in Head Start and Chapter I programs are invited to attend one or more of their sessions. Specifically, the project is designed to teach at-risk parents to read more efficiently and to view reading in a more favorable light. Discussions on positive parenting and the provision of reading activities are essential components of the project. Materials selected for use in the project contain children's literature and related adult material. Concerted efforts are always made to select materials that are accessible and of interest to participants.

Nickse et al. (1988) described an intergenerational adult literacy project that was housed at Boston University. That project focused on activities related to improving children's literacy skills. Participants were parents of children who had reading difficulties. Within the project, tutors modeled learning activities (decoding, vocabulary, reading/listening, comprehension, study skills, and writing) for parents to use with their children. Parents were then given an opportunity to teach some activities to their children and were encouraged to practice the activities in their homes. In addition to the learning activities, parents and children became engaged in additional literacy events.

The aim of the Barbara Bush Foundation for Family Literacy is to support the development of family literacy programs. Such programs may serve to break the intergenerational cycle of illiteracy and establish literacy as a value in the American home (*BCEL Newsletter* 1989).

Other examples of parent/child programs that may be categorized as intergenerational include *Family Focus: Reading and Learning Together; Collaborations for Literacy;* the *Head Start Program;* and *TAPP.* Since October of 1988, *Family Focus* has held over 300 workshops. Some of the workshops were training sessions, while others were parent/child programs. In the parent/child programs, parents worked directly with their children. They learned to involve themselves in their children's reading activities.

Collaborations for Literacy (CFL) was one of the first programs founded on the recognition that the "educationally disadvantaged" parent and child were a learning unit and might benefit from shared learning activities (*BCEL Newsletter* 1989). CFL's objective was to move parents, grandparents, or other surrogates to improve their own reading by reading to children. The adults were the primary target with a *ripple effect* consciously designed for the children. *The Head Start Program* is a multidimensional preschool program that seeks to create a positive experience for both children and parents. "This is a national effort that should be expanded to reach all students who are potentially 'at risk' for school failure" (Kunisawa 1988b, 63). *TAPP* (Teenage Parent Program) is a school support program that encourages pregnant girls to continue regular classes while parenting. TAPP also seeks to combat the high dropout rate among pregnant teens.

Efforts of Businesses

U.S. businesses have responded to the need to create a more literate society by providing incentives to children. For example, Pizza Hut sponsors a national program called *Book It* that awards pizza coupons to students who read a specified number of books. That program has been modified to include awards to youngsters for the completion of five or more hours of leisure reading.

Other fast-food restaurant chains encourage reading in the home by giving away children's books. Last year Carl Jr.'s restaurant gave a series of books, written by Mercer Mayer, to children with their purchased meals. Similarly, Burger King became the exclusive sponsor of the R & R Project. It awarded fast-food items and bookmarks to children who completed a specified number of hours reading.

In Pinellas County, Florida, two businesses awarded coupons for fast foods to participating elementary school children. Pinellas County elementary students read for 205,050 hours between October and December of 1986. More than 233,000 of Pinellas's elementary students, 61 percent of the total enrollment, participated in the program.

The Orange County Register newspaper contains a column entitled "My Best Book" in its Sunday edition. The column features one reader each week and serves as a testimony to the impact of reading in the lives of its subscribers (adults and children). The previously cited businesses are just a few that have sponsored reading incentive programs as well as encouraged families to read together.

As an educator and parent, I am conscious of the effect my values, behavior, and interests have upon my own daughters. Parents realize that they see themselves in their children. They also hear themselves repeated in their children's spoken words. Parents are models for their children, setting the stage for their children's futures, instructing them, providing them with enriching experiences, and encouraging them.

A Personal Perspective on Literacy

My mother began reading stories aloud to us (her children) when we were young. I remember how Tom Sawyer came alive to me as I sat on the edge of my brother's bed listening intently. Mark Twain remains one of my favorite authors.

As a high school student, there was never any question that I would attend college. My father insisted that we (my family) move from a rural area to an urban area because he wanted us (his children) to attend his alma mater. He felt it would provide us with an excellent education and preparation for college.

An avid reader, my father played an important role in my own education. The dinner in our home was more formal than in my friends' homes. Our parents would converse, but we three siblings only entered the conversation when addressed. Sometimes my father would ask, "Have you read any good books lately?" Many of the gifts I have received over the years from him have been books, inscribed with a personal note.

Now, as I read to my youngest daughter, I see the delight in her eyes as a story unfolds for the first time and a smile when she reads a book with increasing fluency and expression. From the observations I have made, I know that she is prudently aware that reading is valued in our household. A story is a must before bedtime. Stacks of books lie on the floor next to her bed. The cabinet that houses art supplies, games, and coloring books also contains a children's book or two. A trip to the library or bookstore is a pleasurable outing.

And as I go to put the towels and sheets away and find no room, I have to laugh! The linen closet has become our daughters' private library. From personal experience, I see what my father passed on to me and what I am passing on to my children—the importance of reading in the home.

Conclusion

Clearly, there is a need for parental involvement in their children's literacy development. Children need adults who share their literacy heritage to lead them into literacy (Cullinan 1989). When parents are unable, due to embarrassment and/or lack of literacy skills, to assist their children in attaining basic reading and writing skills, it creates a climate of scarcity for their children in which to learn—thus, a cycle of intergenerational illiteracy.

To break the intergenerational cycle of illiteracy, society will have to recognize its sources and provide solutions to the problem. One source is illiterate parents. Solutions to the problem of illiteracy for many parents and educators are found in programs like the ones presented earlier in this chapter. I hope educators, in efforts to break the cycle of illiteracy, will use this presentation as they work with parents and children.

References

Anderson, R. C., E. H. Heibert, J. A. Scott, and I. A. Wilkinson. 1985. *Becoming a nation of readers: The report of the commission on reading.* Urbana, IL: Center for the Study of Reading.

BCEL Newsletter. 1989. Literacy begins at home. April, 1–5.

Berney, K. 1988. Can your worker read? *Nation's Business,* October, 26–34.

Blevins, A. L. 1986. *Grandparenting: An intergenerational response to problems of early adolescent parenthood.* An action research report presented at the XVIII World Congress of O.M.E.P., 13–17 July. World Organization for Early Childhood Education. Jerusalem: Israel.

Bristow, P. 1989. *Project BOND: Bonding parents and children together through reading.* Paper presented at the thirty-fourth annual Conference of the International Reading Association, New Orleans, LA.

Business Week. 1988. Needed: Human capital. No. 3037, 19 September, 100–103.

Chisman, F. P. 1989. *Jump start: The federal role in adult literacy.* Final report of the project on Adult Literacy, January. Southport, CT: Southport Institute for Policy Analysis.

Cullinan, B. E. 1989. Literature for young children. In D. S. Strickland and L. M. Morrow, eds., *Emerging literacy: Young children learn to read and write,* 35–51. Newark, DL: International Reading Association.

Darling, S. 1989. *Kenan Family Trust Literacy Project and Program Model.* Paper presented at the thirty-fourth annual Conference of the International Reading Association, New Orleans, LA.

Epstein, J. L. 1986. Parents' reaction to teacher practices of parent involvement. *Elementary School Journal* 86(3):277–94.

Finn, C. E. 1986. *What works: Research about teaching and learning.* Washington, DC: U.S. Department of Education, Office of Educational Research and Development.

Handel, R. D., and E. Goldsmith. 1988. Intergenerational literacy: A community program. *Journal of Reading* 32(3):250–56.

Hargreaves, D. 1980. *Adult literacy and broadcasting: The BBC's experience.* NY: Nichols Publishing.

Hirsch, E. D. 1987. *Cultural literacy: What every American needs to know.* NY: Vintage Books.

Kunisawa, B. 1988a. Who are adult illiterates? In E. R. Kintgen, B. M. Kroll, and M. Rose, eds., *Perspectives on Literacy,* 378–90. Carbondale, IL: Southern Illinois University Press.

Kunisawa, B. 1988b. A nation in crisis: The dropout dilemma. *NEA Today: Issues '88* 6(6):61–65.

Nickse, R. S., A. M. Speicher, and P. C. Buchek. 1988. An intergenerational adult literacy project: A family intervention/prevention model. *Journal of Reading* 31(7):634–42.

Scales, A. M. 1978. Tips for parents on reading. *New Pittsburgh Courier,* March, 13, 70.

Snow, C. E. 1983. Literacy and language: Relationships during the preschool years. *Harvard Educational Review* 53:165–89.

Snow, C. E., and G. Goldfield. 1983. Turn the page please: Situation-specific language acquisition. *Journal of Child Language* 10:551–69.

Strickland, D. S., and L. M. Morrow, eds. 1989. *Emerging literacy: Young children learn to read and write.* Newark, DL: International Reading Association.

Teale, W. 1978. Positive environments for learning to read: What studies of early readers tell us. *Language Arts* 55:992–32.

Teale, W. H., and E. Sulzby, eds. 1986. *Emergent literacy: Writing and reading.* Norwood, NJ: Ablex.

U.S. Department of Education. n.d. *Fact sheet on nationwide functional literacy initiative.* Washington, DC: Office of Vocational and Adult Education, U.S. Department of Education.

Involvement of Industry in Literacy: Past and Present

Debra A. Klimek-Suchla

> No issue is as critical to the future of America as illiteracy in the workforce. We simply cannot allow this nation to enter the 21st century without a literate, skilled, and flexible workforce. From individual businesses, to entire industries, the effect of a workforce unprepared for an information-based, service-orientated economy will be devastating. (Duffy 1988, 19)

This quote accentuates industry's position in literacy education. Without a literate workforce, U.S. firms will lose their competitive edge over other nations possessing a more literate workforce. Fortunately, industries in the past two decades have found a need to participate in the literacy movement. Several factors have caused their participation.

The first factor is the advancing level of technology in the workplace. With a rise in the usage of computers, robotics, and automated equipment, employers are relying on employees with sufficient skill levels to properly operate the equipment. Employers are also using this equipment to perform nonskilled or low-level skilled tasks. This practice is leaving the moderate to highly skilled tasks for the workers. Do all workers possess the necessary skills to operate the equipment and perform higher level skill tasks? Industry's response has not been yes.

A second factor is the shift in the U.S. economy from that of manufacturing or "smokestack" industries to that of service and information industries. About 90 percent of the new jobs created between 1988 and 1995 will be in the service industry with only 8 percent in manufacturing or muscle jobs. That means instead of basing the economy on human physical strength, it will now be based upon the mental abilities of those in the workforce. Can the present and future workforce perform these service jobs? Industry's response has not been yes.

A third factor for industry's involvement in literacy training is the demographic changes. These changes show that due to decreased birthrates in the early 1970s, fewer youth are entering the workforce. This reduced number implies that employers will need to recruit and retrain workers from segments of the population they have not seriously considered as employees. For example, ethnic minorities, immigrants, women, and displaced workers have not been considered as prime employees. Many of them have not been afforded the opportunity, nor have they sought necessary training, to compete in the job market. How might industry's involvement in literacy ready additional populations for the workforce? Moreover, what has been industry's involvement in preparing needed employees? What problems in industry have been caused by illiteracy? These and other questions followed by a discussion of emerging training efforts will be examined in this chapter. Finally, I will highlight suggestions for future involvement by industry.

One example of industry's involvement in employee literacy and basic skills was a training program implemented in 1970 by the Polaroid Corporation. It was the industry's first in-house basic skills program operated in the U.S. (*The Bottom Line: . . .* 1988).

Edwin Land, founder of Polaroid, felt that Polaroid needed to develop an in-house training program for their employees. With growing technological needs, a great number of displaced unskilled workers in the 1950s and 1960s, and the lack of a strong local community college, Land believed that an in-house training program that offered courses in reading, math, science, and computers would increase their employees' skills level (Hull & Sechler 1987). So a program was developed.

Participation in the program was strictly voluntary. Classes were offered in accordance with need on company or employee time. Course curriculum was closely tied to the employee's job. Priority was placed upon skills needed to improve job performance or to prepare for job growth. The curriculum was customized for each employee. Reading materials used in the literacy training included documents and manuals used on the job. Instructors monitored progress of employees by working closely with the company supervisors. Finally, a support group for the employees was part of Polaroid's training program (*The Bottom Line: . . .* 1988).

Britain, in the mid-1970s, experienced a dilemma similar to that of Polaroid; that is, a large segment of their workforce lacked literacy skills. Since there were no governmental funds for literacy training, business and industry took the literacy initiative. Kimberly Clarke and Cadbury Limited pioneered workplace literacy programs in Britain (Adult Illiteracy: . . . 1975). The programs were appreciated and well accepted by employees because classes were held at the workplace and instruction was geared toward their needs. Corporations noticed that program results showed workers that were more productive and promotable. Company interest in continuing their education usually made the workers more successful.

In the mid-1970s the publishing industry in the U.S. noticed a dramatic decline of sales in hardcover books. Newspaper readership and library usage were declining as well. It seemed that a cause was rising illiteracy. An estimate was that millions of people were illiterate. Since the government could not provide enough funding to support all of the needed literacy programs, the publishing industry decided to offer support. B. Dalton (1983) Bookseller joined the literacy battle by establishing a $3 million grant to help 100,000 adults receive literacy tutoring. They also helped form the Coalition for Literacy. The purpose for the Coalition was to generate a media campaign to draw national attention to the illiteracy problem in the U.S. The campaign helped recruit tutors, and it informed people who lacked literacy skills of locations of literacy programs.

In 1983 the Business Council for Effective Literacy (BCEL) was established. According to founder Harold W. McGraw, Jr., BCEL's purpose was to "foster greater corporate awareness of adult functional illiteracy and to increase

Early Industry Involvement

business involvement and support in the literacy field'' (Carter 1985, 35). BCEL was formed shortly after McGraw's retirement from chief executive officer of McGraw-Hill, Inc. McGraw, personally, gave $1 million to start BCEL. Its governing board includes Sherman Swenson, of B. Dalton Booksellers. Late in 1983, the Coalition for Literacy supporters discovered that the organization did not have enough funds needed to conduct its media campaign. BCEL was contacted and subsequently contributed $450,000 to the Coalition's public awareness efforts. Other contributions from BCEL to literacy include quarterly newsletters, brochures, and flyers for the business community. They present the effects of illiteracy on businesses.

The printing and publishing industry has been criticized by some for not facing the literacy problem sooner. But in retrospect, industry, as a whole, has taken responsible steps in addressing the problem of illiteracy.

Evidence of Illiteracy Problems in Industry Today

As the publishing industry realized that illiteracy was affecting bottom-line figures, various other individual firms were discovering, quite by accident, the problems and costs of illiteracy to business. Because illiterates typically are concerned about job security and social status, they hide the fact that they are illiterate. Often illiteracy is undetected when employees are working in manufacturing or muscle-type jobs.

Some business employers, in 1982, realized that there was illiteracy among their workers. For example, the Ypsilanti plant of Ford Motor Company offered training to employees on a new quality control technique called Statistical Process Control (SPC) (Ross 1986). All workers took the course. However, due to low reading levels many did poorly. Ohan Corporation in Frindley, Minnesota, found itself in a similar situation. It spent $50 million on new machinery to boost productivity, then found that many of the workers could not read the training manual. In 1985, the Northern Tube Division of AP Parts Manufacturing Company in Pinconning, Michigan (Berney 1988), discovered their employees could not keep pace with the training program for SPC. Companies, then, are finding that training materials are rendered useless when employees cannot read the training manual or computer screen in a software training package.

Employers are discovering that only a few applicants can qualify for many entry-level positions. For example, at the New York Telephone Company, only 20 percent of those tested passed an operator's examination (*Building a Quality Workforce* 1988); only 20 percent of the job applicants at Motorola could pass a seventh-grade English test or a fifth-grade Math test; over 60 percent of the applicants failed a basic math test at the Chemical Bank in New York between 1983–1987; and at Michigan Bell, only two out of fifteen applicants successfully completed written and typing tests for clerical positions.

Why does it seem the illiteracy problem has crept up from behind and caught the business sector off guard? In all actuality, it is not the literacy skills of the workforce that have seriously declined. It is that the increasing literacy demands of the workplace have significantly risen in the past twenty to thirty years. According to the U.S. Department of Commerce, approximately 90 percent of all scientific knowledge has been generated in the last thirty years. This knowledge level will double again within ten to fifteen years (*Building a Quality Workforce* 1988). Advances in technology allow businesses the opportunity to collect, store, and retrieve an enormous amount of data. Employees need increasingly keen skills to both record and interpret the data correctly. Also, they need sufficient skills to operate more complex equipment than in the past. Finally, as equipment is updated, it is necessary that employees have skill levels high enough to participate in technological training programs.

Between 1985 and 2000, the workforce in the U.S. will increase by 25 million employees (*Workforce 2000: . . .* 1987). Also, during this time period, 75 percent of the jobs created will require postsecondary education. Fifteen percent of the workforce will be European American males and 85 percent will be immigrants, racial and ethnic minorities, and females. Low birth rates during the early 1970s have forced employers to rely on that 85 percent as potential employees. As the number of European American youth shrinks, racial and ethnic minority youth, adults, and women will take a larger portion of the potential employees percentage. One unfortunate note is that 56 percent of Hispanic seventeen year olds and 47 percent of African American seventeen year olds are regarded as functionally illiterate (How business is joining . . . 1984). This percentage of illiterate youth entering the job market will increase the cost of training programs for business.

The converging trends of new knowledge and a changing population are causing the business community in the U.S. to struggle for position in this competitive global economy. The cost to businesses for problems caused by illiteracy, hiring, retraining, low productivity, accidents, equipment repair, downtime, absenteeism, errors, and poor-quality products is estimated to be between $25 and $30 billion annually (Berney 1988). Additionally, the cost of illiteracy is also measured in terms of unemployment figures, reduced gross national product, welfare payments, losses through criminal acts, prison costs, and reduced tax bases. It is estimated by the Department of Labor that those costs in combination with costs of lost productivity stand at $225 billion annually.

Emerging Training Efforts

The need for businesses to become involved in the fight against illiteracy has been presented. In this section of the chapter, I will provide examples of what some businesses have accomplished and are continuing to do as they fight illiteracy in the workplace.

Pratt-Whitney Group of United Technologies, in 1978, started an in-house general education program for their employees. Their program included provisions for earning a high school equivalency diploma and for training functional illiterates. Planters Peanuts in Safford, Virginia, offered an individualized reading program to employees whose reading skills were below the eighth-grade level (Wantuch 1984).

Ford and General Motors in conjunction with the United Auto Workers (UAW) Union provide free in-house training to their employees. Together they operate the largest number of in-house basic skills programs (Ross 1986).

Aetna Life Insurance Company of Hartford, Connecticut, developed a program called the Effective Business Skills School (Petrini 1989). In this program employees were taught oral and written communication, reading, math, and computer skills. Employees can either volunteer to attend classes or a supervisor can send them.

In 1983, the Gillette Company in St. Paul, Minnesota, employed a public school teacher to give after-hours instruction to thirty employees (*How business is joining . . . 1984*). The program was to continue until all employees had fulfilled their goals. Other contributions that businesses have made include donating space and/or equipment for training, cosponsoring job-site training programs, allowing use of computers for instruction after work hours, sponsoring a literacy event, and covering the cost of printing and distributing the materials.

In 1987 the Department of Labor provided grants for organizations to implement the use of technology in workplace literacy efforts (Bernardon 1989). Three projects developed interactive videodisk (IVD) programs. These projects were at Domino's Pizza, UAW/Ford, and UAW/General Motors. Each business had developed programs unique to its individual training needs in literacy and math skills. There exists two packaged IVD courses for adult literacy training programs entitled Principles of Alphabet Literacy (PALS) and SKILLPAC: English for Industry. These two courses, PALS and SKILLPAC, together taught basic literacy skills as well as applied them to job-related situations. While IVDs were expensive, costs became reasonable when spread out over a large number of users. Like any new technology, as the popularity of the product increased production increased, and selling costs decreased.

Suggestions for Future Involvement

Clearly, industry has a huge stake in workplace literacy training. But the stakes are just as large for other segments of society. Since many businesses cannot afford to develop and staff literacy programs, seemingly forming a partnership with educational institutions, state and federal programs such as the Job Training Partnership Act (JTPA), local labor organizations, and the community would be worthwhile.

In *Building a Quality Workforce* (1988), there is strong evidence that schools and businesses need to work more closely together to properly educate the workforce. The "we/they" opposition syndrome, which highlights differences between the two segments, will deteriorate as partnership efforts emerge. Both schools and businesses need to realize they both possess the common goal of a literate workforce. With commitment and cooperation, that goal can be achieved through teamwork.

Businesses also need to project long-term hiring needs and translate those needs into long-range strategies for education. In short, business people need to roll up their sleeves and get involved in the schools. This means talking to the students, providing field trips, hiring teachers for the workplace, and working with school administrators on specific needs, goals, and policies. Involvement in education must include postsecondary programs as well. Over 75 percent of the workforce for the year 2000 is already in the workforce. It is just as important to upgrade the skills of the adults in the existing workforce as it is to sufficiently educate the youth before they enter the workforce.

Education is not the only partnership that businesses can develop. Private Industry Councils (PICs) created through JTPA in 1982 are established local bodies consisting of membership from education, employment services, community-based organizations, labor, and business. The councils provide a forum for all members to discuss and coordinate job-training efforts in the local community. PICs provide the opportunity for these various sectors to learn from one another about available services and projected employment needs. PICs can also be a potential source for employer training funds depending upon local needs and priorities.

There are a whole host of other community resources with which business may wish to consider partnerships. For example, churches, libraries, human service agencies, labor unions, veteran groups, and employment services are available for partnership.

Illiteracy affects everyone, and no one organization can solve the problem. If workplace illiteracy is to be cut in half by 1999, at least 2 million workers will have to be trained annually (Bernardon 1989). That is a major responsibility, but it can be achieved through cooperative efforts by all.

In a service-based economy, human resources determines economic growth. Education and training enhance that growth and increase the resources. Because of the increasing knowledge, skill, and ability levels required of workers by businesses, schools can no longer be the sole source of education. Industry and business must also play an active role either by providing education and training directly or by coordinating training efforts with other local agencies and resources. Illiterates have too few tools to become skilled workers. Yet, a skilled workforce is a key to economic growth. Providing workers with the tools to become literate and skilled is no longer a philanthropic venture. To business and industry, it is an economic survival strategy.

References

Adult Illiteracy: Will Industry Fill the Gap? 1975. *Economist,* November, 31–32.

B. Dalton Launches $3–Million Literacy Campaign. 1983. *Publishers Weekly,* 30 September, 39.

Berney, K. 1988. Can Your Workers Read? *Nation's Business,* October, 26–34.

Bernardon, N. L. 1989. Let's erase illiteracy from the workplace. *Personnel,* January, 29–32.

Berstein, H. R. 1978. June 26. AAF meet hears of threat by illiteracy problem. *Advertising Age,* 26 June, 2.

The bottom line: Basic skills in the workplace. 1988. Washington, DC: U.S. Department of Education and U.S. Department of Labor.

Building a quality workforce. 1988. Washington, DC: Office of Public Affairs.

Carter, R. A. 1985. Mobilizing business for literacy. *Publishers Weekly,* 24 May, 35–38.

Duffy, J. E. 1988. Solving workplace literacy problems. In *The bottom line: Basic skills in the workplace.* Washington, DC: U.S. Department of Education and U.S. Department of Labor, 19.

How business is joining the fight against functional illiteracy. 1984. *Business Week,* 16 April. 94, 98.

Hull, W., and J. Sechler. 1987. *Adult literacy: Skills for the American work force.* Columbus, OH: The National Center for Research in Vocational Education, Ohio State University.

Petrini, C. 1989. How can business fight workplace illiteracy? *Training and Development Journal,* January, 18–25.

Ross, I. 1986. Corporations take aim at illiteracy. *Fortune,* 29 September, 48–50, 52, 54.

Wantuck, M. 1984. Can your employees read this? *Nation's Business,* June, 34–37.

Workforce 2000: Work and workers for the 21st century. 1987, June. Indianapolis, IN: Hudson Institute.

Psychological Perspectives

Psychologists (e.g., Watson, Thorndike, Kohler, and Bruner) have indicated that psychology is that field of study that attempts to understand and explain life as people live it. Seemingly, as educators attempt to understand the lives of people, they naturally increase their knowledge relative to individuals and groups. To learn more about selected groups of people, we pondered many considerations. Overall, the use of tests was the one consideration that seemed to affect all groups of people. Test results, especially psychological tests that require individuals to read test items, can either enhance or destroy individuals' lives. Since the test is so powerful, we decided to begin this section of the volume with a chapter that examines its magnitude (see Condell and Richardson). Second is a discussion of how test results have shown progress of African Americans in the face of problems (see Biggs). Although the remaining chapters are not test specific, in general, we see that tests have affected the populations discussed herein. Specifically, Lloyd discusses issues relative to African Americans. Other chapters present an in-depth look at literacy training for incarcerated inmates (see Ryan), the understanding and feelings of learning disabled adults (see Ross), the value of a literacy education for older adults (see Harvey and Cronan), and the goals and drives of non-English-speaking adults (see Bruder).

Power of Tests on Literacy Education

James F. Condell and F. C. Richardson

The values inherent in a democracy often do not reflect the reality of what occurs in the political, economic, and sociocultural arenas. That is because these values are too frequently sidestepped in the world of education. One tool, tests, helps educators, politicians at all levels, and the general public as they assess what takes place in schools. Tests have been used, historically, for and against persons not in mainstream societies. Data from educational and psychological tests have been employed arbitrarily to assist or avoid, enable or hold back, label or identify, exclude or include, glorify or defame, and so on. One could describe at length instruments that have been used, under the guise of providing a precise measurement, for populations not in the mainstream.

Some tests that have been administered in either the school years or adulthood have been helpful in preparing individuals for a set of feasible goals. Other tests, or maybe the improper use of test data, have not been helpful and, in actuality, have created harmful situations.

The review given herein is intended to provide a summary of aspects of the literature that can offer the reader an introduction to the use of tests. We make no claim of expertise in the field of adult literacy education. We have, however, many years of collective professional experience with adults in higher education and mental health settings. This experience has alerted us to the need for judicious test practices as the U.S. moves to a greater degree of literacy. We are aware of the demand for education for all but even more so for individuals (illiterate adults, mentally disturbed, etc.) whose initial preparation for learning in a formal institution may not have been extensive enough for survival in a contemporary world.

Early developments in psychology did not acknowledge the concept of testing as a possibility for helping to better understand the human mind. More than one hundred years ago, Wilhelm Wundt, as the prime developer of the experimental laboratory method (for the then young science of psychology), gave little evidence that he felt the need to admit the existence of differences among individuals. His work was in the model of existing sciences that were essentially physiology, physics, and chemistry. The data from these disciplines were considered to be lawful. Sigmund Freud, who sought (and a few agree that he did so quite successfully) to unlock the unconscious, obtained his data through such basic analytical techniques as free association and dream analysis. John B. Watson opened new doors for psychological investigations with his theory/system of behaviorism. Here again, like Wundt, it was in the laboratory where the critical research was generated. A much later entry into the realm of psychological theory was labeled humanistic psychology. Abraham H. Maslow was one of the leading figures of that movement. The humanist effort to fathom the more positive elements of behavior led to restatements of the pioneering work of Wundt, Freud, and Watson. Counterattacks were subsequently made on the humanistic theories/models.

One outcome from the historical facets of psychology has been the acceptance of behavior as the proper area of study and research for the behavioral sciences. Ultimately, psychology became open to a variety of methods and approaches. As a result, the field of individual differences/differential psychology earned respectability as an additional source or supplier of behavioral information. The data came mainly from tests. The various research, testing, and statistical manipulations became known as psychometrics. Many new areas of understanding had their inception in that field. An exploration of selected events and ideas from the field of individual differences that hold meaning for adult literacy education follows.

Sir Francis Galton

Charles Darwin, one of the great independent scholars, established the stimulus that aided the scientific community in considering the measurement of the human mind. This he did for his cousin, Sir Francis Galton. Galton's book *Hereditary Genius* (1962) gave him the push he needed. The development of the twin-study method along with Galton's innovations in eugenics opened a Pandora's box. His data collection in the Anthropometric Laboratory in the Kensington Museum of London attracted the attention of those psychologists who did not subscribe to the kind of research emanating from the laboratory of Wundt at the University of Leipzig. Following a period of study with Galton, James McKeen Cattell (an American who completed his doctorate under Wundt) spent the remainder of his life upgrading the mental test movement. Cattell was highly inspired by the productivity of Galton. It was Cattell who later coined the term *mental test*.

Galton carried his instruments on his trip into the heart of Africa. He was a prodigious traveler and published many accounts of his sojourns. He did not refer to his instruments as tests but, instead, preferred the expression anthropometric measures. On the African continent, Galton found the people that he measured did not perform as well on his instruments as the people he measured in England. This could have been the first misunderstanding by scholars of the nature of individual differences. A full treatise on the life and work of Galton and his followers, especially Karl Pearson and Charles Spearmen, has been presented by Kevles (1985) and Forrest (1974).

Alfred Binet

Alfred Binet, a contemporary of Galton, was a part of the cadre of independent scholars who lived in France. Binet received his entire education in his home country and, consequently, seems not to have been influenced by the psychological orientations of Wundt or Freud. Binet must, however, have been aware of their intellectual productivity.

In contrast to the motor-functioning approach of Galton, Binet held an interest in what is referred to as abstract thought or abstract reasoning, or it could be alluded to as critical thinking. Binet functioned in the experimental psychological laboratory and the educational classroom. He crossed the barriers of science to the territory of pedagogy, a trip rarely taken in contemporary times. It should be akin to a bustling highway. Could it be that the separation of science and education established a setback in what was to be the central focus, learning? History cannot attribute the default to Binet or Galton. Both of these sages uttered repeated warnings about the premature applications of their findings/results.

The story is recorded that Binet was asked to develop an instrument, based on his research, that could be used to eliminate from schools those students least likely to succeed. That, under any consideration, was a request that would negatively effect many students who entered schools.

With his collaborators, including Victor Henri and Theodore Simon, Binet gave to the world the *Binet-Simon Scales* in 1905. Revisions were made in 1908 and 1911 (see, Binet 1911; Binet & Simon 1912). It was the administration and interpretation of the Binet, and not the scales in and of themselves, that has led to a host of uses and abuses of the tests. (A case in point would be the overpopulation of ethnic and racial minority groups of children in special education classes in the U.S.). Binet died in the year of the final revision of the scale he created. Before his death, Binet involved himself and a host of others in studying the schools of Paris and assisting in the construction of a well-studied curriculum. Binet developed a psychoeducational clinic in a school building in order to be closer to the sources of his data. Alfred Binet, according to Wolf (1973), could have been designated as the father of educational psychology. However, the title was given to an American psychologist, Edward L. Thorndike.

The Spread of Individual Intelligence Testing

Lewis M. Terman took up the work of Alfred Binet following the introduction of Binet's test to the U.S. by Henry H. Goddard. The scales were standardized and presented to psychologists and educators as the Stanford-Binet Intelligence Scale (Terman & Merrill 1916). Terman, in the style and spirit of test makers from an earlier period, limited the sample to populations that excluded what are referred to as racial and ethnic minorities. A real difficulty with such a procedure was the resultant use of the scale with minority children. It was used to place them in special programs within the schools even though they were not present in the standardization sample.

Martin D. Jenkins, in his studies in educational psychology with Paul Witty, attempted to study the use of the Stanford-Binet with a non-European population. Their findings were astonishing in terms of the numbers of non-Europeans with high Binet intelligence quotients (IQ). Jenkins felt encouraged to extend the sample. However, no funding to do so was ever acquired.

It was David Wechsler who provided an alternative set of tests to the Binet. With a rearrangement of items, the use of three quotients instead of one, and the development of the deviation IQ, additional data could be obtained of further significance for educational as well as clinical programs and institutions. Unfortunately, the Wechlser (1949) Intelligence Scale had similar sampling oversights as the Binet. A rather complete yet understandable explanation of test bias has been compiled by Kaplan and Saccuzzo (1989). As a greater degree of interest is given to the field of individual differences, it is expected that many of the ethnic and racially involved aspects of testing will be eliminated. However, it is conjectured that none of the negative aspects of testing will be improved soon enough. The reader will do well to consult discussions of the issues involved in writings such as those contained in *The Negro Educational Review* (1977, 1987) and Samuda (1975).

World War I

Just a few years after the widespread dissemination of the test techniques of Binet, which held promise for psychologists with a need or desire to place the results in the marketplace, a host of Binet-type imitators and instruments emerged. A group of self-selected psychologists saw an opportunity to apply their testing skills in a large setting, so during World War I they convinced the U.S. military that tests could serve to select officers, rank enlisted personnel, and set up new systems with scientific aura. With sufficient hindsight, a more appropriate term would be scientific zeal.

There are technical terms, such as validity, reliability, difficulty index, discrimination index, test bias, and the like, that psychometricians use to discuss the readiness, or lack of readiness, for tests and test results. Seemingly, many of the terms were not considered when the self-selected psychologist used tests to set up new systems for the U.S. military.

Presently, the most quoted information from the large testing program is related to African and European Americans' racial differences in test scores. Could the tests alone, with limited input from social, anthropological, and cultural sources, account entirely for the range of racial differences that have been charted, graphed, and tabled from the World War I data? Gould (1981) addresses the question in his book *The Mismeasure of Man*.

The Immigration Act of 1924

The immigration issue is mostly about adults who hope to make a start in a new and free place. However, the manner in which immigrants are admitted to the U.S. has become something of an intellectual battleground. There are opposing opinions from psychologists whose brilliance and skills have never been under question. Their views need, however, to be scrutinized by students of adult education.

Snyderman and Herrenstein (1983) have doubts about some of the comments made on the use of tests in the decisions surrounding the Immigration Act of 1924. Kamin (1974) states that there is concern over the use of tests for the rejection of immigrants into the U.S. Whatever the outcome of the opinions and feelings over the issue in the early 1920s, there is an awareness that test data are in evidence as they point to racial and ethnic groups and their various abilities or inabilities to acquire a good education. The issue seems to be centered around placing blame rather than finding solutions for alleviating oppressive conditions. If Galton set the stage for the unending controversy, who is going to ring up the final curtain with a favorable conclusion?

Testing in the Schools

It was in the 1920s that intelligence and achievement group tests were constructed and marketed on a large scale for huge populations. Tests became the order of the day in educational institutions. Many publications in professional education attest to the use of test data in support of curriculum changes, the establishment of educational objectives, the growth of instruments for the assessment of personality and aptitudes, and the spread of counseling and guidance services.

During the 1930s, adult education in the U.S. received a boost from many governmental agencies that provided classes for adults through the existing school system. Today adult classes continue to exist through school systems. Also, a number of adult education centers that offer classes have emerged. One purpose for the classes is to help students prepare for the General Educational Development (GED) examination. Passing that examination validates a high school equivalency for the student.

The number of concerns related to educational and psychological measurement is vast. Resulting factors have included the misclassifying of a representative number of students (particularly African Americans) into special education classes, the denial of admissions to merit programs, and a lack of access to mainstream opportunities. Parents are being given an opportunity to become informed as to what can transpire in favor of, or against, their children after being tested in school. Likewise, adults in literacy classes are aware of how tests have and will continue to influence their lives. The reader is advised to review recent measurement principles and procedures publications for additional tests and testing information. An excellent source for studying the impact of testing upon individuals is *The Negro Educational Review* (1987).

Race and Testing

Probably nothing has blemished the emphasis on educational and psychological testing of African Americans as has the heredity-environment issue. Jensen's (1969) interest in the eugenics movement set off a barrage of fighting words the likes of which have not been heard since the turn of the century. What were the motives behind the impetus to scientifically probe into the race and testing relationship? Perhaps one motive was to promote a race superiority notion. A host of psychologists who preceded and followed Jensen have worked, often diligently, to keep alive the controversy of race superiority based on test data. There are others who have felt that the same or increased effort could have provided some workable programs to help eliminate test pattern discrepancies that exist in the area of personality as well as in intelligence and educational achievement.

The Antidotes

Our views in this chapter have been affected not only by our membership in a group that has felt the effect of the misuse of tests, but by the probability that millions of underrepresented adults have been sidetracked in their quest for equality. We are aware that because of a good education there is a history of accomplishment by intellectuals such as W. E. B. Du Bois, Rayford Logan, Charles Wesley, Carter G. Woodson, Martin D. Jenkins, Kenneth Clark, and

Mamie Clark. In recent years, Robert Williams and other African American psychologists have looked to education for answers as to what has gone right as well as wrong with the equality tenet.

Several theoretical as well as applied steps and positions have been taken in the past that would have helped had they been heeded. Thurstone (1938), in his work on primary mental abilities, attempted to eliminate the concept of the IQ from the testing vocabulary. In using a profile, Thurstone hoped to lessen the impact that a single score had on test takers and test givers.

Guilford (1967), with his structure of the intellect model, provided a large number of possibilities yet to be implemented with formally developed test instruments. His model stands as a possibility for use with adults. Eells, Davis, Havighurst, Herrick, and Cronbach (1951) along with Cattell (1940) offered the culture-free and culture-fair combinations. Their findings have not altered the psychometric process, but their direction is worth continued investigation. Definitions in these areas do need to be reconsidered.

Educators working with adults have both historical and contemporary views to pursue as they turn to psychology for the creation of ideas that will assist in the growth of adult literacy and the eradication of illiteracy. Certainly an understanding of the field of psychological measurement (with intensity) is needed by those who work in adult education.

Psychology does not exist in a vacuum. The social-cultural-economic-political realms are highly involved in whatever becomes the psychological activity of the day. Most, if not all, of the factors discussed in this chapter did not begin or end with psychologists. It was far too often the misuse of psychological instruments that created or led to the havoc. The future for testing seems to lie with psychologists and educators who will combine their efforts to stimulate a greater awareness of the democratization of education for all.

References

Binet, A. 1911. *Les id'ees Modernes Surlesenfants*. Paris: Flammarion.

Binet, A., and T. Simon. 1912. *A Method of measuring the development of the intelligence of young children*. Lincoln, IL: Corier.

Cattell, R. B. 1940. A culture-free intelligence test I. *Journal of Educational Psychology* 31:161–79.

Eells, K., A. Davis, R. Havighurst, R. Herrick, and L. Cronbach. 1951. *Intelligence and cultural differences*. Chicago: University of Chicago Press.

Forrest, D. W. 1974. *Francis Galton: The life and work of a Victorian genius*. NY: Taplinger.

Galton, Sir F. 1962. *Hereditary genius*. Cleveland: Meridian.

Gould, S. J. 1981. *The mismeasure of man*. NY: Norton.

Guilford, J. P. 1967. *The nature of intelligence*. NY: McGraw Hill.

Jensen, A. R. 1969. How much can we boost IQ and scholastic achievement? *Harvard Educational Review* 39:1–123.

Kamin, L. J. 1974. *The science and politics of IQ*. Hillsdale, NJ: Erlbaum.

Kaplan, R. M. and D. P. Saccuzzo. 1989. *Psychological testing: Principles, applications, and issues*. Pacific Grove, CA: Brooks/Cole.

Kevles, D. J. 1985. *In the name of eugenics: Genetics and the uses of human heredity*. NY: Alfred A. Knopf.

The Negro Educational Review. 1977. *XXVIII*(3–4): 142–236.

The Negro Educational Review. 1987. *XXXVIII*(2–3): 35–216.

Samuda, R. J. 1975. *Psychological testing of American minorities: Issues and consequences.* NY: Dodd Mead.

Snyderman, M., R. J. Herrenstein. 1983. Intelligence tests and the immigrant act of 1924. *American Psychologist* 38:986–95.

Terman, L. M. and M. A. Merrill. 1916. *Stanford Binet Intelligence Scale.* Chicago, IL: Riverside Publishing Co.

Thurstone, L. L. 1938. Primary mental abilities. *Psychometric Monographs* 1.

Wechlser, D. 1949. *Intelligence scale for children.* Cleveland, OH: Psychological Corporation.

Wolf, T. H. 1973. *Alfred Binet.* Chicago: The University of Chicago Press.

African American Adult Reading Performance: Progress in the Face of Problems

Shirley A. Biggs

Reading performance, or literacy, is described in this chapter as the ability to read and/or write, as educational attainment, as test performance, and as function. These terms reflect the various ways skill in reading has been measured. Early measures of literacy were based on the ability of an individual to read and/or write one's name. For example, in 1870, it was estimated that 20.1 percent of the non-European American population aged ten years and older were literate based on that definition. A second method for determining achievement in literacy was based on educational attainment, or the number of grades completed. In 1969, an individual was deemed literate if he or she had successfully completed six or more years of school (U.S. Bureau of the Census 1971). A third measure of reading ability was performance on a written test. The test was either designed like those for school-aged children or designed to measure an adult's ability to function on a variety of life tasks. A fourth but less-direct measure of reading ability was performance on tasks that required reading to function productively. In the remainder of this chapter, I will provide an in-depth exploration of the ability to read and write, of educational attainment, of test performance, and of function particularly as they relate to African Americans.

Stedman and Kaestle (1987) wisely suggest to readers in their historical review of reading performance that

> Many of the available data are unreliable, unrepresentative, or noncomparable over time. The attempt to determine trends is therefore perilous. Much skepticism is in order. (P. 10)

Readers are encouraged to approach the following review with similar skepticism.

Ability to Read and Write

Over the years, the U.S. Census Bureau posed questions related to reading and writing ability. Cook (1977) traced the statistical trends from 1900 through 1970, sometimes drawing distinctions about data between African Americans and other groups, and sometimes not. She noted that from 1900 to 1930 the literacy question asked dealt with whether or not respondents could read and/or write. In 1900 and 1930 the concern was whether or not a person could read and write in the native language. In 1910 and 1920 the concern was whether or not the respondent could write in any language. In 1940 literacy was redefined by the census questions as schooling or educational attainment. Surveys conducted in 1950 and 1969 again focused on the ability to read and write.

Based on the definition of literacy as the ability to read and write, U.S. Americans became increasingly literate as the twentieth century progressed. Illiteracy percentages for African Americans went from close to 50 percent down to 3 percent (U.S. Bureau of the Census 1971). The Civilian Conservation Corps alone taught 15,000 African American males to read during the 1930s (Keegan 1986). Further, illiteracy rates were projected to remain low and stable through the 1990s based on the basic ability to read and write (U.S. Bureau of the Census 1982).

While data based on the ability to read and write reveal progress in reducing illiteracy among Americans in the U.S., that data also reveal a difference among racial groups. Over time, that difference favored European Americans showing lower percentages of illiteracy. However, in 1910 of roughly 5.5 million illiterates, 57.7 percent were European Americans and only 40.4 percent were African Americans. But as new immigration laws were enacted that favored more literate northern and western European Americans over less literate groups from other parts of the world, the nature of the difference among races in illiteracy percentages reversed (Cook 1977).

Several problems must be considered in the interpretation of the data. First, the age range of the respondents changed over time. The earlier studies included respondents as young as ten years old. More recent studies defined adults as fourteen, eighteen, or twenty-five years or older. A second problem was that data about literacy and race were not always available in forms that were useful when the purpose was to study African American trends. Early studies often aggregated data about race into European American and non-European American categories. A related problem was that of sorting out aggregated data about native and foreign-born Americans. Cook (1977) cites a third problem inherent in the use of census data.

> Often the assumption was made and recorded that because a person was white [European American] he was literate, or because he was . . . black [African American], he was not . . . . Some people were unwilling to admit their illiteracy and gave faulty information. (P. 24)

These problems made it difficult to confidently identify real trends and make comparisons across the years among groups.

Educational Attainment

Reading performance, or literacy, was measured through the identification of the number of grades or school years completed. The underlying assumption offered for using this approach was that attendance at school (sometimes described as educational attainment) facilitates the development of reading skill. Since individuals at any point in their schooling can vary in their performance from very poor to exceptionally capable, the schooling criterion was most appropriately applied to reading achievement estimates for large populations.

Educational attainment data have been collected by the Census Bureau since 1840. Such data became particularly important in 1940 because the reading/writing criterion was not used to estimate literacy in that year. Schooling figures have appeared since that time. The change in the means of estimating educational attainment further complicated an already confusing picture of adult reading achievement by making comparisons across instructional methods. Also, since 1940 the criterion grade level purported to indicate reading ability has changed. Thus, one assumption for illiteracy or lack of reading achievement was that there had been no schooling. In this instance, no consideration was given to those who learned to read and continued to develop their skill in a nonschool setting. Another assumption set the completion of third grade as necessary for minimal achievement since the teaching of basic reading skills was generally emphasized in the primary grades. However, as reading demands made on individuals increased in complexity, the grade level that represented adequate achievement climbed until completion of high school had come to be seen as minimal attainment. As a result, even high school graduation was questioned as a reliable criterion for demonstrated reading ability.

Still, recent African American adult reading performance measured on the basis of schooling reveals progress. The 1980 census data for noninstitutionalized adults aged fourteen years and older indicate that 9.6 percent of that population completed less than five years of schooling, 49.4 percent completed high school, 19.4 percent completed one or more years of college, 7.9 percent completed four or more years of college, and the median number of school years completed was 11.9 percent. In comparison, the data for European Americans indicated 2.7 percent, 69.7 percent, 32.2 percent, 17.2 percent, and 12.5 percent respectively (U.S. Bureau of the Census 1980). Stedman and Kaestle (1987) reported that scholars and researchers concluded that schooling for the general adult population showed steady progress. They cited data from Grant and Eiden's study. The data showed that adult educational attainment increased by two years from 1960 to 1980 and by four years between 1940 and 1980.

Another view of the historical context of steadily increasing educational attainment reveals several factors that may have stimulated progress. Cook (1977) suggests that perceived industrial, political, and national defense needs, in the U.S., during the decade of the 1940s became the basis for educational efforts that positively affected literacy levels. Industry sought workers who could read well enough to be productive. Political concerns about the spread of communism spurred efforts to educate citizens to embrace democratic ideals. The U.S. Armed Forces worked to prepare a fighting corps that was literate enough to follow directions and effectively protect interests of U.S. citizens. The level of literacy determined to be necessary for achieving these pragmatic objectives was estimated to be five years of schooling (Robinson 1952). Underlying each of these factors was the reality that African Americans lagged behind European Americans essentially because of unequal educational opportunity. One notable effort to address the problem was the establishment of the Project for Adult Education of Negroes, directed by Ambrose Caliver, a noted African American educator. While its primary purpose was to increase the literacy level of young men who would be able to serve during wartime in the U.S. Armed Forces, it ultimately established models of instruction and materials for use in adult education that still influence the field (Cook 1977).

Test Performance

Reading skill is most commonly measured through testing. However, available information that describes adult performance on tests is generally limited to special populations. Prisoners, undereducated students in literacy development programs, members of the U.S. Armed Forces, and other groups of adults whose literacy level is the target of interest are examples. Because the composition of each of the various groups is not generally representative of the total population, generalizations about reading performance results are appropriately limited to those specific groups. For example, Gray (1956) observed that "more objective tests of reading have been given to members of the armed forces than to any other adult group" (p. 38). While literacy information about the U.S. Armed Forces is useful, it provides only a portion of what can be known about the general population or a specific group within that population.

The tests discussed in this section are limited to those administered to national samples since the mid-1960s. Further, since patterns of results of the various tests were similar, only two types are described here. (See Fisher 1978; Kirsch & Guthrie 1977–1978; Stedman & Kaestle 1987 for descriptions of additional tests.)

The Brief Test of Literacy was said to be designed to distinguish readers and writers who had achieved a level of skill comparable to that of most fourth graders from those who had not. It was administered during the last five minutes of the Health Examination Survey given between 1966 and 1970. Responders, aged twelve to seventeen years, were required to read seven brief narrative passages and to answer three multiple-choice questions about each passage. Of interest were the results generated by seventeen-year-old respondents. Their performance as emerging adults may provide some insight into future adult reading behavior. Fisher (1978) reported that African American males earned significantly lower scores than African American females. Overall, 14.8 percent of seventeen-year-old African Americans earned scores comparable to entering fourth graders.

Adult reading has also been measured by the National Assessment of Educational Progress (NAEP). Unlike traditional achievement tests, no test score was generated for individuals; however, score patterns across groups have been described. A multistage probability sampling technique was used to assure that the results were representative of the national population. (Results reported here are from two sources. One source of information is from the three assessments conducted in 1970–1971, 1974–1975, and 1979–1980 when nine, thirteen, and seventeen year olds were assessed so that change in performance over time could be observed.) Data from seventeen-year-old respondents as well as two sets of assessment data from the Mini-Assessment of Functional Literacy (MAFL) with twenty-six to thirty-five year olds are of interest. The MAFL was used to test seventeen year olds who were still in school. The two young adult assessments tapped a population of out-of-school respondents who may have been in the workforce. An analysis of the results revealed that the 1970–71 performances were similar for seventeen year olds and twenty-six to thirty-five year olds, with young adults (twenty-six to thirty-five years old) performing only slightly better than emerging adults. Similar results were obtained when a less comprehensive assessment was conducted.

A study of the pattern of African American reading performance revealed a high percentage of scores among those in the lowest quartile, that is, 54.4 percent in 1971, 48.8 percent in 1975, and 45.4 percent in 1980. Additionally, a low percentage earned scores in the top quartile of all scores earned, that is, 5.8 percent in 1971, 8.4 percent in 1975, and 10.4 percent in 1980. A slight positive but nonsignificant change was evident across assessments. The percentage of lower scores decreased and the percentage of higher scores increased (National Assessment of Educational Progress 1981).

A study of the types of questions successfully answered during the MAFL project revealed similarities and differences between African American and European American respondents. Both groups were similarly successful in answering questions that asked them to demonstrate knowledge of word meanings and understanding of significant facts. However, they differed noticeably in drawing inferences, comprehending main ideas and organization, and reading critically (Fisher 1978).

To fully understand and interpret the results of these tests, it becomes important to again take a historical perspective. The context of the 1960s and 1970s was one of significant change in education. The factors affecting change need to be considered to determine how they might have influenced the scores, either directly or indirectly. Thus it is not enough to note the difference between African American and non-African American scores. Note must also be made of the gains achieved and the specific strengths revealed. In addition, the educational changes brought new opportunities during the decade that produced more time, expertise, and other resources for reading instruction. The newly available resources were used and gains were made. The lesson learned from these data may be that the bleak outlook suggested by a traditional interpretation of the scores may be unnecessarily pessimistic. The gains made point out the importance of the availability of educational opportunity. A careful study of both the data and the context shows that the most significant gains in reading were made by younger African Americans, aged nine and to a lesser degree aged thirteen, toward whom the most rigorous program efforts and largest amount of resources were directed.

Function

Function is yet another way reading skill has been assessed. Two types of functional measures will be discussed. The first are those that have been applied to national or broad-based samples of respondents. The second are those that focus on targeted or narrowly defined groups.

National Groups. The Adult Performance Level Project (APL) is an example of a national or broad-based attempt to identify and describe adults, in the U.S., as they function in day-to-day life situations. APL is based on the assumption that competence is related to income, education, and job status. Items devised for APL measured adult functions that required reading or problem solving. The items were extensively field-tested and modified. Items were also analyzed for relevance and for their relation to successful functioning. With the aid of an independent research firm, APL was administered to a representative sample of individuals from the forty-eight contiguous states of the U.S. Results are reported in terms of three levels of success.

> APL 1—The respondent does not function, or functions with difficulty and has completed 8 or fewer years of school.
> APL 2—The respondent does function, but on a minimal level and has completed 9 to 11 years of school.
> APL 3—The respondent functions proficiently; attaining a high level of income, job status, and education. (Adult Performance Level Project 1975, 5)

Results show that of the 7,500 adults surveyed, 19.7 percent performed at APL 1, 33.9 percent performed at APL 2, and 46.3 percent performed at APL 3. Thus, close to one-half of the population can be described as functioning at the proficient level, approximately one-third at the minimally competent level, and one-fifth at the poorly functioning level. Reading results followed a similar pattern. African Americans and Spanish-surnamed Americans were most heavily represented in low and minimal function levels. European Americans were heavily represented at the proficient level. All groups except Spanish-surnamed Americans were similarly represented at the minimal function level.

Overall, the data reflect the trend that certain demographic factors predicted placement in the APL 1 and APL 3 levels. Low income, limited education, minimal job status, and being African American or Spanish-surnamed predicted placement in APL 1. Extended education, advanced job status, and being a European American predicted placement in APL 3. Again, these findings must be interpreted in a context that takes into account opportunities to compete and obtain well-paying jobs for African and Spanish-surnamed Americans. Even if they managed to obtain a level of education comparable to that of European Americans, comparable job and comparable pay do not necessarily follow.

Function and Targeted Groups. The ability to read in order to function has been measured by studying targeted groups. Such studies focus on specific populations that may be limited to a particular occupation, a geographic area, an ethnic group, an age designation, or a combination of these and/or other variables. A growing body of research (Heath 1980; Heisel 1985; Heisel & Larson, 1984; Mikulecky & Winchester 1983) seems to reflect a trend toward small targeted descriptive studies. These studies appear to reflect the thinking of Szwed (1981) who suggests that research designed to elicit accurate descriptive data about the American reading public should "stay as close as possible to real cases, individual examples, in order to gain the strength of evidence that comes with being able to examine specific cases in great depth and complexity" (p. 21). Further, Heath (1980) challenged the generalizability of findings from national surveys to specific subgroups. She described her ethnographic study. In it, the targeted group lived in an African American working-class community in the southeastern part of the U.S. For five years, careful records were kept of reading and writing behaviors of ninety members of the community as they went about their daily lives.

Several findings emerged from her observations that are of interest here. One finding was that the adults in the community under study used reading as a social rather than an academic tool. For example, written materials were often used to support a point made in an argument during social interaction. Reading for reading's sake appeared to be interpreted by the people under study as an escape from real life; thus, it was not a valued activity. A second and related finding was that this group had the following distinctive uses for reading and writing:

1. Instrumental. Information is provided to manage practical problems of daily life (price tags, checks, bills, advertisement, street signs, traffic signs, house numbers).

2. Socio-international. Information is provided that is pertinent to social relationships (greeting cards, bumper stickers, letters, newspaper features, recipes).

3. News-related. Information is provided about third parties or distant events (newspaper items, political flyers, messages from local city offices about events of vandalism, etc.).

4. Memory supportive. Reading and writing served as a memory aid (messages written on calendars, address and telephone books, inoculation records).

5. Substitutes for oral messages. Reading and writing used when direct oral communication was not possible or would prove embarrassing (notes for tardiness to school, messages left by a parent for child coming home after parent left for work).

6. Provision for permanent record. Reading and writing used when legal records were necessary or required by other institutions (birth certificates, loan notes, tax forms).

7. Confirmation. Reading and writing provided support for attitudes or ideas already held, as in settling disagreements or for one's own reassurance (brochures or cards, directions for putting items together, the Bible). (Heath 1980, 128–29)

A careful review of the uses in the previous list showed that these community residents were selective in what they read. For example, they routinely scanned ''price tag(s) for the critical cue—the decimal point—and then read the price of the item'' (p. 129). They read newspapers in a similarly selective manner. Heath also noted that the African Americans in her study did not need to read on the job very often. Also, most written information was made available through oral explanations or demonstrations.

A second study concerned with local or environment-related reading performance was conducted to demonstrate that group-specific reading behavior can apply to age as well as ethnic or job-related factors. As part of a broad-based longitudinal study, Heisel and Larson (1984) assessed the reading and writing behavior of 132 elderly African American adults in a large northeastern urban area. Using an approach described as naturalistic, the subjects, aged sixty to ninety-four, were randomly selected from a larger group of the same race. No attempt was made to obtain a representative sample since the purpose was to study and describe these specific cases in depth. Demographically, the median school grade completed was sixth, with 5 percent never having attended school. Twenty-five percent completed three grades or less, and 10 percent completed high school. Data were elicited by middle-aged African Americans recruited from the neighborhood who had been working with the subjects for several years. Data were collected by way of structured interviews based on a survey instrument developed for the study. Results of the survey showed that 7 percent identified themselves as nonreaders, 12 percent as poor readers, 11 percent as below-average readers, 51 percent as average readers, 14 percent as above-average readers, and 4 percent as excellent readers. When asked to describe their reading skill development, 65 percent said that they learned to read by the time they were ten years old. Half of them reported that they were taught to read by teachers and the other half were taught by friends or relatives. Forty-eight percent reported that they felt that their reading skill had improved during recent years, while 30 percent believed that their skills had declined. Eighty-five to 90 percent said that they had adequate survival reading skills to satisfy their daily needs. Actual reading performance of the group revealed that 77 percent of the respondents successfully completed a complex task that involved reading a ballot. Only eight subjects declined to participate.

Self-reported and performance-based data revealed similar achievement patterns. Heisel and Larson (1984) point out that by national, large-scale study standards, this group of elderly African American respondents would be classified as hopelessly illiterate and

> unable to cope with the literacy demands of their daily lives. . . . By their own standards, however, seventy percent of this group are average or better readers, and only ten to fifteen percent have any difficulty meeting the functional reading requirements of their social milieu. (P. 69)

Conclusion

This review of the literature describing the reading performance of African Americans indicates that much progress has been made despite the presence of persistent problems. Engs (1987) cited problems for African Americans as prohibition against learning to read and the lack of access to education; freedom for personal benefit versus containment for the benefit of others; and the difficult transition from separate and unequal schools to the not fully desegregated schools currently in existence. In spite of the problems, substantial gains in the ability to read and write by African Americans have been made over the years. Also, they have demonstrated improved reading performance by increasing their levels of education and by increasing their high school graduation rate. Their test performance has either improved or remained stable due to increasing opportunities and added educational resources. More hopeful are results from recent studies that have measured performance of targeted groups as they function in their milieu. Noteworthy are results from studies that reveal practices that reflect wise and productive uses of literacy that satisfy daily needs of many African Americans who may be otherwise assessed as dysfunctional readers. Still the difference between African

Americans and European Americans remains as a persistent problem; it is inextricably bound up in socioeconomic, ethical, and political issues yet to be resolved.

References

Adult Performance Level Project. 1975. *Adult functional competency: A report to the Office of Education dissemination review panel.* Austin, TX: University of Texas.

Cook, W. D. 1977. *Adult literacy education in the United States.* Newark, DE: International Reading Association.

Engs, R. F. 1987. Historical perspectives on the problems of black literacy. *Educational Horizons* 66(1):13–17.

Fisher, D. L. 1978. *Functional literacy and the schools.* Washington, DC: National Institute of Education.

Gray, W. S. 1956. How well do adults read? In N. B. Henry, ed., *Adult reading.* Fifty-fifth yearbook of the National Society for the Study of Education, Part II. Chicago: The University of Chicago Press.

Heath, S. B. 1980. The functions and uses of literacy. *Journal of Communication* 30:123–33.

Heisel, M. A. 1985. Assessment of learning activity level in a group of black aged. *Adult Education Quarterly* 36(1):1–14.

Heisel, M., and G. Larson. 1984. Literacy and social milieu: Reading behavior of the black elderly. *Adult Education Quarterly* 34(2):63–70.

Keegan, A. R. 1986. The CCC: A successful job corps, 1930s style. *American Visions* 5(1):20–25.

Kirsch, I. S., and J. T. Guthrie. 1977–1978. The concept and measurement of functional literacy. *Reading Research Quarterly* 13:485–507.

Mikulecky, L., and D. Winchester. 1983. Job literacy and job performance among nurses at varying employment levels. *Adult Education Quarterly* 34:1–15.

National Assessment of Educational Progress. 1981. *Three national assessments of reading: Changes in performance 1970–1980.* Report no. 11-R-01. Denver, CO: Education Commission of the States.

Robinson, H. M. 1952. Training illiterates in the army. *Elementary School Journal* 54:440–42.

Stedman, L. C., and C. F. Kaestle. 1987. Literacy and reading performance in the United States, from 1880 to the present. *Reading Research Quarterly* 22(1):8–46.

Szwed, J. F. 1981. The ethnography of literacy. In M. F. Whiteman, ed., *Writing: The nature, development, and teaching of written communication, Vol. I,* 13–23. Hillsdale, NJ: Lawrence Erlbaum Associates.

U.S. Bureau of the Census. 1971. Illiteracy in the United States: November 1969. *Current population reports,* ser. P-20, no. 217. Washington, DC: U.S. Government Printing Office.

U.S. Bureau of the Census. 1980. Educational attainment in the United States: March 1978 and 1979. *Current population reports,* ser. P-20, no. 356. Washington, DC: U.S. Government Printing Office.

U.S. Bureau of the Census. 1982. Ancestry and Language in the United States: November 1979. *Current population reports,* ser. P-23, no. 116. Washington, DC: U.S. Government Printing Office.

Issues in Literacy Education: African Americans

R. Grann Lloyd

It is generally estimated that from 20 to 27 million adults in the U.S. who lack basic literacy skills in reading, writing, and mathematics need to function satisfactorily in today's job market. Within these parameters, it seems that a minimum of 23 million adults in the U.S. are functionally illiterate, and at least 4 million are unable to read or write at all. In this connection, it seems significant to observe that an additional 45 million adults read with only a minimal level of understanding. It is very disturbing to note further that a recent U.S. Senate report estimates that 44 percent of all African American adults are functionally illiterate in contrast to about 16 percent European American adults (*Congressional Record* 1990).

Achievement of literacy, especially adult literacy, has been a problem for African Americans throughout their existence in the U.S. From the time they were brought to the U.S. as slaves, to the present, attempts by African American adults to become literate has been an arduous task. Also, progress toward achievement of literacy skills has generally been less than adequate. A disproportionately large number of African American adults have presumably been so lacking in basic literacy skills that they could not qualify for jobs with adequate pay. Hence, many have been condemned to lives of poverty. They exist without adequate food, clothing, shelter, education, health and medical care. Moreover, many unintentionally transmit illiteracy as an enduring legacy to their children.

Adult African Americans grapple with the reality of a need for (*a*) economic efficiency, (*b*) civic responsibility, (*c*) the education of their children, and (*d*) a sense of self. To that end, challenges for them have been to develop mechanisms and techniques that achieve these needs for lasting purposes, also "to command . . . institutions of mankind to serve these purposes more faithfully and fully" (Schneider 1968, 3). Both the enormity of these challenges and the inability of millions of functionally illiterate African American adults to participate effectively in society are psychologically damaging to a far greater proportion of African Americans than is generally realized. The embarrassment and shame caused by illiteracy limits normal participation in society and creates high levels of anxiety for many. This anxiety has caused self-consciousness, and as a means of escape, many African Americans have withdrawn from as much human association as possible.

A cursory glance at the issues examined in this chapter should set forth the need for a literacy education. Further study should place in proper perspective the educational benefits (psychological and otherwise) to both African and non-African Americans.

Economic Efficiency. The quest for economic efficiency by adult African
Americans is not only a psychological and social issue of equity and fairness,
but an economic issue as well. Immediately after World War II, the average
worker with less than a fifth-grade education was able to acquire a fairly good
job in the manufacturing sector. However, for at least the past two decades, the
U.S. has been moving from an industrial manufacturing age into an information
age. During this time period, due primarily to automation and foreign
competition, millions of manufacturing jobs, particularly in the automobile,
rubber, and steel industries, have vanished. Although millions of new jobs have
been, and are being, created in information systems and the service areas, they
require a high level of basic literacy. That high level makes it very difficult for
illiterate workers to fill those jobs (*Fortune* 1982).

The average worker today must have skills far beyond a fifth-grade level.
By the year 2000, three out of four jobs will require educational preparation
above the ninth grade. The majority of new jobs will require some postsecondary
education. Examination of the changing demographics in the U.S. indicates
that, other things being equal, the future labor force will rely more and more on
population groups that typically have disproportionately high levels of illiteracy. Current projections indicate that during the time period from 1986 to
the year 2000 more than 80 percent of the U.S. labor force growth will occur
among African Americans, Asian Americans, Hispanic Americans, other
minority races, and women—a serious matter, since many non-European
Americans are conspicuously prominent among the pool of unskilled and increasingly unused labor. It is predicted that by the turn of the century the
proportion of new jobs in low-skill categories will decline from the current 40
percent to only 27 percent (*Chicago Tribune* 1988).

One of the most distinguishing characteristics of success, among adults, is
the job. When adult workers are chronically unemployed or are employed only
in the lowest skill job categories and in the most menial jobs at the bottom of
the wage scale, they are unable to provide for the necessities, comforts, and
desires of either their families or themselves. This is especially difficult for
adult African American men who cannot provide adequately, if at all, for their
families' needs. Their inability to fulfill the expected and/or normal role as
head of the household often causes them to lose the respect of their wives and
children and to suffer a major loss of self-esteem. As their self-esteem
deteriorates, desertion and divorce often follow; abuse of wives and children
increases. In attempts to avoid reality and to acquire some measure of success
to bolster their sagging sense of self, many of these individuals drift into such
antisocial behaviors as petty crime, alcohol, and drugs. Often the behaviors
cause incarceration. In this connection, it seems appropriate to note from the
Congressional Record (1990) that 75 percent of adults who are incarcerated are
functionally illiterate and that the reading level of the average person in prison
is at the third- or fourth-grade level. Finally, the anxiety that is surely associated with economic inefficiency and/or economic insufficiency may also
trigger physical disorders.

Civic Responsibility. The issue of civic responsibility is wide-ranging and multifaceted. It is concerned with the acceptance of civic duties, loyalty to democratic ideals, respect for the law, sensitivity to matters involving social justice, tolerance, the use of critical judgment, and related matters. Civic participation in public affairs often requires knowledge, courage, and social activity to correct conditions that are unsatisfactory. But can these matters be entrusted to people who are illiterate, since uninformed activity and misdirected knowledge are impediments to civic responsibility? The nineteenth-century American writer Henry Thoreau suggested that democracy is dependent upon individuals who think independently. Yet civic responsibility requires that citizens be informed and capable of bringing a substantial measure of quality to their thinking.

A literacy education may increase African Americans' chances of being socially informed. Likewise, it should increase their willingness to participate, to a greater degree, in civic affairs. As Weinberg and Shabat (1956) pointed out many years ago, "citizens in a democratic society are obligated . . . to participate in civic matters" (p. 30). But rather than participating in civic matters, those who are illiterate often become self-conscious and defensive because they feel incapable of intelligent civic participation and wish to avoid embarrassment. Often, they become evasive and/or withdraw from political discussions, association with community organizations, volunteer community efforts, identification with political parties, and even voting in political elections. Such barriers seem to limit the development and nurturing of human relationships among those with a deficit in literacy skills.

Education. While African American parents have always wanted for themselves and their children the same quality and quantity of education delivered to other Americans by the public school system, they have not always sought to achieve it directly by organized means. In fact, a disproportionately large number of the parents have not been in positions to do so because of their own shortfall in literacy skills. Yet they recognize that the educational system has failed to effectively educate their children. Many of the parents are distressed by the disproportionately large number of African American children being expelled, suspended, and "pushed out" of public schools in the U.S. each year. Also, many parents are frustrated by the disproportionately large number of African American children labeled "educable mentally retarded" and enrolled in "special education classes" (Hale 1981, 1) each year. They want the school system to recognize

> that Black [African American] children grow up in a distinct culture. Black [African American] children therefore need an educational system that recognizes their strengths, their abilities, and their culture and that incorporates them into the learning process. (Hale, 4).

A literacy education for African Americans would enable them to contend more intelligently and vigorously for more quality in the education their children receive and in the jobs they seek. It would prevent the decrease of their self-worth as their children progress through the school system. An education would also prepare them to function and to acquire reasonable jobs in a literate society. Overall, a literacy education should help African Americans give their children a better start in life. First Lady of the U.S. Barbara Bush has stated:

> The home is the child's first school. The parent is the child's first teacher. Reading is the child's first subject. We all know that adults who have problems with literacy tend to raise children who have problems with literacy. (*Congressional Record* 1990, S-729).

Illiteracy affects all U.S. citizens either directly or indirectly. It impedes growth of the economy. It raises the prices of goods and services when business firms must absorb the cost of training and retraining employees who do not have basic literacy skills. It raises the taxes paid to support those who are unemployed because of their incompetence to read, write, and compute with sufficient facility to compete in today's labor market.

Conclusion

As millions of African American adults in the U.S. strive for literacy and seek to obtain at least a modicum of formal education, they often experience numerous psychological and physical problems. These include anxiety and stress, uncomfortable levels of self-consciousness and embarrassment, evasion and withdrawal from association as a means of escape, nervous disorders, and loss of self-esteem. In many cases hypertension is experienced; it seems to lead to high blood pressure, headaches, strokes, and feelings of insecurity. Additionally, psychosomatic maladies frequently develop and often become persistent. Nevertheless, those African Americans who are deficient in literacy skills and/or who have an appetite for learning should not be deterred in their pursuit for an education. Cyril Houle has said, it is

> . . . the process by which men and women (alone, in groups, or in the institutional settings) seek to improve themselves or their society by increasing their skill, their knowledge, or their sensitiveness. . . . [and] any process by which individuals, groups, or institutions try to help men and women improve in these ways. (cited in McGee & Neufeldt 1985, ix)

African Americans have been involved in education almost from the time they arrived in the U.S. Thompson (1974) sums this matter up cogently:

> The Blacks' [African Americans'] struggle to acquire a "good" education has been long, frustrating, and dangerous. Motivating the struggle has been the conviction that education is the key to individual dignity, social status, and equal citizenship. Even during the slave period when the education of Blacks [African Americans] was prohibited by law and when those who violated that law were severely punished, many slaves dared to attend "clandestine" schools and learned to read and write whenever and however they could manage to do so. (P. 168)

Historically, the valiant efforts made by adult African Americans to improve every aspect of their lives, with education receiving the highest priority, must persist through the 1990s and beyond.

References

Chicago Tribune. 1988. 26 December, sec. 4: 5.

Congressional Record. 1990. 5 February, S–729.

Fortune. 1982. 28 June, 58–65.

Hale, J. E. 1981. *Black Children: Their roots, culture, and learning styles.* Provo, UT: Brigham Young University Press.

McGee, L., and H. G. Neufeldt. 1985. *Education of the black adult in the United States.* Westport, CT: Greenwood Press.

Schneider, K. R. 1968. *Destiny of change: How relevant is man in the age of development?* NY: Holt, Rinehart & Winston, Inc.

Thompson, D. C. 1974. *Sociology of the black experience.* Westport, CT: Greenwood Press.

Weinberg, M., and O. E. Shabat. 1956. *Society and man.* Englewood Cliffs, NJ: Prentice-Hall.

Literacy Training for Incarcerated Adults

T. A. Ryan

Former Chief Justice Warren Burger's concern with costs and benefits of warehousing prisoners has gained considerable attention. He has stated repeatedly that the country cannot afford to incarcerate the same people over and over again without giving them skills to function outside the prison. It was his contention that confining offenders without trying to change them was an expensive folly with short-term benefits and long-term costs (Burger 1981). With Burger's concern in mind, I designed this chapter to present an overview of the background, implementation, and psychological impact of literacy training for incarcerated adults.

Prison Setting for Literacy Training. The ultimate mission of the prisons in the U.S. is the protection of society. Individuals who have been apprehended by law enforcement agents and found guilty by the courts for having transgressed against the mores and laws of the country are sentenced to prison. Primary concerns of prison administrators historically have been security of the facility and custody and control of the inmates—prerequisites for successful protection of the citizenry.

Background

Philosophical biases and public demands have dictated the place of literacy training of inmates in correctional systems. When there has been commitment to reform and rehabilitation, education has had a high priority in prisons, and development of literacy training programs has had substantial support. When the prevailing philosophy has been "nothing works" combined with a commitment to punishment, deterrence, and incapacitation, education has been a low-priority concern, and resources for literacy training have been limited.

Prison Population. The number of prisoners under the jurisdiction of U.S. federal and state correctional authorities at year's end 1988 reached a record 527,402. Prisoners with sentences of more than one year accounted for 96 percent of the total prison population at the end of 1988. The remaining prisoners had sentences of a year or less or were unsentenced. The number of sentenced prisoners per 100,000 residents in the general population was 244. Eleven of the seventeen jurisdictions with rates equal to or greater than the rate for the nation were located in the South. Female inmates numbered 32,691, increasing at a faster rate during 1988 (13 percent) than males (7 percent). The rate of incarceration for sentenced males (476 per 100,000 males in the general resident population) was about twenty times higher than for sentenced females (26 per 100,000 females in the general population). There was some evidence that during the period 1980 to 1987 changes in criminal justice policies increased the probability of a criminal being incarcerated over the levels existing in prior years (Bureau of Justice Statistics 1989).

Demographic Profile of Inmates. The individuals making up the prison populations of the U.S. are as diverse in age, experience, aptitude, interests, and personal characteristics as the general population from which they came. A number of distinguishing characteristics for adult inmates have been found. For example, Bell et al. (1979) concluded there was a higher incidence of unstable home backgrounds among offenders compared to nonoffenders. On the whole, adult offenders tended to be predominantly male (96 percent), disproportionately young, African American, unmarried, poor, and unemployed in comparison to the general population.

The Comptroller General of the United States (1979) reported that "the offender population in federal and state correctional institutions is largely young, male, and disproportionately represented by lower social and economic levels and minority groups" (p. 13). Adult offenders typically had emotional and personality problems. A variety of psychological and emotional stresses contributed to their frustrations, defensiveness, and hostility (George & Krist 1980). The typical adult offender was a "school dropout, unemployed, unskilled, functionally illiterate, lacking in self-esteem" (Murray 1980, 3). More than half the adult offenders had learning disabilities. The Education Commission of the States (1976) found 59 percent had learning handicaps, 30 percent had below-average intelligence, 53 percent had emotional problems, and 65 percent lacked motivation. As a group, inmates tended to suffer from low self-esteem, high frustration, and inadequate social responsibility.

Literacy Training in Prisons. Literacy training for adult inmates is meant to prepare them for positive, constructive roles during the time of incarceration and to prepare them for release to society as law-abiding, contributing members.

The American Correctional Association (1988) literacy handbook contends that prisons continue to be places where the young are held. As the population grays, as more workers retire, as the economy grows and more jobs are created, the supply of workers will lag behind the demand. The productivity of the workforce must be increased. Thus, there is a need to capitalize on the potential economic contribution of the nearly 1 million adults who are in prisons. Literacy, job skills, and coping competencies may help curb the growing recidivism rates. Bellardo (1986a), in reviewing the changing philosophies governing the place of education in the prison system, concluded that whatever the quality and effects of correctional education, one result could be predicted: Ex-offenders lacking opportunity to develop new skills would return to old habits, friends, and life-styles.

Many researchers have demonstrated a relationship between employment problems and criminal behavior (Duffy & Vandersteen 1975; Larkin 1975; Railsback 1975; Zivian 1975; Kitchner, Schmidt, & Glaser 1977). Larkin found unemployed or underemployed parolees were less likely to succeed at parole than employed parolees. McKee (1970) established that one of the most frequent reasons cited by employers for not hiring parolees was their lack of education. Ryan (1989) concluded, based on results of a study of female parolees in relation to an educational support program,

... It is not possible to say with certainty that there is a link between ESP and successful completion of parole or probation. ... [However] it should be noted that out of 73 women (who participated in the education program) 67 did not have a parole revocation. (P. 222)

When inmates are released from prison, their chances for law-abiding behavior will not be enhanced if their educational deficiencies are not overcome during the time they are in prison (American Correctional Association 1988).

History of Literacy Training in Prisons. Even though the history of correctional education in the U.S. is only about fifty years old, prisons have existed for some 200 years (Ryan 1982). The genesis of literacy training for inmates can be traced to early attempts by the chaplains to reform the prisoners. Conducted at night or on Sundays,

> correctional education was the chaplain standing in the semi-dark corridor, before the cell door, with a dingy lantern hanging to the grated bars, and teaching to the wretched convict in the darkness beyond the grated door the rudiments of reading or numbers. (Lewis 1922, 141)

In 1827 a law was passed in New York providing for the appointment of secular teachers, supervised by chaplains, to teach in state prisons (Wines & Dwight 1867).

Correctional education progressed slowly during the four decades following the American Prison Association's proclamation in 1870. In 1934 the state of New York and the Federal Prison System introduced compulsory classes for functionally illiterate inmates. The Englehardt Commission (1939) stated that the purpose of prison education was the socialization of inmates through varied activities emphasizing individual inmate needs. Overall, there was little interest in inmate education in the 1940s and 1950s.

A resurgence of interest in inmate education was manifested in the 1960s and 1970s. For example, the U.S. Office of Education through its Adult Education Act made literacy training a national priority. This included the education of inmates. Also, the Manpower Development and Training Act of 1962 provided funds to support intensive educational and vocational training for inmates.

One of the first major efforts to address functional illiteracy of adult inmates was undertaken in 1969 and supported from that time through 1975 by Adult Education in the U.S. Office of Education. This effort resulted in the development and implementation of plans for adult basic education in prisons in forty-five states, and in accompanying training of prison personnel to conduct literacy training programs for inmates (Ryan et al. 1975).

The 1980s witnessed a dramatic increase in interest in literacy training for inmates, as evidenced by American Broadcasting Corporation's (ABC) Project Literacy U.S. (PLUS), Literacy Initiatives, Literacy Volunteers of America, and National Adult Literacy Congress. The Correctional Education Association in concert with ABC's Project PLUS published *Learning Behind Bars*. It described selected educational programs conducted in juvenile, jail, and prison facilities. A literacy guide for correctional administrators was supported by the National Institute of Corrections (Bellardo 1986a).

For the most part, participation in literacy programs in prisons was voluntary throughout the U.S. from about 1940 to 1980. The establishment of the first mandatory adult basic education policy in the U.S. Bureau of Prisons was in 1981. The policy incorporated the following components:

1. Inmates functioning at less than sixth-grade level were required to enroll in an adult basic literacy program for ninety days.
2. Inmates could not be promoted to jobs above the lowest level until they met the sixth-grade standard.
3. Institutions developed needs lists to follow each inmate's progress.
4. Institutions developed incentives and awards for inmate progress.

After three years it became apparent that the sixth grade level was not high enough to meet employers' rising expectations and comparable community standards. [So] . . . in July 1985, a pilot program was initiated in the Northeast Region to test the establishment of the 8th grade as the new standard; a year later that standard became nationwide. (McCollum 1989, 9–10)

McCollum attributed success of the literacy training program in the Federal Bureau of Prisons to two factors:

1. *Connection between literacy achievement and income.* The difference between a prison industries entry level grade of twenty-two cents an hour and the top grade of $1.10 per hour was a significant motivator.
2. *Increased availability of computer-assisted instruction.* The use of computers allowed for drill and practice, and teachers were able to manage enlarged enrollments without losing one-on-one contact.

The American Correctional Association (1988) in the "Offender Programs Handbook" noted that the establishment of a mandatory literacy level could serve as a motivator for enrolling students in literacy training. Nine states (Maryland, Arizona, Arkansas, Massachusetts, Michigan, Montana, New Jersey, Ohio, and Texas) had established required literacy levels in 1988 ranging from second- to eighth-grade level. Other states adopted programs that related literacy to parole considerations or other entitlements.

Implementation of Literacy Training in Prisons

Extent of Literacy Training in Prisons. Studies have been conducted to survey enrollment in correctional education programs and administration of programs (Ryan 1973; Dell'Apa 1973; Bell et al. 1979; Conrad 1981; Contact Inc. 1982; Ryan & Woodard 1987). Generally, results from the surveys have shown agreement in terms of availability of adult basic education (literacy) programs and the percent of total inmate populations enrolled in the programs. Also, results have shown that roughly 96 percent of the prisons for adult inmates offered adult basic education. In 1973 Dell'Apa found that one-third of the inmates in state institutions and an average of 41 percent of the inmates in federal institutions participated in educational programs. Reasons for nonparticipation were lack of interest, inadequate facilities or funds.

The data from a survey of prisons in 1979 by Lehigh University indicated that (*a*) only 38 percent of inmates were enrolled in some type of educational program and (*b*) peer pressure worked against an inmate enrolling in school. Another reason for low enrollment in 62 percent of the institutions surveyed was that inmates working in prison industries were paid more than those going to school (Bell et al. 1979).

In a national survey of forty-five states, Ryan and Woodard (1987) found that 98 percent of the states (forty-four out of forty-five) reported offering adult basic education programs for adult inmates. The number of inmates enrolled in these programs ranged from zero to 11,932. The average was 849 per state, representing 9 percent of the total adult inmate population. States with the largest enrollments were Texas (11,832), New York (2,000), and Florida (1,894). States with the smallest or zero enrollments were Hawaii, Idaho, and Nevada. The number of hours per week inmates participated in literacy training ranged from five to forty-three, with the average being eighteen. Out of forty-four states offering adult basic education, forty states (91 percent) offered these programs at the correctional facilities; four states offered literacy training both at the prison and through community resources.

Nature of Prison Literacy Training Programs. The *development, implementation,* and *evaluation* of literacy training programs for adult inmates can be accomplished by using a generalized planning model that employs a systems approach. Following is a brief presentation of the model.

1. *Development of Literacy Training.* The use of systems approach in development of prison literacy training requires: (*a*) an analysis of the prison setting to establish prerequisites for assessing needs with attention to facilities, staffing, and scheduling of activities, resources, and budgetary constraints; (*b*) the definition of goals and objectives that state the desired end results of the program; and (*c*) an evaluation of alternative instructional techniques to include teleconferencing, videos, and computer technology for delivery of the training needed to achieve program objectives.

2. *Implementation of Literacy Training.* The second major component in the model is implementation of the day-to-day activities involved in the literacy program. This implementation requires: (*a*) the use of advisory groups to advise and counsel about the latest educational technology, employment trends, job opportunities, and new ideas from public schools that might be applicable for prisons; (*b*) the conduct of public relations to obtain support for programs and to keep informed about legislation that could impact literacy programs at the local, state, and federal levels; (*c*) the establishment of an organizational structure that shows how personnel involved in literacy training relate to other prison staff; (*d*) the scheduling of tasks and activities to minimize potential conflicts with work assignments, protective custody or segregation of inmates, and hospitalization; (*e*) the determination of the cost of literacy training programs and the identification of sources

of financial support for the operation of programs; (*f*) the provision of facilities that are conducive to learning; (*g*) the recruiting, selecting, and training of staff who are knowledgeable in their subject areas and knowledgeable about inmates; and (*h*) the development of curriculum that includes instructional hardware and software, scope and sequence, methods and techniques, and incentives and rewards.

3. *Evaluation of Literacy Training in Prison.* There must be ongoing daily evaluation focusing on the process of literacy training in order to detect possible areas where changes need to be made in the curriculum, staffing, or facilities where the program is offered. Also, each year there should be an evaluation of the program to determine the extent to which the objectives have been achieved and to establish accountability. Review of this kind of immediate feedback on a regular basis can help correct deficiencies in the program as it is being conducted.

A generalized planning model for literacy training has been adapted from the model developed initially by Ryan et al. (1975) and subsequently implemented throughout prisons in the U.S. The model is compatible with the practical suggestions for developing successful literacy programs set forth in the Guide for Correctional Educators developed by the Far West Regional Laboratory for Educational Research and Development. This guide emphasizes that program goals, student assessment, student motivation, teaching methods, materials, linkage with business and community, and program evaluation are essential for literacy training in prisons (Bellardo 1986a).

Sample Literacy Programs in Prisons. A survey (Bellardo 1986a) that investigated 225 prison literacy programs in the U.S. found that although most prisons offered programs for inmates at the low-literacy level, many lacked formally developed programs. Among the formal model programs were those characterized as individualized, staffed by trained reading teachers and tutors, supplemented with computer technology, and using a flexible curriculum. These literacy programs were integral parts of a total educational program for prison inmates. Following are descriptions of *model literacy programs* that illustrate a range of creative solutions that may be implemented in the development and delivery of literacy training for adult inmates (Bellardo, 1986b).

1. *Buena Vista Correctional Facility, Buena Vista, Colorado.* This is a medium security facility for male inmates, average age twenty-six years, with a total population of 740 inmates. The staff included one director, eleven instructors, and inmate aides.

   The philosophy of the institution reflected promotion of social responsibility, personal initiative, and positive motivation as ways to redirect inmates into noncriminal roles. Teachers were encouraged to be innovative. There was a strong emphasis on communication with staff in other departments, and teachers served as role models for the inmates. Academic teachers also served as counselors. Noteworthy features of this program included (*a*) incentive system; (*b*) staff communication across components; (*c*) courses in social responsibility, marriage, and family; and (*d*) prerelease.

2. *Maryland Correctional Institution, Hagerstown, Maryland.* This is a minimum to medium security facility for male inmates, average age twenty-three years, with a total population of 2,480 inmates. The staff included one supervisor, two assistant principals, seventeen instructors, one librarian, and inmate aides.

In 1978 the Maryland Department of Education assumed responsibility for the state's correctional education program, previously managed by the State Department of Corrections. The program's philosophy emphasized provision of basic skills, job preparation, and personal development. The program used individualized instruction. Adult basic education was mandatory for ninety days for inmates scoring less than fifth-grade level. Noteworthy features of this program included (*a*) peer tutoring, (*b*) related subjects in vocational education, (*c*) computer laboratory, and (*d*) employability skills.

3. *Muskegon Correctional Facility, Muskegon, Michigan.* This is a medium security facility for male inmates, average age twenty-seven years, with a total population of 850 inmates. The staff included one principal, twelve instructors, teacher aides, inmate aides, and volunteer tutors. The program was structured to help inmates acquire basic academic and vocational skills and to apply these skills to solve real problems and gain self-confidence. The teaching approaches included one-on-one, small group, programmed instruction, formal classes, and independent study. The adult basic education classes offered for students below sixth-grade level were highly individualized and provided remediation in English, mathematics, and reading. An inmate lacking basic academic skills could progress through a sequence of instructional experiences. Examples are fundamental reading, writing, and mathematics; survival reading, writing, mathematics, and career awareness; occupational exploration; specific occupational training; and job readiness. Noteworthy features of this program included (*a*) student education groups, (*b*) skills application, and (*c*) student newspaper.

4. *Oklahoma Prison Literacy Project.* In 1986 a Literacy Task Force was formed to study inmate literacy needs and to determine alternatives for meeting the needs. The task force recommended development of a statewide literacy project including all correctional facilities. The State Departments of Education and Libraries and literacy volunteers throughout the state of Oklahoma cooperated with the State Department of Corrections to develop and implement the Oklahoma Prison Literacy Project. A Laubach training team was installed in each correctional center to provide initial literacy training

workshops, develop a basic library of materials, and select staff for each facility to serve as an ongoing training team.

The Department of Corrections granted released time for staff to attend training sessions. The Department of Education provided funds to purchase literacy workbooks and materials. The Department of Libraries provided basic start-up packets for each facility, recruited literacy volunteers, provided honoraria and travel expenses for participating trainers. Two incentives were provided for inmate participation in the literacy program: (a) the Pardon and Parole Board proclaimed full support and acknowledged that inmate program participation would weigh favorably for parole decisions; and (b) the governor supported consideration of inmate program participation as an important variable on the parole application. This project was awarded the 1988 national Laubach Literacy Action Award.

Psychological Impact of Literacy Training

The psychological impact of literacy training for adult inmates is probably greater than any other educational program experienced by them. This is not to say that the other educational programs are unimportant. Far from that. Rather, literacy training provides the foundation for participation in all other programs and thereby contributes to benefits that come from all program involvement.

Most inmates have the ability to learn. Studies indicate the learning potential of low-achieving inmates is equivalent to that of inmates achieving at high school level and beyond in the U.S. Most adult inmates with low levels of literacy have experienced a history of school failures. Some have limited English fluency or are non-English speaking. They tend to have poor self-esteem and are easily frustrated. They are usually interested more in learning content that has immediate application to their lives than to less practical instructional materials. All available evidence suggests that inmates, for the most part, have poor academic and vocational skills, have low self-esteem, and do not take responsibility for their lives. To address these needs, an ideal literacy program should stress mathematics, reading, writing, vocational and job-seeking skills. It should also attempt to increase inmates' self-esteem and promote positive social behaviors.

Sensitivity to ethnic, cultural, and class differences should be provided in basic literacy programs. Many studies have indicated the importance of sensitivity to incarcerated Native Americans' customs and values. Cultural conflicts can be frustrating and can lead to alienation of inmates. Such could add to the already powerful frustrations that come from being functionally illiterate. In Juneau, Alaska, where 75 percent of the inmate students were native Alaskans, teaching methods in the literacy program were adapted to compliment the inmates' cultural styles. Hispanic, Asian, and African American inmates may experience learning problems related to cultural conflicts.

Major problems for most inmates are the lack of job skills and a history of being unable to support themselves and their dependents in socially acceptable and civically responsible manners. Literacy programs that link problems of inmates to the acquisition of basic skills with vocational training, job readiness, and prerelease can make a significant psychological difference in their lives.

A literacy program should recognize the need for inmates to develop and implement parenting roles effectively. It is difficult to be a role model for one's children if a person cannot read the newspaper, cannot read a street sign, and cannot read the labels on medicine bottles. Always to be in a position of having to make excuses for one's inability to read or write, to be seen by one's children as a failure, to experience the inner torment of knowing there are hard and fast barriers precluding participation in the mainstream of society—these are the facts of life that mark functionally illiterate inmates as outcasts and failures. Add to this the social stigma of being branded a prisoner and the result is a totally devastating destructive psychological impact on adult inmates. Literacy training programs should hold out hope for functionally illiterate inmates and give them promise of rewarding lives for themselves and their children.

Functional illiteracy is one of the most costly problems facing the U.S in the closing decade of the twentieth century. This problem is magnified manyfold for incarcerated adults. These adults are doubly handicapped within the prison environment where the options are more limited than in the free world and the rewards are more apt to be available for those who can read, write, and compute.

Education is one primary activity that a correctional system can provide. The program resources are accessible at relatively low cost; the inmates who are the potential students are available and have time for education. The benefits of literacy training are great, both for individual inmates and for society in general.

Conclusion

References

American Correctional Association. 1988. *Literacy: A concept for all seasons.* Washington, DC: St. Mary's Press.

Bell, R., E. Conrad, T. Laffey, J. C. Lutz, F. V. Miller, C. Simon, A. E. Stakelon, and J. J. Wilson. 1979. *National evaluation program: Correctional education programs for inmates.* Washington, DC: Law Enforcement Assistance Administration.

Bellardo, D. 1986a. *Making literacy programs work: Practical guide for correctional educators.* Vol. I. Washington, DC: U.S. Government Printing Office.

Bellardo, D. 1986b. *Directory of prison literacy programs in the United States.* Vol. II. Washington, DC: U.S. Government Office.

Bureau of Justice Statistics. 1989. *Prisoners in 1988.* Washington, DC: U.S. Department of Justice.

Burger, W. E. 1981. An agenda for crime prevention and correctional reform. *American Bar Association Journal* 67:988–91.

Comptroller General of the United States. 1979. *Report to the Congress: Correctional institutions can do more to improve the employability of offenders.* Washington, DC: Author.

Conrad, J. P. 1981. *Adult offender education programs.* Cambridge, MA: Abt Associates, Inc.

Contact, Inc. 1982. *Correctional education.* Lincoln, NE: Author.

Dell'Apa, F. 1973. *Educational programs in adult correctional institutions: A survey.* Boulder, CO: Western Interstate Commission on Higher Education.

Duffy, J., and E. Vandersteen. 1975. Wisconsin job service goes to prison. *Journal of Employment Counseling* 12:175–82.

Education Commission of the States. 1976. *Correctional education: A forgotten service.* Denver, CO: Author.

Englehardt Commission. 1939. *Report.* Washington, DC: U.S. Government Printing Office.

George, P. S., and G. Krist. 1980. A unique educational experience: Teaching in a correctional institution. *Corrections Today* 42:58–60.

Kitchner, H., A. K. Schmidt, and D. Glaser. 1977. How persistent is post-prison success: *Federal Probation* 41:9–15.

Larkin, T. 1975. Removing the ex-offenders catch-22. *Manpower* 7:18–22.

Lewis, O. F. 1922. *The development of American prisons and prison customs, 1776–1845.* Albany, NY: Prison Association of New York.

McCollum, S. G. 1989. Mandatory literacy for prisons. *Federal Prison Journal* 1:9–10.

McKee, J. M. 1970. The use of programmed instruction in correctional institutions. In T. A. Ryan, ed., *Collection of papers prepared for 1970 national seminars: Adult basic education in corrections.* Honolulu, HI: University of Hawaii.

Murray, L. 1980. Public hearings on the status of vocational education in correctional institutions. *Journal of Correctional Education* 31:8–11.

Railsback, T. 1975. Corrections: A long way to go. *Federal Probation* 39:48–51.

Ryan, T. A. 1973. A model for correctional education. In M. V. Reagen, D. M. Stoughton, T. E. Smith, and J. C. Davis, eds., *School behind bars: A descriptive overview of correctional education in the American prison system.* Syracuse, NY: Syracuse University Research Corp.

Ryan, T. A. 1982. Correctional education. In H. Mitzel, ed., *Encyclopedia of educational research,* 5th ed., 370–74. NY: Free Press.

Ryan, T. A. 1989. A transitional program for female offenders. In S. Duguid, ed., *Yearbook of correctional education,* 209–23. Burnaby, BC, Canada: Simon Fraser University.

Ryan, T. A., D. W. Clark, R. S. Hatrak, D. Hinders, J. C. V. Keeney, J. Oresic, J. B. Orrell, A. R. Sessions, J. L. Streed, and H. G. Wells. 1975. *Model of adult basic education in corrections.* Honolulu, HI: University of Hawaii.

Ryan, T. A. and J. C. Woodard, Jr. 1987. *Correctional education: A state of the art analysis.* Washington, DC: U.S. Department of Justice.

Wines, E. C., and T. A. Dwight. 1867. *Report on the prisons and reformatories of the United States and Canada.* Albany, NY: Van Benthuysen & Sons.

Zivian, M. 1975. State rehabilitation services for adult offenders. *Journal of Rehabilitation* 41:27–30.

Literacy and the Adult with Specific Learning Disabilities

Jovita M. Ross-Gordon

Why, one might ask, is there a chapter on learning disabilities in a book about adult literacy. Are learning disabilities considered developmental disabilities that affect children? Do children get the special education they need to overcome these disabilities before they reach adulthood? Have questions been raised about the theoretical basis of specific learning disabilities and the methods used to identify them? Although one might reply yes to each of these questions, such an answer would be overly simplistic in each case. The fact remains that thousands of children in the U.S. previously identified as having specific learning disabilities have reached adulthood and seek a variety of adult services, including literacy instruction and adult basic education (ABE).

Discussion with any experienced provider of adult basic education will suggest the presence of adults who do not carry the learning disabled label but fail to make progress in traditional basic skills programs despite seemingly normal ability levels. Some of these adults attended school at a time when learning disabilities (LD) were said not to exist; others attended school since the growth of LD as a field of study and a special education category, yet escaped labeling and the special services associated with it. The presence of adults identified as learning disabled or suspected to have specific learning disabilities in adult literacy programs compels the intelligent discussion of a variety of issues surrounding literacy and learning disabilities in adulthood. More questions may be provided than answers, but they are, nonetheless, questions that must be raised. Those involved in providing literacy instruction must be prepared to thoughtfully consider the issues before either carelessly labeling adults as learning disabled or dismissing the possibility that individually based learning disabilities do exist.

A discussion of adult learning disabilities must begin with a discussion of concepts and history. Conceptually, the term *learning disabilities* is best distinguished from the more generic term *learning problems*. Some use the adjective *specific* in conjunction with learning disabilities to make this distinction. There can be many reasons for an adult to exhibit learning problems. Some of these reasons are intrinsic to the learner, including diminished sensory acuity, limited intellectual ability, acquired brain injury, emotional disturbance, chemical dependency, and lack of motivation to learn. Other reasons are external to the learner, including ineffective instruction, limited exposure to necessary background knowledge, and environmental stresses. Historically, the term *learning disability* has been used to describe a heterogeneous group of learning difficulties when the previously listed reasons do not explain the learning problem. Most definitions have emphasized three elements: (*a*) a discrepancy between ability and performance, (*b*) an absence of other primary handicapping conditions, and (*c*) factors intrinsic to the individual (Johnson & Blalock 1987).

In recent years, a definition proposed in 1981 by a joint committee representing six professional fields concerned with learning disabilities has gained increasing acceptance though not official sanction. While still emphasizing that the learning disability is intrinsic to the individual, this definition deemphasizes the medical terminology and leaves room for the coexistence of learning disabilities along with other handicapping conditions.

> Learning Disabilities is a generic term that refers to a heterogeneous group of disorders manifested by significant difficulties in the acquisition and use of listening, speaking, writing, reasoning, or mathematical abilities. These disorders are intrinsic to the individual and presumed to be due to central nervous system dysfunctions. Even though a learning disability may occur concomitantly with other handicapping conditions (e.g. cultural differences, insufficient/inappropriate instruction, psychogenic factors), it is not the direct result of those influences. (Hammill, Leigh, McNutt & Larsen 1981, 336)

Since this definition makes reference to presumed "central nervous system dysfunctions," it does not eliminate the diagnostic dilemma of deciding what constitutes sufficient evidence of such dysfunction. It is this kind of dilemma that led the Rehabilitation Services Administration (RSA) to at first require neuropsychological evidence following its 1981 decision to serve learning disabled clients under a mental disorder code, then later to accept educational evidence of learning disability while classifying it under a neuropsychological (physical) disorder code (Biller 1988). This is the tangled path of differential diagnosis awaiting the adult educator who seeks to identify learning disabilities in a student.

Prevalence of Adult Learning Disabilities

Prevalence (Kavale 1988) is the number of times of a given condition in a given population at a given time. Just how concerned should adult educators involved with literacy programs be about the prevalence of LD? One's judgment on this question is likely to be influenced by knowledge of the number of such students likely to be served in adult education programs.

Kavale observes that at the time PL 94–142 was written it was suggested that as many as 2 percent of the school population would be learning disabled. At that time, LD represented 17 percent of the handicapped students served in schools; by 1984 the number of LD students had increased 119 percent (Kavale 1988). By the 1983–1984 school year, the percentage of school-age students served as learning disabled rose to 4.57 percent, and they represented 42 percent of those in special education programs (Hallahan, Keller, & Ball 1986).

It is difficult to determine how accurately these figures reflect the actual prevalence of learning disabilities in school-age children, with most estimates ranging from 2 percent to 15 percent. Analyses of identification processes used by schools suggest that many social, legal, and organizational factors impinge on diagnosis; and certain types of students may, more likely, be identified than others in particular settings (Ysseldyke, Thurlow, Graden, Wesson, Deno, & Algozzine 1983). It is even more difficult to estimate the number of individuals with specific learning disabilities in the adult population who may be in need of literacy instruction.

Accepting a given prevalence figure among children and extrapolating it to the adult population may not be meaningful, since variable ability levels and adult living demands have a great influence on the number of learning disabled adults likely to seek any kind of educational assistance. These adults may appear in a wide variety of adult learning environments and may or may not require support in areas associated with literacy acquisition. There is at least some basis for suspecting that LD adults are more likely to seek assistance in the arena of adult basic skills or General Educational Development (GED) preparation, given evidence that learning disabled youth are less likely to attain a high school diploma while attending school (Thornton & Zigmond 1987; White, Schumaker, Warner, Alley, & Deshler 1980). Yet, estimates that 80 to 95 percent of those in ABE programs (Jordon & Weisel's work cited in Travis 1979) have learning disabilities must be interpreted with extreme caution.

Assessment

At least one reason for conservatism in interpreting estimates of LD in the ABE population has been criticism of some of the instruments used to assess the processing disorders associated with learning disabilities (Coles 1980; O'Donnell & Wood 1981; Travis 1979). The entry of the Woodcock-Johnson Psychoeducational Battery (Woodcock & Johnson 1977) onto the scene has at least provided a reliable measure normed for adults. Yet, the nature of leading definitions of learning disabilities suggest no one instrument can appropriately be used to identify learning disability. At a minimum, an individually administered test of intellectual ability is required, along with achievement tests to determine whether there is a discrepancy between ability and performance. The Wechsler Adult Intelligence Scale-Revised (WAIS-R) (Wechsler 1981) is the measure of overall ability most widely used in diagnosis of learning disabilities. It is favored because it gives separate scores for verbal and performance abilities, along with standard scores for a number of subscales.

Assuming a processing-based definition is accepted, assessment also normally includes interpretation of WAIS-R subscale scores and likely administration of the Cognitive volume of the Woodcock-Johnson Psychoeducational Battery and/or other measures of cognitive processing. Such measures are used to pinpoint difficulties in perception, memory, conception, or higher level cognitive processes and to determine which sensory systems are most affected (auditory, visual, haptic, kinesthetic). Johnson (1987a) describes informal procedures that can be used during evaluation and diagnostic teaching with adults to pinpoint underlying process weaknesses according to the level of cognition affected, the particular sense(s) involved, and the difficulty with intrasensory, intersensory, or multisensory learning. While these procedures might be criticized from a measurement standpoint, they can be useful for suggesting both modes of remediation and compensation.

Any serious attempt to exclude other primary causes of the learning difficulty require acuity screening and a detailed learning history. Adults can typically give this history themselves through an interview, although corroboration through school records may be helpful. In taking a history, it is important to include questions that will elicit information about frequent moves, chronic absenteeism or critical gaps in school attendance, severe emotional instability, family history of learning problems, and primary modes of reading instruction. While some might question the learner's assessment of instructional adequacy, at least one study suggests low-literate adults can make cogent statements about both their own role in their learning histories and instructors that have aided or hindered their learning (Taylor, Wade, Jackson, Blum, & Gold 1980).

The main point to be made in this discussion of assessment is that appropriate evaluation of learning disability cannot be accomplished through any single measure. It is important that checklists or instruments developed to serve as a screening mechanism, to suggest *possible* learning disabilities, be treated as such. The benefits of diagnosis must be weighed against the psychological impact of a thorough evaluation and possible resulting labels. More appropriately, the decision to evaluate should be made carefully in light of anticipated outcomes of the process. Benefits such as an understanding of the reason for previous learning difficulties, improved instructional and learning strategies, and employment training and support through the Office of Vocational Rehabilitation (OVR) must be considered against possible ramifications of being labeled "learning disabled."

Learning Disabilities in Adulthood: Real or Irrelevant?

You may ask, is it really necessary to identify adults as having learning disabilities or to provide specialized services to those previously identified as learning disabled? Numerous studies have suggested that learning disabilities do persist into adulthood and that they do affect many aspects of adult life (Gottfredson, Finucci, & Childs 1984; Horn, O'Donnell, & Vitulano 1983; Johnson & Blalock 1987). There is evidence that the impact of learning disabilities is manifested during adulthood in continuing academic deficits (Johnson & Blalock 1987; Rogan & Hartman 1976), language and nonverbal processing problems (Johnson & Blalock 1987), vocational training and employment problems (Biller 1987; Brown 1984; Cheslar 1982; Cummings & Maddux 1982; Faford & Haubrich 1981; Geist & McGrath 1983; Lean 1983; White 1985), and social and family living problems (Cummings & Maddux 1982; Johnson & Blalock 1987; Kroll 1984; Lenkowsky & Saposnek 1978). While little research has been reported to date investigating the relationship between learning disabilities and social problems like homelessness, the indications that LD adults may be ill prepared for vocations may have caused underemployment, frequent job changes, and dependency on others for their survival.

It is important to note that learning disabled adults exhibit learning strengths that permit many of them to skillfully compensate for their learning disabilities (Barsch 1981; Johnson & Blalock 1987; Ross 1987; Smith 1985), often escaping unnoticed in adult life and requiring no help from well-meaning professionals. Some young adults who have received services in the past welcome, or even depend on, the kind of support attached to their LD label; others want no part of the label and avoid association with programs for the LD even when it means sacrificing helpful services. Some adults not previously identified may shy away from the suggestion that they have a learning disability, while others refer themselves for testing just to gain a better understanding of their learning difficulties. So there is no simple answer to the question whether specialized services are needed by the learning disabled adult. It depends greatly on the individual, his/her life circumstances and aspirations. It is known that LD adults are likely to place a greater value on the need for assistance with social relationships and skill, career counseling, developing self-esteem, vocational training, and job getting and holding than they are on assistance with academic skills in isolation (Cheslar 1982). These concerns are important to keep in mind in planning comprehensive intervention approaches that address literacy needs of learning disabled adults from a broad perspective.

Just as definitional and measurement problems have fraught the discussion of learning disabilities, so too the discussion of adult literacy has been hampered by a lack of consensus on the definition of literacy and the resulting discrepancies in figures cited regarding the incidence of illiteracy. In the recent National Assessment of Educational Progress (NAEP) study conducted in 1985 where young adults' competencies were measured in three areas (prose literacy, document literacy, and quantitative literacy), literacy was defined as "the ability to use printed and written information to function in society, to achieve one's goals, and to develop one's knowledge and potential" (Kirsch & Jungeblut 1986, 3–4).

Literacy and the Learning Disabled

This general definition can aid in the examination of the areas in which an adult's specific learning disabilities might have an impact on his/her reading skills. There are a variety of learning disabilities that might differentially affect the reading process. For example, Johnson (1987b) indicated that an individual with general language problems might experience difficulties with phonemic discrimination, memory, syntax, oral reading, decoding, and comprehension, while the individual with only oral expressive language problems might only have difficulty with retrieval and pronunciation in oral reading. Also, a person with primary decoding and spelling problems may exhibit no language-based reading errors but may appear unable to master the orthographic code. One with general comprehension problems may master phonological and orthographic rules necessary for decoding, demonstrating a relatively high score on single word oral reading tests, yet may struggle with comprehension whether at the single word level (vocabulary), sentence level, or discourse level. Problems isolated to memory may be manifest in the individual who decodes adequately and shows adequate comprehension on tasks related to word vocabulary and inferential reading but who fails to recall specific details from a reading selection. The person with multisensory processing problems that create difficulty in integrating auditory and visual systems may see one thing yet say another during oral reading; thus, they may perform much more effectively on a silent reading task for which extraction of meaning is predominant.

Because distinct language and processing problems can be indicated by different kinds of reading problems, multiple measures of reading skill should be used in assessing learning disabled students, including oral and silent reading at the single word, sentence, and paragraph levels (Johnson 1987b). For example, informal reading measures (see Scales 1980, 1987) and specially structured tasks can be useful for assessing phonetic analysis and structural analysis skills in a more detailed fashion, or for assessing comprehension of more extended discourse than typically included in formal reading tests.

The concept of a hierarchy of language skills (Johnson & Myklebust 1967) suggests those who experience difficulties with oral receptive or expressive language or with visual receptive language (reading) can be expected to experience problems with written language. Gregg and Hoy (1984) suggest procedures for assessing written language difficulties in a manner that translates into remedial suggestions based on whether error patterns indicate auditory deficits, visual deficits, auditory and visual deficits, problems with punctuation and capitalization, written syntax deficits, or problems generating ideas and organizing thoughts. The suggested procedures emphasize creating an environment where creativity is encouraged while students are also helped to improve their ability to monitor their errors.

While the scope of this chapter prohibits an adequate discussion of computational literacy among learning disabled students, it is important to note that many LD students do experience problems in math as well as reading and writing, while others may experience mathematical deficits without accompanying reading and writing problems. Johnson and Blalock (1987) describe one pattern of learning disabilities that is characterized by quantitative, nonverbal, and visual-spatial disorders. Such students frequently come to their clinic reporting problems with handwriting and arithmetic. Despite adequate reading skills, these individuals may have real difficulty with everyday living skills and job performance due to their poor sense of time, direction, and organization. They are mentioned here because narrow definitions of literacy are likely to exclude them from a target population, although they may be among those greatly in need of help.

Intervention

Discussion of learning disabilities and their impact on literacy acquisition may be informative, but if it is to be ultimately useful, knowledge about adult learning disabilities must translate into suggestions for intervention. One way of classifying intervention approaches in the field of learning disabilities relates to theoretical perspectives. Kavale and Forness (1985) used such a scheme in designing and reporting a meta-analysis of studies of intervention effectiveness with LD children. The interventions examined included simply reducing class size, special class placement, early intervention, behavior modification, psycholinguistic training, perceptual-motor training, modality instruction, stimulant drugs, and diet intervention. Average effect size was reported for each type of study, with an effect size of +1.00 equivalent to one standard deviation on an achievement measure, which in turn means a one year increase. For studies reporting results in percentiles, an improvement from the fiftieth percentile to the eighty-fourth percentile was equated with an effect size of +1.00. The greatest effect size was found for behavior modification interventions (.93), although the forty-one studies using that form of intervention were characterized by the biggest standard deviation (1.16). Early intervention and psycholinguistic training were the next most effective interventions with seventy-four early intervention studies averaging an effect size of .40 and thirty-four studies of psycholinguistic training averaging an effect size of .39. It is worth noting that simply reducing class size yielded a greater average effect size (.31 for seventy-seven studies; standard deviation .70) than modality instruction, diet intervention, or perceptual motor training. Negative average effect sizes were reported for fifty studies of special class placement and 135 studies of stimulant drugs, suggesting these interventions did not overall lead to achievement gains.

It might be noted that the students in special class placements are likely to be more severely learning disabled than those provided other interventions within a resource room or regular classroom context, providing a partial explanation for the lack of overall progress in that setting. Kavale (1988) observed that standard deviations are as large as the effect sizes for all treatment types except stimulant drugs, suggesting that success or failure of the studied interventions is contingent upon relatively uncontrolled (and unknown) factors.

Approaches. Intervention approaches used with LD adolescents and adults can be categorized according to the primary goals of instruction that include basic skills remediation, subject area tutoring, compensatory modifications, cognitive training, and vocational exploration and training (Deshler, Schumaker, Lenz, & Ellis 1983; Johnston 1984; Ross 1987). Instruction begins at approximately the current achievement level, most often focusing on reading, math, and writing skills, with the intent of improving levels of performance through individualized instruction.

Many previous discussions of teaching reading to the learning disabled adult share an emphasis on remediation (Bowren 1981; Gold 1981; Peterson 1981; Thistlewaite 1983), although they vary in the techniques used and the relative emphasis on decoding (and perceptual learning disabilities) versus comprehension-based instructional strategies. There is a danger that learning disabled adults entering programs relying solely on remedial approaches may become discouraged and drop out when they see limited progress. Their frustration may be even greater when a purely diagnostic-prescriptive model is followed and they are not involved in selecting relevant goals (Hamilton 1983).

Another approach (often observed in secondary, college, and sometimes vocational training settings) uses compensatory techniques. They are designed to change the setting or conditions for learning rather than changing the learners. Although compensatory techniques are rarely used as the only form of intervention, Johnson and Myklebust (1967) long ago suggested a combined approach of remediating areas of weakness while teaching skills through stronger learning modalities, suggesting the importance of compensation. The practice of compensatory techniques is observed in college programs for the learning disabled when reading disabled students are given access to taped texts and instructors administer oral examinations. Other compensatory aids include use of a typewriter or computer by those with handwriting difficulties and use of a calculator. With such techniques, students with severe reading disabilities have been able to graduate from college. The wide range of compensatory or coping strategies exhibited by successful learning disabled adults suggests that the ability to develop or select compensatory techniques can be highly adaptive.

Models. A current learning need, addressed through a tutorial intervention model, was designed to provide direct assistance to the LD individual in mastery of particular content. This model is probably more relevant to GED and workplace literacy settings than ABE and the volunteer tutor environments. For instance, the tutor/instructor might help the student learn vocabulary and text reading strategies specific to a welding course or to the social studies section of the GED examination. A concern expressed by Deshler et al. (1983) is that the learner taught using the tutorial model is not taught how to learn independently of the tutor. Thus, this intervention model does not optimally facilitate the self-directedness seen as a goal for adult learners (Knowles 1980; Brookfield 1986).

Another model that has been successfully applied with LD adolescents is that of learning-strategies development. This model is based on the assumption that LD learners must use such cognitive strategies as planning and problem solving. Those who advocate this model, including Deshler et al. (1983), maintain that it uniquely prepares the learner for dealing with future learning situations.

No one approach or model has been demonstrated as ideal. In fact, the most successful programs for LD adults are likely to combine two or more approaches. For example, Project ABLE, a program designed for learning disabled adults, combined both remedial and compensatory approaches. Other approaches have combined compensatory techniques, counseling, remediation, and consultation with family members of LD adults.

This overview of intervention approaches and models suggests some methods for working with individual LD learners. It does not, however, suggest a comprehensive systems approach for assisting LD adults, literacy and basic education instructors, and family members as they attempt to respond to the diverse LD adult learning needs. In view of the previous information, I am suggesting a Multilevel Service Model that can provide a framework for additional intervention. It has specific applications to ABE/GED programs since it grew out of a study of ABE/GED teachers' perceptions of learning disabilities (Ross & Smith 1987).

The Multilevel Model has three major components. *Level one* includes *preservice training and staff development.* It begins when teachers are hired to teach within ABE/GED programs. As preservice and in-service training programs are developed, the teachers should be prepared to modify their instructional strategies to fit a variety of learning styles. Supplementary instruction should address the identification of learning disabilities and accommodations for LD students that can be made in the ABE/GED classroom.

Level two includes *ongoing consultation with teachers.* Specialists in the areas of reading and learning disabilities should consult with teachers to help them interpret diagnostic information. That information should be translated into teaching plans for use with LD students. Such specialists could also consult with trained volunteer tutors assigned to a particular LD student. An identified pool of external consultants consisting of professionals not typically involved in literacy and basic education programs would also be valuable. This should include physicians, psychologists, neurologists, rehabilitation counselors, and others who have demonstrated a specific interest in applying the knowledge and skills of their disciplines to learning disabilities.

Level three includes *direct services.* This service would be used to supplement levels one and two in cases where it was needed. The most frequent form of direct service would be diagnostic evaluation for learning disabilities. With some students, an extended period of diagnostic teaching might be necessary before appropriate recommendations for the mainstream class could be provided. Other students may benefit most from ongoing assignment to individual or group instruction that is led by someone extensively trained to work with this population. As in the mainstream class, multiple intervention strategies may be employed, including assistance in development of compensatory and learning strategies. The LD adult, whether in the mainstream class or specialized class, must ultimately be prepared for applying literacy skills to adult living needs.

Conclusion

Adults labeled as LD and others not labeled but who demonstrate the disabilities as those labeled are numerous. Adult educators who work with the LD population should find the following to be of value.

1. New models will have to be developed for service delivery, rather than simply transferring special education models developed for children in public school. Such models should emphasize the notion of education in the least restrictive environment and should incorporate contemporary knowledge about philosophy, psychology, and sociology of adult learning and teaching.
2. A unifocal model is less likely to be effective than one that includes a variety of intervention approaches to be selected based on the individual's learning needs and goals.
3. Recent knowledge about the social context of adult literacy (Kazemek 1988) should be considered in planning literacy programs for the adult learning disabled. While individualized instruction may be necessary for some portions of the adult's learning program, group exposure to learning groups should also be an integral part of the programming, especially for those adults who need to learn appropriate social behavior or want group support. The existing social

support networks of LD adults should also be taken into account in the comprehensive program-planning process.

4. The LD individual must be considered as a whole person who may need to develop literacy skills in multiple aspects of adult living, but also as a person who brings individual learning strengths. LD individuals are capable of developing effective learning and coping strategies and making their own contributions to their social networks (Ross 1988).

References

Barsch, J. 1981. The learning disabled adult: Self-concept revisited. *Adult Literacy and Basic Education* 5:172–77.

Biller, E. F. 1987. *Career decision making for adolescents and young adults with learning disabilities.* Springfield, IL: Charles C. Thomas, Publisher.

Biller, E. F. 1988. *Understanding adolescents and young adults with learning disabilities: A focus on employability and career placement.* Springfield, IL: Charles Thomas, Publisher.

Bowren, F. 1981. Teaching the learning disabled adult to read. *Adult Literacy and Basic Education* 5:179–85.

Brookfield, S. 1986. *Understanding and facilitating adult learning.* San Francisco: Jossey-Bass.

Brown, D. 1984. Employment considerations for learning disabled adults. *Journal of Rehabilitation* 50(2):74–77.

Cheslar, B. 1982. ACLD vocational committee completes survey on LD adult. *ACLD Newsbriefs* (146)5:20–23.

Coles, G. S. 1980. Can ABE students be identified as learning disabled? *Adult Literacy and Basic Education* 4:170–81.

Cummings, R. W., and C. D. Maddux. 1985. *Parenting the learning disabled: A realistic approach.* Springfield, IL: Thomas.

Deshler, D. D., J. B. Schumaker, B. K. Lenz, and E. Ellis. 1983. Academic and cognitive intervention for LD adolescents: Part II. *Journal of Learning Disabilities* 17:170–79.

Faford, M., and P. Haubrich. 1981. Vocational and social adjustment of learning disabled young adults: A follow-up study. *Learning Disability Quarterly* 4:122–30.

Geist, C. S., and C. McGrath. 1983. Psychological aspects of the adult learning disabled person in the world of work: A vocational rehabilitation perspective. *Rehabilitation Literature* 44:210–13.

Gold, P. C. 1981. The DL-LEA: A remedial approach for nonreaders with a language deficiency handicap. *Adult Literacy and Basic Education* 5:185–92.

Gottfredson, L. S., J. M. Finucci, and B. Childs. 1984. *The adult occupations of dyslexic boys: Results of a long-term follow-up and implications for research and counseling.* Baltimore, MD: The Johns Hopkins University, Center for Social Organization of Schools.

Gregg N., and C. Hoy. 1984. *Assessment and remediation of written language academic assessment and remediation of adults with learning disabilities: A resource series for adult basic education teachers.* Five County Adult Education Program. Athens, GA: Clarke Co. Board of Education. ERIC Document Reproduction Service no. ED 285–354.

Hallahan, D. P., C. E. Keller, and D. W. Ball. 1986. A comparison of prevalence rate variability from state to state for each of the categories of special education. *Remedial and Special Education* 7(2):8–14.

Hamilton, E. 1983. Language and reading comprehension: A strategy for planning programs with learning disabled adults. *Adult Literacy and Basic Education* 7:129–37.

Hammill, D. D., J. Leigh, G. McNutt, and S. Larsen. 1981. A new definition of learning disabilities. *Learning Disability Quarterly* 4:836–42.

Horn, W. F., J. R. O'Donnell, and L. A. Vitulano. 1983 Long-term follow-up studies of learning-disabled persons. *Journal of Learning Disabilities* 16:542–55.

Johnson, D. J. 1987a. Principles of assessment. In D. J. Johnson and J. W. Blalock, eds., *Adults with learning disabilities: Clinical studies,* 9–30. Orlando: Grune & Stratton.

Johnson, D. J. 1987b. Reading disabilities. In D. J. Johnson and W. J. Blalock, eds., *Adults with learning disabilities: Clinical studies* 145–62. Orlando: Grune & Stratton.

Johnson, D. J., and W. J. Blalock. 1987. *Adults with learning disabilities: Clinical studies.* Orlando: Grune & Stratton.

Johnson, D. J., and H. Myklebust. 1967. *Learning disabilities: Educational principles and practices.* NY: Grune & Stratton.

Johnston, C. L. 1984. The learning disabled adolescent and young adult: An overview and critique of current practices. *Journal of Learning Disabilities* 17:386–91.

Kavale, K. A., ed. 1988. *Learning disabilities: State of the art and practice.* Boston: College Hill Press.

Kavale, K. A., and S. R. Forness. 1985. *The science of learning disabilities.* San Diego, CA: College-Hill Press.

Kazemek, F. E. 1988. Necessary changes: Professional involvement in adult literacy programs. *Harvard Educational Review* 58:464–87.

Kirsch, I. S., and A. Jungeblut, A. 1986. *Literacy: Profiles of America's young adults.* Princeton, Educational Testing Service. ERIC Document Reproduction Service no. ED 275–701.

Knowles, M. 1980. *The modern practice of adult education.* Chicago: Follett.

Kroll, L. G. 1984. LD's—What happens when they are no longer children? *Academic Therapy* 20(2):133–48.

Lean, E. 1983. Learning disabled trainees: Finding and helping the hidden handicapped. *Training and Development Journal* 37(9):56–65.

Lenkowsky, L. K., and D. T. Saposnek. 1978. Family consequences of parental dyslexia. *Journal of Learning Disabilities* 11(1):59–65.

O'Donnell, M. P., and M. Wood. 1981. Adult learning problems: A critique of the London Procedure. *Adult Literacy and Basic Education* 5:243–49.

Peterson, B. L. 1981. One approach to teaching the specific language disabled adult language arts. *Adult Literacy and Basic Education* 5:251–55.

Rogan, L. L., and L. D. Hartman. 1976. *A follow-up study of learning disabled children as adults.* Final report. Evanston, IL: Cove School Research Office. ERIC Document Reproduction Service no. ED 163–728.

Ross, J. M. 1987. Learning disabled adults: Who are they and what do we do with them? *Lifelong learning: An omnibus of practice and research* 11(3):4–7, 11.

Ross, J. M. 1988. Learning and coping strategies used by learning disabled ABE students. *Adult Literacy and Basic Education* 12(2):78–90.

Ross, J. M., and J. Smith. 1987. *ABE and GED staff perceptions regarding learning disabled students.* A final report of the 310 Special Project 88–98–8034. University Park, PA: Penn State University, Institute for the Study of Adult Literacy.

Scales, A. M. 1980. The informal reading assessment inventory. *The Reading Instruction Journal* 24:5–7.

Scales, A. M. 1987. Alternatives to standardized tests in reading education: Cognitive styles and informal measures. *The Negro Educational Review.* XXXVIII (April–July):99–106.

Smith, S. L. 1985. Falling through the cracks: Learning disabled adults at night school. *The Pointer* 30(1):25–27.

Taylor, N., P. Wade, S. Jackson, I. Blum, I., and L. Gold. 1980. A study of low-literate adults: Personal, environmental and program considerations. *The Urban Review* 12(2):69–77.

Thistlewaite, L. 1983. Teaching reading to the ABE students who cannot read. *Lifelong Learning: The Adult Years* 7(1):5–7, 28.

Thornton, H. S., and N. Zigmond. 1987. *Predictors of dropout and unemployment among LD high school youth: The holding power of secondary vocational education for LD students.* Paper presented at the annual meeting of the American Educational Research Association, April, Washington, DC.

Travis, G. Y. 1979. An adult educator views learning disabilities. *Adult Literacy and Basic Education* 3:85–93.

Wechsler, D. 1981. *Wechsler Adult Intelligence Scale-Revised.* NY: Psychological Corporation.

White, W. J. 1985. Perspectives on the education and training of learning disabled adults. *Learning Disability Quarterly* 8:231–35.

White, W., J. Schumaker, M. Warner, G. Alley, and D. Deshler. 1980. *The current status of young adults identified as learning disabled during their school careers.* Research report no. 21. Lawrence: University of Kansas, Institute for Research in Learning Disabilities.

Woodcock, R. W., and M. B. Johnson. 1977. *Woodcock-Johnson Psycho-Educational Battery.* Bingham, MA: Teaching Resources Corp.

Ysseldyke, J. E., M. L. Thurlow, J. L. Graden, C. Wesson, S. L. Deno, and B. Algozzine, 1983. Generalizations from five years of research on assessment and decision making. *Exceptional Education Quarterly* 4:75–93.

Psychological Implications of Literacy Education for the Older Adult

Rhonda L. Harvey and Theresa Cronan

Education for the elderly population has never received a high priority. The public perception is that there is no need to provide older adults with an education, since they are beyond their productive years. Thus, education for later life has probably been the most neglected area of the educational system (Sekhon, Cox, & Rathee 1983) in the U.S. To that end, we will explore the value of a literacy education, particularly in the area of reading, as well as the psychological implications of its absence and presence in the lives of older adults. We have sectioned this chapter to present a profile of the illiterate elderly, the value of reading for the elderly, a need for the elderly to participate in literacy programs, and the need for an educational response to illiteracy as it has effected older adults.

According to Sekhon et al. (1983), in general, there has been a slight shift in basic values of society with the postindustrial era. There is a greater emphasis on quality of life. African Americans demand an improvement in the quality of their lives through the civil rights movement. Women demand improvement in the quality of their lives through the women's liberation movement. The "Gray Panthers" demand improvement in the quality of life for older adults (Sekhon et al. 1983) through various political structures. Since learning was recognized as a means of providing older adults with the capacity to deal with problems of aging (White House Conference on Aging 1981), both the value of reading and other literacy needs of older adults must be regarded in a discussion of quality of life.

Profile of the Illiterate Elderly

While the exact number of illiterate adults over sixty-five is unknown (Hunter & Harmon 1979), Jacobs and Ventura-Merkel (1986) cite United States Department of Education statistics that reveal the seriousness of illiteracy among today's elderly population. They indicate that the elderly comprise 38 percent of the total U.S. illiterate population. Even after fifty, sixty, or seventy years of coping with illiteracy, it remains a problem that cannot go away by itself (Jacobs & Ventura-Merkel 1986).

Older adulthood is often characterized by loss of employment through retirement, loss of significant others through death and relocation, loss of mobility, and loss of time-restructuring and meaning-affirming mechanisms that take away those people and routines upon which effective coping is often based. Thus, questions such as the following persist about the well-being of the older adult nonreader:

. . . how does the older adult nonreader receive and transmit information? What impact has literacy on successful aging? As the role of the older adult in society changes with respect to the use of greater amounts of leisure time, to the probability of retirement centers, and to a greater emphasis on home-based care, may increases in literacy skill result in economic, social, or other benefits? (Fisher 1987, 47)

Social isolation, loneliness, and poor self-image are examples cited by Jacobs and Ventura-Merkel (1986) of the psychological impact of illiteracy on older adults. A summary of their discussion of each concern follows.

Social Isolation. Literacy problems can affect older adults in their ability to get around. If they are unable to pass a driver's test, they have to depend on others for transportation. If these significant people move away or die, those who depend on them cannot travel. Mobility, Jacobs and Ventura-Merkel point out, is affected in other ways. The older adult may have trouble reading bus or subway maps and schedules and finding out about transportation programs that serve elderly persons.

Loneliness. People with literacy problems may feel increasingly alone as they age. They may lose, through relocation or death, those who helped them read and write. Without these people, older adults may not hear about services for the elderly or community cultural and recreational programs publicized in newspapers.

Poor Self-image. Illiteracy is bound to affect self-image, according to Jacobs and Ventura-Merkel. Some older adults may feel inadequate or inferior because of their lack of literacy skills, particularly if people judge them by their literacy skills. Other older adults may have rewarding personal relationships that help make up for this lack.

Kingston (1981) reported that there is increasing evidence of the following: (*a*) Senior citizens spend little time in reading. Comparatively few of the elderly spend more time than one hour per day reading. Few read more than the daily paper, personal correspondence, or a magazine. The elderly spend considerably more time before the television set than in reading. (*b*) Many adults who are able to read do not do so. (*c*) Those who read as senior citizens learned to read well as children, and those who read regularly tend to have a somewhat higher level of education and social status than those who rarely read. On the contrary, adults who had difficulty mastering reading skills and who failed to develop a love for it during early adulthood or middle age are not likely to suddenly develop extensive reading habits after retirement. (*d*) Some gerontologists and social workers appear to feel that senior citizens who are active in many social groups are displaying better mental and social attitudes than those who prefer solitary, sedentary activities such as reading. (*e*) Most literacy programs are highly oriented toward the achievement of fundamental reading skills and functional reading competency, and rarely move participants beyond functional literacy.

Value of Reading

In spite of the reported negatives listed by Kingston (1981), he recognized that if people abandon the belief that reading helps bridge the gap of the ages so that the thoughts of previous generations can be discovered or if people fail to recognize that through reading one interacts with the great thinkers of this generation, educators will be unable to help elderly citizens develop their full intellectual potential. Educators will not be content to develop functional alliterates; instead, they will seek to develop in people facing retirement the necessary ability and zeal for reading. Then, Kingston contends, "reading will be a genuine means of enhancing the lives of the elderly" (p. 171).

Most reading educators believe that literacy does enhance the lives of senior citizens and cite the obvious examples of the value of reading. Surviving in this complex world, stretching limited incomes through careful purchases, avoiding rip-offs by carefully perusing contracts, obtaining information about community activities through the newspaper, and forgetting personal worries through fiction are some of the examples noted (Kingston 1981).

Additional sources seem to dispute the concept that reading is necessarily associated with isolation in later years. One of the consistent themes in Wolf's (1977) findings on the worth of reading as perceived by older adults inter-viewed was that "reading does provide many elderly persons with a coping mechanism pertinent to the problems of aging" (p. 16). In discussions with the older adults, it was seen that those interested in reading participated more in social activities and wanted to be active and involved. Wolf and his elderly respondents saw reading activities as providing relaxation, "a chance to con-verse with others, a means to strengthen inner resources," and help in adjusting "to states of social change and ambiguity. Reading is a means to perpetuate an ongoing communication with life" (p. 17).

The growing population of elderly brings with it concern for maintaining and enhancing the quality of extended life spans. One aspect of quality of life is active participation in varied activities. Whereas young adults spend a sig-nificant amount of time engaged in jobs and professional endeavors, later life brings added time to plan for retirement. For many of the elderly, this presents a problem. How can they spend this time in an interesting, productive, or aes-thetically satisfying manner? Scales and Biggs (1987) asked and then answered the question as follows. Reading appears to offer a partial solution to the prob-lem of using the extra time accompanying retirement. Robinson's study of the time-use habits of more than 2,000 subjects aged eighteen to sixty-five in which reading was found to be a significant factor in the quality of life was cited by them. Other studies by Biggs, Glenn, Scales and Glenn, and Sharon that support the importance of the role played by reading in the lives of elderly adults were also cited.

Gentile, Haase, and Robinson (1985) pointed out that learning to read or enhancing one's reading ability is an activity that can add zest to life.

> Integrating the content of education with social aspects of living increases the benefits to the aged, for is not the sine qua non of successful living to be wanted and useful, and is not the goal of education to understand how to use all of oneself? (P. 111)

Unfortunately, these writers note that the advancement of reading and thinking processes are seldom seen as weapons against senility or some of the other infirmities that plague many people during retirement.

Frenkel-Brunswick (1968) indicated that numerous anatomical processes, such as knowledge and experience, are influenced by one's inner life and also that these processes actually impede biological decline. If this is true, Gentile et al. (1985) claim reading and writing pursuits deserve high priority among the aged. "Their emotional, psychic, spiritual, and corporeal energy may be rekindled through the avenues of literary enterprise, thereby opening the possibility of a significant future" (p. 115).

Educational Need versus Participation

Many researchers have noted the high level of illiteracy among older adults, in contrast to their low level of participation in literacy classes. Kasworm (1982) points out that in adult basic education and other literacy efforts, adults aged sixty-five and older represent the highest level of the undereducated when years of educational attainment are considered, as well as the highest level of functional illiteracy of any age cohort (Kasworm, 1982).

Fisher (1987) investigated the low level of participation in adult basic education programs/classes, attended by large numbers of older adults with minimal education. He invited consideration of the impact that illiteracy has on older adults. Little evidence exists, according to Fisher, to assess the severity of the problem or to measure the impact of low-level literacy on the well-being of older adults. This paucity of research findings, he contended, demands a careful investigation of the degree to which the presence or absence of literacy skills may be related to successful aging and to the ability of an older adult to adapt.

In examining the implications for practitioners regarding the discrepancy between the apparent need for literacy services by a large proportion of the older adult population and the lack of response of those who possess this need, Fisher (1987) further invited consideration of the following: (a) perceptions of needs of older adults by professionals working with them may be different from actual needs of the older adult population; (b) needed educational programs may be inappropriately planned or delivered; and (c) present living conditions of older adults may not be supportive of, or conducive to, literacy or educational efforts. In addressing the question of whether or not the literacy level among older adults is a problem, Fisher concluded:

> solutions to the problem of increasing participation by older adults in literacy training will become more apparent when a more precise understanding has been developed of the literacy needs of older adults and of the impact of the presence of literacy skills on their aging. (P. 48)

Need for Educational Response

Kasworm and Courtenay (1982) addressed a significant concern—that the adult learning community has had minimal involvement, much less a proactive stance regarding literacy outreach to the older learner population. Their statistics reveal that approximately one-third of adults age fifty-five and above are functionally illiterate, while only 5 percent of current adult basic education activities are serving this group. According to Gutknecht (1986), gerontological research and practice which deals with not only the physical, but psychological and sociological aspects as well, is only now beginning to develop and have an effect on educational practices employed with the aged. (P. 3)

In examining literacy studies, Courtenay, Stevenson, and Suhart (1982) found that the literacy needs of the elderly have largely been ignored by educators. Their review and analysis of the literature on functional literacy and the elderly also found that there is no adequate definition nor measure of functional literacy for the older adult. Their findings suggest that the elderly are less advantaged than younger people in meeting literacy demands for this society and that little attention has been given to older age groups in terms of measurement criterion and treatment of data. They contend that educators of older adults need to focus attention on revising literacy education to improve the abilities of older adults. In spite of incomplete measurement at present, current research indicates that older adults have the greatest need for literacy learning opportunities. "To wait for improved measures and/or future generations of older adults who are expected to be 'literate' is an injustice to the existing generation of older persons" (p. 350).

According to Fisher (1986), the main problem confronting researchers in considering the role of literacy among older adults is the irrelevance of the tools that are available.

The use of grade level or grade level equivalency to describe the level of literacy of an older adult relies on a measure designed for another purpose applied to the person approximately one-half century earlier. (P. 95)

Rigg and Kazemek (1983) also noted the paucity of research-based information about the literacy of the aged. They contend that educators, researchers, and authors develop reading programs and suggest teaching techniques and materials based on little more than assumptions that are all too often based upon stereotypical notions of what the "typical" elderly reader needs and wants. Thus, literacy programs for the elderly are developed by those who think they know what is best for the elderly. They conclude that educators must look at what elders themselves want to do with reading and writing.

The positive impact of existing adult basic education programs on participants was reported by Kasworm (1982). Senior learners (aged sixty-five and above) interviewed in her survey reported personal value reasons for entering an adult basic education (ABE) program. The socializing aspects of the classroom, the program as an outlet for expression, and the program for its "inwardly directed reasons," such as "a source for self-renewal, for gaining a new lease on life" (p. 203) were personal value reasons cited. The impact of instruction as reported by the seniors was summarized by Kasworm as a generalized renewed interest in life, an improved self-worth and increased independence, and a stronger sense of life control and stability. The program was seen by many to renew interest in self, life, and learning.

Snider and Houser (cited by Gutknecht 1986) noted that while much research and development funding from various sources is directed toward solving problems of the aged, little support is available that focuses on the positive aspects of aging.

Gutknecht (1986) cited education as one of the more positive aspects of aging:

> Education for older persons is based on the premise that adults of all ages need knowledge and/or skills because: 1. Education relates to self-fulfillment, 2. It is necessary to learn to cope with changes in later life, 3. There is a vocational advantage to education, and 4. Through education the aged will be allowed to continue their contribution to society. (P. 4)

The growing elderly population creates concerns for maintaining and enhancing quality of extended life spans. Whereas young adults spend significant amounts of time in career endeavors, later life brings retirement. This additional time presents the problem of how to spend it in an interesting, productive, satisfying manner. Reading appears to offer at least a partial solution to the problem of using the extra time (Scales & Biggs 1987). Wolf (1977) cited strong evidence of the importance of reading for the older person seeking entertainment, knowledge, satisfaction of intellectual curiosity, cultural development, and companionship.

Gentile et al. (1985) noted that much of the knowledge on reading habits, interests, and problems of the elderly is based on data gathered primarily from surveys of the general population and on studies detailing the use of library services, especially among older persons living in retirement centers and health care facilities. They contend that instead of providing a comprehensive view of the older reader, much of this research is fragmentary and contradictory in nature.

Gentile et al. (1985) recognized that, until recently, aged adults have been on the periphery of the educational system with minimal concern shown for their educational development. With the shift in the age of the population and with recognition of the contributions of the aged to society, a change in attitude has begun.

What is needed, according to Gentile et al. (1985), is a model of the aged reader that is descriptive, positive, interactive, and representative—a model that comes from studies without preconceptions of the aged reader in industrial and postindustrial societies. This model will also come from living and working with people who are aging and from studying them and younger people, for the young, too, are aging. Also needed are appropriate reading materials, the exploration of teaching strategies for the elderly, and the identification of educational needs and interests of the elderly so that reading programs offered are relevant and attended.

Kasworm and Medina (1989) synthesized the literature on literacy in the senior adult years. They note that literacy in the senior adult years has historically been defined by concepts created for youth and young adult literacy research and programs. They explore alternative perspectives of literacy in the senior adult years and conclude that literacy, in terms of a certain level of reading, writing, and computation, may not reflect the true reality of older adult connectedness with their worlds and their needs. They conclude that the need for a specified level of literacy is more self-denied with increasing age than within the broad societal driven notions of literacy for younger adults.

What then are the psychological implications of literacy among the elderly? It appears that reading may offer an opportunity for social interaction, increased participation in community and cultural events, enhanced self-esteem, intellectual stimulation, entertainment, and enjoyment of increased leisure time. Reading may offer a partial solution to extending quality of life in the later years.

However, educators will have to seriously consider reading needs and interests of the elderly and not automatically base program offerings and opportunities on back-to-basics programs designed for youth or on stereotypical notions of what is best for the elderly. Rigg and Kazemek (1983) caution that educators cannot assume elders are "old children" who need "back-to-basics" instruction, nor that older adults share the same needs and interests as a college-educated public. Instead the research, such as that conducted by Scales (1989), must look specifically at the elders themselves and investigate their perceptions of reading and writing.

The potential of reading to enhance quality of life seems to be present for the elderly. To impose upon the elderly programs based upon distorted, stereotypical notions of them held by much of society will not enhance quality of life.

References

Courtenay, B. C., R. T. Stevenson, and M. P. Suhart. 1982. Functional literacy among the elderly: Where we are(nt). *Educational Gerontology* 8:339–52.

Fisher, J. C. 1986. Literacy usage among older adults. In K. Landers, ed., *Proceedings for the Annual Adult Educational Research Conference* 94–99. Syracuse, NY. ERIC Document Reproduction Service no. ED 269–571.

Fisher, J. C. 1987. The literacy level among older adults: Is it a problem? *Adult Literacy and Basic Education* 11(1):41–50.

Frenkel-Brunswick, E. 1968. Adjustment and reorientations in the course of the life span. In B. Neugarten, ed., *Middle age and aging.* Chicago: University of Chicago.

Gentile, L. M., A. M. B. Haase, and R. D. Robinson. 1985. The older adult as reader. In D. B. Lumsden, ed., *The older adult as learner* 99–117. NY: Hemisphere Publishing Corporation.

Gutknecht, B. 1986. *Developing successful learning experiences for older adults.* Paper presented at the Conference of the Association of Teacher Educators, February, Atlanta, GA. ERIC Document Reproduction Service no. ED 268–293.

Hunter, C. S. J., and D. Harmon. 1979. *Adult illiteracy in the United States: A report to the Ford Foundation.* NY: McGraw-Hill.

Jacobs, B., and C. Ventura-Merkel. 1986. *Tutoring older adults in literacy programs.* Washington, DC: National Council on the Aging, Inc. ERIC Document Reproduction Service no. ED 286–001.

Kasworm, C. E. 1982. Older learners in adult basic education. *Adult Literacy and Basic Education* 6(4):195–207.

Kasworm, C. E., and B. C. Courtenay. 1982. *Functional literacy in older adults: Proactive approaches to research and teaching.* Paper presented at the National Adult Education Conference, November, San Antonio, TX. ERIC Document Reproduction Service no. ED 229–559.

Kasworm, C. E., and R. A. Medina. 1988. Perspectives of literacy in the senior adult years. *Educational Gerontology* 15:65–79.

Kingston, A. J. 1981. Does literacy really enhance the lives of the elderly? *Reading World* 20:169–72.

Rigg, P., and F. Kazemek. 1983. Literacy and elders: What we know and what we need to know. *Educational Gerontology* 9:417–24.

Scales, A. M. 1989. Reading perceptions of the elderly adult. *Reading Improvement* 26:225–30.

Scales, A. M., and S. A. Biggs. 1987. Reading habits of elderly adults: Implications for instruction. *Educational Gerontology* 13:521–32.

Sekhon, G. A., H. G. Cox, and R. S. Rathee. 1983. Education and the elderly in America. *Indiana Academy of Social Science Proceedings* 18:158–166.

White House Conference on Aging. 1981. *Report of mini-conferencing on life-long learning for self-sufficiency,* October. Government Document Y 3:W 58/4: 10 L 47.

Wolf, R. E. 1977. What is reading good for? Perspectives from senior citizens. *Journal of Reading* 21(1):15–17.

The Adult Non-English
Speaker and Literacy

Mary Newton Bruder

The information presented in this chapter represents nearly twenty years of teaching experience in foreign languages, English as a foreign language (EFL), English as a second language (ESL), and literacy education, both for native speakers of English and non-English speakers. It has a very practical orientation and is meant to offer advice and encouragement to the nonspecialist attempting to instruct non-English speakers in learning to read and function in English.

In this chapter, definitions of the terms *EFL, ESL,* and *literacy* will be presented. Additionally, similarities and differences in teaching adults who are native English speakers and who are nonnative English speakers as well as the range of differences to be found in nonnative speakers will be examined. Finally, I will discuss how culture conflicts can confound normal progress in learning a foreign language. I will finish the chapter with a short discussion of instructional considerations for the teacher/tutor of adult nonnative speakers.

Definitions

EFL and ESL are often used interchangeably. However, there is a distinction not commonly made that I think is crucial in working with adult non-English speakers. For example, an EFL speaker learns English for travel or study in an English-speaking country, even if such travel or study is going to take place over an extended period of time. Ultimately, the EFL speaker's ties to a native language and country will take precedence and she/he will return to her/his native land.

The ESL speaker, on the other hand, learns the language in order to partake fully of the goods and services available in a new society. In addition to learning the language, the ESL speaker must learn a broad range of language skills so that she/he can pay or avoid paying taxes, deal with the various chores of having a job, raise and educate a family, pay bills, use the telephone, etc. That speaker usually remains in the new society because she/he is an immigrant or a refugee. (An examination of the immigrant/refugee status can reveal an enormous psychological difference that literally "not being able to go home again" can make.) My focus in this chapter is the ESL speaker.

The next term is literacy. For the ESL adult, the operative distinction is literacy versus illiteracy. I define illiteracy as the state of not being able to read or write in one's native language, and literacy as the possession of that ability.

Similarities and Differences in Teaching

Similarities. The similarities of speakers revolve around their all being adults in what is essentially a situation reserved for children, that is, learning to speak or learning to read in classrooms. Many adults find the classroom situation stressful. Techniques used to reduce stress in general adult education situations may be used equally with native English and ESL speakers as long as cultural conflicts do not interfere. Other similarities include such experiences as taking care of families, going to work, and/or attending adult literacy classes. In classes, both the native English and nonnative speakers need to have their life experiences acknowledged.

As much as possible, class lessons should focus on the students' experiences plus everyday survival skills. These adults, both native English and ESL speakers, are no different from all others in their need to succeed and see ongoing progress.

Differences. Native English speakers in the U.S. who have failed to learn to read in school have a history usually marked by shame and fear of discovery, as well as a dislike for the school setting that failed them. Usually this is not the case for ESL speakers. They do not dislike school. In fact, most have a high respect for education and school settings.

Usually, native English speakers who are unable to read have very good oral language skills. In fact often their skills are so good that it comes as a great shock to discover that they cannot read. The reverse generalization should not be made for non-English speakers. Even though many cannot express themselves fluently in oral language, it does not mean that they cannot read in English. Many Chinese and Japanese speakers who have learned to read and write English well may speak little English. Speakers from the Arab countries may not be able to read English but may be quite fluent orally. A caution—do not make assumptions about the reading ability of speakers on the basis of their oral speech.

To summarize, the differences between a native English-speaking illiterate adult and a non-English-speaking adult who cannot read English are potentially much more important than the similarities and must be considered carefully in devising an instructional program.

Range of Differences among Adult ESL Speakers

Many parts of the world now have access to U.S. television (TV) programs, which may not be a plus in exporting U.S. values but can provide help in listening to English speakers—unless, of course, the native language is dubbed for the English. Some non-English speakers do listen to U.S. TV. In general though, speakers from Europe and Africa are stronger in listening to and speaking English than are speakers from the Asian countries. Traditionally, speakers in these parts of the world have had more access to speakers of English than those of Asia. ESL speakers from the Asian countries are generally much better at reading, memorizing vocabulary, and learning grammar rules than their Western colleagues. Partly, this is because reading, memorizing, and learning rules are emphasized in their study of English, and also, because that is the general mode of learning used in these cultures.

Another factor to be considered is the student's knowledge of the grammar of their native language. When students need to learn from a grammar-based curriculum, knowledge of the grammar of the native language makes learning easier (Bruder 1979). I once had an Algerian student who knew French as well as his native Berber language, but he was having a great deal of trouble with the grammar of English. When I pointed out to him that the point in question paralleled the same point in French, he had no more trouble. Another student from Venezuela was having trouble with the passive voice in English, which has exactly the same formation in Spanish. When the teacher pointed this out to him, the student looked even more puzzled and declared, "There is no such thing in Spanish!" Aside from the obvious point that the instructional methods should be based upon what the student brings to class, a knowledge of the grammar of one's language usually makes the formal learning of grammar easier.

Culture Shock. Oberg (1960) described culture shock as the anxiety resulting from losing the familiar signs and symbols of social intercourse. People in new cultures often learn that their familiar ways of judging what is right and wrong may not be accurate.

Cultural Conflict

There are fairly predictable stages of cultural shock that vary in time and in duration from individual to individual. Individuals who escape culture shock are usually quite young or are tourists who are in the new culture for a limited time. Some variables related to the severity of culture shock that I have observed over the years are as follows.

1. *Language Proficiency.* Generally, the higher the language proficiency upon arrival, the more severe is the culture shock. I think this has to do with expectations. When one is fluent in a foreign language, she/he expects to be able to get along fairly well. Negative situations for the fluent speaker can lead to self-doubt, anxiety, and culture shock. On the other hand, when one does not speak the language well, there are fewer expectations of being able to function well.

2. *Role Reversal.* When a person undergoes a dramatic role change in a new culture, the severity of culture shock is likely to be high. Consider a professional man in a male dominant society who enters a beginning language class in the new culture taught by young women. For him, learning the new language taught by women indicates a childlike dependency; it can cause a great deal of emotional stress.

3. *Location.* If the surroundings and climate in the new culture are very different from one's home, the change can be stressful. For example, once my program had a group of Algerian students arrive in Pittsburgh in January. It was cold, and they were wearing lightweight clothes. The first thing we did was shop for clothes. They insisted on having long underwear. They knew it would snow, so they automatically assumed it would be terribly cold as well. Another group of students from Venezuela were from very rural areas of their country and had a very difficult time adjusting to Pittsburgh's urban life.

4. *Cultural Constraints.* Societies generally seem to be organized to regulate individual behavior on the basis of shame (external control) or guilt (internal control). In the U.S. most people do what is right

because they feel guilty if they do not. It took many hours of training by parents to achieve this internal control, and it works quite well most of the time. Some other cultures use the presence of other people's attention to externally control their behavior. People who come from cultures that exercise external control often have difficulty learning to function in a culture that uses primarily internal controls.

The adjustment to another culture comprises three fairly clear-cut stages. First, on arrival in the new culture (if one has entered the culture willingly) everything is wonderful: life is an adventure, the people are nice, the food is delicious, etc. Then comes a phase when everything is awful in the host society. During this phase, the visitor can reject the host culture and glorify the one she/he left behind.

The second stage might include such physical symptoms as an upset stomach, the inability to sleep or sleeping much more than necessary, the desire to be alone, fear, and/or general symptoms of depression. It is at this point that the visitor needs help. Conversations with a fellow countryman who has recovered from this stage is recommended. Together they could speak in their native language for an extended period of time. Basically, the visitor needs to know that her/his malady has a name and that it will go away if she/he will give it enough time.

The third stage is one of realistic adjustment to the new culture. As the language proficiency improves, the positives and negatives in the new culture will be placed in a proper perspective. Ultimately, good choices for one's life will be made.

Problems in Cross-Cultural Communications. Since an in-depth treatment of this topic has been documented in a large body of existing literature, here I will present several anecdotes that will illustrate the range of misunderstandings that can arise when two cultures meet.

1. *Words That Do Not Fit the Action.* Native speakers have knowledge of the subtle nuances of their language that elude even fluent nonnative speakers. For example, U.S. speakers know that "let's get together" does not imply an engagement or an invitation; but the words themselves and others like them (Why don't we do lunch?) confuse people who do not know that an invitation must be accompanied by a specific time and date. Many visitors who had thought of Americans in the U.S. as friendly and open come to the conclusion after a few such instances as the previously mentioned that they are "insincere" and "do not say what they mean." One visitor complained: "Ask an American how he is and you get a weather report!" I was perplexed by the remark until I realized how often Americans in the U.S. open casual conversations with concerns about the weather.

ESL learners need to know such uses of language that are used for establishing conversational parameters but are largely empty of actual meaning. When someone is asked how are you feeling, a list of illnesses is not expected. This is not insincerity, but the way the conventions of American English operate. I deliberately said American English to distinguish it from the British variety. British English does not follow the same conventions and may add to the difficulties of ESL learners who have prior exposure to British English.

2. *Incomplete Information Can Be Harmful.* A visitor on an exchange program from Eastern Europe presented me, her hostess, with towels she had brought from home and a box of imported laundry detergent. I was puzzled at the inclusion of these items in strictly limited baggage weight, so I asked my guest about it. "We were told before we left that Americans do not share these items," she explained. Luckily, I was able to help her to understand that some Americans in the U.S. do not use the same towel as another person, even among family members. For the laundry detergent I found out that she would consider it begging to ask for soap to launder her clothes.

3. *Familiar Landmarks May Have Different Meanings.* The most common phenomenon is in the area of gestures. What we consider as "waving goodbye" using our fingers (especially to children) is a "come hither" gesture in Spanish-speaking Latin America. Smiling can mean happiness, but it can also indicate embarrassment in Asian cultures. Silence in response to a question does not mean ignorance of the answer in Asian cultures. In these cultures, it is not considered good to bring attention to oneself. Also, for people brought up in these cultures, it is very difficult for them to ask questions. It is a loss of face to admit not knowing something, and to ask a question after an explanation would be an indication that the explanation was faulty in some way. The question, "Do you have any questions?" will always be answered in the negative; the question, "Do you understand?" will always be answered in the affirmative, no matter what the actual knowledge.

4. *Personal Questions.* Questions defined as personal, that is, not casually discussed among acquaintances, vary from culture to culture. One does not, for example, ask after the health of an Arab man's wife, but one must know the salary of a Japanese person in order to know which forms of address to use. Working with ESL adults requires tact, sensitivity, and attention to their reactions in many situations.

In summary, it is not possible to avoid all cross-cultural misunderstandings any more than it is possible to avoid misunderstandings with other native speakers of English. The best thing to do is to establish a strong feeling of trust in which questions can be asked and answered as openly as possible in pursuit of knowledge and human understanding.

Matching Teacher or Tutor with Learner. Many cultures have strict restrictions about men and women working together; men of some cultures have difficulties

Instructional
Considerations

learning from women. Therefore, I would recommend that the teacher or tutor and learner be of the same gender if possible. For similar reasons, the tutor should be approximately the same age or older than the learner. It is helpful if the tutor has an interest in, or some knowledge about, the learner's native land and if they have some common interests as well. It gives the pair something to discuss apart from the lesson at hand. Additional lessons can be built on their commonalities.

Materials. Probably the most important skills for the newly arrived ESL adult learner are listening and reading. They must be able to understand directions and explanations from native speakers, and they must be able to read labels and directions, job applications, bus schedules, bank forms, want ads, etc. The materials, therefore, should include the items that they need to read.

Many believe that exposure to TV and radio will increase listening ability very quickly. Unfortunately, sustained listening when one does not understand at all is very difficult and frustrating. The result is that adults who do not understand the language simply do not listen to the radio or watch TV very much.

With the help of a teacher, the adult ESL learner can learn to use TV and radio as a tool for learning. Soap operas are very good programs for learning English. They go slowly along the story line; the characters are easily identified as to character types; the same words and phrases are repeated again and again; the emotions are easily identified. The teacher should pick a soap opera to use for instruction. The first few lessons could be spent on character, role identification, and understanding of the story line. Names should be written for easy reference. A bilingual dictionary could be used to help understand unknown words. As the soap opera becomes easier for the student to understand, the teacher should point out such things as cultural clues, gestures, and sarcasm.

The radio can be used in a similar manner, but there needs to be even more structure because there is no accompanying picture. Discerning individual voices in a foreign language is not easy. If the ESL adult has a particular interest or need to listen for the weather or traffic reports, one station should be chosen. The adult should listen for structure of such reports. Sometimes there is a headline statement, followed by an advertisement before the actual report. ESL adults need to be able to anticipate how to listen to the radio.

Whenever an ESL adult cannot recode in English, teachers should choose a text with a systematic presentation of the letters and their sounds (see, e.g., Bruder & Williams 1986). Notice that uppercase and lowercase letters sometimes look very different (R/r G/g Q/q) and that cursive letters look different from manuscript ones. An adult at this stage should be taught only one form, probably manuscript is the easiest.

As the adult's reading ability progresses, a daily newspaper can be used to create lessons centered on her/his interests and needs. Perhaps there are English classics that the adult has read in translation. With the teacher's help, the adult might be able to read the originals, especially if there is an accompanying videotape available.

Teaching Strategies. Following are a few general strategies for tutors or teachers to use as they teach ESL adults.

1. Specify a teaching point for each lesson and state the reason why it should be taught. For example: Write the words for the numbers from twenty to forty (twenty, twenty-one, etc.) The reason is so that the ESL adult can write checks to pay bills. If the tutor cannot instantly identify *why* a skill is being taught, it probably is not worth teaching.

2. Teach only one new thing at a time. When teaching about a new situation or concept, use language the student already knows. New language material should be put in a familiar context. If there is more than one new thing, it will be difficult to pinpoint an error when one occurs.

3. In communicating with the ESL student, use formal standard English with full verb forms, for example, going not goin', being not bein'. Ask questions using the question words *"Do you want a drink? Is he coming with us?"* rather than by the rising voice intonation *"Want a drink? He coming with us?"* This standard spoken style is the nearest to written English and will be the easiest for her/him to understand. For the same reason, use Latin-based vocabulary rather than Anglo-Saxon. *Examination* is a much longer word than *test,* but it is more transparent to speakers of Indo-European languages and people who have studied formal grammar.

4. The teacher or tutor might learn some greetings and common commands in the ESL adult's native language. Greeting the ESL adult in his/her language could provide a more comfortable class setting.

5. The teacher should simplify the syntax of his/her speech. Use simple subject + verb + object sentences without relative clauses. Teachers should learn to listen to themselves. Notice if a puzzled look appears on the ESL student's face. If so, the sentences should be examined for complexity. I am not suggesting that these adults be spoken to as if they were children; I am suggesting ways to make English as a second language more accessible to them.

6. Whenever a grammar-based method is used to teach ESL adults, the teacher or tutor should have a good foundation in English grammar and a good ESL reference grammar text (see Crowell 1964; Quirk & Greenbaum 1973; Warriner & Griffith 1977). If the teacher, or tutor, has to say "I do not know" in response to grammar questions, the learner will become discouraged.

7. One's rate of speaking should not be slowed down. Slowed speech introduces distortions that make it difficult to be understood. Instead, pausing between sentences will give listeners time to process what was said. Whenever sentences are repeated, they must be in exactly the same words as the first message. If paraphrasing occurs, the listener is likely to be presented with two varying messages, neither of which she/he understands.

8. Teachers and tutors should relax and have a good time getting to know the emerging personality of the ESL adult learner for whom they are doing a wonderful deed.

References

Bruder, M. N. 1979. *The Relationship of metalinguistic skills to proficiency in foreign language learning.* Unpublished Doctoral Dissertation, University of Pittsburgh, PA.

Bruder, M. N., and E. Williams. 1986. *Cracking the code: Learning to read and write in English.* Pittsburgh, PA: University of Pittsburgh Press.

Crowell, T. L., Jr. 1964. *Index to modern English.* NY: McGraw-Hill.

Oberg, K. 1960. Cultural shock: Adjustment to new cultural environments. *Practical Anthropology* 7(4):177–82.

Quirk, R., and S. Greenbaum. 1973. *A concise grammar of contemporary English.* NY: Harcourt Brace Jovanovich, Inc.

Warriner, J. E., and F. Griffith. 1977. *Warriner's English grammar and composition: Complete course.* Orlando: Harcourt Brace Jovanovich, Inc.

Sociological Perspectives

Sociological perspectives for adult literacy education can be examined through conditions that include change in life-styles, development of self-esteem, relationships with other people, forms of communication, and remedies for illiteracy. Such conditions may be viewed as problems that affect the social lives of many people.

In this section of the volume, adult literacy programs that have been used to affect the lives of people are described. Authors have estimated dimensions of the illiteracy problem, discussed conditions that seem amenable to remedies, and presented solutions that have been successful. The common thread running through these programs is the desired goal of positive change by low-literate adults. Park opens this section by discussing and offering solutions to illiteracy in the workplace. Next, Anderson discusses literacy education in the military. A technology-based program developed for the military and used with civilians is described by Branson. Revilla and Sotillo's chapter follows with a discussion of bilingual education for adults. Attention is given to an urban college's community-based programs for urban dwellers by Hall. Another college's program that is designed primarily for women is presented by Burley. Kofmehl describes a Christian literacy program that has been used internationally for a number of years. Finally, literacy education programs for the homeless are described by Scales, and a literacy education program for the miseducated is described by Hoover, Mc-Phail, and Ginyard.

Workplace Literacy
Rosemarie J. Park

> There is no way in which the United States can remain competitive in a global economy, maintain its standard of living, and shoulder the burden of the retirement of the baby boom generation unless we mount a forceful national effort to help adults upgrade their basic skills in the very near future. (Chisman 1989, iii)

Adult literacy has become a major issue with implications for educational, social, and economic policy. There are many who view the decrease in U.S. economic importance and the increase in the influence of the Japanese as a direct result of educational inadequacy on the part of the U.S. workforce. The failure of many individuals to leave the welfare system and become productive members of the workforce is also blamed on educational inadequacy. Such concern has fueled an already well-developed educational reform movement and focused national and international attention on the area of workplace literacy.

In this chapter I will define workplace literacy and examine the research on literacy as it impacts job productivity and job safety. Next, I will discuss solutions that are available to employees as they seek to avoid or remedy their literacy problems in the workforce.

Definitions

Definitions of workplace literacy must encompass those elements of workplace reading and writing that are unique to the technical or occupational situation. Current research in reading and writing point to the fact that both reading and writing are context dependent. A view that reading was a generic skill that once learned could be transferred to any context is no longer accepted. Thus, reading in the workplace involves knowledge of the specific content of an occupation and utilizes a different set of processes than typical classroom reading. Students in high school are predominantly concerned with reading-to-learn activities. Reading for leisure or vocational reading does not necessarily involve learning. Reading on the job is primarily reading-to-do (Sticht 1976; Mikulecky 1982). In order to read the electrician's manual, for example, the vocational student would need to know the basic concepts and allied vocabulary on which the field of electronics depends. If that student had come to the U.S. from an agricultural village in the Cambodian mountains and had never been exposed to electricity, then he/she would have a great deal of difficulty grasping enough of the content to understand even the first part of the manual. The student would experience difficulty even if his/her decoding skills and English were advanced. Reading depends on a shared base of knowledge between writer and reader. Without this shared informational base, the reader cannot hope to fully "read and understand" a text (Smith 1982).

Thus, workplace literacy involves more than acquiring a general set of reading skills equivalent to any particular reading grade level as measured by standardized reading tests. Such reading levels may be necessary prerequisites for acquiring a specific knowledge base, but these levels do not, of themselves, imply proficiency in any given vocational area. Analyzing workplace literacy almost always involves some type of task analysis to determine what types of reading are necessary to a given job in the workplace, the frequency and importance of the specific reading to the job, and the strategy needed to apply reading to the work situation.

Workplace literacy is not, then, simple literacy instruction provided for employees in the hope of increasing overall literacy and, hence, job productivity. Workplace literacy must be related to the specific demands of each workplace.

Two most recent reviews of workplace literacy by Sticht (1988) and Collino, Aderman, and Askov (1988) failed to find any research that draws a direct connection between literacy levels and measured improvement in productivity of individual workers. Relationships between workers' ratings on their jobs and reading skill are cited as evidence of a link between reading ability and productivity. Sticht (1988) draws attention to the work of industrial psychologists and human factors in connecting communications and cognitive skill requirements for job training and job performance. He points out that industrial psychologists have conducted extensive research on vocational aptitude batteries such as the General Aptitude Test Battery (GATB), which depend greatly on, and correlate highly with, literacy skill. Sticht notes with reference to Carroll that at the more advanced levels, literacy tests of the National Assessment of Educational Progress appear to resemble the more traditional verbal intelligence or verbal aptitude measures (Sticht 1988).

Job Productivity

Further review of the literature on basic skills and job performance (Collino et al. 1988) reports somewhat contradictory findings of two research studies that attempt to link reading and job performance. For example, workers in a dairy did not perform any differently regardless of reading skill level. Findings from another study reported that workers who read more than two years below the measured readability of reading material on their job performed significantly less well than their peers.

Is this lack of research evidence surprising? Probably not. The demonstration of a link between reading level and job productivity depends on the acceptance of a very simple set of assumptions. The first of these is that reading is a single skill or trait that can be measured irrespective of functional context. Reading achievement tests depend to an extent on this assumption, and because the tests rely heavily on school curriculum for content, they are successful in discriminating between children's reading performances in school. Evidence suggests reading comprehension beyond basic decoding skill depends on a number of cognitive factors as skill levels increase. Advance measures of reading comprehension are, as Sticht suggests, linked to measures of *verbal intelligence*. Thus, reading is not a unitary skill. It is very difficult to separate out from a variety of factors which ones also influence worker productivity.

The interrelationship between reading achievement, job knowledge and experience, and some measures of verbal intelligence also make it difficult to determine which elements determine successful job performance.

Job productivity, although seemingly attractive as a measurable outcome, is likewise determined by a variety of factors. The assumption that worker productivity is determined by individual factors that can be identified and measured by researchers with relative ease may not apply to all situations. For example, those products that depend on factors that are less tangible or measurable would have to be excluded. The number of pounds of cheese dairy workers produce might depend on such unpredictable factors as the weather, changes in feed supplies, federal price-support changes, and even changes in the production process itself. Jobs that depend on creativity or inspiration for a successful outcome would be impossible to measure as a function of reading ability.

A final assumption is that since nearly all jobs utilize reading to some extent, then workers must use reading on the job in similar ways. Different jobs certainly utilize written materials differently and depend more or less on them for successful performance. Changes in processes, modernization, and introduction of computerized machinery may temporarily increase workers' reliance on written material. Some jobs require very little reading, such as the production of fast foods using premeasured ingredients. Other clerical jobs depend almost entirely on reading and writing skills.

Researchers who hope to be successful in this type of research must begin by identifying the reading skills they believe are relevant, the job type the skills apply to, and the elements of productivity the skills theoretically impact.

Job Safety

One major rationale for increasing the reading skills of the workforce has been to decrease accidents and errors made on the job. Nearly all of the evidence cited for the relationship between increased reading and decreased errors on the job is anecdotal. For example, Chisman (1989) in the latest report on adult literacy in the U.S. quotes what he hopes is an apocryphal story of a secret visit by managers of a nuclear power plant. The manager had discovered that some of their maintenance crews could not read warning signals that might indicate the reactor was overheating. It should be pointed out here that no research evidence exists to back up what is a commonsense assumption that literate workers make fewer errors on the job, whether safety related or otherwise.

Available Solutions

Many employers are aware of the problems that marginally literate employees pose to the production process, to their own safety, and to the safety of others. Identifying illiterate employees brings employers face-to-face with a myriad of legal questions that surround the use of literacy tests to hire or screen workers whose literacy skills could put them or their fellow workers at risk. This section will explore the use of literacy tests in the workplace and discuss the possible implications of having a workforce unable to read crucial safety and warning information.

Most employers, if given an option, might prefer simply not to hire employees whose reading skills are too low to properly perform on the job. However, such a solution is not as simple as it seems. There are a number of questions that need answering before any action can be taken. First, what is the appropriate reading level required on any job? How can employers determine the minimum necessary reading requirement for a given occupation? Many employers have resorted to the use of readability formulas as an indication of the relative difficulty of job-related material.

Establishing Minimum Reading Requirements for Jobs. Readability analyses of job-related reading materials are often used as an indicator of the minimum reading levels needed in order to perform jobs successfully. Although these formulas are important in providing some indication of the relative difficulty of job-related reading, they are not always fully understood in terms of strengths or limitations.

There is little documented research as to what the minimum reading requirements for jobs are. Among the few available studies are those by Sticht (1976); Moe, Rush, and Storlie (1980); and Diehl and Mikulecky (1980), who have studied the reading requirements in a number of occupations. In this research, readability formulas have typically been used to assess the reading difficulty of work-related reading material. However, research shows the readability levels of such material are not necessarily the reading levels needed to complete job training successfully.

Readability formulas are methods of obtaining the approximate difficulty of reading materials by measuring certain variables. Most formulas use the average sentence length combined with a measure of either word length or word familiarity in randomly selected 100 word segments. The figure for an average sentence length and word length, as measured by the number of syllables or the number of unfamiliar words, is fed into a mathematical regression formula. The resulting number is then translated into an approximate grade at which a student could understand the reading with 75 percent accuracy on a comprehension test.

The weaknesses of readability formulas have been documented in an excellent article by Duffy (1987). Formulas, generally, work less well on technical materials. Partially, this is because they cannot be used on text containing few words and incomplete sentences, such as text frequently used on computers. Much workplace reading and writing, especially involving forms and notices, fits into this category. Secondly, formulas do not take into account the background knowledge the experienced worker brings to the written material. Readability formulas tend to overestimate the difficulty of technical material. Research has shown that workers on the job can perform adequately with reading levels of one to two years below the estimated readability level of the reading material used on the job (Diehl & Mikulecky 1980).

Consequently, the reading difficulty of texts as measured by formulas cannot be used in conjunction with an assessment of worker reading ability to identify who can and cannot enter a training program or do certain jobs. Such practices lead to screening out workers who might well be successful based on previous work experience. The practices also tend to limit the upward mobility of persons covered by affirmative action suits (Park, Storlie, Rengel, & Dawis 1985).

In order to establish an approximate difficulty level for reading in any job, an employer needs to survey the reading materials and have employees rate them as to the relative importance to the job and the frequency of use. Readability formulas may be used to set an approximate reading level, allowing for at least a two-year margin.

Establishing the Reading Ability of Potential Employees. Once an approximate reading level has been identified, then a suitable method for assessing a potential employee's reading ability relative to that level must be found. Standardized adult reading tests provide one such method, but they are not without problems. If a standardized reading test is selected to measure the reading level of employees or potential employees, it must be validated. Not all reading tests are suitable or even legal. The process for test validation poses several problems if the requirements of the law and the Uniform Guidelines on Employee Selection Procedures (*Federal Register* 1979) are to be followed.

The uniform guidelines require that tests used in employee selection relate directly to the tasks performed on the job and that their application not discriminate against women and other underrepresented groups. As yet, there has been no published demonstration of validity for any commercially available reading test with respect to reading, other than college student populations. Although a test has been validated for use with government civil service employees (Park et al. 1985), the field is still very limited. Consequently, employers have a problem in selecting a test that they can legally use.

Screening Current Workers with Literacy Problems. Hiring and promotion on the basis of measuring literacy skill through tests present a myriad of problems in complying with antidiscrimination law. However, identifying workers with literacy problems with the intention of providing help rather than a job dismissal notice is far less problematical. A number of tests can be used to screen employees who are at-risk.

Which employees can be considered at-risk? Short of taking a reading inventory of each particular job for the reading required, there are some generally accepted levels of literacy that are regarded as minimum. Most frequently, an eighth-grade level is an approximate yardstick for "functional" literacy in almost any job or job-training situation. Employers could then use one level below eighth as the one that employees could be considered at-risk. Once the required reading level is established, the use of any adult normed test should do the job. The Adult Basic Learning Examination (Karlsen & Gardner 1986) or the Test of Adult Basic Education (1976) are both suitable. A caution on using these tests is in order. It is more humane and efficient to select a half-hour reading and math subtest from the several tests provided than risk the trauma of giving the entire test, which may take several hours.

Employers can also design job-related reading task tests that use the types of reading materials workers would use daily on the job. Developing such tests takes more time and effort and some expert advice. These tests are more popular with employees since they can be seen to relate directly to the job in question. They may also be a more valid measure of the actual skills people need in order to perform the job. Once potential employees with low reading skills have been identified, the next task is to persuade employees to participate in work-related literacy programs.

Finding Sufficient Literate Employees. Even if employers did have a test that might be safely used to screen out marginally literate employees, the dramatic decline in the numbers of young people entering the workforce may give them little option in hiring. For example, from 1980 to 1985, 125,000 workers were added to the Minnesota labor force. Only 94,000 workers will be added between 1990 and 1995. This trend is reflected nationally (Collino et al. 1988).

The most rapidly growing segment of the youth population is Hispanic, increasing from 20 percent of the eighteen to twenty-four year olds in 1984 to 24 percent in 1994 (Venezky, Kaestle, & Sum 1987). Hispanic American youth have the highest school dropout rates of any group. According to the Census Bureau, 57 percent of African Americans and 49 percent of Hispanics live in central cities, whereas 75 percent of the new jobs are in the suburbs, and often there is no good public transportation linking the two areas (Bernstein, Anderson, Zellner, & Hammonds 1988).

The dearth of younger workers entering the workforce means employers must fill gaps by retraining the existing employees. Thus, employers are faced with having to retrain workers whose last experience of school might well have taken place twenty years ago. The high replacement costs and sheer difficulty of replacing experienced workers may make dismissing illiterate employees unfeasible. Solutions for closing the literacy gap will be discussed next, starting with one relatively simple solution.

Rewriting Technical Material at Lower Reading Levels. It is difficult to ensure hiring only literate personnel. Initiating literacy programs for employees, as presented in the following paragraphs, is a long-term proposition. One way to help close the literacy gap between employees and work-related reading materials is to rewrite the material in a simpler form.

Most problems involving uninitiated persons reading technical information, whether that information is highly technical information from the field of electronic engineering or instructions on using a new software program on a personal computer, lie with an incorrect set of assumptions on the part of the writer. For example, what is perfectly plain and simple to the engineer, who wrote the directions for how to use a computer part, is unintelligible to the nonengineer who has to use the part. The rapid explosion of technical information puts the new or uninitiated employee, not to mention those with marginal reading skill, at risk. As jobs change, employees are expected to read and understand all types of technical information that did not even exist when they were in school. Where possible, this new information has to be translated to a simple form that the uninitiated can understand.

Those who write technical information are only slowly coming to the realization that a substantial portion of those they write for may not read and understand the written information they are receiving. Unfortunately, the failure to read the information may only be apparent when some accident or costly error has occurred. The legal aspects of who is responsible when an employee causes damage either to himself/herself, others, or costly machinery have not been litigated in terms of the employee's ability to read safety warnings or instructions. Employers are also extremely wary of admitting the existence of employees with substandard skills. What if an employee with less than adequate reading skill causes an accident in which members of the general public are injured? Would the employer, if he/she knew about the reading deficit, be legally responsible? As implied in the previous section on reading and job safety, there is little research or legal case law to act as a guide.

Impacting Literacy through Federal Job-Training Programs. Many of the *Jump Start* (Chisman 1989) recommendations, which are the latest set of recommendations to the U.S. federal government on adult literacy, involve refocusing current federal job-training programs on the needs of the marginally literate. Most of these recommendations involve little or no increase in funding. Should the federal government and state governments target existing funds that are designed to meet the job-training needs of economically disadvantaged youth toward those with low-literacy skills?

Targeting seems simple on the surface, but it is not the simple solution it first appears. Targeting scarce resources inevitably means funds are diverted from one group of those in need to another. This sets up competition within programs and alters the client group. In job-training programs, targeting funds to the low-literacy group means favoring clients who need long-term programs to get them employed at jobs paying more than poverty-level wages. Is it wise to spend more resources on a few clients who are most in need, or should many who need less in terms of becoming employable get the bulk of scarce resources? Federal programs in the past have been accused of ignoring those most in need and skimming off the most able. Certainly if future program funding depends on the number of clients placed successfully in employment, such practices are almost mandatory for continued program survival.

Developing Workplace Literacy Programs. Employers may find that workplace literacy programs must be a constant in employee upgrading and renewal. They can no longer depend on the school system to turn out sufficient numbers of highly literate potential employees. Demographic factors have sharply diminished the size of the potential workforce. Changes within the workforce itself have changed the nature of work so that higher level skills, such as problem solving, are increasingly demanded in work situations. Once an employer has decided to institute workplace literacy programs, what guidelines should be instituted, and what problems might be encountered?

Lack of Employee Participation. The major stumbling block to literacy programs for adults in the U.S. is that most of the eligible adults simply do not participate in them. Nationally, only about 6 percent of the target population enters literacy training. Once entered, most stay for less than three months (Delker 1986).

Workplace literacy programs whether military or civilian have similar problems, even in what might be considered favorable circumstances for the implementation of programs (Sticht 1976). Why are adults so reticent to join programs? Here are some possible conclusions based on an in-depth survey and a yearlong follow-up of workers who had lost their jobs in the steel, computer manufacturing, truck manufacturing, and lumber industries in Minnesota (see table 3.1) (Park, Dawis, & Storlie 1986).

By and large, workers were aware of the need to upgrade their skills. Sixty percent of the total group and 75 percent of lumber workers, who were in the lowest job skill group, thought more reading would be required in future jobs than in the jobs they had held. All had used reading to a greater or lesser degree on their jobs. Of the total group, more than 80 percent thought others they had worked with would benefit from reading and mathematics brushup programs. More than one-half were interested in taking some retraining program (54 percent), and most thought retraining would increase chances of reemployment (85 percent). How did this group feel about actually attending reading and mathematics brushup classes?

Although 80 percent thought others needed to attend such classes, only 15 percent would admit that they themselves lacked the reading skill and that they needed to retrain. A slightly higher percent said they would be interested in a reading program (39 percent) if one were offered. More felt their math skills were inadequate (27 percent) and 47 percent showed interest in a math program if offered. It seems that most workers feel very reluctant to admit that their reading and math skills are insufficient. Although not ready to admit to the problem, more could be talked into attending brushup programs if offered the opportunity.

Is it surprising that people are unwilling to own up to a literacy problem? One of the unfortunate effects of the current literacy initiative has been to label almost one-third of the U.S. adult population illiterate. This label has pejorative implications; it is associated in the public mind with stupidity, ignorance, and possibly antisocial behavior. Small wonder that literacy providers relate stories of adults driving great distances across town to attend literacy programs so no one they know will recognize them there. Clearly programs have to be destigmatized so that it becomes legitimate to attend them.

Altering the name or calling programs a different name will not mask their true nature. I, along with others, decided on the label *brushup* for our literacy programs for dislocated workers. Most went along with this, but all understood that this was a polite euphemism.

Table 3.1   The Need for Basic Skills Programs

	Lumber	Manufac-turing (1)	Manufac-turing (2)	Mining	Agriculture	Total
Do others need brushup? (Yes)	92%	85%	60%	73%	90%	80%
Would others benefit from such a program? (Yes)	94%	96%	63%	85%	98%	87%
To be successful in training:						
Do you have the reading skills you need? (Yes)++	77%	78%	90%	90%	86%	85%
Do you have the math skills you need? (Yes)	66%	56%	83%	70%	86%	73%
Do you have the writing skills you need? (Yes)	77%	72%	83%	87%	70%	79%
Would you be interested in a:						
reading program? (Yes)	31%	33%	33%	39%	58%	39%
Math program? (Yes)+	50%	69%	34%	39%	46%	47%
*Writing program (Yes)**	25%	29%	30%	36%	65%	37%
How likely are you to attend? (Numbers listed here are means.)#+*	6.6	7.6	4.7	4.1	6.5	6.0

(1) Heavy manufacturing.
(2) Computer-related manufacturing.
Rated on a scale of 1–10, where 10 is definitely will attend.
* Significant differences exist between groups (significant at .05 or more).
+ Answers correlate with intention to seek training.
++ Answers correlate with years of education.

Ensuring Participation. Certain steps can be taken that make employee participation more likely. Sticht (1976) found that U.S. Navy employees were more likely to attend programs that paid them and were on the employer's time, than unpaid and on the workers' own time.

Incentives, either financial or in terms of promotion prospects, seem a necessary ingredient of workplace programs. Most continuing education in business either functions on an incentive system or becomes a mandatory part of the job.

Employee participation in the planning and development of programs is, in my experience and in the research, an important factor in program success. Former union officials were successful in attracting participants in plant-specific dislocated worker programs that offered basic skills classes. They were able to do this because they were known and trusted by their fellow workers. Employee participation is becoming more and more recognized as a beneficial element in successful businesses. If employees feel some ownership in a program, they will be more willing to support it.

Basic skills programs should be considered an integrated and ongoing part of the business in in-house training programs. An International Labour Organization discussion paper on vocational training strongly supports the idea that training programs for the "low-literate" be part of the larger system of human resources development (Barbee 1986, 27). This integration together with the integration of literacy training into vocational training will do much to break down employee reluctance to enter programs. If literacy training is not separated out but becomes an expected, integral part of ongoing job-retraining programs, which in turn are part of the conditions of employment for all employees, the problem of participation should be greatly ameliorated.

Program Efficiency. Throughout this chapter, the point has been made that reading, especially at the higher levels, cannot be separated out from the knowledge base that underlies it. In the workplace, this knowledge base changes as jobs become more complex. Reading for working increasingly implies accessing highly technical material. Reading, writing, and mathematics have to be applied to technical text. As Mikulecky (1982) and Sticht (1976) have pointed out, reading skills learned in general contexts do not necessarily transfer to technical contexts. The reader has to build the relevant knowledge base. Building this knowledge base can be accomplished using a variety of multimedia approaches. However, such a task is bound to take time.

Assessments of evaluative data show that it takes approximately 100 hours to raise adults' skill levels one grade level as measured by standardized achievement tests. However, such gains may be illusory for purely technical reasons. Even the most recent tests are carefully standardized versions of adult achievement tests that have very large standard deviations and standard error measurements (SEM) (Park In press). Regression effects combined with large SEMs make it difficult to show short-term gains with any degree of confidence. Adults who enter programs and are immediately tested are fearful and have forgotten much of their test-taking skills. After a few hours of instruction, they recall much they had forgotten since leaving school. Only when new knowledge enters the picture does adult learning stall. Too short an interval between tests shows rapid gains that cannot endure. Too many sellers of computerized software programs extrapolate rapid gains made in the first twenty hours of instruction to extremely high estimates of what an adult might learn in forty or sixty hours. Such claims are highly questionable, but they are rarely questioned because program operators do not know what questions to ask.

Effective workplace literacy programs must use functional context methods that teach the reading, writing, and math skills. Only about a quarter of the performance on general reading tasks transfers to context-specific reading tasks (Mikulecky 1986). Efficiency demands that the reading, writing, and math tasks taught in workplace literacy programs are explicitly those that are needed on the job. Emphasis should be placed on problem-solving skills that relate directly to problems met on the job. These specific skills will secondarily improve general reading and problem-solving skills, but the opposite is not the case.

Conclusion

Workplace literacy is not a simple subject and does not lend itself to simple solutions. Over the last few years, literacy has been seen as the precipitating cause of such diverse and global phenomena as economic decline, increased dependence on welfare, and increased incarceration rates. Because education is seen as a key ingredient of social and economic health, it does not necessarily follow that improving education will result in the desired economic and social change. This is not an argument for doing nothing. The reasons for adopting workplace literacy programs are strong. But they must be implemented without unrealistic expectations and the type of overblown claims currently in vogue.

Improving literacy skill cannot be accomplished with a "quick fix." Customized job-related literacy programs must be integrated into worker upgrade and training on a regular basis. Improving reading means expanding the knowledge base of the worker, and building knowledge takes time. Emphasis needs to be placed on higher level cognitive skills to prepare workers for the ongoing learning needed in the changing workforce. Workers will not voluntarily participate in programs that they do not view as central to their jobs. Hence, reading programs must be specifically work related and not tied to outmoded methods and techniques directly taken from elementary reading classes.

Finally, some way must be found of financing workplace literacy. Should businesses who ultimately stand to profit from an improved workforce take on the entire burden? Is there a public interest in the improvement of the workforce that would give the federal or state governments an interest in either direct grants or tax rebates to businesses who undertake workplace literacy programs? Should individuals contribute to their own further education? The answer lies in the will of individuals and of corporations to better themselves and to prepare for the future.

References

Barbee, D. 1986. Methods of providing vocational skills to individuals with low literacy levels: The U.S. experience. *International Labour Office*. October. Geneva.

Bernstein, A., R. Anderson, W. Zellner, and K. Hammonds. 1988. In G. Collino, E. Aderman, and E. Askov, eds., *Literacy and job performance: A perspective*, 18. Institute for the Study of Adult Literacy, The Pennsylvania State University.

Chisman, F. P. 1989. *Jump Start: The federal role in adult literacy*. Final report of Project on Adult Literacy, January, The Southport Institute for Policy Analysis.

Collino, G., E. Aderman, and E. Askov. 1988. *Literacy and job performance: A perspective*. Institute for the Study of Adult Literacy, Pennsylvania State University.

Delker, P. 1986. *Beyond literacy in an uncertain world*. Knoxville, TN: The Commission of Adult Basic Education. ERIC Document Reproduction Service no. ED 272–715.

Diehl, W., and L. Mikulecky. 1980. The nature of reading at work. *Journal of Reading* 24.

Duffy T. M. 1987. Readability formulas: What is the use? In T. Duffy and R. Waller, eds., *Designing usable texts,* 113–43. San Diego, CA: Academic Press.

Federal Registrar. 1979. 1978 federal uniform guidelines on employee selection procedures 44(43): 2 March.

Karlsen, B., and E. F. Gardner. 1986. *Adult basic learning examination.* NY: The Psychological Corporation; Harcourt Brace Jovanovich, Inc.

Mikulecky, L. 1982. Job literacy: The relationship between school preparation and workplace actuality. *Reading Research Quarterly* 17:400–19.

Mikulecky, L. 1986. *The status of literacy in our society.* Paper presented at the National Reading Conference, 5 Dec., Austin, TX.

Moe, A., T. Rush, and R. Storlie. 1980. *The reading requirements* for *10 occupations.* Newark, DE: International Reading Association.

Park, R. J. In press. Commentary on three programs for intergenerational transfer of cognition. In T. Sticht, B. McDonald, and M. J. Beeler, eds., *The intergenerational transfer of cognitive skills.* Norwood, NJ: Ablex Publishers.

Park, R., R. Dawis, and R. Storlie. 1986. *The educational needs of dislocated workers in Minnesota.* Center for Urban and Regional Affairs, University of Minnesota, Minneapolis.

Park, R., R. Storlie, E. Rengel, and R. Dawis. 1985. The validation of a reading test for civil service employees. *International Personnel Management Journal* 14:3.

Smith, F. 1982. *Understanding reading.* NY: Holt, Rinehart & Winston.

Sticht, T. 1976. *Reading for working.* Alexandria, VA: Human Resources Research Organization.

Sticht, T. 1988. Adult literacy education. In E. Z. Rothkopf, ed., *Review of research in education* 15. Washington, DC: American Educational Research Association.

Test of Adult Basic Education. 1976. Monterey, CA: CTB/McGraw-Hill.

Venezky, R., C. Kaestle, and A. Sum. 1987. *The subtle danger reflections on the literacy abilities of America's young adults.* Princeton, NJ: NAEP, Educational Testing Center.

Literacy Education in the Military

Clinton L. Anderson

The concept of literacy education in the military emerged during the earliest days of the U.S. Army. In 1778 General George Washington recognized the need for providing basic academic instruction to illiterate, convalescent soldiers following the bitter winter at Valley Forge (Wilds 1938). The purpose of this instruction appeared to have nothing to do with requirements for any basic educational skills to perform military jobs. Instead, it was aimed at providing enlisted men with the ability to read and recite their Bible in hopes of spiritual enrichment and a better life in the future. How has literacy education in the military provided a better way of life for enlisted men and women? The answer lies in my following discussion of the history of literacy education in the military; strategies and instructional programs designed to address the problems of illiterates in the military; and issues that include tailoring instructional programs to enlistees' needs, using educational credentials for advancement, and recognizing the military as a responsible educator.

History

The history of literacy education within the U.S. military services is continuous since those early days with periods of emphasis occurring during such wartimes as the Civil War, World War I, World War II, the Korean War, and the Vietnam War (Anderson 1986; Sticht 1982). In 1918, the army introduced the first massive paper and pencil intelligence testing program (Duffy 1985). The results of this testing provided the first tangible evidence of a literacy problem. For example, the U.S. War Department found that 30 percent of the 1.7 million soldiers taking the Army Beta Test could not understand the form due to their lack of reading skills (Resnick & Resnick 1977). At this point, literacy became reading comprehension instead of oration.

The primary philosophy of the World War I army leadership was rooted in the conviction that development of literacy was not their responsibility, but rather the responsibility of the civilian community (Strehlow 1967). The educational work in the American Expeditionary Force was developed early in 1919 under the Young Men's Christian Association (YMCA), which provided standardized methods, books, and courses. The YMCA also provided "expert advisors and assistants for schools for officers and men" (Munson 1921, 477).

By the beginning of World War II, the military leadership seemed to have forgotten the lessons learned during World War I about testing and identification of illiterates and low literates. Between October 1940 and May 15, 1941, soldiers were inducted into the army not by having their literacy skills tested, but on their acknowledgment that they could comprehend simple orders given in the English language (Goldberg 1951). Such was determined by asking them if they could read or write. Quickly, the U.S. Armed Forces realized that illiterates and low literates had extreme difficulty adjusting to military service and performing military jobs satisfactorily. So restrictions were placed on the induction of illiterates. Next, massive in-service literacy education programs were established and maintained. Instructional materials included the *Soldier's Reader* and later the *Army Reader* as basic texts, supplemented by numerous pamphlets that included a regular cartoon strip that told of the experiences of "Private Pete" and his friend "Daffey." Examples of these cartoon strip titles include: "Marksman Pete," "Pete Meets Gas," and "Private Pete Keeps Healthy." These materials were used extensively in special training units designed, in part, to upgrade literacy and English language skills of inductees.

The American Council on Education commissioned some of the most exhaustive studies involving education of military personnel during World War II. One of these studies (Houle, Burr, Hamilton, & Yale 1947) reviewed literacy training during this period in the overall context of adult education in the War Department. Ginzberg and Bray (1953) provided considerable information on the problems of illiteracy confronting the army in World War II and efforts to overcome them. Their work was particularly noteworthy in identifying a deep conviction held by many leaders of the armed forces that development of literacy was not a responsibility of the military but of the civilian education community. Perhaps the most comprehensive effort in documenting army training of illiterates during World War II was done by Goldberg (1951). His work is valuable for its detail of program development, philosophy and purpose, actual content, and evaluation efforts.

On December 24, 1941, the War Department authorized the establishment of a correspondence school for army-enlisted soldiers. The Army Institute began operations on April 1, 1942, at Madison, Wisconsin, in facilities donated by the University of Wisconsin. By February 1943, its name had been changed to the United States Armed Forces Institute (USAFI) to reflect the extension of services to the U.S. Navy, Marines, and Coast Guard. Literacy and high school as well as college and vocational courses were developed and offered by correspondence, using the U.S. Postal Service and the military postal systems overseas. This method of study was an attractive and efficient method of instruction for service members at permanent duty stations scattered throughout the world. As USAFI developed, so did its need for self-teaching and self-testing materials. USAFI produced numerous adult basic education instructional materials. The *On Your Mark, Get Set, Go* series and the Metropolitan Achievement Test served as important course materials for military literacy programs until USAFI's disestablishment in 1974.

Manpower requirements for the Vietnam War required a serious look, by the military services, at the use and training of illiterates and low-literates. During 1967, the Department of Defense (DOD) conducted Project 100,000. Through this project many of the approximately 400,000 men who had failed selective service mental examinations between October 1, 1966, and October 1, 1967, were accepted into the military services. The principal thrust was on the use of these low-level recruits, not on their literacy development. As an outgrowth of Project 100,000, the Human Resources Research Organization (HumRRO) was tasked in the early 1970s to identify literacy demands inherent in army jobs. After studying reading demands of jobs, HumRRO was again tasked by the army to study ways to train people to reach those demands in some kind of literacy program. HumRRO developed the Functional Literacy Program (FLIT) (Sticht 1975). From this effort emerged the concept of literacy training directly related to military job training and duty performance.

In 1977, the post-Vietnam era, after the armed services again had become an all-volunteer force, the United States General Accounting Office documented a need for the U.S. government to address illiteracy programs in the military services. Its findings showed that when compared to normal recruit population ". . . poor readers tend to have higher discharge rates, experience more difficulty in training, perform less satisfactorily on the job, and lack the potential for career development" (General Accounting Office 1977, Front Cover Page).

During the first half of the 1980s, the army's standard was, generally, below fifth-grade level for illiterate and below ninth-grade level for marginally literate soldiers, as measured by a commercially procured standardized test (Army Regulation 621—5, 1983). During the mid-1980s, below tenth-grade level became a commonly used standard for marginal literacy.

Paul Chatelier (1980), an assistant for training and personnel systems technology in the U.S. Office of the Under Secretary of Defense for Research and Engineering, indicated that "Technologically sophisticated hardware doesn't mean much if people can't operate or maintain it" (p. 3). Consequently, DOD, in conjunction with the military services, instituted a Training and Personnel Systems Technology Program with four major areas of emphasis:

1. Human factors to improve the design of weapons and support systems so personnel can operate equipment with the minimum of training; actions being taken in this area include human studies, man-machine studies, and man-machine mission studies.
2. Simulation and training devices to improve services' ability to train military personnel; actions taken in this area include visual simulation, force/motion cue simulation, sensor simulation, weapons fire simulation, maintenance training simulation, instructional features, and specialized training devices.
3. Education and training to instruct military personnel so they will be effective in performing job assignments throughout their careers; actions being taken in this area include curriculum development, methods and media, management systems, effectiveness evaluation, technology transfer, and special applications.
4. Manpower and personnel to improve DOD's ability to forecast manpower needs and to recruit manpower in sufficient numbers; actions taken in this area include occupational requirements and structures, resources management, recruitment, accession and placement, career development, productivity and effectiveness, and civilian and military work force development (Chatelier, 1980).

In general, all the military services (Army, Air Force, Navy, Marine Corps, Coast Guard) have maintained a history of providing in-service basic education programs and related activities such as counseling, testing, and high school completion. Such efforts were to help undereducated or low-aptitude personnel increase their basic skills and knowledge so they can complete initial entry training, perform their military jobs effectively, compete for retention and promotion, and meet individual goals and aspirations (Sticht 1982; Duffy 1985). In 1988, the total force strength of the DOD stood at 3.4 million personnel; 1.6 million were members of the U.S. reserve component, that is, Army Reserve, Army National Guard, Air National Guard, Air Force Reserve, Navy Reserve, Marine Corps Reserve, and U.S. Coast Guard Reserve (McNeilly 1988). It seems reasonable to suspect that the military will have to continue its literacy education programs to help its personnel perform their tasks satisfactorily.

In their efforts to address illiteracy and marginal literacy problems, the military services seem to have adopted a fourfold strategy. First, English is the standard work language. This policy was set forth by the army in a letter to the United States Senate, March 15, 1979.

The Grand Strategy

> Army policy does not restrict soldiers to the use of the English language when communicating with each other. However, they must have sufficient skills in the English language to perform their military duties. Our policy recognizes that members of the Army must be able to communicate with their supervisors, subordinates, and fellow soldiers. It also acknowledges that the very nature of our equipment and procedures dictates the need for all soldiers to be completely functional even if English is their second language. (Department of the Army, Alexander Letter 1979, 1)

Second, literacy requirements for service members and civilian employees are minimized by maintaining strict readability standards for military publications, by maximizing the use of graphics and multimedia training materials, and by developing and implementing realistic simulations and simulators.

Third, the military services are maintaining high enlistment standards for recruits entering the military services and for retaining personnel once in service. Recruiters target high school diploma graduates. In essence, they search out healthy young people with above-average literacy, vocational skills, and knowledge as measured by the Armed Services Vocational Aptitude Battery (ASVAB). Each of the armed services uses educational incentive packages to entice people into their employment.

Fourth, the military services have instructional programs in adult basic education aimed at assisting active service members to meet job requirements and to advance professionally in their branch of service. In effect, these instructional programs are used to resolve literacy and related skill development problems not eliminated by other actions.

Overall, the fourfold armed services appear reasonably satisfied with this strategy for resolving their literacy problem. For example, in 1982, the army's Deputy Assistant Secretary for Human Systems and Resources testified before a congressional Subcommittee on PostSecondary Education concerning the impact of illiteracy in the army by saying: "Today I conclude that the Army is not significantly adversely affected by illiteracy" (Department of the Army, Kinzer Statement 1982).

Instructional Programs

The military services have historically incorporated many diverse elements within adult basic education for service personnel. Generally, the common thrust has been in the area of basic educational skills, for example, reading, writing, and arithmetic, for the English-speaking member. But for service personnel whose first and primary language is other than English, the effort has been on developing speaking and listening skills using the English language.

The military services have also been heavily involved in high school completion for those service members who have entered the armed services without a high school diploma. Since 1980, the few non-high school graduates who have been accepted into the military services have generally scored above average in their ASVAB. Consequently many of these individuals are encouraged to take the General Educational Development (GED) examination as soon as practical and receive a high school equivalency certificate. Some, however, will work with supporting educational institutions and actually achieve a high school diploma.

Under DOD Directive 1322.8 (Department of Defense 1987), all the military services operate voluntary education programs for their personnel. Among these educational opportunities are bridging or advanced skills courses in reading, writing, and mathematics that are designed to prepare military students for regular college-level instruction. Courses in computer literacy, computer operations and programming, and information systems management are also readily available for many military personnel.

In addition, the military services, particularly the army, conduct host-nation language orientation courses for service members stationed in foreign countries for whom English is not the primary language. These host-nation language courses, such as German, Turkish, Greek, Korean, are presented at a very basic or survival level and are designed to assist the service member to live and travel in that host nation with a minimum of language and cultural difficulties. (Even though many different adult basic education elements exist within the military services for service personnel, this chapter will concentrate on basic educational skills for English-speaking personnel.)

With regard strictly to basic skills programs in the military, also operated under DOD Directive 1322.8, there is a kaleidoscopic array of programs in various stages of continuing development and implementation (see table 3.2). Each service component has different kinds of on-duty programs and educational services, with different criteria for entry and for exiting, different assessment devices and lengths of instruction, decentralized management, little systematic evaluation, and assorted materials. These programs serve a multiplicity of functions (Sticht 1982). Generally, the programs are delivered by civilian educational institutions or companies under contract to the military. Fiscal year 1988 statistics indicate the following individual enrollments: Army—66,448; Navy—

Table 3.2   Basic Skills Education Programs in the Military: 1980–1981

DOD Preenlistment Programs	Recruit Training Programs	Job Technical School Programs	Unit/Duty Station Programs
	ARMY		
ABE	Basic Skills	BSEP II	BSEP II
Job Corps	Education	BSEP	IBSEP I
ESL	Program		ASEP
	(BSEP I)		Off-Duty HSC
	AIR FORCE		
	BMT Reading	STEP	IDEA
	Proficiency	ASP	Off-Duty HSC
	Program	PLATO-SIP	
		MSIP	
		TT-IDEA	
	NAVY		
	Academic	JOBS	FST
	Remedial		BEST
	Training		Off-Duty HSC
	MARINE CORPS		
	None	None	BSEP
			Off-Duty HSC

Acronyms: DOD: ABE—Adult Basic Education; ESL—English as a Second Language; Army: BSEP—Basic Skills Education Program; ASEP—Advanced Skills Education Program; Air Force: BMT—Basic Military Training; STEP—Skill Training Enhancement Program; ASP—Academic Skills Program; PLATO-SIP—PLATO Skills Improvement Programs; MSIP—Math Skills Improvement Programs; TT-IDEA—Technical Training Individualized Development and Educational Advancement Program; IDEA—Duty Station IDEA; Navy: JOBS-Job—Oriented Basic Skills; FST—Functional Skills Training; BEST—Behavioral Skills Training; Marine Corps: BSEP—Basic Skills Education Program (Sticht 1982, 32).

20,341; Marine Corps—11,166; Air Force—1,705; Total DOD—99,660 (DANTES 1989).

Each of the many basic skills programs in DOD have their own development history. Only the Job Skills Education Program (JSEP), developed by the army, is briefly discussed. (A complete description of JSEP appears in the following chapter of this volume.) JSEP is the outgrowth of a comprehensive series of educational initiatives begun by Secretary of the Army Clifford Alexander and his staff in 1979. It is the army's attempt to shift from general literacy instruction to a more functionally oriented program based on prerequisite basic educational skills. The skills were identified in an analysis conducted by the U.S. Army Training and Doctrine Command, under a contract with the RCA Service Company. This analysis was called the Military Occupational Specialty Baseline Skills Project. It focused on two areas: (*a*) identification of initial entry training course survival skills, and (*b*) an extended task analysis of ninety-four most densely populated military occupational specialties and the common tasks required of all soldiers. Based on findings of this analysis, the goal of JSEP was to design, develop, and field-test a job-related curriculum for armywide adoption, using advanced instructional technologies.

The American Institute for Research's (AIR) evaluation of the army's field-testing of JSEP found that

> Soldiers almost invariably liked JSEP. They stated that the computer-based instruction was enjoyable, held their attention, allowed them to progress at their own pace, forced them to persevere in a task until they had mastered it, allowed them to make mistakes in private. Soldiers said they had enrolled in JSEP to improve their GT scores (General-Technical scores on ASVAB), and generally thought the program would help to do this, even though it was not designed to improve GT and the empirical data indicated that it did not do so. All of the JSEP instructors and educational administrators who were interviewed were aware that JSEP's purpose was to teach soldiers the verbal and quantitative skills prerequisite to MOS performance. However, these educators said that neither the soldiers nor the commanders who referred them to continuing education perceived this to be a need, and job performance improvement was not cited as a reason for enrolling in continuing education by any of the soldiers or their supervisors interviewed for the evaluation. (Hoffman, Hahn, Hoffman, & Dean 1988, ix)

Based on the AIR evaluation reports (Hoffman et al. 1988; Hoffman 1988), it appears that the army has a standardized curriculum that enhances academic knowledge and skills required for military job performance as recommended by the General Accounting Office (1983) and stipulated in congressional budget guidance for the army's basic skills education effort. But the army's leadership emphasizes scores on ASVAB to select soldiers for retention, for additional job training, and possibly for soldier promotion. Soldiers who have low General Technical or Armed Forces Qualification Test scores want to prepare themselves to retake the ASVAB to enhance their ability to compete successfully in the army's military personnel management system. So, similar to a college-bound student's quest for a preparation course for the Scholastic Aptitude Test (SAT), soldiers want a preparation course for taking the ASVAB.

Issues

Tailoring Programs to Enlistees' Needs. Adult and continuing education, as currently implemented in the military services, is an integral function of the local military commands at installations, posts, bases, ships, communities, fleets, and major command levels around the world. Commanders operate within the military structure under mountains of policy directives, regulations, and specifications aimed at centralization and standardization. Military rationale for standardization is that because of uncontrolled proliferation of computers, telecommunication systems and other technology-oriented media, and systems with their incompatible hardware, software, and data bases, excessive time is required for the development of education and training programs and their implementation. Perhaps, a more basic rationale is that service members are mobile with a tour of duty lasting from under twelve months to as long as thirty-six months at one location with numerous job changes occurring at that site. Even while assigned at a permanent duty station, many service members are subject to long temporary duty assignments away from that location. For example, soldiers stationed at Fort Bragg, North Carolina, are routinely placed on temporary duty in the Sinai Peninsula. In changing duty stations and while on temporary duty, soldiers in literacy education often participate in programs operated as a function of different commands. The necessity for some standardization of curriculum and centralization of management is recognized in order not to confuse soldiers and to allow them to proceed in their learning process with minimum disruptions and unproductive duplication of effort.

On the other hand, commanders must have a certain degree of flexibility to function effectively to accomplish the unit's mission as well as to care for the troops and their families. Hence, commanders tailor their training and education programs to meet needs and priorities as they perceive them. It is the local education services officer or specialist, and his/her staff, who works under local command guidance and tailors the adult basic education programs to meet both the perceived needs of the command structure as well as the assessed needs of service members. In this regard, there must be sufficient flexibility in the armed services' adult basic education efforts for local initiatives and for command imprint, which shows that this specific effort belongs to that particular command. Perhaps the bureaucratic support (including regulations, information management, and curriculum) should be standardized and centralized at least within each military service, but sufficient flexibility should remain at the local level to create, tailor, and engineer adult basic education efforts to meet human needs.

Use of Education Credentials. Motivation for learning may be extrinsic, intrinsic, or both with some interconnectedness. Many service members in adult basic education classes appear highly motivated to learn (Anderson 1986). But when this is observed, service members have some tangible goals they are striving toward, such as ASVAB scores that will allow the service member to be rated a Mental Category IIIA, a seventy on the English Comprehension Level Test, a certificate of course completion in a learning center, a high school diploma, or a high school GED certificate. Most of these tangible goals are, in a sense, credentials the military services have established as important marks of personal achievement in the education arena. By gaining these goals, "good" things including promotion, better jobs, reenlistment, and opportunities for further education may occur. The lack of these marks of achievement means very low probability of good things happening. In some ways, the military services' use of extrinsic motivation in education reflects its larger system of awards and decorations as visible evidence of achievement.

In some instances, as in the case with a high school diploma or GED certificate, the credential carries an added valve—that of acceptance in the civilian society. The award (including the ceremony) of a high school diploma through a military-sponsored program represents tangible evidence of success to the service member's family and to friends in the civilian community. It is not only evidence that the service member has reached an important goal, but that the military service, as an organization, facilitated its occurrence.

The Military as a Responsible Educator. Historically, a prevailing attitude among many military leaders has been that basic education is really the responsibility of the civilian sector and the military organization should not be concerned with it. In many ways, the military would like to assume the role of an employer who chooses and retains only those employees capable of doing the job and meeting rather stringent criteria for promotion and reenlistment. Yet, recruitment and retention of military personnel are dependent on the available manpower pool willing to enlist and remain on duty. A large segment of that pool, coming as they do from disadvantaged backgrounds and poor civilian educational environments, seek opportunities for better education and job training. As a result, the military services have had to provide educational services for the illiterate, marginal literate, and those who are not fluent in English.

In times of mobilization and war, problems have been more acute. In peacetime with smaller manpower requirements, the problems of illiteracy seem to have receded essentially through recruitment and retention standards and, in recent years, aided by GI Bill educational incentive packages. *Marginal Man and the Military Service* (Department of the Army 1965) makes a case for the military accepting illiterates and marginal literates during peacetime; so in mobilization and war, the military services will know how to train and use these manpower resources to execute the wartime mission. This, in part, was the rationale behind Project 100,000.

Several factors weigh heavily against the military being able to avoid enlisting men and women with basic educational deficiencies. First, there is the shrinking seventeen- to twenty-one-year-old manpower pool well documented by the Census Bureau. Second, serious quality problems exist within the U.S. secondary school system as documented by a series of education studies and reports published during the 1980s. No apparent national strategy exists that can effectively resolve illiteracy and marginal literacy problems within the civilian sector. Third, demographers point to the increasingly large percentage of the reduced manpower pool that will be young people whose first language is other than English. Fourth, military trainers, regardless of the best man-machine interface efforts, are being confronted with finding effective ways to train individuals to operate and maintain more complex, lethal, and expensive equipment than ever before. Basic education, then, for military job performance should be focused on reading, writing, verbal communication, mathematics, computer literacy, information management, and the abilities to think, reason, and solve problems under stress.

Conclusion

Requirements for adult basic education in the U.S. military are not expected to diminish. But with the current strategy to resolve literacy problems, the in-service emphasis is on the marginally literate service member. Manpower availability problems, combined with increased military-training requirements, may even expand the need for such programs and services. Consequently, adult basic education activities are encompassing an increasingly large spectrum of organizational training, personal management, and human needs for basic education.

The history of literacy education in the military is long and complex. Current instructional program efforts are based on a variety of goals and purposes that have not been well defined nor commonly understood among personnel operating these programs, by researchers attempting to improve them, or by commanders who sponsor them. Yet, these programs continue to be conducted by adult and continuing educators located throughout the military services to meet a variety of human and organizational goals. Visibility of program efforts tends to wax and wane with the interests of military leaders, their beliefs in education, and their perceptions of how education can be used to help service members and the organization. Continuity of literacy education efforts rests primarily on in-service directors of education, education services officers, specialists, and counselors; it rests on their abilities, will to plan, develop, procure, and implement instructional programs that meet educational needs, and then on their ability to get service members to participate successfully in those programs.

References

Anderson, C. L. 1986. *Historical profile of adult basic education programs in the United States Army.* Unpublished Doctoral Dissertation, Teachers College, Columbia University, NY.

Army Regulation 621—5. 1983. *Army Continuing Education System(ACES).* Washington, DC: The Adjutant General's Office, Headquarters, Department of the Army.

Chatelier, P. R. 1980. Training and personnel systems technology: A boost to readiness. *Defense Management Journal* (second quarter):2–5.

DANTES. 1989. Voluntary education program fact sheet (FY 1988). *Information Bulletin,* 152. Supplement 4. Pensacola, FL: Defense Activity for Non-Traditional Education Support.

Department of Defense. 1987. *DOD Directive 1322.8: Voluntary educational program for military personnel.* Washington, DC: Office of the Assistant Secretary of Defense for Manpower, Reserve Affairs and Logistics.

Department of the Army. Alexander Letter. 1979. *Letter from Clifford Alexander, Secretary of the Army, to Sam Nunn, Chairman of the Subcommittee on Manpower and Personnel, Armed Services Committee, United States Senate.* Washington, DC: Office of the Deputy Chief of Staff for Personnel.

Department of the Army. Kinzer Statement. 1982. *Statement before Subcommittee on Education and Labor. House.* 97th Cong. 2d sess. 21 September. Washington, DC: Office of the Assistant Secretary of the Army, Manpower and Reserve Affairs.

Department of the Army. 1965. *Marginal man and military service.* Washington, DC: Department of the Army.

Duffy, T. M. 1985. Literacy instruction in the military. *Armed Forces & Society* 11:437–64.

General Accounting Office. 1977. *A need to address illiteracy problems in the military services.* USGAO report FPCD–77–13. Washington, DC: U.S. General Accounting Office.

General Accounting Office. 1983. *Poor design and management hamper army's basic skill education program.* USGAO report FPCD-83–19. Washington, DC: U.S. General Accounting Office.

Ginzberg, S., and D. W. Bray. 1953. *The uneducated.* NY: Columbia University.

Goldberg, S. 1951. *Army training of illiterates in World War II.* NY: Teachers College, Columbia University.

Hoffman, D. M. 1988. *Evaluation of the job skills education program: Part II curriculum review.* AIR-55600–FR-8/88. Vol. 2. Washington DC: American Institutes for Research.

Hoffman, L. M., C. P. Hahn, D. M. Hoffman, and R. A. Dean. 1988. *Evaluation of the job skills education program: Part I learning outcomes.* AIR-55600–FR-8/88. Vol. 1. Washington, DC: American Institutes for Research.

Houle, C. O., E. W. Burr, T. H. Hamilton, and J. R. Yale. 1974. *The armed services and adult education*. Washington, DC: The American Council on Education.

McNeilly, D. 1988. *Notes from briefing provided by the Office of the Deputy Assistant Secretary of Defense (Guard, Reserve Readiness and Training)*. Pentagon, June 22, 1988.

Munson, E. L. 1921. *The management of men: A handbook on the systematic development of morale and control of human behavior*. NY: Henry Holt & Company.

Resnick, D., and L. Resnick. 1977. The nature of literacy and historical exploration. *Harvard Educational Review* 47:370–85.

Sticht, T. G. 1975. *A program of army functional job reading training: Development, implementation, and delivery systems*. Report no. FR-WD (CA)-75-77. Alexandria, VA: Human Resources Research Organization.

Sticht, T. G. 1982. *Basic skills in defense*. Report no. FR-ETSD-82–86. Alexandria, VA: Human Resources Research Organization.

Strehlow, L. H. 1967. *History of the army general education program: Origin, significance, and implication*. Unpublished Doctoral Dissertation. George Washington University, Washington, DC.

Wilds, H. E. 1938. *Valley Forge*. NY: MacMillan.

Technology in Adult Basic Skills: The Job Skills Education Program

Robert K. Branson

As technology in adult basic skills education becomes more capable, it can be used to address a growing number of applications in the education and training communities. This chapter presents the design, development, and field-testing of a large technology-based functional basic skills program called the Job Skills Education Program (JSEP—"jay-sepp"). It illustrates a paradigm for instruction that has been supported for many years. Herein, I will show how it originated in the U.S. Army and was successfully demonstrated in civilian adult education settings.

JSEP is a program designed for large numbers of people who require a substantial course of study to reach a level of competency that will enable them to profit from structured training programs. The instruction is offered on a computer system having both keyboard and light-pen student input devices. The students are managed through the program by an internal student management system that keeps track of the lessons they are supposed to take, those they have taken, and how long it took them to complete each. The student workstations are networked to a host that contains the course ware and management system. A typical JSEP system has eighteen to twenty workstations, though the computer can be assembled to handle many more.

Technology-based literacy and basic skills programs for adults may be the only reasonable option considering the magnitude of the problems and the number of adults requiring such programs. There are three key reasons that I believe justify this assertion. First, there are not enough trained teachers to address the problem. Most teachers are needed in programs not amenable to technology. Second, literacy and basic skills instructional strategies require extensive drill and practice before students reach a level of automaticity. This instruction can be provided by technology. Third, many adults miss classes because of family problems, sporadic transportation, work, and illness. With technology-based programs, they do not fall behind in their studies.

In the following sections, a brief history, the major issues in design, the development and implementation, and the use of the JSEP model with civilians will be discussed. I believe that this model offers high promise for adult literacy and basic skills programs.

Need for JSEP. In the mid-1970s, U.S. Army field commanders identified what appeared to be basic skills deficiencies in soldiers reporting for duty assignments. Subsequent investigation by the army's Training and Doctrine Command revealed that a significant proportion of soldiers were having job performance difficulties because they lacked the skills to use army manuals,

JSEP History

make routine calculations, and follow maintenance and repair instructions (Lieutenant Colonel R. R. Begland, personal communication 1988).

Most of the army's technical training schools are in the Training and Doctrine Command. They were contacted to find out whether basic skills deficiencies were impacting the quality of training. It was found that when the instructors in the training programs had difficult content to teach, they spent training time on basic skills to ensure that deficient soldiers were able to understand the training. In so doing, they were also teaching basic skills to soldiers who had already mastered them, an inefficient practice. To avoid giving redundant remedial education in technical training courses, the army decided to develop a basic skills program that would prepare entering soldiers for technical training to be given before or during their technical training courses (Major R. Tarr, personal communication 1988).

Because the U.S. Army has so many jobs and so many possible uses of functional basic skills, it decided to undertake a job analysis to find out which jobs required which basic educational skills. Sticht (1975) and Philippi (1988) have described similar kinds of analyses. Incidentally, the army distinguishes between education and training because of organizational assignments and because education is not usually permitted to occur on regular duty time.

Job Analysis. The JSEP model requires that any basic skills included must be directly used on the job before instruction is designed to teach the skills. As a consequence, it was essential to have a complete job and task analysis to identify which jobs required what skills. To obtain that analysis, the army issued a request for proposal (RFP) in the late 1970s that would result in analyses of ninety-four jobs that covered about 85 percent of the entering soldiers; the remaining 15 percent of the soldiers were in the other 200 jobs.

The team of RCA Educational Services (RCA), Educational Testing Service (ETS), and Florida State University (FSU) was successful in winning the contract. RCA conducted the massive job and task analysis, ETS developed the tests, and FSU provided training and support to RCA. To do the analysis, RCA had to identify all of the tasks that comprised any job that might be performed by entering soldiers. This analysis involved about 8,000 tasks and required input from about 1,500 subject matter experts (Ed Shepherd, personal communication 1988). Having identified the tasks, they used a task analysis procedure that resulted in identification of instances where a basic skill was found on a job. These instances were called Indicator Statements. The analysts were required to interview people who had both performed the tasks and taught them in an army school to be sure that the Indicator Statements were accurate.

To make the analysis more manageable, RCA grouped similar Indicator Statements into general categories of skill called Prerequisite Competencies (PCs). In all, they identified some 200 PCs in the ninety-four jobs they analyzed. Examples of PCs and Indicator Statements are found in Table 3.3.

Army jobs are called Military Occupational Specialties (MOS). The MOSs that were analyzed ranged from basic combat infantry, to cooks, to all kinds of maintenance and communications specialists. When the job and task analyses

Table 3.3   Prerequisite Competencies and Illustrative Indicator Statements from the RCA Job and Task Analysis

PC 41b.   Use and interpret hand and arm signals.
- Signal operator to swing load out when clear of vehicle.
- Clasp hands together to have driver stop tank when lifter is straight up and down over connector with road wheel off the center guides.

PC 15a.   Draw plane geometric figures.
- Draw the areas of operation on the map using the platoon leader's map as a reference.
- Draw a triangle over grid intersection.

PC 02c.   Measure lengths of objects or distances using a ruler, yardstick, meter stick, or scale.
- Determine the center point of the FPF.
- Measure along azimuth the estimated distance.
- Read micrometer.

PC 19d.   Use tables of trigonometric functions (degrees).
- Extract log sin for value of 1/2 (latitude of station-apparent declination of sun).
- Determine log sin vertical angle.

were complete, the documentation, including computer tapes and printouts were delivered to the army. About forty linear shelf feet of 8 1/2-by-11-inch computer sheets in binders were required to hold these printouts.

Starting the JSEP Project. Following the job and task analyses the army developed the procurement specifications for the design and development of JSEP. It was during this critical time that the U.S. Army Research Institute realized the necessity for implementing JSEP with the improved technology that was becoming available at that time (circa 1982). The army required that all soldiers be given the same job-related instruction no matter where they were stationed. Technology provided a means of controlling the quality and content of that instruction.

In 1982, the team of Florida State University and Ford Aerospace Corporation (FSU-Ford) was awarded the JSEP design and development contract. The army had an existing PLATO computer system and wanted JSEP hosted on that system. FSU-Ford proposed TICCIT as the second system. TICCIT is a computer-based instruction (CBI) system controlled by a host that operates the individual workstations through a network. Both systems have internal student management systems that control and keep track of what lessons the students should have and which ones they have completed.

The fundamental mission of JSEP is to prepare soldiers to succeed in training   **JSEP Design**
programs for their individual MOS. In that context, JSEP is a *training* program for soldiers to learn their MOS. If soldiers go through JSEP and are more

successful students than those soldiers who do not, then the program will have met its design objectives. Even though the longitudinal follow-up data are not available for JSEP, Baker and Hamovitch (1983) reported that the U.S. Navy's Job-Oriented Basic Skills (JOBS) program improved performance in training programs, subsequent job performance in the fleet, and increased the number of sailors who were retained in the navy.

Design considerations. First, because soldiers are adults, JSEP designers believed that the basic skills instruction should be presented in an army context. The RCA analysis provided the documentation of what should be included in each MOS, and the army literature provided the specific instances and examples to do that (Branson & Farr 1984).

Second, since the vast majority of soldiers entering the army were high school graduates, it was assumed that the preponderance of instruction would be *remedial;* soldiers would have been taught the material before (Dick 1985).

Third, many of the entering soldiers would not be adept at those skills necessary to be successful students; they would profit from the training (Derry & Murphy 1986).

Fourth, many soldiers would not perform well on the kinds of tests they were accustomed to taking. Accordingly, they would be provided a brief review of subject matter before being given tests (see Gagne, Briggs, & Wager 1988).

Fifth, soldiers' duty assignments would take precedence over education. Accordingly, JSEP must be designed to fit the reality of the army. JSEP designers had to ensure that soldiers could miss days or weeks without getting behind in class or losing important instruction. These design considerations will be discussed more fully in the following sections.

Common Past Experience. One significant problem in many adult education and literacy programs is that students come from so many different backgrounds and cultures that it is difficult to find examples relevant to all of them. Even though entering soldiers come from diverse backgrounds and communities, the army provides basic training as an experience that greatly reduces the diversity. Basic training teaches a vocabulary of army terms; names and functions of numerous tools and pieces of equipment; names and examples of individual and group formations and movements; and shared feelings of fear, excitement, exhaustion, accomplishment, pride, and satisfaction. Soldiers are also required to be proficient in basic soldiering as defined in the *Soldier's Manual of Common Tasks.* During basic training, soldiers perform these common tasks.

From analyses of the basic training tasks, designers identified sources of situations, examples, problems, and requirements that applied to all soldiers. These were used to form the context of instruction in the basic skills necessary to learn more technical jobs. Sticht's (1975) classic studies in functional literacy were based on a context similar to basic training (see also Sticht 1988).

Army Literature. The army publishes substantial amounts of literature to support training and job performance in each MOS. Soldier's manuals provide details of what the soldier is expected to know and be able to do to be proficient in each MOS. Technical manuals describe the maintenance and operation of tools, instruments, and equipment. General periodicals on maintenance and soldiering are sent to all army units. Training extension courses and audiovisual lessons that teach soldiers how to perform tasks have been developed in each MOS. There is also a variety of videotapes, videodiscs, films, and other media that address attitudes, morale, and maintenance and operation of equipment. Again, soldiers are expected to use and learn from this literature and media.

Lesson Design. JSEP designers decided early in the design process that it would be more efficient to permit soldiers to demonstrate proficiency after a short review than to begin with a series of tests. This decision was based, in part, on reports in the literature about test anxiety and on the specifications for events of instruction as elaborated by Gagne and Briggs (1974). Consequently, lessons were divided into (*a*) the Diagnostic Review Lesson category and (*b*) the Skill Development Lesson category. The former contained a brief review of the prerequisite competency, the minimum practice, and a test of the lesson objectives. If soldiers passed the test after the Diagnostic Review Lesson, they were sent to the next lesson. If they did not pass, they were immediately assigned the Skill Development Lesson that contained detailed instruction and practice in the PCs.

Soldiers were permitted to take the Skill Development Lesson twice. If they failed on their second attempt at the lesson, the computer signaled the instructor to provide additional tutoring (Dick 1985).

One design decision, made early, was not to have soldiers begin JSEP with a long series of diagnostic tests. Tests are not welcome parts of soldiers' lives. Because only at-risk soldiers were sent to JSEP, it was believed best to let them start getting instruction before taking any tests—a design decision that has been challenged by third-party evaluators (see Hoffman, Hahn, Hoffman, & Dean 1988).

Lesson Assignment. As was indicated earlier, the common tasks from basic training provide excellent examples for the context of instruction. The lessons based on common tasks make up the core curriculum; they are commonly assigned to all soldiers.

Unfortunately, many MOS have basic skills requirements that are not found in the common tasks. For those MOS, specific lessons were designed to address deficiencies. For example, many mathematics lessons, such as trigonometry, were restricted to only a few MOS. On the average, soldiers would take about 80 percent of their lessons from the common core and the remainder from MOS specific. Being able to assign individual lessons only to those whose jobs required them was a fundamental advantage of this technology-based system.

One problem with implementation in the army was that when MOS lessons were referred to, the impression was created that the lessons were actually teaching job tasks rather than subordinate basic skills. This confusion continued in the civilian demonstration; it will be described later.

When lessons were found to be dependent on prior knowledge, thus forming a learning hierarchy, these lessons were linked to the terminal lesson so that when soldiers did not pass the test at the conclusion of the Diagnostic Review Lesson, they were sent to the prerequisite lessons. True hierarchies were rare, however, and most lesson sequences were assigned mostly by logic. Quite often, instructional designers and untrained teachers confused the *order of job performance* with the concept of a learning hierarchy, which is a true dependency of one intellectual skill on another (see Gagne 1985).

Paper Lessons. Even though it is important to have a CBI system that manages all instruction, some PCs cannot be well taught on the computer. Report writing and form completion are examples. When requirements that could best be met by pencil and paper lessons were discovered, they were designed in that form. Such lessons were assigned and tracked by the student management system.

Learner Strategies. An interpretation of the literature on metacognition (see Baker & Brown 1984; Scales 1988) and the development of learning abilities suggested that soldiers fell into many of the classes of students who could profit from direct instruction on how to manage self-learning (Derry & Kellis 1986; Derry & Murphy 1986). Learner strategies were designed for JSEP in two ways: by direct instruction and by a series of embedded prompts in the lessons to remind soldiers when to use a particular strategy. Reminders were in the form of icons displayed on the lesson screen when soldiers appeared to be having trouble with the content (Derry, Jacobs, & Murphy 1986–87). Learner strategies' modules dealt with self-motivational training, time management, reading comprehension, and problem solving.

Soldier Management System. One of the major design features of JSEP that was presented at the outset was that the entire system should be managed by the computer. The alternative would have been to have multiple copies of more than 300 floppy disks that would require considerable clerical activity to manage and file. Consequently, a soldier management system (SMS) that enrolled soldiers, collected background data, assigned lessons based on the MOS, kept track of the lessons completed, prepared reports on soldiers and other administrative details, and routed soldiers back to their previous stopping point regardless of how long they had been away was designed.

In addition to the automatic and routine functions, the SMS also permitted local instructors to add or delete lessons from an individual soldier's assignments. Further, it was also possible for new lesson assignments to be prepared and entered into the system as army requirements changed. New lessons could be added and obsolete ones deleted. For example, when changes in army jobs occurred, MOSs were added or deleted from the SMS.

Finally, an advantage of SMS for soldiers was that when the soldiers transferred, their JSEP records could be printed out and forwarded to their next duty stations. Their study could then be resumed.

At the outset, it was estimated that the JSEP curriculum would contain about 400 hours of instruction. While it was never intended that any soldier would receive all lessons, it was decided that 400 hours would accommodate the common tasks and the MOS's specific requirements. This was probably the largest CBI basic skills curriculum ever developed and, certainly, the largest developed simultaneously for two computer systems.

JSEP Development

While there were many challenges during the development process, one of the most significant was that of keeping all lessons in the system internally consistent. Many lessons on related topics were under development at the same time. Instructional designers would frequently approach the instruction of a topic in different ways. Even though differences among teachers were tolerated, when two similar lessons on a computer had different slants, soldiers became confused. Thus, keeping lessons within the same form and configuration became a massive coordination and management problem.

Early trials. When a rough approximation to the SMS had been determined and about 10 percent of the lessons completed in a first draft, a field trial of the system was arranged, in the learning center at Fort Rucker, Alabama. Both PLATO and TICCIT systems were field-tested at the same time. As the soldiers progressed through the lessons, designers and instructors paid careful attention to any errors or problems and provided assistance where necessary to the soldiers. It was on the basis of these trial results that major design, development, and scheduling decisions were made (Peterson & Farr 1984).

Even though there were many problems with the individual lessons plus a management system that was quite crude, the trials gave solid evidence that the systems would work and meet the initial design requirements. Soldiers gave excellent feedback about problems they encountered, and subsequent interviews permitted detection of any positive or negative reactions to the total experience. The results were far more positive than expected. Even the students with limited English proficiency did well on the lessons because they were able to take the time to understand the text; they were not at the mercy of an instructor covering the material at a fixed pace.

Development continued for a year. New sites that were planned to be in continuous operation after development were opened. The new sites had either PLATO or TICCIT, but not both. Lesson and system tryouts continued at these sites for about two years until the final versions of both systems were completed.

Each system had the capacity to run two four-hour shifts daily; they were not regularly scheduled to operate in the evenings. A typical soldier's JSEP assignment might include about 120 hours of instruction. At that rate of usage, and with each site having sixteen terminals, about 267 soldiers per year could be given JSEP at each tryout site. Soldiers were not scheduled for more than four hours per day. More detailed descriptions of JSEP design, development, implementation, and evaluations can be found in Branson (1989, In press), Derry and Murphy (1986), Derry et al. (1986–87), Dick (1985), and Hoffman et al. (1988).

**Transferring JSEP
to Civilian Use**

The U.S. Departments of Education, Labor, and Defense decided that JSEP should be considered for use in the civilian job-training, adult education, and vocational education communities. They planned to sponsor a demonstration of selected portions of JSEP at a cooperating civilian tryout site. The RFP necessary to initiate this demonstration was issued in 1987. The contract for the civilian project was awarded to the FSU-Ford team in 1988. Work began in May of that year. The major issues raised and their resolutions are presented in the next sections.

Selecting Occupations. To be convincing, the demonstration had to address the basic skills requirements in several occupations; twenty occupations were chosen. To be selected, an occupation's requirements had to be available in the existing JSEP curriculum, since no new development was planned. In addition, the occupation had to be one in which there were openings and in which growth was expected in the tryout area. It did not make sense to provide instruction for occupations in which there would be no jobs.

The U.S. Department of Labor's *Dictionary of Occupational Titles* was consulted to identify potential jobs. Earlier, the National Occupational Information Coordination Committee (NOICC) prepared a "crosswalk" that matched civilian job titles to military jobs. By going through that process, far more civilian jobs were identified than could be used in the demonstration. It was then necessary to begin a process of deciding the criteria to use for the selection of the final twenty occupations.

Changing to a Civilian Context. Earlier, I described the rather elaborate process that was followed to ensure that the lessons were presented in an appropriate army context. These included special situations, vocabulary, familiar tasks, and specific examples selected from the job and task analyses. There were no similarly detailed task analyses for the civilian occupations. These had to be inferred.

After the original version was developed, the instructional designers developed the lesson format and wrote specifications for the problems and examples to be used. It was the job of the "greeners" (those who searched the army literature for examples and situations) to ensure that the correct army language and artwork was used. To develop the civilian version, a decision on how much "degreening" was necessary to make the lessons acceptable and effective in civilian applications was made.

Some of the lessons were totally inappropriate. For example, civilians rarely need to identify combat aircraft and armored vehicles by their shapes. Some lessons were substantially different. For example, army cooks must use electronic diagnostic instruments to maintain the electric power to their field kitchens; civilian cooks do not. Conversely, a military police officer issues a traffic citation in about the same way a state trooper does. Such lessons required little change.

Much of the artwork used in the screen displays showed equipment that soldiers use daily. This artwork and the language to describe it would be totally unfamiliar to the civilians, and much of it had to be changed. However, changes in the lessons were not made when the army context was intelligible to civilians, even though the examples were from army problems. The army has specific spellings for common words: *gage* vs. *gauge, inclosure* vs. *enclosure,* and many more. These annoying and incorrect usages were changed.

Reading Level. I believe that standard reading grade level and reading level formula are inappropriate for vocational training applications, particularly when this training is technologically based and will become completely obsolete when newer intelligent tutoring systems are marketed. Consider the number of syllables in *howitzer*—a complex word, yet every soldier in the army knows it. Other polysyllabic words known to all soldiers include: *disassemble* and *assemble, tracked vehicle* (tank), *quarter-ton truck* (jeep), *maintenance, radio-teletypewriter, communications channel,* and many more. Every attempt to change these words in the civilian version was made, for example, *disassemble* became *take apart, quarter-ton truck* became *jeep, watercraft* became *boat,* and so on. However, in the final civilian configuration of JSEP, which should include two or three students at each terminal in a collaborative learning mode, reading level should not be a significant problem.

Adding Occupations. Studying the occupational literature to find which occupations required what basic skills was labor intensive and expensive. What was needed was a relatively quick and efficient way to identify which objectives in the JSEP curriculum were actually required in any occupation. So a review of the military research and training products that would be useful to civilian education and training was studied for potential solutions.

The U.S. Air Force has been a leader in occupational analysis research for many years (Christal 1974). One facet of that research has been to develop rating scales that measure attributes of job tasks called task factors. Some of these task factors include: probable consequences of inadequate performance, task learning difficulty, relative time spent, and training emphasis. The latter task factor seemed particularly appropriate for identifying JSEP objectives that should be included in occupational preparatory programs.

Training emphasis refers to the amount of emphasis a particular task should be given in the training program. Senior job incumbents, instructors, and supervisors know which tasks are unimportant. Some are easy to learn, some are highly consequential, and some are performed so infrequently that including them in the training program for everyone would be a waste (Ruck, Thompson, & Thomson 1978; Goldman & Kerner-Hoeg 1984).

Vocational instructors, who were subject matter experts in their own fields, were asked to rate each of the JSEP objectives in each lesson on the developed Training Emphasis Scale. A seven-point scale that ranged from "well above average emphasis" to "average emphasis" to "well below average emphasis" was used. When these data were analyzed, it was then possible to use the results to make lesson assignments in each of the occupations rated. Thus, a lesson prescription for an electronics inspector might include 100 of the 300 JSEP lessons, while the prescription for a floral arranger might contain only sixty of the lessons. One disadvantage to this approach was that it would not identify basic skills requirements not found in the JSEP curriculum.

Tryout Sites. In the early summer of 1989, tryout sites were opened in White Plains, New York, at the White Plains Adult Education Center Rochambeau School and at Meridian Community College in Meridian, Mississippi. The population at White Plains included welfare mothers, ESL students, vocational students, and those eligible to participate in the Job Training Partnership Act.

The Meridian site represented a unique coalition of the college, the office of the governor, and Peavey Electronics (a large electronics firm that makes guitars, amplifiers, speakers, sound mixers, and other products sold throughout the world to the music industry). Peavey had a significant problem recruiting employees who could learn more complex jobs required for the company to stay internationally competitive. Peavey was one of the very few U.S. American firms competing well in the international electronics markets. Therefore, the governor's office was highly interested in keeping the company in the state.

Seeing both of these civilian installations operating successfully with undereducated students provided a sense of great satisfaction to the JSEP development staff who had worked so long to make it all come true. It took about ten years from the inception of the job analysis concept in the army to the civilian implementation. What remains is to see that JSEP is made available to those in need of it.

Conclusion

Through the example provided by the Job Skills Education Program, I have tried to show the developmental sequence and logic that made the program work. In particular, the issues of design and development have been elaborated to show the level of effort required for JSEP's operation.

It will require every bit as much professional effort to implement JSEP successfully on a continuing basis. Note that it is in implementation that most programs gradually fail. The erosion of success in programs is due to many factors, but staff turnover, lack of training, and obtaining agreement are significant factors. I believe that many of these deficiencies, identified from conventional programs, will be reduced or eliminated by technology-based systems.

References

Baker, M., and M. Hamovitch. 1983. *Job-oriented basic skills (JOBS) training program: An evaluation.* NPRDC Tech. Report 83–5, January. San Diego: Navy Personnel Research and Development Center. AD A124 150.

Baker, L., and A. L. Brown. 1984. Metacognitive skills and reading. In P. D. Pearson, ed., *Handbook of reading research,* 357–94. NY: Longman.

Branson, R. K. 1989. Large scale ISD projects: Two case studies. In W. Hannum and C. Hansen, eds., *Instructional systems development in large organizations.* Englewood Cliffs, NJ: Educational Technology Publications.

Branson, R. K. In press. Design, development, and technology transfer in the Job Skills Education Program. In T. Shlechter, ed., *Problems and promises of computer-based training.* Norwood, NJ: Ablex Publishing Company.

Branson, R. K., and B. J. Farr. 1984. The Job Skills Education Program: Issues in design and development. In *Proceedings 26th Annual Conference of the Military Testing Association,* 791–96. Munich. AD BO96 442.

Christal, R. E. 1974. *The United States Air Force Occupational Research Project.* Lackland AFB, TX: Air Force Human Resources Laboratory. AD A774–574.

Derry, S. J., J. J. Jacobs, and D. A. Murphy. 1986–87. The JSEP Learning Skills Training System. *Journal of Educational Technology Systems* 15(4):273–84.

Derry, S. J., and A. Kellis. 1986. A prescriptive analysis of low-ability problem-solving behavior. *Instructional Science* 15:49–65.

Derry, S. J., and D. A. Murphy. 1986. Designing systems that train learning ability: From theory to practice. *Review of Educational Research* 56(1):1–39.

Dick, W. 1985. *The design and development of the U.S. Army computer-based Job Skills Education Program.* Paper presented at a seminar on Multimedia Authoring Systems, London, England.

Gagne, R. R. 1985. *The conditions of learning.* 4th ed. NY: Holt, Rinehart and Winston.

Gagne, R. M., and L. J. Briggs. 1974. *Principles of instructional design.* NY: Holt, Rinehart and Winston.

Gagne, R. M., L. J. Briggs, and W. W. Wager. 1988. *Principles of instructional design. 3d ed. NY: Holt, Rinehart and Winston.*

Goldman L. A., and S. Kerner-Hoeg. 1984. The instructional systems development (ISD) 8 factor model revisited. In *Proceedings 26th Annual Conference of the Military Testing Association,* 397–402. Munich. AD BO96 442.

Hoffman, L. M., C. P. Hahn, D. M. Hoffman, and R. A. Dean. 1988. *Evaluation of the Job Skills Education Program: Part I, learning outcomes.* American Institutes for Research, Washington, DC.

Peterson, G. W., and B. J. Farr. 1984. The Job Skills Education Program: Results from preliminary tryouts. In *Proceedings 26th Annual Conference of the Military Testing Association,* 797–802. Munich. AD BO96 442.

Philippi, J. W. 1988. Matching literacy to job training: Some applications from military programs. *Journal of Reading* 31(7):658–66 (April).

Ruck H. W., N. A. Thompson, and D. C. Thomson. 1978. The collection and prediction of training emphasis ratings for curriculum development. In *Proceedings of the 20th Annual Conference of the Military Testing Association.* Oklahoma City, OK: U.S. Coast Guard.

Scales, A. M. 1988. Using a metacognitive-schema approach to teach college reading and study skills. In T. J. Betenbough and S. A. Biggs, eds., *Innovative learning strategies,* 73–91. College Reading Improvement, International Reading Association.

Sticht, T. G. 1975. *A program of army functional job reading training: Development, implementation, and delivery systems.* HumRRO Tech. Report. Alexandria, VA: Human Resources Research Association. AD A012 272.

Sticht, T. G. 1988. Adult literacy education. In E. Rothkopf, ed., *Review of research in education* 15. Washington, DC: American Educational Research Association.

Bilingual Education for Adult Learners

Vincenne Revilla Beltran and Susana M. Sotillo

As the twenty-first century approaches, bilingual education for adult learners has renewed significance in the U.S. for political, social, educational, and economical reasons. Since the mid-1980s demographers have predicted the changing population picture of the U.S. (Hodgkinson 1985; Statistical Abstract of the United States 1985). These predictions have included (*a*) an increasing older population and (*b*) a population comprised of greater percentages of Hispanic Americans, African Americans, Asian Americans, and recent immigrants who are, or will be, needing access to a variety of educational opportunities.

Over the last several decades, college educators have been witnessing what they perceive to be the decline of basic English, mathematics, and reading skills of their entering freshman classes. There has been a gap between teachers' expectations and student performance and display of knowledge. In an effort to deal with this situation, special developmental and remedial programs have surfaced at colleges and universities across the nation, including some of the most prestigious institutions of higher learning. In addition, both profit and nonprofit community-based programs have been serving ever-increasing numbers of individuals seeking to enhance their basic skills. The need for remediation has been primarily in the areas of English, reading, and mathematics.

For years, basic literacy skills have been viewed by professional educators as the cornerstone of academic skills needed by an individual in order to survive, compete, and advance in a technologically based information society. Moreover, since members of underrepresented populations are often ignored in mainstream society, the importance of literacy skills cannot be overemphasized.

Addressing the educational needs of an ethnically and racially diverse adult population will be costly and challenging. It will require an accepted national agenda specifically designed for this purpose and a formal commitment that involves political, educational, and social infrastructures.

Because of the importance of bilingual education (i.e., instruction in first language until English is learned, plus the development of reading, writing, and math skills) for adult learners, our intent is to present an examination of contemporary issues related to this topic. The interested reader is provided with a brief historical overview of bilingual education with special emphasis on political and contemporary issues. Also, we have presented a discussion of the unique characteristics and needs of bilingual learners along with qualifications for instructors. Future issues and recommendations conclude the discussion and serve to offer suggestions for consideration when addressing the needs of the twenty-first century adult bilingual learner in the U.S.

In the eighteenth century, bilingual education in the German language was widespread in the U.S. Benjamin Franklin (inventor, writer, and prominent statesman) was adamantly opposed to the use of German in the Pennsylvania school system. He vigorously campaigned against the use of languages other than English for purposes of education. His thinking reflected many of the biases commonly held by educators and social scientists today.

With the onset of World War I, public sentiment in the U.S. turned against instruction in the German language. Individuals were jailed or fired if they refused to comply with the antibilingual education laws passed. Bilingual education through German was eventually abandoned. The same legal battles concerning the use of languages other than English in the education of children and adults that were fought during the first two decades of the twentieth century (Myers vs. Nebraska as cited in Castellanos 1983) must continue to be fought into the twenty-first century.

Interest in multilingual instruction was revived during World War II. The intelligence agencies needed qualified multilingual individuals who could gather vital information for strategic purposes. This period of world history saw the development of prestigious institutes of foreign language training throughout the U.S. (Castellanos 1983). But it was not until the late 1960s that bilingual education, as it is known today, became a widespread educational practice in Florida, California, and other states with large Spanish-speaking populations (Ravitch 1983). With the large influx of immigrants and refugees from countries in Southeast Asia and Eastern Europe, Ethiopia, Afghanistan, and various other countries in the early 1970s and mid-1980s, the efficacy and cost-effectiveness of bilingual education came into question. English-as-a-second language (ESL) (teaching American English to non-English speakers) programs were gradually developed and expanded and have largely displaced previous bilingual education programs (Baker & deKanter 1981).

Political versus Educational Issues. Bilingualism is a concept that evokes mixed reactions in the U.S. In general, academicians tend to consider it a valuable resource, to be cherished and developed (Grosjean 1982). In contrast to this view, many primary and secondary school educators and administrators, as well as those in college settings, regard bilingualism as being synonymous with lack of education, cognitive deficiencies, and low socioeconomic status. As Haugen (1979) has stated, if we look around at

> the countries where bilingualism has risen to the status of a national problem—say Belgium, Canada, Finland, Ireland, Wales, Yugoslavia—it has usually been due to the refusal of a dominated social group to submit to the imposition of the language of a social group. (p. 73)

He goes on to emphasize that the power relationships of victor over vanquished, of native over immigrant, of upper class over lower class have bred bilingualism as it is commonly understood. The fact that it is a label unilaterally imposed by a dominant group is a major source of pejorative connotations where these exist (see also Bernbaum 1979).

Historical Background

The current mood in the U.S. with respect to bilingualism and bilingual education is clearly reflected in the xenophobic pursuit by U.S. English, a Washington-based organization, for a constitutional amendment to enshrine English as the sole official language of the U.S. This movement was once spearheaded by S. I. Hayakawa, the septuagenarian former senator from California. The results of the San Francisco, California November 1983 elections, where Proposition O (a nonbinding referendum opposing the practice of printing city ballots in Spanish and Chinese, as well as English) passed by two to one, provided encouragement for what is now known as Hayakawa's backlash.

Newspaper reports and editorials carried the message of U.S. English to the English-speaking U.S. public, warning them that bilingual education was an insidious separatist movement gaining in strength at a time when the U.S. was receiving the largest wave of immigration in its history. This backlash quickly spread to Florida, Arizona, Kentucky, Pennsylvania, Nebraska, Indiana, Illinois, Virginia, and many other states. In Florida, a group called Florida English, led by the former republican state representative Robert Melby of St. Petersburg, successfully collected petitions to place an amendment in the 1986 Florida ballot to make English the state's official language. As of this writing, a total of thirteen states have designated English as the only official language.

Other well-financed organizations, such as the American Federation of Teachers and the National Association of State Boards of Education, openly declared their opposition to bilingual education by rejecting the 1980 proposed rules for compliance with the Lau remedies (transitional bilingual programs) (White 1984). What is perhaps most distressing about these organizations and movements claiming to protect the English language and the public good is that they have succeeded in disseminating and perpetuating linguistic, educational, and historical myths. Examples of such myths, propagated by U.S. English, are the claims that societal bilingualism will eventually lead to ethnic separatism and that the use of languages other than English will undermine the purity and unity of the English language in the U.S.

Hayakawa's claims that the English we share is at the core of our identity as citizens and that it is our ticket to full participation in American political life (*Newsweek* 1984) insinuate the beginnings of a revival of historical romanticism as exemplified in the philosophical writings of Herder and von Humboldt. Herder's conception of language as the tool, the content, and the form of human thoughts led him to the conclusion that an examination of the different languages of the world would reveal the ways of thinking and speaking of every nation (cited in Cassirer 1950). Thus, language for Herder was a reflection of a national mentality. But it was von Humboldt who went further in espousing his theories on languages when he proclaimed:

> language reacts more obviously and more intensively upon individuality, and the concept of a nation must be based especially upon language. Since the development of man's human nature depends upon the nature of language, the concept of the nation as a host of people constructing a language in a definite manner is directly manifest through language. (von Humboldt 1971, 131)

It is unfortunate that the prevailing theories of the nineteenth and eighteenth centuries were used in the 1980s to suppress the concept of diversity and multilingualism. The current emphasis on the unity and purity of the English language as reflections of a nation's moral and political strength represents a serious distortion of the nationalism and romanticism of Herderian thought. The central thesis of Herder's philosophy of history and politics rested on the realization that the principle of plurality and diversity that he so strongly advocated implied the recognition and acceptance of inherent tensions and conflicts. Such was the price of diversity for Herder (see Barnard 1969).

Overall, it seems as if the philosophical speculations and pronouncements on the subject of cultural diversity and plurality of languages as reflected in the media (newspapers, magazines, television) betray a profound ignorance of historical and philosophical facts.

Contemporary Focus Adult Programs. Bilingual adult education programs in the U.S. are primarily found in immigrant and refugee community agencies and organizations. They are often funded through state and city grants. These programs serve culturally and linguistically diverse individuals, who are primarily interested in entering training programs or attending the two-year community colleges. These adults seek assistance in improving their productive and receptive skills in English and in acquiring training in specific fields. Many of them aspire to graduate from college or two-year vocational-technical programs. Unfortunately, their aspirations are not matched by the linguistic and computational skills that they possess. A large percentage of the adults served by bilingual educational programs have limited functional literacy skills in the first language (see Cummins 1981 for a review of primary language development and cognitive skills). This becomes a problem in terms of developing appropriate instructional activities and educational frameworks that would help these students learn English and specific computational skills that are prerequisites for successful vocational or two-year college-level work.

Among the adult educational programs serving large numbers of Spanish-speaking individuals in the state of Pennsylvania are the Lighthouse, Congreso de Latinos Unidos, and Taller Puertorriqueño. These three organizations are located in a large urban center (Philadelphia), with citywide resources at their disposal. Their approach to teaching skills for adults is primarily through the use of Spanish—the adults' first language. At the Lighthouse, teaching social sciences, mathematics, and natural sciences is conducted in Spanish. English is taught by qualified ESL instructors. Students, who attend, study to pass the General Educational Development (GED) examination. Most plan to pursue postsecondary education at either a local community college or in a technical institute.

What makes these programs unique is that there is a commitment on the part of the instructors and administrators to enhancing the individual's Spanish literacy skills while at the same time allowing the student to develop and master reading, writing, and listening comprehension skills in English. A coordinated effort is made in order to incorporate the students' linguistic resources into the teaching/learning process. At Taller Puertorriqueño, the emphasis has been primarily on developing artistic and literary skills among young Puerto Ricans. Their main goal is to keep Puerto Rican culture alive and disseminate their numerous artistic and literary accomplishments throughout the English-speaking Philadelphia community. Congreso de Latinos Unidos has also been instrumental in actively encouraging young people to further their education by providing a variety of bilingual services and educational opportunities through their GED and Spanish literacy programs.

These approaches to bilingual education for adult learners are duplicated in numerous urban areas in Pennsylvania, the areas include Harrisburg, Lancaster, and Bethlehem. Similar approaches to the education of adults are being used by Polish, Vietnamese, Cambodian, and Chinese community agencies and organizations. Their approaches to, and support of, bilingual instruction varies. In most of these linguistic communities, emphasis is placed on learning English as a second language. There are, however, classes being taught in Vietnamese, Chinese, and Cambodian to youngsters who have not had formal exposure to those languages.

A limited number of educational agencies use a bilingual approach as a means of encouraging non-English-speaking youth to pursue postsecondary or vocational education. Very few colleges or universities provide bilingual education to their students. One of the few exceptions was the Community College of Philadelphia, where psychology, sociology, and basic math were generally taught in Spanish. With the large influx of Southeast Asian refugees and multilingual immigrant groups, most classes, such as biology, taught in Spanish or in a bilingual mode were eventually phased out. A drastic decline in the enrollment of Spanish-speaking students undermined the support for bilingual education. Instructors advocating ESL instruction as the only alternative became instrumental in changing faculty and administrative perceptions of bilingual education. With the increasing visibility of the English-only movement as it spread across the nation, some board members proposed changes to the college's policy of allowing sociology, psychology, and mathematics to be taught in Spanish. This issue divided board members and, as of this writing, has not been resolved. Intolerance to bilingual education has replaced a once enlightened attitude toward multiple approaches to the education of culturally and linguistically different individuals. In the meantime, enrollment of Spanish-speaking students in postsecondary institutions (Duran 1983) continues to decline.

Although many colleges and universities claim to have bilingual education programs for those in need of linguistic assistance, a close examination of their educational services would often reveal that these are primarily ESL programs. It takes commitment, professional training, institutional support, and funding to develop and implement viable bilingual education programs for adults. History has shown that educational institutions are resistant to change. It is very difficult to change faculty and staff perceptions of the value of bilingual or multilingual education. Since this is the reality in most educational environments, bilingual adult education remains in the planning stages. There are many philosophical and bureaucratic obstacles that must be overcome in order to develop national guidelines and policy regarding adult bilingual education.

Characteristics and Needs. To today's professional educator, it is evident that different assumptions and processes are employed when teaching adults than when teaching children. This notion becomes even more apparent when an educator is faced with the challenge of teaching an adult population that has very specialized characteristics, such as differences in language, culture, and customs. In such an instance, it is critical that the instructor design effective learning and teaching strategies to address specific characteristics and needs of adult learners. This basic premise is one of the keystones of adult learning theory. Briefly stated, contemporary adult learning theory takes into account the mature characteristics of the adult learner, most important of which is that of being self-directed.

Bilingual Learners and Instructors

May it suffice to say that pedagogy is the theoretical framework and practice of teaching children where the learning process is primarily teacher directed. On the other hand, andragogy is defined as the art of helping adults learn and is primarily self-directed in nature. These two theoretical models represent two ends of a continuum whereby effective strategies may be selected according to their appropriateness for given learners and situations.

Knowles (1975) discusses the assumptions underlying pedagogy and andragogy regarding the learner, role of the learner's experience, readiness to learn, orientation to learning, and motivation. The differences in the assumptions are striking as one reviews the variables between the two theories. For the purposes of the adult educator, one can easily see how important these assumptions can be in planning a course of study for adult learners. The andragogical approach assumes the adult learner is self-directing, can serve as a resource, and is internally motivated compared to young learners who are teacher dependent and motivated by external factors. Further, Knowles presents the process elements of pedagogy and andragogy. Of particular importance to the adult educator, the process elements illustrate basic classroom components, including climate, planning, diagnosis of needs, setting objectives, learning designs, activities, and evaluation procedures. However, a universal incorporation of all process elements is not necessarily advocated nor appropriate for all circumstances. More suitable is an incorporation of process elements that are specifically designed for the characteristics of a particular group of adult learners based on their needs, experience, abilities, etc.

A synthesis of the literature focuses on characteristics of adult learners, motivation, curriculum design, classroom environment, and evaluation methods. In recent years there has been an increase in the number of books and articles that have addressed adult learning theory, and because the field is continuing to grow, this trend will most likely continue. Nevertheless, the field of adult education is still in its early stages of development and more research is needed to adequately meet the needs of its increasing number of practicing professionals in various settings. Likewise, the number and variety of adult learners further necessitate additional research, particularly in the area of bilingual education (Language Policy Task Force 1982). New professionals, as well as those who are established, are cautioned not to overly simplify their view of a specific group of adult learners, particularly the bilingual population; operating under assumptions that may be grounded in stereotypes tends to leave one with blind spots about adult learners, particularly those from underrepresented groups or those who are disadvantaged and who have been historically neglected by educational systems.

Ovando and Collier (1985) discuss the notion of *discovering the student*. For an instructor, the importance of taking time to know and understand one's students cannot be overemphasized. When adult students enter the classroom environment, they enter with a whole history of personal and cultural experiences, values, and predispositions. To ignore these unique aspects about one's students is to ignore their importance in contributing to the learning process. When instructors understand their students, they are more likely to better address the needs of those students.

In an initial assessment of adult bilingual learners, an instructor may wish to examine such variables as how and under what circumstances did the individual come into the country; do they have a family or community support system that helps encourage their education and use of the new language; are they employed; have they had prior language instruction experience (where, when, level); what future short-term and long-term goals do they have. An initial assessment can prove profitable in the long run for an instructor in the development of course objectives, instructional strategies, evaluation techniques, etc. (see Clarke 1981; Dave 1984).

Instructors. In order to maximize effectiveness, instructors of adult bilingual learners must be prepared to deal with the complex variables present in the learning environment. This preparation should include formal and informal training and an openness to language and cultural diversity. Often the instructor is charting new classroom territory and must be prepared to access a variety of resources during the process.

Suggested teacher preparation may include such areas as

1. Formal academic preparation that includes theoretical and applied linguistics as well as knowledge of, and competence in, a second language.
2. Field experience in teaching non-English-speaking adults with limited or nonexistent formal schooling through community organizations or agencies.
3. Opportunities for internships, placements, and/or student teaching at both the graduate and undergraduate levels.
4. Forming language policy and education task forces at the state level in order to develop guidelines for implementing and monitoring adult bilingual education programs.

5. Continued personal and career development through specialized seminars, workshops, regional and national conferences, and in-service training.
6. Contact with professionals from an involvement with educational institutions and community agencies that provide services to adult bilingual learners or related populations.
7. Participation in the professional development of the discipline by presenting papers at conferences, serving on boards and task forces, writing articles for refereed journals, etc.
8. Networking with professional colleagues in adult and bilingual education.

In addition, instructors of adult bilingual learners must have an openness in frame of reference to meeting students' needs in a variety of ways that will translate into effective learning. This openness extends to such areas as the following:

1. The understanding and appropriate application of adult learning theory, specifically assumptions and process elements as presented by Knowles (1984).
2. A sincere appreciation and understanding of cultural diversity in the broadest sense, which includes the aspects of values, customs, and socioeconomic factors relevant to one's students (refer to Hymes 1974).
3. A willingness to live and teach in a bilingual or immigrant community where English is not the primary language of communication.
4. An understanding of teaching as empowering individuals to deal with the U.S. educational and societal systems (see Giroux 1981).
5. A broad-based preparation in bilingual education that includes theory as well as the social and political dynamics present in establishing, funding, and maintaining such programs.
6. A strong commitment to the pursuit of quality and effectiveness in bilingual education programming.

Fanselow and Light (1977, 46–51) present Guidelines for the Preparation and Certification of Teachers of Bilingual/Bicultural Education. These guidelines detail personal qualities as well as training in language proficiency, linguistics, culture, instructional methods, curriculum utilization and adaptation, assessment (general, language, content, and self), school-community relations, and supervised teaching. These professional guidelines are detailed and provide a comprehensive base for teacher preparation.

A compilation by Zemke and Zemke (1981) lists thirty items derived from a review of the literature regarding adult learning. Their categories cover motivation, curriculum design, and maximization of classroom experience. Their review serves to provide a general overview of key issues important for the professional educator who teaches adults.

Recommendations

In concluding this overview of adult bilingual education, the following recommendations are offered as pertinent points for consideration in regard to implementing such programming.

1. This form of literacy instruction (i.e., using a bilingual approach), if offered to adults of limited English proficiency who also possess limited formal schooling, should be provided through a community center, using the various community agencies and resources, such as bilingual job counselors, to provide students intensive and comprehensive support services. Counselors at a local college or university cannot do an adequate job because of their limited or nonexistent links with community agencies and neighborhood cultures.

2. Ethnographic studies should be carried out prior to the implementation of any so-called literacy projects (Hymes 1974). The real importance of ethnographic fieldwork, especially with respect to bilingual education, lies in the fact that it facilitates the process of language planning, program design, and policy formulation.

3. With respect to the teaching of ESL, the provision of second-language (L^2) input may be facilitated by encouraging (a) neighborhood activities and real interaction between English-speaking participants (regardless of language variety) and non-English-speaking participants; (b) outings with English-speaking neighbors; (c) visits to the neighborhood library where ESL workshops could be organized so as to encourage community participation and exposure to the printed media in English.

4. English for specific purposes should be spoken at community sites. Adults need to develop communicative skills and enhance their work-related vocabulary. Exposure to the printed media and to comprehensible input in the L^2 is vital in terms of increasing their employability. (See Krashen 1981 for an overview of comprehensible input and second-language acquisition.)

5. Job training for specific purposes should have an integrated ESL component that incorporates the skills and prior experiences of individual participants.

6. Individuals who wish to pursue postsecondary education should be encouraged to attend a local college after specific reading, writing, and study skills have been mastered at the community learning centers. Furthering their educational goals should be a realistic expectation following a period of intensive preparation in a supportive environment (Sotillo 1985).

References

Baker, K., and A. deKanter. 1981. *Effectiveness of bilingual education: A review of the literature.* Washington, DC: Department of Education, Office of Planning, Budget and Evaluation, 25 September.

Barnard, F. M. 1969. *Herder on social and political culture.* NY: Cambridge University Press.

Bernbaum, G. 1979. *Bilingualism in society.* Cambridge, Massachusetts: National Assessment and Dissemination Center for Bilingual/Bicultural Education.

Cassirer, E. 1950. *The problem of knowledge: Philosophy, science, and history since Hegel.* Translated by W. H. Woglom, M.D., and C. W. Hendel. New Haven: Yale University Press.

Castellanos, D. 1983. *The best of two worlds: Bilingual bicultural education in the U.S.* Trenton, NJ: New Jersey Department of Education. CN 500.

Clarke, M. A. 1981. Reading in Spanish and English: Evidence from adult ESL students. In S. Hudleson, ed., *Learning to read in different languages.* Linguistics and Literacy, Series I. Washington, DC: Center for Applied Linguistics.

Cummins, J. 1981. The role of primary language development in promoting educational success for language minority students. *Schooling and language minority students: A theoretical framework.* Los Angeles, CA: Evaluation, Dissemination and Assessment Center, California State University.

Dave, L. 1984. A theoretical framework for the study of the effects of bilingualism on mathematics teaching and learning. *Fifth International Congress on Mathematical Education,* Adelaide, Australia.

Duran, R. P. 1983. *Hispanics' education and background: Predictors of college achievement.* NY: College Entrance Examination Board.

Fanselow, J. F., and R. L. Light, eds. 1977. *Bilingual, E.S.O.L. and foreign language teacher preparation.* Washington, DC: Teachers of English to Speakers of Other Languages.

Giroux, H. 1981. *Ideology, culture and the process of schooling.* Philadelphia, PA: Temple University Press.

Grosjean, F. 1982. *Life with two languages.* Cambridge, MA: Harvard University Press.

Haugen, E. 1979. The stigma of bilingualism. In J. B. Pride, ed., *Sociolinguistic aspects of language learning and teaching.* Oxford, England: Oxford University Press.

Hodgkinson, H. L. 1985. Demographics and the economy: Understanding a changing marketplace. *The Admissions Strategist,* no. 3, Special issue on adult recruitment, 1–6.

Hymes, D. 1974. *Foundations in sociolinguistics.* Philadelphia, PA: University of Pennsylvania Press.

Knowles, M. S. 1975. *Self-directed learning: A guide for learners and teachers.* NJ: Prentice-Hall.

Knowles, M., and Associates. 1984. *Andragogy in action.* San Francisco: Jossey-Bass.

Krashen, S. D. 1981. *Second language acquisition and second language learning.* Oxford, England: Pergamon Press.

Language Policy Task Force. 1982. *Intergenerational perspectives on bilingualism: From community to classroom.* Center for Puerto Rican Studies. NY: Hunter College.

Newsweek. 1984. English spoken here, please. J. Alter with L. Howard in Washington; R. Sandza in San Francisco; L. R. Prout in Miami, and Bureau Reports, 2 January, 24–25.

Ovando, J. O. and V. P. Collier. 1985. *Bilingual and ESL classrooms.* NY: McGraw-Hill.

Ravitch, D. 1983. *The troubled crusade: American education, 1945–1980.* NY: Basic Books, Inc.

Sotillo, S. 1985. Bilingual instruction in a college setting: Serving adult second language learners who possess limited formal schooling. *Hispanic Leadership Fellows.* Project report. New Jersey Department of Education.

Statistical Abstract of the United States. 1985. U.S. Department of Commerce, Bureau of the Census, 105th edition.

von Humboldt, W. 1971. *Linguistic variability and intellectual development.* Translated by G. C. Buck and F. A. Raven. Philadelphia, PA: University of Pennsylvania Press.

White, E. 1984. Law and policy in the Lau Era: The emerging politics of language. *Education Week,* 8 February, 15–17.

Zemke, R., and S. Zemke. 1981. 30 things we know for sure about adult learning. *Training/H.R.D.* 18(6):45–52.

Community-Based Programs for Adults

James C. Hall, Jr.

Adult Literacy; English as a Second Language; High School Equivalency; Basic Skills; Education Counseling and Tutorial Services for In-School and Out-of-School Youth; Survival Skills for Older Adults; Career Training for Young Adults; Career Counseling; Adolescent Vocational Exploration; Parenting for Single Mothers; Community Leadership; Technical Assistance to Women and Minority Small Business Owners; Citizenship Education; Consumerism; Cultural, Educational, Recreational Facility and Program Management; Health; Drugs; and AIDS Education—these activities are but a partial list of the expanding spectrum of community-based programs that are increasingly being operated by a number of urban higher education institutions. The response of these institutions to their surrounding communities most often operated through their Divisions of Adult and Continuing Education is a complex, fascinating, and potentially, extremely beneficial educational phenomenon that deserves careful examination, understanding, and enthusiastic support.

In this chapter my purpose will be to explore various aspects of these urban adult and continuing education programs. Moreover, I will present why and how urban institutions might become involved in community-based programs and provide a brief description of several community-based programs, followed by a discussion of the procedures and outcomes of each program.

At this point, it is vital to recognize that, traditionally, the phrase community-based programs has referred only to programs operated by community organizations and not to those operated by educational institutions, agencies, government, etc. However, in this chapter, the concept of community based will be expanded to focus more on outcome and process, than on a limited definition restricted to one type of program sponsor or operator.

Community Based: Why Become Involved?

The increased involvement of urban higher education institutions in community-based programs is a fact and is considered, by most, to be a good thing for all involved. The reasons why higher education institutions have become involved, however, are numerous and vary from institution to institution. To understand some of these reasons is important and may help clarify and delineate the value and benefits of such programs for urban higher education institutions. Further, such understanding can supply a sound rationale for community-based programs at a particular institution and point out strategies for gaining support for such activities.

Institutions across the U.S. have become involved in community-based programs for reason related to institutional survival, social responsibility, political survival, public relations, and community enhancement.

The rationale for being involved in community-based programs is comprehensive. The concept of community based encompasses all aspects of survival in today's urban world. It is an exciting, though obviously challenging, new mission for an urban college or university. And while it may threaten the conservative, the staid, the traditional, and the elite, community-based involvement presents a window of opportunity to a more dynamic, relevant role and relationship for all involved. Further, the evidence is clear that community-based involvement is no longer a choice. Rather it is more and more becoming a necessity for colleges who wish to survive in an urban environment.

College or University Involvement

If a college or university is to be successful and act as a *means* for achieving program success, it must be willing to broker and facilitate services. This means that colleges must accept a number of roles and different relationships with cooperating community entities. The college may be the primary provider of the service, work in partnership, be a subcontractor, act as an advisor, act as a monitor, be a pass-through, or be one among many resources to a program.

The key to exercising its role effectively is that the urban institution must be humble, open, and secure enough to dignify others with trust and respect. The college must see its partners as equals. The power of being the deliverer of the educational service, usually a jealously guarded prerogative of higher education institutions, must be generously shared and, in some instances, even given up for community-based programs to be truly successful.

Programs

Herein I have presented examples of five selected community-based programs, followed by a discussion of the concerns, critical decisions, and outcomes. The examples are of actual programs that have been implemented by a U.S.-based urban institution of higher education that is deeply involved with the community in which it is located. The programs were selected because they clearly illustrate what can be achieved in each of the basic service areas—instruction, training, technical assistance, counseling, and assessment/referral. Some of the benefits as well as the liabilities involved in implementing these programs will also be discussed. It should be noted that while adult literacy education is one of the highly visible programs being focused upon currently in higher education, it is but one of many important community-based programs that are being undertaken by Divisions of Adult and Continuing Education.

The State Legalization Impact Assistance Program

This program offers English-as-a-second-language and citizenship classes to individuals wishing to become permanent residents under the provisions of the new federal Immigration Reform and Control Act. The funding for the program is provided by the federal government. At the state level, it is administered jointly by the State Department of Social Service and the State Education Department. The initial grant received by this particular institution provided for sixty hours of instruction for 420 participants who were placed in twenty-four classes. Numerous community groups were involved in the recruitment of participants. Several classes were provided at an off-site location in a community-based organization.

Discussion. The changing demographics of the college's local community were such that there were increasing numbers of foreign-born residents who were coming to the college for a variety of services that would directly help them survive in the U.S., improve their employability, resolve specific immigration problems, and enhance the quality of their lives. While these varied groups of people from over two dozen different countries were not a political force, in the traditional sense, there were many influential individuals in the community who were sympathetic to their needs. Haitians, Caribbeans, Central and South Americans, Asians, individuals from Africa and Europe were all part of the constituency that had regularly come forward over the years to participate in the college's Adult and Continuing Education programs. Now, many others came forward as a result of the new legalization program. Classes filled rapidly and a waiting list developed. There was no need for a formal recruitment drive as individuals learned about the program by word of mouth. Through the college's Community Learning Center programs, a relationship of trust had been developed with community residents, who now used their networks to inform people about this opportunity. Within months of the program's beginning, classes were successfully graduated, bus trips to Washington, D.C. were undertaken, and a vast number of community residents were becoming new, avid supporters of the college and enthusiastic members of the community. All involved in the program have deemed it a huge success.

- The state funders and the university's central coordinating office were pleased for the program had met all of its goals and used funds appropriately. Such a situation has direct implications for the college's future relative to receiving further support for this and other programs.

- Community groups were pleased. The program provided a vital and real opportunity for diverse segments of the community that were traditionally isolated from each other to work and learn together and to develop a spirit of mutual cooperation, respect, and enthusiasm for learning. Such attitudes could only benefit all involved.

- The college perceived the program's value. It provided opportunities for the college to reach out and work with new community-based ethnic, religious, and cultural groups. These groups, in turn, saw the opportunity to work with a college as a way to enhance their image with their constituencies. They were appreciative of the chance to work together and have become active supporters of the institution.

- Local political officials readily confirmed their deep belief in, and support of, the program citing their confidence in the college and the appropriateness of its involvement in such programs. Such support will be a valuable asset in the future.

• Finally, the participants were pleased. They had learned what they needed to know and had achieved the necessary documentation to move to the next step in the process of becoming legalized U.S. citizens.

It is clear that careful planning and effective implementation reaped a host of benefits for all involved that far outweighed any difficulties the college experienced in mounting this community-based program. Though it risked the liability of building a demand for services that might have rapidly exceeded its ability to respond, this potential problem was readily perceived by the college, and plans were made immediately to mount additional services should the need arise.

This program, conducted in partnership with a major airline industry-sponsored community-based organization, was designed to train one hundred youth in the fields of clerk/typing and bank telling. The college was a subcontractor in this program and provided occupational training and basic skills instruction. The community-based organization recruited participants, provided counseling services, and handled job placement. Almost on a daily basis, the program was funded and monitored by its city's Department of Employment.

Job Training Partnership Act (JTPA) 78 Percent Youth Employment Training Program

Discussion. The community in which the college was located was severely impacted by a high rate of high school dropouts and youth unemployment. Community-based organizations and ethnic, cultural, religious, and business groups, along with government and municipal agencies, shared deep concern about how to mount education and training programs that could successfully address the needs of at-risk youth. Crime, drugs, and other related problems plagued the community. Everyone was interested in doing something, but what to do and how to do it were another matter.

A job-training program for out-of-school youth was finally funded in the community by a municipal agency. The program was heavily regulated, with almost all aspects of the program including recruitment, instructional curricula, counseling, and placement outcomes mandated and specified by the funding source. Almost immediately problems developed, as subtle and not so subtle conflicts arose among the various groups cooperating to mount the program. For example, the local community-based organization, whose responsibility it was to place students in jobs, saw placement as the program's main objective. This often meant pulling individuals out of the training program prematurely if a job opportunity arose. The college, which provided the training and basic education, felt this short-circuited their efforts and reduced the students' chances for long-term employment success. Unfortunately, the college was a subcontractor in the program and had to adhere to the contractor's wishes. The situation culminated in the funder citing the college for failing to retain students in training. Needless to say, this increased the tension between the college and the community-based organization.

Other pressures also contributed to the tension. The community-based organization was under pressure from its backers, the airlines, many of whom did not feel that youth-training programs were their highest priority. Faculty and staff of the college, outside the Division for Adult/Continuing Education, felt the institution's image was being seriously damaged by serving what was generally considered a hard-core, less-desirable, underrepresented youth population. There were conflicts between the staffs of the community-based organization and the college. There were problems of schedules, priorities, variance of pay patterns for staff, and distribution of funds. Clearly, this program was complicated, to say the least, and impacted by a host of controllable and uncontrollable variables.

A major point illustrated by this experience is that while all agreed generally about the overall goal and value of the program, there was not enough preparation, analysis, and planning before moving forward with the program to ensure maximum success. Despite its difficulties, the program achieved modest success as evidenced by its repeated funding over a number of years. The program did have some tangible benefits:

- A modest training/job placement program was established in the community. This program became a viable alternative to local proprietary schools that had the reputation of being dishonest with the underrepresented youth of the community.
- Many local youth were successfully trained and placed in employment.
- Through perseverance, some influence was successfully exerted on the funders that resulted in constructive modification of their rigid guidelines and procedures.
- A number of local adults were hired in professional positions in the program. Several became permanent members of the college's Community Learning Center staff.
- Relationships among the parties involved were worked through and a degree of trust was increased.
- Through proximity and contact, the antiprogram forces within the college diminished their fears about, and objections to, working with hard-core youth.
- Significant monies and resources were brought into the community.

Clearly there were benefits, but also some problems. The liability of frustration, confusion, and resentment was a real problem. There remains some ill feeling and resentment among some of the individuals who worked in the program. What was learned, what was gained, and what was established, however, through this joint effort has value far beyond the negatives experienced. Particularly for the college, the program helped it become significantly more sophisticated about, and skilled in knowing, what it can and cannot do; how to work with community agencies more effectively; and how to better plan to ensure success.

The college's Small Business Development Center (SBDC), cosponsored by the state and the U.S. Small Business Administration is administered through the state university system and provides technical assistance to start-up and existing small businesses. The SBDC specializes in providing direct one-to-one counseling on small-business problems and offers training and instructional programs targeted to the needs and interests of small-business persons. As part of this structure, the program has an advisory board comprised of individuals that represent private and public organizations concerned with the business, economic growth, and development of the local community. The start-up funds for the center came from a combination of sources including the U.S. Small Business Administration, the state, the college, and the local city/county government.

Discussion. The local chamber of commerce; the local Community Development Corporation; the local Community Planning Board; several independent, ethnic minority organizations; local banks; local and citywide offices of economic development; an academic department of the college; a state-funded Regional Education Center; statewide offices of Economic Development; federal programs of the Small Business Administration; the state Department of Labor; individual local community businessmen; local politicians; several militant ethnic groups; student clubs; a congressman; and others too numerous to mention—all were interested in getting more technical assistance to the local business person. In mapping the community, it became clear that the confusion, conflict, redundancy, and competition among all those working in the name of economic development was mammoth. The single neutral force in the whole picture appeared to be the local college, which with its prestige and apolitical nature, was well positioned to provide the needed assistance. Here was a perfect opportunity for the college to bring order to an area of vast disorder through successful involvement in a community-based program.

A Small Business Development Center was established and quickly became the coordinating body for all the entities concerned with local economic development. A communitywide board/committee that met periodically was established with broad representation. Agreement was reached as to who did what, who received what funds, who referred whom to whom, how cooperation was to be achieved. In no time it was evident that this community-based effort was a success and would have a positive impact not only on the small businesses in the community, but also on the constituencies concerned with local economic development.

There were many benefits to all concerned:

- Dozens of local individuals received help in completing business plans, securing loans, obtaining bonding, securing contacts, controlling inventory, and developing marketing and personnel management skills.

- More productive relationships were developed that allowed the numerous entities in this area to work together more effectively.

Small Business Development Center (A Technical Assistance Program)

- Major sources of funding support were convinced of the value of investing additional resources in the local community.

- The image and credibility of all involved rose significantly.

- New opportunities developed for college business majors, co-op students, and college faculty to become meaningfully involved in "real-world" activities closely akin to the related academic curriculum being offered.

- A new spectrum of adult/continuing education courses and activities were developed to support the center's activities that enhanced the overall education services provided by the college.

- A specific community problem was solved that involved an uncontrolled, underground van transportation system that was raising havoc with the local community. The center helped establish this van system as a workable, alternative, supplementary transportation system that became recognized by the authorities, was properly regulated, and was made compatible with the municipal transit authority.

This community-based effort, while tremendously successful, did have one major liability for the college, which only through careful vigilance was prevented from materializing into a full-blown disaster. Due to the history of conflict about the vans among businesses, community residents, politicians, transportation unions, police, and regulatory agencies, there was a potential that no matter what neutral, objective role the college played, someone would be offended and accuse the college of *taking sides*. With patience, care, and a reputation built upon credible prior community-based experience, the college remained relatively unscathed and was perceived as having delivered a truly significant service to community residents.

The Adult Career Advisory Program (An Assessment and Referral Program)

This unique program is funded by the Alliance for Employee Growth and Development, a joint venture of AT&T (American Telephone and Telegraph), CWA (Communication Workers of America), and IBEW (International Brotherhood of Electrical Workers). The university, of which the college is a member, was contracted by the alliance to conduct a program to help union members reflect on their current career, get help with career planning and decision making, explore new career opportunities, and find out more information about employment opportunities where they worked as well as elsewhere. Staff from the college's Division for Adult/Continuing Education attended special training in career counseling and assessment to conduct the program's seminars and individual counseling activities. The college was compensated for its participation.

Discussion. Industries, agencies, unions, utilities, and businesses employ many local residents and thus have a direct impact on the local community. Obviously, these institutions also have power and political influence beyond the community and can be powerful allies for a college. In recent times, industry, unions, and large business organizations have not been consistently pleased by urban institutions' enthusiasm, competency, or responsiveness to helping address issues not traditionally seen as the business of academics. As a result, these institutions have had to circumvent colleges and universities to get business-related training or counseling services. When this occurs, the college, its students, its faculty, and the local community lose out. In this case, however, the university and the local college responded quickly, enthusiastically, and competently. The benefits were immediate and impressive. Some of them were:

- The stock of the university rose significantly with both the union and management of this nationwide business.
- Substantial money was provided to the university and the local college to fund the program.
- The staff training provided in this program had positive implications for other college community-based programs.
- Many of the participants recognized the college and university as a viable choice for further study.
- People from a broader geographic and different ethnic/cultural and demographic base became aware of the local urban college and viewed it with an increased level of respect and relevancy.

A program such as this, when successfully implemented, can significantly alter a negative view of an institution and generate favor it needs for survival from the broader community constituency.

An inherent danger of becoming involved in such a program is that it involves high risk and high gain. If the program is well executed, the college's reputation can be instantly enhanced, and other unions, businesses, and agencies will more readily consider using the college for a variety of services. On the other hand, if the program is poorly executed, a bad reputation will evolve that can be devastating. The tragedy in this situation, as well as in other similar community-based programs, is that often variables beyond the control of the local college or university may result in the acquisition of a negative reputation, despite the fact that the reputation may be undeserved. There is no solution to this problem, but a warning to be extremely careful to do well with those variables and elements that one can control.

Adult Literacy (An Instructional Program)

Often known as ABE (adult basic education), this program is designed to provide basic literacy skills and English-as-a-second-language instruction to community adults. Supplemental program activities include career and vocational counseling, data collection, staff development, and computer-assisted instruction. Day, evening, and weekend classes are provided by this institution at several off-site locations as well as at the college's Community Learning Center. The program is funded by a combination of federal funding from the Adult Education Act, Adult Literacy Education funding from the state, and state and city tax-levy funding. Currently, the institution's program provides over 12,000 instructional hours and serves over 1,200 participants. The institution cooperates with six community-based civic, senior, private, ethnic/cultural, and substance abuse organizations in delivering its services.

Discussion. Concern about adult literacy is growing in the U.S. and around the world. Today it is widely accepted that basic education is critical to human survival, especially in a world increasingly impacted by various economic, sociological, and cultural changes. As higher education institutions face the inadequate academic preparation of their entering freshmen, they have become more empathetic to the severity of the problems experienced by community adults who lack basic skills, as well as the problems experienced by business, industry, and others who seek a workforce that can keep pace with rapid technological change and increased competition. Thus, despite certain reluctance on the part of some institutions of higher education, many urban and other institutions are more frequently recognizing that it makes good sense to be involved in adult literacy.

Sometimes individuals who seek such instruction are embarrassed that they have problems reading or speaking English and are reluctant to return to the elementary or secondary school system where they may have previously failed. The college becomes for them a prestigious and somewhat more trusted site at which to learn. There is generally support from community organizations for a college to operate an adult literacy program. There is increasing attention to the development and dissemination of appropriate, effective curricula materials and instructional methods that have been successful with a variety of populations. There are new sources of funding for such programs, and unfortunately there are endless numbers of potential program participants. Most everything is in place to help an urban institution of higher education that wishes to implement an adult literacy program.

Among the many benefits of implementing such a community-based program are:

- Adult literacy programs result in recognizable, immediately usable outcomes for participants.

- Generally such a program brings positive recognition, appreciation, and support from many groups in the community.

- The content of an adult literacy program can be developed to address issues critically important to individuals' daily survival, and it is uniquely suited to incorporating a "second agenda" related to social goals.

- Instructional expertise can be developed that has direct implications for colleges and universities involved in responding to the remedial needs of matriculated students.

- The nature of an adult literacy program is such that it provides a foundation for developing solid cooperative relationships with other community agencies that are necessary to the development of comprehensive community-based programming.

The potential liability of such a program lies in the degree to which the institution takes it seriously. Adult literacy programs require administrative and instructional expertise. Sometimes an assumption is made that anyone who has taught at the college or high school level can function successfully in an adult literacy program or, worse, that a program can be operated loosely with a number of volunteers. Such an assumption is a serious mistake. Many programs have fallen apart as a result of poor instruction. Further, good instruction alone does not guarantee success, for counseling, careful placement, and consistent follow-up must be present to ensure that students are supported adequately through the learning process.

Successful programs require effective instructional methods, relevant curricula, adequate student support services, accessible classes, convenient schedules, a variety of materials, and cooperative community relationships. A college that has put all these variables together in the implementation of an effective adult literacy program signals its potential for expanded community involvement and real human service. Adult literacy programs teach more than reading and writing. When implemented effectively, they result in individuals becoming empowered and gaining greater control over their own lives. Such empowerment is at the core of all community-based programs.

Conclusion

These programs illustrate only a small segment of the broad spectrum of successful community-based efforts currently taking place in urban institutions of higher education. It should be noted that the college whose programs have just been described is also actively involved with other community-based programs, including High School Equivalency Preparation; Basic Skills for a City Volunteer Corps; an Adult Career Counseling project; an Adolescent Vocational Exploration program; a JTPA 8 percent Basic Skills program; a summer computer-assisted instructional program for high school youth; an out-of-school youth-training program; a parenting program for single mothers; and the development of its center into a state-designed ACCESS Center for comprehensive educational services. These and other programs receive approximately $2 million in grants and other support from almost two dozen different sources including the federal, state, and city governments, private agencies, banks, businesses, utilities, unions, local community-based organizations, private donations, industry, and foundations. In the process, the center works closely with forty to fifty individual entities, both communitywide and citywide on an almost daily basis. This college, as do other similarly enlightened and committed urban colleges, has community-based programs that serve and impact almost an equal or greater number of individuals than the college's regular academic programs. What is accomplished through this program is awe inspiring.

The college is part of a large urban university suffering the ongoing problems of budget, enrollment, student unrest, fluctuating political support, and the need for updating and making relevant its curriculum. Several years ago, in this milieu of stress and problems, the college was first threatened with total extinction, then slated for reorganization to a community college, and finally faced with severe restrictions on the building of its critically needed campus. Today, this four-year college has moved into an exceptionally fine new campus, is actively pursuing development of graduate programs, and has increased enrollment to the point where it is rapidly developing a shortage of space on the new campus. There have been steady increases in the grant and foundation monies coming to the institution as well as increases in other kinds of support. The racial, ethnic, and demographic composition of the school's enrollees has significantly expanded. The content, quality, and relevance of its academic programs have changed in a very positive manner. The reputation of the institution continues to improve, and the community, though still relatively not college oriented, is a devoted, a fierce, and an effective supporter and an advocate for the college. The college is considered by all to be a vital, valuable, indispensable "family member" of the community, which has shared in a most beneficial process of mutual enhancement. This was made possible by the willingness of the college to take its social responsibilities seriously and to devote itself to a mission of community-based involvement, though it did so originally out of an almost desperate need for economic and political survival. The college survived and now continues its course of involvement because it believes that this is the best of good educational business.

The Chatham College-Bethesda Model: An Approach to Literacy Education for Women

JoAnne E. Burley

There is an increasing body of knowledge reported every year on adult literacy programs. Often these programs are designed for underrepresented groups of the population, for example, racial and ethnic minority groups, elementary and high school dropouts, and nonnative speakers of English. In recent years women have been identified worldwide as a group in need of special attention for literacy development. McCall (1987) reports that as much as two-thirds of the world's illiterates are women and that illiteracy among adult females often remains hidden until they have to enter the workforce. In these situations, illiteracy is often defined in relation to the demands society places upon them.

McCall (1987) further states that in the U.S., 27 million adults (20 percent of the population) are functionally illiterate and a higher percentage of those defined as illiterates are women (23 percent) rather than men (17 percent). Furthermore, 75 percent of all households headed by women are without a high school diploma and living below the poverty line. This information would suggest an urgent need for situational relief that might be achieved first, by the development of adult literacy programs designed to recruit and instruct women, and secondly, by instructional programs that maximize women's ability to relate and instruct each through peer instruction.

A peer-tutoring model, inspired by the intergenerational model (Nickse, Speicher, & Buchek 1988), employed college students as literacy workers. They were paid with funds from the Federal College Work-Study Program.

A similar model of college students tutoring adult learners has been encouraged by the U.S. federal government through the Student Literacy Corps program (*Federal Register* 1989). In this program the goals were to

1. Identify students currently enrolled at a college or university who wish to participate in the Student Literacy Corps. Corps members tutor in an adult literacy program with a structured classroom setting. The program, located in a public community agency, services educationally or economically disadvantaged individuals;

2. Provide an opportunity for corps members to gain practical experience in such academic areas as the social sciences, economics, or education by combining formal study with the undergraduate experience as literacy tutors; and

3. Provide the opportunity for corps members to receive academic credit for at least six hours of voluntary, uncompensated service each week of the semester in a public community agency.

Regardless of how innovative an adult literacy program design may be or which populations such programs are designed to serve, there are factors associated with *recruitment, instruction,* and *retention* that should be considered in order to identify and instruct adult learners.

Recruitment. Of the many methods used to recruit adult learners for literacy and adult basic education classes, Balmuth (1988) suggests personal referrals to be the most successful. Often such referrals are made by guidance counselors who work with recruitment programs for high school dropouts between the ages of sixteen and twenty-four and by employers, parents, friends, relatives, and correctional officers. Word of mouth, home visits, and even door-to-door canvassing has proven more successful than television (TV) or radio advertisements. Perhaps the most successful method of recruiting has been by students in a literacy program or those who have been in a program that they regard as successful.

Instruction. Adult literacy and adult basic education (ABE) programs traditionally have been developed to operate in a manner similar to the educational and instructional programs for children. Bowren (1987) suggests that some teachers make adjustments in instruction and materials, which gives recognition to the fact that adults' interests and experiences differ from those of children. Also, organizational patterns and instructional strategies should be altered in recognition of adults' maturity and responsibility for their own life-style. Within the past years, scholars such as Knowles (1980) and Ulmer and Dinnan (1981) have supported andragogy (teacher facilitated instruction) as an instructional technique, rather than the continued dependency on pedagogy (teacher directed instruction). Guides have been established for in-service training for ABE instructors that focus on the nature of the ABE program, the general characteristics of the ABE student, the objectives of an ABE program, and an introduction to some of the instructional techniques found to be most successful (Burley 1986). What has been learned has been used to provide the type of instructional adult literacy program that specifically addresses the needs of adult learners.

Retention. In the U.S., only about 50 percent of those in ABE programs remain for one year (Balmuth 1988). Research examining the ways of improving retention for adults in literacy programs has made significant strides. Such research reported by Balmuth (1988) has included data collected on absenteeism and reading achievement. There are of course, many reasons why adults do not come forward to join ABE and adult literacy classes. Lehr (1983) cites Cross' three classifications of obstacles that deter adults. First, there are *situational barriers,* which are defined as those arising from one's situation in life. Such would include job responsibilities, finances, home and family, transportation, and other responsibilities. Second, there are *dispositional barriers,* which are those attitudes and perceptions about oneself as a learner that might prevent or inhibit academic success. Third, there are *institutional barriers,* which are those practices and procedures that discourage working adults. Examples might include fees, location, selection, and content of courses. There is also the reality that some adults are not ready to resume academic learning. For the adult who is making sufficient money for himself or herself to support a family, stopping to attend school or a formalized educational program may, in the short-term, retard the entire family's growth or survival. Long-term goals may be a luxury that the adult simply cannot afford to consider at the time. More often, this may be true for women and one-parent family households in a lower socioeconomic bracket than for others. Other adults may not consider themselves ready due to specific family pressures.

Fingeret (1982) suggests that the reason many adult learners stop, start, and discontinue their participation in literacy programs is because the program sponsors oftentimes force the participants to choose between their place in the community and their personal independence. Hunter and Harman (1979) concluded that the most effective literacy programs are those that focus on persons in their communities and those that involve the adults in the program design. Such programs help gain the confidence of adult learners. With this in mind, the Chatham College-Bethesda Adult Literacy Program was developed. The program became a joint venture between a college and a nearby local community center. The primary concerns were (a) to focus on and encourage as many women as possible to improve their literacy skills; (b) to use a young female adult peer-tutoring model to both provide tutors for the women and to have the women model positive reading behavior and attitudes; (c) to provide opportunities for college students, faculty, and staff members to contribute in a meaningful way to the educational attainment of adults outside the traditional higher education curriculum; and (d) to improve community relations between the institution of higher learning and the neighboring community.

Chatham College, a small private liberal arts college for women, and the Bethesda Community Center located in the Homewood-Brushton section of Pittsburgh, Pennsylvania, became partners to establish the Chatham College-Bethesda Adult Literacy Program (CC-BALP). The union between the two was quite appropriate since logistically they were approximately two and one-half miles apart. In addition, both had demonstrated for years a deep and sincere effort to address the needs and concerns of the Pittsburgh community. At the time of the proposed venture, Bethesda Community Center had provided needed social services to the local residents for the past twenty-six uninterrupted years. Likewise, Chatham College with a well-established reputation for community service had been providing educational opportunities for women for a number of uninterrupted years. Both partners were dedicated to improving the quality of life for the local residents. They recognized the special needs of the women and children of the community. Their desired focus, then, became that of improving educational opportunities for women in that community.

Chatham College-Bethesda Model

The community of Homewood-Brushton is approximately 5.6 miles east of downtown Pittsburgh. It is estimated to be 712 acres in size, containing 2.1

Community Background

percent of the city's land and approximately 3 percent of the city's population (*Bureau of the Census* 1980). In 1980 Homewood-Brushton's total population was 15,158, of which 97 percent were African American, 2 percent were European American and 1 percent was identified as other (*Bureau of the Census* 1980).

According to the 1980 census, 55.3 percent of the Homewood-Brushton population were female and 44.7 percent were male. The median income in Homewood-Brushton was $6,615 in 1970 and $11,249 in 1980. Sources of income according to households in the Homewood-Brushton area were reported as (*a*) earned income—60.6 percent; (*b*) self-employed—2.3 percent; (*c*) investment income—15.6 percent; (*d*) social security—36.6 percent; (*e*) public assistance—35.5 percent; and (*f*) other—29.3 percent. Twenty-eight percent of Homewood-Brushton families have incomes below the poverty level. Roughly, 35 percent of Homewood-Brushton women are employed, 5 percent unemployed, and 60 percent are not in the workforce. Forty-two percent of the men are employed, 10 percent are unemployed, and 47.3 percent are not in the workforce (*Bureau of the Census* 1980).

According to the 1980 census, the educational attainment of the Homewood-Brushton population for persons twenty-five years and over was that 22 percent had an educational level of elementary school or less, 50 percent were high school graduates, 14.9 percent had one or more years of college, 4.5 percent were college graduates, and 8.6 percent were not counted.

Most national studies point to the important role that education plays in future employment. The quality, quantity, and demonstrated mastery of educational experiences determine the lifelong work patterns and earnings of people in Pittsburgh. The need, then, to provide an adult literacy program in the Homewood-Brushton section of Pittsburgh was based partly on the census data.

Program Participants

In 1987 eighteen women and two men with an age range of nineteen to sixty-seven years from the Homewood-Brushton section of Pittsburgh were accepted into CC-BALPs first program. Seventeen participants were African American and three were European American. Each participant met the eligibility criteria for being (*a*) a resident of the state of Pennsylvania, (*b*) seventeen years of age or older, (*c*) not currently enrolled in another adult literacy program funded by the state of Pennsylvania, and (*d*) not having earned a high school diploma or a General Educational Development (GED) certificate.

Recruitment strategies for the program included word of mouth, neighborhood canvassing, and referrals by local social services agencies, ministers, physicians, and friends. The literacy program personnel, aided by the Bethesda Community Center staff, carried out the recruitment strategies.

Program Description

CC-BALP, funded through a grant from the Pennsylvania Department of Education, was designed to instruct approximately twenty adult learners per year from the Homewood-Brushton community. The program offered instruction in reading, mathematics, and language two days a week from 9:00 A.M. to 2:00 P.M. Career and personal counseling were offered in the afternoon.

At the beginning of the program, all adult learners were tested using the Adult Basic Learning Examination (Karlsen & Gardner 1986). Other assessment instruments were used if additional screening was necessary. After testing, prescriptive folders (Scales & Biggs 1977) for each adult learner were prepared and filed.

Each session began with the learner and his/her tutor reviewing the academic prescription and assessing the goals for the day. Tuesday and Thursday morning sessions from 9:00 A.M. to 11:50 A.M. consisted of three fifty-minute instructional sessions on reading, writing, and mathematics. A typical prescription resembled the following:

NAME _____ DATE _____ TUTOR(S)_____

TIME	SUBJECT	ASSIGNMENT	EVALUATION
9–9:50	Reading	Sequence of events Text:	Oral retell of story
10–10:50	Math	Understanding percentages; review vocabulary terms (see attached sheet)	Workbook pages 23–45
11–11:50	Writing/ Language	Paragraph development Main idea & supporting details	Tutor-review

At the end of each session, the learner's performance was evaluated, and a new prescription was written by the literacy instructor before the next session. Reinforcement was given in the form of outside readings, homework assignments or specific assignments, such as locating information, interviewing friends or family members, and listening to a program on the radio or television.

Afternoon sessions from 12:00 to 2:00 P.M. allowed adult learners to work independently. They used computer-assisted instruction (CAI) or met with the program counselor to gain greater insight into their personal and career goals.

Tutor Training

The selection of approximately forty tutors was from Chatham College's students, faculty, and staff. Students could elect to use the experience of tutoring adult learners as a field-placement experience. That experience provided partial college credit for students majoring in education, psychology, economics, and human services. All tutors were screened for academic suitability. In addition, personal interviews were conducted to determine the appropriateness of personality for the program and for the matching process with prospective adult learners.

Tutor-training sessions were required for all who tutored. Approximately twelve hours of direct instruction were given; an additional three to five hours of independent instruction were available through videos, films, or counseling sessions. Consultants were hired to teach a multiplicity of instructional strategies (see Scales & Burley 1988; Scales & Biggs 1983; Bowren & Zintz 1977) to the tutors and other program personnel. In-service programming was developed according to the needs and desires of the program personnel. Additional training was suggested for a tutor whose performance indicated such a need.

Personnel

Presented in this section is a list followed by a description of the program's personnel, their credentials, salary status, and a description of each position.

Personnel	Credentials	Salary
Program Director & Reading Specialist	Ph.D.	Paid
Instructor/ Coordinator	B.A./B.S.	Paid
Secretary	Certificated Program	Paid
Tutors	High School Diploma	Volunteers
Tutor Coordinators	2 yrs. college	Work-study funds
Van Driver	PA license	Paid
Recruiter/Counselor	B.A./B.S./M.A./M.S.	Paid
Child-Care Coordinator	Previous Experience	Paid

Program Director. The program director was responsible for the overall operation of the adult literacy program. That included hiring staff, planning the instructional program, training tutors, conducting the internal evaluation, and securing adequate funds for program operation.

Instructor. The program instructor was responsible for conducting adult learner interviews, interviewing tutors, administering tests, preparing individualized prescriptions for adult learners, matching tutors to the adult learners, and providing periodic progress reports to the learners.

Tutors. All tutors, including college students, faculty, and staff, were volunteers. Each tutor had to agree to spend at least three hours per week with her adult learner. Tutors were interviewed for suitability prior to receiving tutor training.

Tutor Coordinators. Tutor coordinators were junior- and senior-level college students who were in good academic standing and who had tutored for at least one full year. Tutor coordinators prepared materials, corrected papers, and coordinated activities among the tutors, adult learners, and program instructor. Tutor coordinators also assisted in the tutor-training program.

Van Driver. The van driver was needed to transport adult learners from the Homewood-Brushton community to the adult literacy program site on Chatham College's campus.

Recruiter/Counselor. The recruiter/counselor was responsible for publicizing, screening, and keeping records for the adult literacy program. Contact with the adult learners included counseling (career and personal), providing referrals to community and social service agencies, guiding the adult learners through realistic goal setting, and maintaining close and continuous contact.

Child-Care Coordinator. The child-care coordinator provided daily activities for the children of the adult learners. This service was provided free to any adult learner in the Chatham College-Bethesda Adult Literacy program.

The adult literacy program was housed on the campus of Chatham College. Classrooms, computer center annex, and lounge facilities for the program were housed in one building. Adult learners were encouraged to use the library, computer center, laboratory, cafeteria, and student center. Textbooks, materials, and other supplies were provided without cost.

Facility

Transportation and child care were provided without cost to all adult learners. A minivan was provided by Chatham College to pick up adult learners at prearranged locations throughout the Homewood-Brushton community. One such location was the Bethesda Community Center where the child-care facility was located.

Transportation and Child Care

The Pennsylvania Department of Adult and Basic Education was the principle funding source. Chatham College provided additional funds and in-kind contributions. Funds were also provided by the Bethesda Community Center, Nabisco Brands of Pittsburgh, and the Pepsi-Cola Company.

Funding

Two types of evaluation procedures were undertaken for the program. First, the Pennsylvania State Department of Education conducted the external evaluation. This consisted of written reports, statistical data sheets, and a budget report being submitted both midyear and year end. In addition, a representative for the department made at least two site visits per year. A written summary report was given to the program director for immediate review.

Program Evaluation

Second, the literacy program director conducted an internal review that evaluated the adult learner's performance and attitudes, instructional techniques, materials, facility accommodations, and program record keeping. Assessment of attitudes was obtained both through personal interviews with the adult learners and anonymous questionnaires.

Each tutor and the instructor determined at the end of every three months whether or not his/her adult learner's short- and/or long-term goals had been met. Discussion between the tutors and the adult learners were prompted through such questions as

1*a.* (Short-Term) Have I made a commitment to completing each assignment to the best of my ability?

1*b.* (Long-Term) Have I made a commitment to taking and passing the GED examination?

2*a.* (Short-Term) Have I been realistic in my goal setting?

2b. (Long-Term) In planning for my future, can I afford to continue on at this time?

The literacy program evaluation is continuous throughout the life of the program.

Program Outcomes

1. Adult learners were enthusiastic and eager to attend an adult literacy program located on a college campus. While most adult learners did not dislike the idea of attending an adult literacy program at more traditional sites such as libraries, churches, elementary schools, or community centers, most were impressed that a college would sponsor an adult literacy program for persons who had not yet earned their high school diploma.
2. The use of college students, faculty, and staff as tutors proved to be an excellent incentive for the adult learners. These volunteer tutors were dedicated, motivated, and responsible workers.
3. Conducting the adult literacy program on a college campus provided all of the material, space, resources, and personnel that was needed.
4. College students were given an opportunity to experience firsthand the conditions of life for those persons whose literacy levels were insufficient to afford them the independence and opportunities afforded others who are more able.
5. The retention level for adult learners for two years was 80 percent. A significant factor was the small number of adult learners and the very strong interest the tutors took in the program.
6. The adult literacy program provided a very different but interesting field placement experience for college students majoring in education, psychology, human services, and economics.
7. The adult literacy program was affordable. Without concerns for cost, transportation, and child care, the program remained very desirable to the adult learners.
8. The adult learners liked the flexibility of applying more time to their areas of greatest need. Many were relieved that the program did not operate like regular school and that they could work on improving other skills such as mathematics and composition as well as learning to read and speak well.
9. The majority of the adult learners would have preferred to attend class more often than twice weekly.
10. The program operated for ten months per year rather than twelve months. Some students did not want the summer break in their instruction.
11. Tutors could not always remain with an adult learner for the entire year. Obligations to their studies, changes in course selection, or job responsibilities often permitted the tutor to commit only for one academic semester rather than for the year.

12. Finally, a no-cost program made some of the adult learners feel as though they had no way to contribute to their own educational advancement.

If the program's success is measured in student retention, program awards, or the number of adult learners who finally received their GED certificates, then success on a modest scale has been achieved. Perhaps the real success is the uniqueness of this program. It supported the cooperative spirit of a local community center and a small college by generating an idea, developing a plan, and furnishing, in part, funds, personnel, space, and resources to make a small, but significant, contribution to a group of people who wanted to improve their education.

References

Balmuth, M. 1988. Recruitment and retention in adult basic education: What does the research say? *Journal of Reading* 31(7):620–23.

Bowren, F. 1987. Adult reading needs adult research models. *Journal of Reading* 31(3):208–12.

Bowren, F. R., and M. B. Zintz. 1977. *Teaching reading in adult basic education.* Dubuque, IA: William C. Brown Company Publishers.

Bureau of the Census. 1980. The United States Department of Commerce, Washington, DC.

Burley, J. 1986. *Andragogy: Implications for preservice-inservice training.* ERIC Document Reproduction Service no. ED 264–386.

Federal Register. 1989. 1 June, Thursday. Vol. 54, no. 104.

Fingeret, A. 1982. *Through the looking glass: Literacy as perceived by illiterate adults.* Paper presented at the American Educational Research Association annual meeting. New York, NY. ERIC Document Reproduction Service no. ED 222–698.

Hunter, C., and J. Harman. 1979. *Adult illiteracy in the United States: A report to the Ford Foundation.* NY: McGraw Hill. ERIC Document Reproduction Service no. ED 173–775.

Karlsen, B., and E. F. Gardner. 1986. *Adult basic learning examination.* NY: The Psychological Corporation; Harcourt Brace Jovanovich, Inc.

Knowles, M. 1980. *The modern practice of adult education: Andragogy versus pedagogy.* NY: Association Press.

Lehr, F. 1983. Adult literacy. *Journal of Reading* 27(2):176–79.

McCall, C. 1987. Women and literacy: The Cuban experience. *Journal of Reading* 30 (4):318–24.

Nickes, R., A. Speicher, and P. Buchek. 1988. An intergenerational adult literacy project: A family intervention/prevention model. *Journal of Reading* 31(7):634–42.

Scales, A. M., and S. A. Biggs. 1977. College reading and study skills: An assessment-prescriptive model. In O. Clapp, ed., *Classroom practices in teaching English 1977–1978: Teaching the basic—really!*, 22–28. Urbana, IL: National Council of Teachers of English.

Scales, A. M., and S. A. Biggs. 1983. *Reading to achieve: Strategies for adult/college learners.* Columbus, OH: Charles E. Merrill Publishing Company.

Scales, A., and J. Burley. 1988. A holistic approach to teaching adult literacy techniques. *Lifelong learning: An omnibus of practice and research* 12:26–28.

Ulmer, C., and J. Dinnan. 1981. *Adults learn again.* GA: State of Georgia Department of Education.

A Christian Literacy Program for Adults

William E. Kofmehl, Jr.

Christian churches have played an important role in American education since colonial times. The theocracy of Massachusetts, for example, passed the "Old Deluder Satan" Act in 1647. This law required all towns with over fifty families to establish elementary schools, so that the "Old Deluder Satan" would not be able to keep mankind in ignorance. To ensure widespread ability to read the Bible, an earlier law of 1642 required that all be taught to read either by masters or parents.

After the establishment of the United States of America, the federal government made use of the churches to further its own educational agenda. In a treaty of 1803 with the Kaskaskia Indians, the U.S. agreed to contribute $100 per year for seven years to support a priest who would "instruct as many of their [Indian] children as possible in the rudiments of literature" (Berry 1968, 14).

Throughout the nineteenth century, the U.S. Army hired chaplains to perform the duties of schoolmasters and usual religious activities. Their duties included the instruction of children of officers and private soldiers during the day, and the instruction of the men themselves during night school (U.S. War Department 1838). The Bureau of Refugees, Freedmen, and Abandoned Lands (commonly known as the Freedmen's Bureau), established under the control of the War Department in 1865, made further use of the chaplains as well as many religious agencies to educate former slaves (Franklin 1961). In more recent times the Lutheran Church took on the responsibility of providing basic literacy education for adults. Specifically, it donated resources to establish the Allegheny County Literacy Council (ACLC), Inc. Since I was unable to locate other church efforts in the literature that supported literacy education with a structured program like ACLC, my discussion is herein focused. Specifically, my chapter will examine ACLC's development and teaching materials, present profiles of a few ACLC students, and describe how similar programs can be developed and sustained through Christian literacy outreach efforts.

Background

ACLC, now a U.S.-based model program within Christian Literacy Associates (CLA), was established in 1976. A small grant obtained from the Lutheran Church in western Pennsylvania and the West Virginia Synod was used to establish the program. Currently, funds for ACLC come from various churches. One of ACLC's strengths is the volunteers who work in the program. As of June 1989, ACLC had trained over 2,800 volunteer tutors in its U.S. program. From 1978 to 1983, through a project funded by World Vision, ACLC trained 20,000 volunteers in Haiti to teach from its Christian Literacy Series (CLS). In various countries throughout the African, Asian, and Latin American continents, CLA volunteer consultants developed CLA's Basic Primers

(1978–1989). The primers were written in seventeen different languages. Two of these primers, written in Spanish and Haitian Creole, are in use with illiterate immigrants in the U.S.

All teaching materials in CLS (Kofmehl 1983) were specifically developed to be used by tutors (nonprofessional educators). Essentially, tutors must be able to read well themselves, have patience, and be able to commit two single one-hour periods per week for a series of twelve weeks.

The program's offices are housed in St. John's Lutheran Church of Highland in Pittsburgh, Pennsylvania. Staff consists of over forty part-time volunteers. They include computer operators, reading specialists, artists, cartoonists, mimeograph and binding machine operators, newsletter editors, and a prayer fellowship. Two Vista workers were available for the 1988–1989 year to provide more continuity in matching and follow-up of tutors and students.

Literacy Series

CLS is a unique Bible-content basic reading program that makes provisions for one-on-one instruction to functionally illiterate students. Instruction can begin, if necessary, at zero level (nonfamiliarity with the alphabet) and progress up to a sixth-grade or functional level (able to enter high school equivalency, Adult Basic Education, or job skill-training classes). CLS consists of the *Pre-Reading Program* plus four books. The *Pre-Reading Program* uses sixteen steps to teach students the English alphabet and the forty most common English words (Kucera & Francis 1967). The first three steps form a model for the tutor, and the remaining thirteen simply use the model's framework with new information substituted. Step one focuses on nine letters of the English alphabet (A, D, E, F, H, I, N, O, T) that can be combined to form the six most common English words. To begin, students are given three letters on a 3 x 3 grid along with transparent red plastic markers. Next, they are instructed to place markers on specific letters. They go through the 3 x 3 grid of six lines, three boxes per line, to reinforce the left-to-right pattern of reading. Emphasis is placed on proceeding from left to right—one box at a time, one row at a time—and from the top of the grid to its bottom. The student makes two passes through the grid. In the first pass she/he is to find the letter that looks like the one identified by the tutor. In the second pass she/he marks each letter and reads it orally (see fig. 3.1).

Step two utilizes a similar grid that contains the three most common English letter groups (the, of, and). Again, the student makes two passes (left to right, one box at a time) through the grid. Initially she/he is finding a box that contains one of the letter groups. Prior to the second pass the student is asked to say the letters in selected letter groups and mark the letter group as she/he proceeds from left to right through the grid. (Step two is excellent for reinforcing the spelling of the forty most common English words).

Step three introduces six words (the, of, and, to, a, in) in the context of sentences. One sentence, with repeated repetitions, is used for each word. Each sentence uses one of the words plus pictures and diagrams to represent nouns, verbs, and adjectives. This enables a sentence to be built with no sight words

Part 3

Figure 3.1 3 × 3 Grid.

a	d	e
d	e	a
e	a	d
a	d	e
d	e	a
e	a	d

other than those of the forty most common already taught or the one word from
among the forty that is being studied at a given time. After the words have
been taught, the student is introduced to a three-sentence story that uses all six
words. The student is asked to read the story silently, is questioned to determine his/her comprehension, and is then asked to read the story orally. As was
previously mentioned, the thirteen steps following the initial three make use of
the same basic framework. Subsequently, the remaining letters of the English
alphabet are taught, the final thirty-four of the forty most common letter groups
are presented and taught, and stories for practice are provided.

Upon completion of the *Pre-Reading Program,* the student is ready to
begin the first of 114 lessons, divided among four books. A *Teacher's Guide*
with specific instructions for each lesson is built into the front of each of the
four books. The lessons are designed to teach the pronunciation and spelling
patterns used in the 1,000 most common English words (Thorndike-Lorge
1944). One sample lesson provides the tutor with the techniques necessary for
teaching all 114 lessons. For example, all lessons are divided between two
facing pages. The left-hand page presents the spelling pattern, being taught,
with pictures that illustrate key words and a five-box drill technique. The first
drill box presents the spelling pattern. The second box builds different words or
syllables using the pattern. The third box shows that what looks the same and
sounds the same is the letter or spelling pattern. The fourth box substitutes different letters or spelling patterns and contrasts the resulting words. Finally, the
fifth box serves as a builder, building new words using previously taught syllables and word parts plus the lesson's letter group or spelling pattern. All new
vocabulary words developed in the drill boxes are listed at the bottom of the
page (see fig. 3.2).

Figure 3.2. Drill Box.

The right-hand page of each lesson has two stories for reading practice. The first story makes use of the vocabulary words learned from the drill boxes. The second story, one with religious content, uses some of the new vocabulary but primarily serves as a review mechanism for words from previous lessons. The student is asked to read each story silently. The tutor then asks questions to determine comprehension, either using questions from the *Teacher's Guide* for that lesson or questions that she/he makes up. Oral reading of the religious story then follows. Next, a Scripture passage is read by the tutor, to further illustrate its meaning. A writing exercise that requires the student to use the new vocabulary in sentences, along with words from previous lessons, completes the lesson. Rapidity of advancement is geared to the desires and achievements of each student. Many students have experienced success in CLS. Following are profiles of four such students.

Student Profiles

Kate, a single twenty-three-year-old African American parent of two small children, lived in a metropolitan city. Even though she received government assistance, she wanted more for herself and her children. Her ultimate goal was to become a practical nurse. Realistically, she knew that this could not happen with her current reading skills. So, she called the Christian Literacy Associates' program. Kate was matched immediately with a tutor from one predominately African American Christian group.

Kate joined her tutor's Christian group. Her tutor became her personal friend. Eventually, this friend assisted her in winning a court case that involved adequate housing.

Kate completed CLS, earned her General Educational Development (GED) certificate, and eventually took her training as a practical nurse.

A second student was Clark, married, European American, and working as a foreman on a roofing crew. He was in his late thirties and lived in a blue-collar section of a metropolitan city. His wife, who was completing a degree in nursing, was unaware of his illiteracy at the time of their marriage. Since Clark could not read, not even recognize all of the letters of the alphabet, his wife served as his translator or buffer to the literate world. With her support, Clark sought help and was assigned a tutor in the Christian Literacy Associates' program.

Clark's tutor, in his midseventies, could easily relate to Clark's current situation. His tutor was a ninth-grade school dropout himself, from more than fifty years ago. With his tutor's help Clark completed the CLS reading series and pursued further schooling toward high school completion.

A third student, Bob, was in his late forties, was European American, and described himself as a junior executive. When he began the CLS series, he was in charge of the display department for a large suburban department store. The reason Bob came to CLA for tutoring was his lack of decoding skills. A quick summary of his life explains his lack of reading ability.

A child of alcoholic parents, he became a ward of the court and went to many different elementary schools. When he reached minimum dropout age, he joined the U.S. Army. After he completed his enlistment, he began washing windows. He established his own company, with his wife handling the paper work and bookkeeping. Later on, a hospital accountant asked him to become their supervisor of housekeeping. That job experience prepared him for the position he held at the department store. Bob was in constant fear that someone would discover his inability to read. If that happened, he knew he would lose his job, home, boat, truck, and all that he had worked for.

Tutoring brought Bob up to a functional reading level. Now he serves as Director of Plant Operations for a large metropolitan area hospital. He finally feels secure in the business world. Noteworthy is the fact that the Christian aspect of CLS brought about a reconciliation with his oldest son, who had moved away from home.

Martha was an eighty-four-year-old European American student. She left Poland seventy years ago, raised thirteen children, and eventually realized that her only regret in life was that she could not read the Scriptures. Martha entered the Christian Literacy program because she wanted to learn to read her Bible. The tutor, assigned to help Martha achieve her goal, was a patient middle-aged Presbyterian housewife. Upon achieving that goal, Martha became a celebrity of sorts. A local newspaper ran a front-page story of her life and her triumph over illiteracy. Finally, a local television station interviewed her as part of a documentary on literacy.

Literacy Outreach

A preliminary step in planning for a Christian Literacy Outreach Program (CLOP) is to discover by statistical analysis or by survey the need for a literacy program. In spite of the surveys, studies, and census reports available, there is no accurate means of determining the exact number of functionally illiterate adults in a city, a county, or the entire U.S. One reason for the difficulty in determining the number of illiterates is the way "functional illiteracy" for adults has been defined. A functionally illiterate adult has been defined as one who is over sixteen years of age and has less than six years of formal education. Also, as one who is unable to read, write, and compute well enough to function (Scales 1985) as a U.S. citizen.

How can the number of illiterates be estimated in an area? One way is to review the latest U.S. Census of Population and Housing statistics. That document will show conservative figures. In it is listed a breakdown of educational attainment levels. The levels might be used to infer illiteracy. Better sources for obtaining estimates are the public schools, door-to-door questionnaires, telephone interviews, and adult basic education programs in selected areas.

Once the need for a CLOP has been established, individuals might then examine their churches and their neighborhoods; make contacts to recruit tutors and students; train tutors; and administer and secure funds for their programs as follows.

Church

1. What type of people make up my church—socially, economically, ethnically?
2. Are there those within the congregation who might need reading help—adults, children, non-English speaking, physically or mentally handicapped?
3. Are there those who might wish to serve as tutors—retired men and women, husband and wife teams who can alternate weeks, teenagers or college students who would do peer tutoring?
4. Can my church provide a meeting place for tutors and students—once a week, twice a week, daytime, evening, etc.?
5. Can it provide space for a library/reading center?
6. Can it provide initial funds for materials or for a part-time or full-time literacy supervisor?
7. What other social ministry efforts is my church involved in? What contacts does it have with community welfare/social service agencies? What degree of cooperation exists with other churches in this field? How can I use these contacts and personnel to further a Christian Literacy Outreach?

Neighborhood

1. Is my church located in a stable, declining, or transient neighborhood?
2. What is the racial and ethnic mix? Is there a need for English-as-a-second-language (ESL) tutoring?
3. Should I contact human services agencies, or other churches to locate those in the neighborhood who could benefit from a literacy program?
4. Can students get from their homes to literacy centers easily?
5. Will the media (radio, television [TV], newspapers) provide free publicity for a literacy effort?

Making Contacts

Tutors. Contacts to get tutors and students should be made in person or by phone, mail, media, agencies, and so on. Tutors should be drawn from all denominations of the Christian church in an area. Efforts for recruiting tutors should be aimed solely at the churches. Non-Christians who apply should be informed of the purpose of the effort, be trained if they so desire, and be encouraged to set up their own organizations.

The primary source for volunteer tutors should be the area churches. Suggestions for contacting them include

1. Call the church; ask to speak to the pastor.
2. Explain the purpose of CLOP, for example, need for Christian tutors, need for meeting places.
3. Ask how you might contact the women's organization, mission committee, senior citizens' group, etc.
4. Suggest the possibility of a personal meeting with the pastor and/or an interested member of the congregation.
5. Send a packet of information describing CLOP.
6. Suggest the possibility of a full presentation to the church.
7. Send a letter that describes the need, goal, resources, and administration of CLOP.

Students. Adults who read at less than a fifth-grade level are the main target for CLOP. The media and other referral sources can be used to attract the attention of friends of potential students as well as students themselves. Free publicity is often available from radio and TV stations. Normally, stations will give thirty seconds of airtime. That is not enough time to convince an adult who has been illiterate for thirty years that she/he should learn to read and write. However, within that thirty seconds, an appeal could be made to friends, relatives, or employers of the illiterate. The problem of illiteracy should be described as well as an indication of how CLOP is designed to teach illiterate adults to read and write. An address and a telephone number should be given. Such announcements should be aired as often as possible.

Welfare and social service organizations in communities are excellent referral sources and should, like the media, be well utilized. Counselors in these agencies encounter adult illiterates every day. Even when the problem is recognized, little is done about it. One task for CLOP is to contact every social service or welfare agency in the area. Make them aware of the illiteracy problem and convince them that CLOP has the capability of successfully handling referrals. Contact with agencies should be continuous. Monthly telephone calls should be made to keep new staff members aware of CLOP's existence. Records of all contacts should be kept.

Workshops for Christian Literacy tutors are conducted by CLA consultants. *Training Tutors*
They have been designed to train tutors in CLS to teach adults to read. In approximately four hours, a minimum of fifteen tutors can be taught the instructional techniques needed in both the *Pre-Reading* portion of CLS and the remaining four books. Tutors also learn how to print the manuscript-style letters used in the writing exercises and to complete a written assignment using the forty most common English words. Sources for supplementary reading materials, both Christian and secular, are given to tutors. Tutors learn how to become a Christian witness to their student.

The workshop exposes tutors to the complete picture of the Christian Literacy Outreach, enabling them to see how they may become part of a ministry that reaches far beyond the borders of the U.S. At the end of the workshop, tutors receive a certificate showing their completion of a basic workshop, the number of hours involved, the date, and the place where the workshop was held.

There must be some record-keeping system and organization for the program to *Administration*
succeed and grow. Records on tutors, agencies, and students should be kept in a card file. Student cards should be arranged in categories such as active, inactive, or graduated. Schedules of regular contact with agencies, tutors, churches, etc., should be kept. Contact with tutors should be made at least bimonthly. New contacts with churches for the purpose of recruiting tutors and with agencies for the referral of students should be made on a continuing basis. Though personal contacts are always best, the telephone might remain the major contact tool due to time and money. Often CLOPs find it necessary, for communication purposes, to publish a tutor newsletter.

As CLOPs grow, there may be a need for the assistance of part-time or full-time paid help. Active senior citizens might be able to devote twenty to forty hours to the administrative tasks of keeping records, telephoning, mailings, or supervision of volunteers.

In a Christian Literacy program's early stages, money is necessary for *Funding*
textbooks and office supplies, literacy library, publicity materials, brochures, and telephone with metropolitan service capability. Funding can come from Christian foundations, churches, and individuals. No money should be accepted from other sources unless they agree that emphasis on Christian witness can continue unchanged. Government funding will lead to the death of any Christian purpose in the program. CLOPs can obtain tax-deductible status.

Are You Ready?

Do you and those who have shown interest in your church really want to start a CLOP at your church? Your effort should be twofold: (*a*) to reach the adults and children within your area who are functionally illiterate and to help them develop the reading skills necessary to operate in society, and (*b*) to expose the students to the message contained in the holy Scriptures through the example and witness of a Christian tutor and through the basic reading materials and supplements. Bear in mind the biblical warning about calculating costs:

> For which one of you, when he wants to build a tower, does not first sit down and calculate the cost, to see if he has enough to complete it? Otherwise, when he has laid a foundation, and is not able to finish, all who observe it begin to ridicule him, saying, "This man began to build and was not able to finish." (Luke 14:28–30)

Are you and other members of your congregation willing to devote the time and effort necessary to make this program a success? If so, then you are ready to proceed prayerfully.

Conclusion

Illiteracy is a problem that will require the efforts of all forces in society to conquer. The churches form one of the most powerful groups whose efforts could be brought to bear on the subject. They have the resources of leadership, volunteers, and building space that can enable a literacy program to be established quickly and at little cost. In order to motivate the broadest spectrum of churches to become involved, however, requires more than an appeal to social concern. It requires Christian content as well. A Christian Literacy Outreach Program has that appeal.

References

Berry, B. 1968. *The education of American Indians: A survey of the literature.* Ohio State University, December. ERIC Document Reproduction Service no. ED 026–545.

CLA's Basic Primers. 1978–1989. *The light is coming* (Series). Pittsburgh: PA: Christian Literacy Associates.

Franklin, J. H. 1961. *Reconstruction after the Civil War.* Chicago: University of Chicago Press.

Kofmehl, W. E., Jr. 1983. *The Christian literacy series.* rev. ed. Pittsburgh, PA: Christian Literacy Associates.

Kucera, H., and W. N. Francis. 1967. *Computational analysis of present day American English.* Providence, RI: Brown University Press.

Scales, A. M. 1985. Diagnostic-instructional profile of a functionally illiterate adult. *PAACE-SETTER* 2:44–45.

Thorndike, E. L., and I. Lorge. 1944. *The teacher's word book of 30,000 words.* NY: Teachers College, Columbia University.

U.S. War Department. 1938. *General Order Number 29,* 18 August.

Literacy Education for the Homeless

Alice M. Scales

Homeless individuals in urban and rural areas have become more noticeable over the years. The perceived instability of them by employers and landlords is only one factor that has prevented many homeless individuals from obtaining meaningful employment and adequate housing. Not since the Great Depression of the 1930s has the U.S. witnessed such a dramatic increase in their numbers. I have assumed that without massive intervention, these numbers will continue to grow well into the 1990s. With intervention in mind, I developed this chapter to present a brief overview of homeless individuals, trends, types of support, and literacy programs designed to counteract these trends. Also presented will be recommendations for volunteers and other concerned individuals who may want to assist in the provision of enhanced program services for the homeless.

Overview

Until recently, homeless individuals were thought to be derelict men commonly referred to as hobos, vagabonds, and ramblers. Their mobility was normally restricted to walking, hitchhiking, or hitching rides in freight railroad cars. Often they slept or lounged on park benches, in doorways, in bus and train stations, or on the streets. They foraged for food from garbage dumpsters. In rural areas they wandered by farm homes and begged or offered to work for food and a place to sleep for a night or two. Such men were always dressed shabbily and were in need of hygienic care. Once it was believed that many homeless in the U.S. chose that way of life even though evidence about incomes, shelter, etc., have shown the contrary. "Reported cash incomes (including income from public benefits) put the average individual homeless person at 25 percent of the Federal poverty level and the average homeless family at 50 percent of the Federal poverty level" (*A nation concerned: . . . 1988*, part 5, 10). Proper shelter, nutritious food, and health care were main shortcomings of the homeless. Finally, their rates of acute and chronic disease were found to be substantially higher than the average U.S. citizen (*A nation concerned: . . . 1988*).

Trends

Since the early 1980s, studies have shown that the homeless population includes single and married men and women, children, and families. U.S. estimates, from studies conducted of homeless individuals between 1983 and 1988, range from 250,000 to 735,000. The most recent studies show a range of 500,000 to 600,000. The mean and median ages of homeless adults range from thirty-two to forty years old. Three to 12 percent are considered elderly, that is, over sixty years old (*A nation concerned: . . . 1988*).

Results from a survey of twenty-seven U.S. urban cities indicate that their average homeless population includes, on the average, 49 percent single men,

34 percent family members, 13 percent single women, and 5 percent unaccompanied youth. The survey also indicates that, on the average, 34 percent are substance abusers, 25 percent are mentally ill, 26 percent are veterans, and 23 percent are employed in full-time or part-time jobs (Conference survey finds continued . . . 1989).

The homeless population in rural areas is more difficult to measure because there are fewer social services available to measure it. However, it is known that the loss of farms in rural areas, similar to the closing of steel mills in urban areas, has caused severe unemployment and loss of homes. Farm loss may be one of the major reasons for homelessness in rural areas. Without the farms, individuals (farm owners and their families, immigrants, and young men who hired themselves out as farmhands), are unable to earn enough income. This lessens their chances of having enough shelter, food, and clothing.

Recent causes for homelessness have ranged from unaffordable housing to inadequate public policy. More and more it seems as if low-income housing has become unimportant to policy makers. Landlords who rent apartments in low-, middle-, and high-income areas have had to steadily increase their rental fees to offset such rising costs as maintenance and security. This has made it more difficult for many individuals to secure housing. The Rental Housing Crisis Index shows that in 1985 the number of very low income U.S. renter households exceeded the number of very low income renter units by 93.7 percent. Further, the federal housing assistance budget was cut from $30 billion to $7.5 billion between 1980 and 1988 (*Lives in the balance: . . .* 1988).

Types of Support

In one attempt to offset part of the housing crisis, the U.S. Department of Defense (DOD) initiated three programs to assist the homeless. First, in 1983 it made facilities available for emergency shelter to individuals and families who were moving from city to city in search of employment. Second, in 1984 DOD was authorized by the Shelter for the Homeless Statue to turn unused buildings on military installations into shelters for the homeless as long as they did not interfere with military functions. DOD spent $4 million on shelters in such places as Seattle, WA; Middlesex County, NJ; Albuquerque, NM; and Washington, DC. Problems inherent in this program included too few military installations with unused buildings that were accessible to homeless persons. Also, there was a lack of sufficient funds from cities and local governments to operate the shelters. Nevertheless, DOD was successful in making fifteen shelters available to the homeless. Third, beginning in 1984, DOD provided thousands of free blankets, cots, and articles of bedding to shelters throughout the country. In fiscal year (FY) 1988 it provided more than $1.3 million worth of bedding to shelters and, since the program began, more than $3.9 million worth of blankets (*A nation concerned: . . .* 1988).

The U.S. government's attempt to assist homeless and poor individuals has been through Supplemental Security Income (SSI), Aid to Families with Dependent Children (AFDC), and food stamp programs. These subsidies remain well below the poverty line. Also, when there are mentally ill, physically handicapped, and/or elderly individuals living with a family, their special care reduces the income spending to an even lower level.

A most recent government effort to assist homeless individuals was signing the Stewart B. McKinney Homeless Assistance Act of 1987 into law. The purpose of the McKinney Act was to provide funds for programs to serve homeless individuals. For FY 1987 $7,500,000 and for FY 1988 $10,000,000 were authorized to be appropriated for the adult literacy and basic skills remediation programs (Public Law 100–77, 1987). In August of 1988, the House voted in legislation that provided $642.5 million for FY 1989 to continue programs that provide emergency services to the homeless (Hunger, homeless legislation moving . . . 1988). The programs include Food and Shelter—administered by local United Way agencies or statewide or local homeless coalitions; Housing—administered by HUD; Adult Literacy Training—administered by the U.S. Department of Education; and Job Training—administered by the U.S. Department of Labor (*Lives in the balance:* . . . 1988). A cursory glance at the endeavors of the federal government might give the impression that the problems of the homeless are being addressed. However, much remains for the government, state, and local programs to do before the homeless are more than minimally served.

Literacy programs might be a partial answer to ending homelessness if they are administered from a holistic perspective. Holistic literacy programs (see Scales & Burley 1988) for the homeless must entail and reflect the life-styles of those who are to be served. Basic reading, writing, and math skills are important for employment and general independence in life. Of immediate importance to most homeless people is the need of a meal, a bed, and a job. Mentally ill and substance-abusing individuals might have additional goals and needs. Programs designed to serve the homeless will have to address such needs.

A plethora of adult literacy programs have become operational within the past twenty-five years. Types of programs have included adult basic education (ABE); general educational development (GED); English-as-a-second language (ESL); a combination of ABE, GED, and ESL; Laubach, and Christian Literacy. For the most part, programs focus heavily on teaching reading, writing, and math skills. Some include the teaching of typing, oral speaking, and other specific job skills (Scales 1990). Many programs are housed in educational institutions, libraries, rooms donated by companies, churches, and recreational centers. Funds for these programs are obtained from private, state, and federal sources. Even though many of the previously cited programs are excellent, they have not included services that are appropriate for the homeless. However, examples of programs that have focused their attention on the needs of the homeless follow.

Projective Adaptive Literacy (PAL). In 1986 Volunteers of America (VOA), with support from Literacy Volunteers of America (LVA), began its PAL program. VOA continues to operate PAL today. PAL is holistic in that its aim is to service the whole individual. Housed in two New York City residential

Literacy Programs

shelters for recovering alcoholic homeless men, PAL is an integral part of the overall social, psychological, recreational, medical, and vocational services offered at the VOA shelters. PAL includes the following seven components.

1. *Accessibility.* All services recommended for homeless residents residing in a VOA shelter are provided at that shelter.

2. *Screening Procedures.* Volunteer tutors and students are screened. Tutors must be at least twenty-one years old. They are interviewed by telephone to discuss and assess their needs, interests, and motivations. If it is determined that they are suitable for the PAL program, then a personal interview with the VOA Director of Volunteers is held. Screening for students begins after residents have been accepted into one of VOA's shelters. Initially, they are given a description of program activities that are available to them. Next, their educational background, work history, and substance abuse history are discussed and assessed. Finally, residents interested in the PAL program are considered after an observation period of one to three months. That observation period is used to determine whether residents pose no threat to themselves or other individuals in the program.

3. *Selection Process.* In order for volunteer tutors to be selected, they must express a sincere desire to help the less fortunate, speak and write fluent English, have a high school education, show a willingness and ability to interact with and to respect homeless adults, make a minimum six-month commitment to provide one and one-half hours of tutorial services per week, attend all training workshops, and be certified as a basic literacy tutor. Selected students must be residents of VOA programs, be nondependent on chemical drugs, demonstrate a need and desire for tutorial services, commit a minimum of three months to the PAL program, and not pose a danger to self or to others.

4. *Training.* Volunteer tutors are trained within four phases of VOA's PAL program. First, they attend a two- to three-hour orientation session during which they are presented the history of VOA, a presentation on PAL, the characteristics of alcoholism, the myths and realities on homelessness, a presentation by current tutors and students, a presentation on cooperative efforts with other organizations, and an introduction of new volunteers. Second, tutors attend a sixteen-hour Literacy Tutor Certification Workshop. At the end of the workshop they are given a take-home test. If they pass the test, they are awarded a Literacy Volunteers of America certification card. Third, in a two-hour follow-up orientation, tutors prepare lesson plans, administer LVA's READ test, review VOA's policies and procedures, review results from the administration of VOA's PAL Student Interest and Skills Inventory, and schedule a time to meet the students. Fourth, tutors are provided with ongoing training and monitoring techniques. Once every two weeks they are contacted to address and

remediate any difficulties or to identify areas of growth. Once every three months, tutors meet to exchange information, resources, etc. They are also provided relevant information regarding events, materials, literacy trends, etc.

5. *Matching Process.* The Director of Volunteers and the VOA Program Director match students with tutors. Information gathered from interviews of students and tutors is used in the matching process. Considered in the process are the personalities, interests, hobbies, work, and personal background of both student and tutor.

6. *Development of an Individual Education Plan.* Here curricula for students are developed by the individual student and his assigned tutor. Curricula choices for instruction may include basic reading, writing, math, public speaking, pre-GED, college/trade preparation, typing, business machines, computer literacy, and life skills. Progress of each student is monitored through weekly or monthly lessons by student and tutor. The tutor submits a written report.

7. *Cost-Effectiveness.* Training of volunteer tutors is provided by volunteers at no cost. Volunteer tutors pay only for basic workshop materials and registration cost. They then keep the materials to use with their students. Library books are donated to PAL. Sites for the PAL program are provided by VOA (*Volunteers of America of greater New York: . . .* 1988).

Results indicate that PAL is a successful program. It has made use of education in conjunction with other social services. Its holistic perspective has included needs expressed by homeless individuals. Since 1986 it has helped approximately fifty students. Of the fifty, 94% have either found employment and housing, rejoined their families, achieved their goal, or are continuing in PAL. PAL is a model program that is being replicated for homeless people in other states.

On the whole, literacy programs for the homeless in the U.S. are just getting started and are relatively new. Therefore, detailed descriptions of such programs and data that present their outcomes are not yet available. However, I did secure brief descriptions of plans for homeless literacy programs from California and Florida. That information follows.

California. In that state, new programs for the homeless have been initiated in Lancaster, Acton, San Francisco, Fresno, San Diego, and Santa Rosa. An estimated statewide homeless population of 145,526 exists in California, and at least 11,250 of those homeless lack basic literacy and other skills. Informal assessments and individual interviews conducted by shelter providers showed that homeless adults in California lacked readiness skills for literacy, self-esteem and personal responsibility, life skills, financial responsibility, parenting skills, employment preparation, and health and safety precautions. The Regional Task Force of San Diego and United Way of Los Angeles estimated that nearly one-third of the homeless population in those cities have either alcohol or drug abuse problems. These findings were the basis for planning to conduct homeless literacy programs through an instructional model that builds self-esteem. California's purpose was to increase the literacy level among homeless illiterate adults; it did so by creating a consortium between local literacy providers and homeless shelter providers (*Adult education for the homeless:* . . . 1989).

Florida. Florida is a state that expects its population to reach 13.2 million between 1990 and 2000 and expects its homeless population to increase at an alarming rate. In 1985 the state of Florida authorized the Department of Health and Rehabilitative Services and its statewide Task Force on the Homeless to assess the homeless problem in that state. From the assessment it was reported that on any given day from 10,000 to 13,000 persons are homeless. In 1987 the figures were revised to show that from 15,000 to 18,000 persons per day were homeless. Overall, the homeless seem to be located in Florida's seven largest metropolitan areas.

In 1989 programs for the homeless were begun in three large school districts (Dade, Broward, and Orange Counties) and the Florida Community College at Jacksonville. In Dade County, part-time and full-time teachers and counselors were employed. However, planning for transportation of students, for child care, and for shelter matters are continuing. In Broward County, program personnel take literacy to the streets and shelters in backpacks. They teach the homeless wherever they find them. In Orange County, a designated curriculum resource teacher visits homeless shelters and conducts interviews to find potential homeless students. Basic self-help and academic skills seem to be the primary need of the students. The Florida Community College program serves as a liaison between the literacy for the homeless program and various media outlets and agencies. Other responsibilities include administering tests and instructing students in an individualized setting. Their advanced students are given the opportunity to work as tutors in the program (*State of Florida:* . . . 1989).

Recommendations

With the number of homeless individuals increasing, the lack of enough private resources to care for them, and the limited support received from the U.S. government for homelessness, it seems necessary to set forth challenges that might serve to encourage many to assist those less fortunate than themselves.

Recently, the Interagency Council on the Homeless indicated that the local service delivery systems run by nonprofit organizations are the most effective way to provide services to the homeless. A reason for that conclusion was that local service systems have caretakers who are close to the homeless. That closeness seems suited to involving homeless people in planning for successful programs. Thus, a recommendation is that local governments, private voluntary agencies, and states should continue to be the primary vehicle for delivering assistance to the homeless (*A nation concerned:* . . . 1988). A continued implementation of this recommendation will require services from many volunteers.

Seemingly, many homeless programs could not function without volunteers. Therefore, a second recommendation is to encourage those who would like to volunteer to telephone their local volunteer agency to find out where homeless shelters are located. A telephone conversation with an administrator in a shelter for the homeless will provide an introduction of the shelter's procedures and policies for volunteers. Volunteers can perform basic responsibilities. For example, they can boil water for coffee, find clean sheets for beds, and make sure that guests of the shelter follow appropriate procedures when they enter the shelter. Also, volunteers can help guests solve some of their problems by looking for services that might protect their rights and entitlements (Haus 1988). Recommendations, such as the ones just presented, might ensure participation by local governing bodies and individuals. I support and strongly urge individuals to become volunteers for homeless programs.

References

Adult education for the homeless. 1989. Adult Education Unit: Youth, Adult and Alternative Educational Services Division. 8 September. California State Department of Education.

A nation concerned: A report to the president and the Congress on the response to homelessness in America. 1988. Washington, DC: Interagency Council on the Homeless.

Conference survey finds continued growth of hunger, homelessness, housing shortages in cities. 1989. *The Mayor,* January, 5.

Haus, A. 1988. *Working with homeless people: A guide for staff and volunteers.* NY: Columbia University Community Services.

Hunger, homeless legislation moving through congress. 1988. *The Mayor,* September, 2.

Lives in the balance: Establishing programs for the homeless. 1988. Columbus, OH: Ohio Coalition for the Homeless.

Public Law 100–77. 1987. *Stewart B. McKinney Homeless Assistance Act of 1987.* Sec. 702. 100th U.S. Congress.

Scales, A. M. 1990. Influence of learning theories and reading research on adult education programs. *PAACESETTER* 6, 6–14.

Scales, A., and J. Burley. 1988. A holistic approach to teaching adult literacy techniques. *Lifelong learning: An omnibus of practice and research* 12:26–28.

State of Florida: Adult homeless literacy training and basic skills assistance project. 1989. Division of Vocational, Adult and Community Education Bureau of Adult and Community Education. Tallahassee, FL: Department of Education.

Volunteers of America of greater New York: Project adaptive literacy. 1988. NY: Volunteers of America.

The Nairobi Method:
A Culturally Appropriate
Literacy Approach

Mary Rhodes Hoover, Irving J. McPhail, and Laura Ginyard

Adult literacy as it applies to African Americans is at an abysmally low level in the United States (Bradshaw & Paulu 1986). Forty-eight percent of African Americans are illiterate by the age of seventeen, and overall, 44 percent are functionally illiterate (Kozol 1985). Despite tremendous efforts made to improve reading achievement in schools, 10 to 30 percent of the student population fails to read at satisfactory levels (Biggs 1981). A disproportionate number of the failed students are African Americans. Many are denied instruction in methodology proven to be successful in teaching them—which may be a major cause of the high illiteracy rate.

What is ironic about these statistics is that Africans and African Americans have a long history of literacy (Hoover, Lewis, Daniel, Blackburn, Fowles, & Moloi 1986). Not only did the first forms of writing develop out of ancient African cultures (Williams 1974; Van Sertima 1983; Jackson 1974), but written communication manifested itself in such cultural art forms as weaving, designs of Ashanti gold weights, hair braids, and architecture (McPhail 1987).

African American slaves went through incredibly difficult rituals to acquire literacy (Cornelius 1983). For example, Frederick Douglass (1845) bribed little European American boys with bread to teach him how to read. Additionally, public schools were founded by African Americans in the South during Reconstruction (Du Bois 1973). And during the civil rights and black power movements, many successful literacy campaigns were launched (Brown 1986; Coombs 1973; Heins 1972). One such campaign, focused to improve literacy among African Americans, resulted in the construction of the Nairobi Method. One reason why a method was needed for black or African Americans is because they are the most disadvantaged by illiteracy and the only group in the U.S. with a castelike status (Ogbu 1978).

Development of the method began in 1969 in a community-oriented independent African American college (Nairobi) that was located in East Palo Alto, CA. In particular, it was designed to educate miseducated, culturally and linguistically different African American adults. Miseducated implies that instruction proven to be effective for African Americans had not been provided to them in school. That was a problem that had been caused by the system, not by African Americans.

To date we have verified that the Nairobi Method has been used in a variety of adult education settings and with special adult populations. Examples of settings include adult literacy centers (Hoover 1979), General Educational Development (GED) programs, two- and four-year colleges, remedial programs (Hoover 1982; Berg & Axtell 1968), reading labs (McPhail 1981a), prisons, community agencies, and CETA/JTPA programs. Special populations include second-dialect speakers, second-language speakers, single-parent family heads, and at-risk African American males.

Our purposes, as we continue in this chapter, will be to explore philosophies that contributed to the development of the Nairobi Method, describe responsibilities of the staff who implement the method, present the method as described through its techniques, indicate why the method is important, and conclude with a few recommendations.

Philosophy

In order for a literacy program to be successful, it must first be based on a strong philosophy and a solid social, cultural, and political foundation. For example, the ideology of "conscientization" put forth by the Brazilian educator and philosopher Paulo Freire was the foundation of his literacy program. In his philosophy, individuals and/or groups who were unable to read or write were considered "victims" of society. They were powerless and they were poor. It was by gaining literacy skills that they became, as Freire says, "subjects" rather than "objects" of the society. Instead of having decisions about the quality of their lives made for them, they became the decision makers.

Conscientization was rooted in the culture of the Brazilian people. Freire (1970) found that the people, when motivated by this philosophy, became "more fully human," which speeded up their motor and cognitive activities!

Julius Nyerere (1968) motivated adult students in his literacy program with a philosophy called "Education for Self-Reliance." He stated that

> . . . this is what our educational system has to encourage . . . it has to prepare our people to play a dynamic and constructive part in the development of a society in which all members share fairly in the good or bad fortune of the group, and in which progress is measured in terms of human well-being, not prestige buildings, cars, or other such things, whether privately or publicly owned. Our education must therefore inculcate a sense of commitment to the total community, and help the students to accept the values appropriate to our kind of future, not those appropriate to our colonial past. (P. 52)

Likewise, the Nairobi Method is rooted in a philosophy that is designed to encourage miseducated, culturally and linguistically different adults to believe that a literacy education can make a positive difference in the way they live their lives. The philosophy recognizes that a lack of promotion of the miseducated's culture and history suggest that they do not have a background from which to grow and develop.

Another aspect of the philosophy recognizes that miseducated adults can be motivated through intellectual excitement, knowledge of the educational system, and their history. Intellectual excitement is manifested through lessons, slogans, posters, speakers, and pep talks in classes. Such excitement was seen in the Nairobi Method by Coombs (1973, 42). He states: "I was taken by their interest, their enthusiasm for their work, and their refusal to be intimidated even if they knew their answers were incorrect . . . ." Students were taught to cope with the system by developing upper-level literacy and survival skills. Also, they were taught to use their skills to help others who were less fortunate. Finally, learning about the history of African Americans was a must in the Nairobi Method. In academic courses and in assemblies, students were constantly exposed to the history of Africans' and African Americans' achievements (Van Sertima 1983). They were introduced to the fact that the first alphabet with vowels was invented by Ethiopians (Williams 1974); that universities existed in Timbuktu while other groups were living in "cultural deprivation"; and that the belief that African American and other underrepresented groups in the U.S. come from illiterate cultures is not true.

A third aspect of this method's philosophy includes "going the extra mile" to convince students that someone has a genuine concern for them. That concern includes (a) calling students every day to remind them of their classes; (b) picking up students in order to counsel with them to and from their classes; (c) helping with all details of the students' lives, for example, doctor's appointments, delivery of children, personal problems; and (d) immersing the students with pep talks (Hoover & Fabian 1979).

Finally, the method's philosophy promotes a value system oriented toward the masses of African Americans—the expelled, suspended, and alienated (View from Nairobi 1969). Every student was encouraged to commit himself/herself to a lifelong goal of helping others. To get started, students became engaged in such community service projects as tutoring in the public schools, helping organize community forums, and running errands for the elderly.

Staff

To ensure an all-staff endorsement of high expectations, the staff was given a series of workshops to instill in them a strong belief in students' ability to learn. Students were thus imbued by every staff person in classes and assemblies with these high expectations. Students were informed that though they have been deprived of basic skills in the past, these skills will be provided now. They were encouraged to adopt Malcolm X's vigilance in pursuing upper-level literacy (X & Haley 1966).

Techniques of Nairobi Method

Audience and Language. The techniques used in the Nairobi Method stressed audience participation. While most adult literacy programs value individualization, most of the activities in the Nairobi Method were group oriented and geared to an audience participatory style. For example, students read pattern-practice word lists with partners, played prefix/suffix games, corrected dictation with partners, and paraphrase read. Paraphrase reading was one of the major comprehension exercises. For practice, students were placed in small groups where they read a sentence of a paragraph orally and then paraphrased the sentence in their own words. This exercise not only improved comprehension skills, but vocabulary skills as well.

Because most of the students in classes for miseducated adults were bidialectical (i.e., exposed to two dialects, usually standard English and another variety such as Ebonics—language variety spoken by African and other

Americans), a semiforeign language approach (Hoover, Politzer, & Lewis 1980) to reading was used. With this approach, a systematic exposure to the most regular and frequent spelling patterns in English was provided. This language approach has been effective in teaching African American and other bidialectical students to read (McPhail 1982; McPhail 1983; Weber 1971; Hoover 1978; Guthrie, Martuza, & Seifert 1979).

Before students were assigned compositions to write, they learned how features of their spoken language might influence their written language. To do that, students studied Ebonics; it includes features of West African language patterns (Scales & Brown 1981). Their study enabled them to understand why certain language patterns such as "he come" might appear in their written work. Further, they learned that the reason why there is no third person singular *s* on many of their verbs is because there are very few syllables ending in consonants in most West African languages. Once students understood their language, that is, realized that their language pattern was rule governed like any other language pattern, they wrote freely.

Word Attack. In the Nairobi Method, students were provided a systematic programmed linguistic approach to acquire word attack skills. A linguistic sequence (140 English spelling patterns), with selections written in the pattern provided, was used to avoid failure inherent in presenting a long list of phonic skills with no opportunity for practice in actual reading situations. A linguistic sequence also gives adults many patterns beyond the usual consonants, blends, short vowels, etc. Morphemic, accent, and syllabication patterns were presented for use in analyzing multisyllabic words. Finally, spelling practice of pattern words was provided through dictation by the teacher.

Structured Vocabulary. Students were provided with a structured approach to word attack, spelling, and vocabulary through the presentation of 200 Greek and Latin prefixes, suffixes, and roots. They were given five to ten affixes or roots each day and quizzed on them the following day. An evaluation of their knowledge of these word parts was handled through tests. Afterwards the word parts were discussed in whole words with a given context.

A game, "Automatic Flash" (Hoover & Fabian 1979), designed to assist students' memories was played daily. The affixes/roots thus provide several skill benefits. Among them were (*a*) *word attack*—the affixes/roots were presented according to their spelling patterns, that is, short vowels first, then long vowels, then *r*'s. Students thus improved their knowledge of English orthography and spelling; (*b*) *vocabulary*—the affixes/roots also represented meaning units so the students' vocabulary level increased; (*c*) *security*—students previously taught by an ineffective reading method did not realize that English had a structure and set of rules. They enjoyed discovering the structure and patterns of words.

Reading Comprehension. Most of the reading comprehension materials used in the method incorporated generative words and themes (Freire 1970). An example of a generative word is *cadillac*. From cadillac, students generated discussion of the term and generated such syllables as *cad, ked, kid, cod, cud, dall, dell, dill, doll, dull, lack, leck, lick, dock* for study. Other reading materials included themes that were culturally and politically relevant. Culturally relevant books, for example, included *The Color Purple* (Walker 1982) and *The Earth Did Not Devour Him* (Rivera 1987). Other formats and genres of interest to adults used were magazines, newspapers, and job-related materials. These materials related to students' personal struggles with illiteracy, the educational system, and sexism and racism.

Controlled Composition for Motivation. Students were given a program of controlled composition. The daily composition assignments were designed to give miseducated students a sense of security. As a first assignment, students orally composed a paragraph on the topic: "I Have a Number of Strengths." Techniques from the Language Experience Approach (Van Allen 1976) were incorporated as a guide for students. They learned that, collectively, they had a number of strengths. They recited their strengths and put them into a form letter. The following example, taken from such an oral composition activity, demonstrates this process:

> I have a number of strengths. I am a hard worker. I learn quickly and I am very dependable. As listed above, I am a hard worker. For example, I improved my vocabulary skills in a program I attended six hours a day. At the same time, I was raising my family as a single parent and working part-time as a babysitter.
>
> Another strength I have is that I learn quickly. Though I never tutored before, I picked up the skills to tutor my own children by attending Project Success.
>
> My third strength is that I am very dependable. In my last job, I never missed a day unless I was extremely ill—and that was only once.

This form letter was modified to fit each student's circumstances. Students then used the letter (*a*) as a model of English grammar and organization; (*b*) as the basis for several questions usually asked on applications and interviews for jobs; and (*c*) for self-esteem purposes.

Students memorized the letter so that they would always have a few perfect paragraphs for job interviews and as introductions or conclusions to papers they must write. The letter was also used as a vehicle for grammatical practice. One activity was for students to rewrite the entire paragraph in the past tense, change the "I" to "we," thus changing from singular to plural, and other similar exercises.

Other topics for controlled composition were "Why I Am Unique," "Why My Culture Is Unique," "Why This Program Is Unusual."

Composition Based on Generative Themes. Not only reading but also composition methodologies were used in the Nairobi Method. The composition methodology (Hoover et al. 1986; Hoover & Politzer 1981; Lewis 1981) stressed the use of prose, poetry, and speeches from African American authors. They also stressed such topics as Apartheid, Racism, Miseducation, Protest, and Ebonics. The method combined emphasis on a writing process with work on grammar in the context of African American literature.

Test-Wiseness. Teaching students to develop questions and find answers to the questions were the core components of a test-wiseness strategy taught to students in the Nairobi Method. Specifically, students read a passage, asked questions about the passage, and found answers to their questions. Secondly, for each question written about the passage, students wrote statements that they believed answered their questions. Only one statement was considered as the most complete answer. Third, students wrote questions based on such comprehension skills as main ideas, details, and vocabulary in the passage. Finally, they reviewed their questions in the context of the passage (McPhail 1981b).

By the year 2000, it is predicted that there will be a shortage of workers in the labor force, and, also, that the number of new workers entering the workforce will be from underrepresented groups. They will encompass single-parent families and the functionally illiterate (*Workforce 2000: . . .* 1987). It is also predicted that most new jobs will be nonmanufacturing-type jobs that require higher levels of basic and analytical skills. **Conclusion**

The current workforce is in need of upgrading. Those currently outside of the workforce, the underclass, could provide the much needed increase in workers required by the year 2000. However, this group is largely functionally illiterate. This group, and those who will add themselves to its ranks, are in need of intensive literacy training.

To help improve their chances in the workforce, adult literacy programs could use the Nairobi Method as an instructional technique. The effectiveness of it has been cited in the literature, and its description has been available in the ERIC documents for some time (Coombs 1973; Egerton 1974; Hoover 1982; McPhail 1983).

References

Berg, E., and D. Axtell. 1968. *Programs for disadvantaged students in the California community colleges.* San Mateo, CA: Peralta Junior College District.

Biggs, S. A. 1981. Strategy-based reading instruction. In S. A. Biggs, H. W. Sartain, and A. E. Werdmann, eds., *Thumbprints and thoughtprints: Every learner unique,* 33–44. Proceedings of the 32nd Annual Pittsburgh Conference on Reading and Writing. Pittsburgh, PA: School of Education, University of Pittsburgh.

Bradshaw, J., and N. Paulu. 1986. *Our literacy report card: Research in brief.* Washington, DC: Office of Educational Research and Improvement.

Brown, C. S., ed. 1986. *Reading from within: Septima Clark and the civil rights movement.* Navarro, CA: Wild Tree Press.

Coombs, O. 1973. The necessity of excellence: Nairobi College. *Change* 5(3):39–43.

Cornelius, J. 1983. We slipped and learned to read: Slave accounts of the literacy process, 1820–1865. *Phlon* 44:171–86.

Douglass, F. 1845. *Narrative of the life of Frederick Douglass, an American slave, written by himself.* Boston: Anti-Slavery Office. Also B. Quarles, ed. 1960. Cambridge: Bellnap Press.

Du Bois, W. E. B. 1973. *Black reconstruction in America: 1860–1880.* NY: Atheneum.

Egerton, J. 1974. Nairobi College. In L. Hall, ed., *New colleges for new students, 110–19.* San Francisco: Jossey-Bass.

Freire, P. 1970. *Pedagogy of the oppressed.* NY: Seabury Press.

Guthrie, J. T., N. Martuza, and M. Seifert. 1979. Impact of instructional time in reading. In L. Resnick and P. Weaver, eds., *Theory and practice of early reading,* 153–78. Hillsdale, NJ: Lawrence Erhlbaum.

Heins, M. 1972. *Strictly ghetto property.* Berkeley, CA: Ramparts Press.

Hoover, M. R. 1978. Characteristics of black schools at grade level: A description. *Reading Teacher* 31:757–62.

Hoover, M. R. 1979. *Skills to educate people for survival: Steps curriculum.* Chicago: Chicago Urban Skills Institute.

Hoover, M. R. 1982. A culturally appropriate approach to teaching basic (and other) critical communication skills to black college students. *Negro Educational Review* 33:14–27.

Hoover, M. R., and M. Fabian. 1979. *Patterns for reading manual.* Belmont, CA: Star Publishing Company.

Hoover, M. R., S. Lewis, D. Daniel, R. Blackburn, O. Fowles, and A. Moloi. 1986. *The one/two/three method: A writing process for bidialectical students.* Edina, MN: Bellweather Press.

Hoover, M. R., and R. R. Politizer. 1981. A culturally-appropriate composition assessment: The Nairobi method. In M. Whiteman, ed., *Variations in writing: Functional and linguistic-cultural differences.* Hillsdale, NJ: Lawrence Ehrlbaum.

Hoover, M. R., R. L. Politzer, and S. Lewis. 1980. A semiforeign language approach to teaching reading to bidialectical children. In R. Shafer, ed., *Applied linguistics and reading,* 63–71. Newark, DE: International Reading Association.

Jackson, J. 1974. *Introduction to African civilization.* Secaucaus, NJ: Citadel Press.

Kozol, J. 1985. *Illiterate America.* NJ: Anhor Press.

Lewis, S. 1981. Practical aspects of teaching composition to bidialectical students: The Nairobi Method. In M. Whiteman, ed., *Variations in writing: Functional and linguistic-cultural differences.* Hillsdale, NJ: Lawrence Ehrlbaum.

McPhail, I. P. 1981a. *Faculty institute emphasizes basic skills in the content areas.* Baltimore, MD: Morgan State University, Freshman Reading Program. ERIC Document Reproduction Service no. ED 193–695.

McPhail, I. P. 1981b. Why teach test-wiseness? *Journal of Reading* 25:32–38.

McPhail, I. P. 1982. Toward an agenda for urban literacy: The study of schools where low-income black children read at grade level. *Reading World* 22:132–49.

McPhail, I. P. 1983. A critical evaluation of George Weber's classic study of schools where low-income minority children read at grade level. In L. M. Gentile, M. Kamil, and J. Blanchard, eds., *Reading research revisited,* 549–58. Columbus, OH: Charles E. Merrill.

McPhail, I. P. 1987. Literacy as a liberating experience. *English Quarterly* 20:9–15.

Nyerere, J. 1968. *Ujamaa: Essays on socialism.* NY: Oxford University Press.

Ogbu, J. 1978. *Minority education and caste.* NY: Academic Press.

Rivera, T. 1987. *Y no se lo trago la terra/And the earth did not devour him.* Houston, TX: Arte Publico Press.

Scales, A. M., and B. G. Brown. 1981. Ebonics: An English language pattern. *The Negro Educational Review. XXXII,* 252–57.

Van Allen, R. 1976. *Language experiences in communication.* Boston: Houghton Mifflin Company.

Van Sertima, I. 1983. *Blacks in science.* New Brunswick, NJ: Transaction Books.

View form Nairobi. 1969. *Newsweek,* 6 December, 74, 79.

Walker, A. 1982. *The color purple.* NY: Pocket Press.

Weber, G. 1971. *Inner-city children can be taught to read: Four successful schools.* Occasional Papers no. 18. Washington, DC: Council for Basic Education.

Williams, C. 1974. *The destruction of black civilization.* Chicago: Third World Press.

Workforce 2000: Work and workers for the 21st century. 1987 June. Indianapolis, IN: Hudson Institute.

X, M., and A. Haley. 1966. *The autobiography of Malcolm X.* NY: Grove Press.

Economical Perspectives

A basic understanding of the science of economics and the economic system can enable potential literacy providers to realistically develop programs, seek adequate funding, and evaluate their efforts in order to continue serving a given population. Literacy providers who already subscribe to certain philosophical beliefs and who recognize certain sociological conditions can focus on economic systems that may be explained simply as having to do with the production, distribution, and use of wealth, goods, and services. Introduction

Many who provide literacy services depend on the private and public sectors to fund their programs. Thus, decisions are made concerning the allocation of resources by those persons who represent each sector. Recently, adult literacy education programs have received unprecedented attention from the private sector. That sector does not necessarily want to pay to educate its employees in literacy skills, but illiteracy costs them millions annually.

Several ways and means of addressing the cost are offered through chapters in this section of the volume. Although each chapter is written from a different audience perspective, similarity was unavoidable. First, cost-effectiveness of adult basic skills programs is addressed by Mikulecky. Next, proposal writing to secure funding is addressed by Gardner. While Richardson's chapter examines how much monetary and what voluntary contributions have been made to literacy education, Norton's chapter examines why and how such contributions from the private sector have been made. Springer's chapter, from a corporation's perspective, follows with a discussion of why, when, and directly to whom corporations should contribute monetary and in-kind support. Finally, the need to evaluate the success or failure of adult literacy programs for continued funding is presented by Harris.

Effectiveness and Cost-Effectiveness of Adult Basic Skills Education

Larry Mikulecky

Millions of adult citizens in the U.S. find they need a second chance to improve or refurbish their basic literacy and computational skills. In part, this is due to a gap between the basic skills abilities needed to be productive in the workplace and the ability levels of a significant percentage of workers.

Many adults find that their basic reading, writing, computation, and problem-solving skills are insufficient for life's current demands. They enroll in no-charge basic skills programs—some attempting to complete their high school education, others to brush up on skills in a specific area, and still others who struggle to keep ahead of their own school-age children. All are partaking of *second-chance basic skills education.*

Individuals needing this education are recent high school graduates with a poor education, school dropouts, and mature adults facing retraining in mid-career. The overall target population encompasses those who are employed, underemployed, and unemployed. They have numerous problems. In this chapter I will examine their problems in the context of programs and populations, professional instructors and volunteers, program effectiveness, and problems and policy options for adult second-chance basic skills education.

Programs and Populations

Programs. Second-chance basic skills programs are offered by a wide variety of providers. The vast majority of these programs are free to users. Most learners in the programs are served by U.S. federal- and state-funded adult basic education (ABE) classes held in settings that include school buildings, community centers, correctional institutions, YMCAs, and shopping centers. During a one-month period in the spring of 1985, a survey of state-funded adult literacy programs in the fifty states and Washington, DC, was conducted. At that time, over 729,000 adults were reported as receiving services (Bowker 1987). Since there is a good deal of turnover among learners in adult basic skills programs, the total number of learners served in programs over the period of a full year is likely to be considerably higher.

Comprehensive national demographic data are not available on who attends these basic skills classes. The Literacy Assistance Center, however, has compiled data on the 40,000 learners involved in basic skills programs in New York City (Cook 1986). Of the 40,000 New York City learners, nearly 52 percent were enrolled in classes to learn English as a second or other language. Of the basic education students, 10.7 percent were reported to read below a third-grade level and 25.3 percent read below a fifth-grade level. In New York City, 41 percent of the students were male, and 59 percent female. The typical learner was likely to be female, a member of an under-represented group (89 percent), and between the ages of twenty-five and forty-two (52 percent). One-third of the learners were between the ages of sixteen and twenty-four.

In addition to state-funded ABE programs, adults with low basic skills are served by volunteer organizations, private industry programs, college- and university-sponsored basic education classes, and basic skills classes attached to job-training programs. Several programs are also offered informally by private citizens and community and church organizations. No full census of learners has been compiled, and a complete census of all programs is probably impossible since many programs keep inadequate records either as a result of low funding or to ensure learner anonymity. A recent public policy report estimates that as many as three to four million learners may be served by the total of all public and private, formal and informal groups (Chisman 1989).

Potential Populations versus Served Populations. Most U.S. program reports in the research literature estimate *potential* local learner populations by extending estimates of the percentage of functional illiterates taken from national studies. Depending on the literacy level selected as constituting functional literacy and the national studies, national figures of adults experiencing literacy difficulty range from 20 million to over 40 million. Examples of typical local estimate projections from these national data include 90,000 functional illiterates projected in Delaware County, Pennsylvania (Gaul 1987), to over 2 million illiterates in the state of Illinois (Illinois Community College Board 1987).

Populations actually served by programs rarely amount to more than a minuscule fraction of the estimated target populations. Percentages of low-literates served range from less than 1 percent reported by California and Washington State programs (Lane 1984; Carbone 1987) to nearly 5 percent reported by a local Reno, Nevada, program (Bear 1987).

Problems occur when using national population estimates of illiteracy to determine local populations of low-literates. First, some locations vary considerably from national averages. For example, the percentage of low-literates in Louisiana or Mississippi or Texas is nearly triple that of Utah (Brizius & Foster 1987). Secondly, the criteria for being a member of the target population may be inappropriate. Researchers have recommended caution in determining who *needs* literacy education help. Fingeret (1983), for example, maintains that many low-literates use social networks of friends and relatives to help them with daily basic skills demands and therefore may not need additional help. Other researchers argue that simply because someone has managed, through the help of others to function in society, it does not mean that this individual is productive, safe, or guaranteed to continue functioning (Mikulecky 1987).

Though conclusions about need are arguable, it does seem clear that many adults do not perceive themselves as needing or wanting help. In reference to

Canadians, strong indications about low self-perception of need for help among low-literates has been cited by Jones (1988). The Canadian version of the recent U.S. national assessment of adult literacy (Kirsch & Jungeblut 1986) added an item asking adults if they thought they needed help with literacy. The Canadian study (Calamai 1987) found that nearly 90 percent of adults who failed the test *thought they didn't need help* (Jones 1988). This does not, of course, mean that adults who score poorly on basic skills tasks do not need help. It simply means that they are not likely to seek help since they do not perceive themselves as needing it.

Professional Instructors and Volunteers

For the most part, basic skills instruction in the U.S. is provided by part-time teachers and by volunteers. For fiscal year (FY) 1985–1986, the U.S. Office of Adult Education reports that service was provided by over 82,000 instructors in its programs. Of these instructors, only 8 percent were full-time, while 67 percent were part-time and 25 percent were volunteers (Pugsley 1987).

Paid Instructors' Qualification and Training. Levels of training and certification among instructors is quite low (Harman 1985). Skagen (1986) notes that most paid ABE instructors are part-time elementary and secondary teachers who have no special training in teaching adults. Chall, Heron, and Hilferty (1987) observe that staff turnover is very high. Most instructors hold more than one job, and some even shuttle between two or more local literacy centers. Instructors who have little training upon entering programs are unlikely to get much new training from the programs that employ them. Monies for travel and in-service rarely exceed 1 percent of total literacy program budgets (Vorst 1988; Illinois Community College Board 1987). Because resources are spread thinly, part-time instructors often work without immediate supervision and interactions with other instructors who are part-time.

Volunteer Tutors' Level of Participation and Training. A 1985 survey of volunteer use, in the U.S., indicates that volunteer tutors were used, to some degree, by nearly half of state- and federal-funded adult education programs and nearly all local adult literacy programs (Bowker 1987). The vast majority (92 percent) serve as one-on-one tutors, while 39 percent teach small groups, and 8 percent teach classes. The contribution of these volunteers in terms of time and energy is significant. The Literacy Volunteers of America (LVA) report having nearly 29,000 volunteers who averaged fifty hours of service per volunteer during 1987–1988. Also, LVA reported having nearly a thousand more tutors than learners. This suggests that not all tutors are equally involved and some may be inactive (Wright 1989).

Volunteers typically receive from ten to fifteen hours of training, a good deal of which is directed toward pragmatic issues such as where materials are located, where to meet with learners, and how to contact supervisors. There is considerable concern that such meager training is insufficient when one must work with adults who have severe learning problems. Keefe and Meyer (1988) used a battery of professional diagnostic tests to screen 114 adult learners in an ABE program. Of low-literates below the third-grade reading level, over 70 percent had uncorrected or uncorrectable vision problems and half had auditory discrimination problems that confounded their abilities to learn to read. These sorts of learner problems are not easily diagnosed by untrained volunteers and often frustrate teaching techniques learned in superficial training.

Second-chance basic skills programs document effectiveness using a variety of indicators. Among these indicators are the ability to recruit and retain learners, funding, volunteer efforts, and impact of training on earnings or other learner-identified goals.

Program Effectiveness

Recruitment and Retention. Second-chance basic skills programs have not done very well at either attracting or retaining a significant number of learners. Recruitment appears to be improving, but there is no current evidence for improved retention.

Though current media campaigns have helped in the recruitment of adult learners, the general consensus among adult educators is that personal sources such as teachers, counselors, friends, and relatives are more effective for recruitment than impersonal sources such as the media (Balmuth 1988). Carbone (1987) reports that even in the light of a national television literacy awareness campaign, only 17 percent of the clients attending Washington State literacy programs reported becoming aware of literacy help through the media. Teachers, counselors, social-welfare agencies, as well as friends and relatives, were all ranked higher by learners as resources of knowledge about programs. It may be that media advertising is more effective in recruiting tutors than those needing basic skills help.

Retaining learners long enough for programs to have an impact is a major problem (Balmuth 1988). Military data (Sticht 1982) and large program data such as that of New York City (Denny 1988) indicate that it takes an average of approximately 100 contact hours for a learner to improve a single grade level. Military programs described by Sticht (1982) are usually much more intensive (i.e., approximately twenty hours per week) than traditional ABE programs, which provide two to three hours of instruction to a learner per week. Less-intensive programs have sometimes been identified as exemplary and have demonstrated the ability to accomplish the equivalent of one year's gain in approximately fifty hours (Darling 1984; Pasch & Oakley 1985).

High-quality instruction helps a good deal, but a significant amount of time is needed for even the best programs to have an impact. No program in the literature reports holding average learners as long as even 100 hours per year. It takes several hundred hours of learning time to move a learner from sounding out words on road signs to being able to comprehend most newspaper stories. In typical state-funded ABE programs, learners voluntarily attend two to three hours per week with high rates of absenteeism. Only 20 percent of learners persist a year or longer (Darkenwald & Valentine

1985; Developmental Associates 1980; Diekhoff & Diekhoff 1984; Pasch & Oakley 1985).

Programs without state funding and using only volunteer tutors may fare even worse. LVA reports having approximately one tutor for each learner. The organization estimates that tutors averaged fifty hours of contributed time during 1987–1988. This estimate would indicate that most learners receive less than an hour of instruction per week. An alternative explanation would be that most learners leave volunteer tutoring programs well before fifty hours of instruction. In either case, time spent in volunteer tutoring programs suggests that major basic skill gains by learners are unlikely.

Diekhoff (1988) analyzed the records of 194 former participants in a community-based adult literacy program in Texas. The program was above average in effectiveness in that the average reading gain from entry to exit was 1.6 grade levels in 9.8 months. Diekhoff finds the significance of the gain questionable since only 12 percent of the learners left the program able to read above the 7.5 grade level.

Data on learner gain in measured competence are difficult to find. It is much more typical for programs to report effectiveness in terms of general statements. For example, the Commonwealth of Pennsylvania reports that for 1985, 29,409 learners were enrolled in programs, and 25,531 (87 percent) learners met their personal objectives. What the personal objectives might be or how meeting them was determined is not clear (Pennsylvania Department of Education 1986).

Funding and Cost-Effectiveness. Bowker (1987) reports that 83 percent of literacy instruction was received by adults in state-funded adult education programs. Funding in such programs comes primarily through the U.S. federal Adult Education Act of 1966 with amendments in 1978 to extend services throughout the public and private sector. The Adult Education Act provides mainly federal funding (90 percent) with a required 10 percent state contribution of funds (Delker 1984). In 1985, this amounted to approximately $81 million (Congress of the United States 1987).

In May of 1986, a congressional staff study was undertaken to analyze the Literacy Management Information Project Report (LMIPR), which claimed to itemize federal funding for adult literacy programs. The LMIPR indicated that there are seventy-nine literacy-related programs administered by fourteen federal agencies and that $347.6 million were spent on adult literacy activities in 1985. In order to verify the LMIPR report, the committee surveyed seventy-nine literacy-related program directors by telephone and randomly contacted twenty state directors. A good deal in the LMIPR figures appears to be questionable. The congressional study found that (*a*) of the seventy-nine programs in fourteen federal agencies reported in the LMIPR, only ten programs (13 percent) in five federal agencies reported actually conducting literacy activities; (*b*) several programs reported receiving no funding for literacy programs; and (*c*) in FY 1985, only $126.5 million

(36 percent) of the reported $347.6 million was spent on literacy activities for adults (Congress of the United States 1987).

Even though the Canadian population is approximately 10 percent the size of the U.S. population, its government spends considerably more than the U.S. per capita. Sparks (1989) of the Ontario Ministry of Skills Development reports that the Canadian federal government is scheduled to spend $110 million on adult literacy in 1989. Instead of the 10 percent matching funds provided by most states in the U.S., Canadian provinces provide significant funding for adult literacy at the provincial level. Ontario, for example, will spend $50 million on adult literacy programs in 1989. If the same ratio of spending were present in the U.S., adult literacy budgets between $1 billion and $2 billion would be in order.

Funding for most ABE programs in the U.S. is usually a combination of state and federal monies, augmented by a variety of contributed resources. Though many programs rely almost entirely on state and federal support, some programs are able to generate additional resources and accomplish a good deal more than state and federal funding could possibly support alone.

An example of this type of expanded support can be found in the Lafayette Adult Reading Academy (LARA), which recently won a U.S. Department of Education award for Outstanding Adult Education. In 1987, the LARA provided nearly 50,000 learner-contact hours and nearly 7,000 hours of paid instruction. Over 800 learners averaged fifty-eight hours of contact per year at an average cost of $4.59 per hour or $266 per registrant. Federal and state monies of approximately $55,000 covered administrative costs and salaries of the academy's part-time teaching staff. The academy's staff has extended its resources base. They have (a) trained 150 volunteer tutors; (b) solicited grants from Target, Alcoa, and Pillsbury for offering specialized on-the-job literacy training; and (c) received small donations of money, materials, and goods from local businesses, agencies, school corporations, clubs, and individuals (Vorst 1988). Most adult basic skills programs have narrower support, rely more heavily on state and federal funding, and work with fewer learners.

Reported costs per learner in other programs are of the same order or magnitude as the Lafayette program, though the cost per instructional hour is often slightly less. Average learner costs per year in New York and Nevada are $272 and $184, respectively, and costs per hour of instruction are $1.85 and $2.60, respectively (New York State Education Department 1987; Bear 1987). Higher program costs per hour of instruction in the Lafayette program can be attributed to more highly trained and expensive instructors, instructors' time spent helping write grant proposals to generate resources, and noninstructional time spent training and supervising volunteer tutors.

Another perspective on ABE costs is to compare them to the costs of private tutoring and of public school education. The International Reading Association (Committee reports . . . 1989) reports results of a survey of private reading clinics and tutoring services. The average private service charges from $21 to $30 per hour for individual basic skills instruction. A year's worth of instruction at three hours per week would cost from $3,276 to $4,680. The public schools spend an average of $4,000 per child each year (Chisman 1989). This purchases approximately 1,000 hours of instruction per year in classes of twenty-five to thirty students at a cost of approximately $4.00 per instructional hour. Adult basic education programs are not able to provide anywhere near 1,000 hours of instruction per year for each learner. The instructional hour cost of providing one-on-one or small group instruction in ABE centers is close to, or below, public schools' costs for providing large-group instruction. The cost of ABE is a minuscule fraction of private tutoring or public schooling costs. The ineffectiveness of much adult basic education instruction may well be a "you get what you pay for" phenomenon with some magnificent exceptions to the general rule.

Cost-Effectiveness of Volunteer Tutoring. Volunteer tutors have contributed a significant amount of time to helping others learn to read. It is not clear how effective they have been compared to social expectations or even compared to paid instructors. Because volunteers provide their time without charge, policy makers sometimes conclude that volunteers are a simple and cheap solution for adult literacy problems.

There are, however, significant costs in providing volunteer tutoring. For example, volunteers must be properly recruited and trained, and trainers of volunteers must themselves be trained. Moreover, volunteers must be supervised and supported by experts and other professional personnel—especially when dealing with low literates with severe learning disabilities (Harman 1985). In addition, volunteers need to be provided with appropriate instructional materials, provided work space, provided help in solving tutoring problems, and evaluated. A ratio of one supervisor to four volunteer tutors is commonly needed (Woods 1988).

Often the resources invested in recruiting, training, and developing volunteer tutors has limited impact. Many tutors work with only one or two learners during a year and then leave programs. The dropout rate among tutors is quite high, so recruiting and training resources are often wasted. Rogers (1984) notes that one LVA program trained 244 tutors in a six-year period. At the end of that period, 91 percent of the tutors had dropped out of the program. For the most part, each year sees a new contingent of untrained tutors with only a few carryover tutors.

In summary, since the effectiveness of volunteer tutors is unclear, the cost-effectiveness is not possible to determine. It is clear, however, that volunteer tutoring programs are not cost free and, given the high dropout rates of tutors, may not be particularly cost-efficient. There may be intangible benefits to volunteer tutor programs in terms of the tutors' heightened sensitivity and awareness of literacy problems.

Impact on Earnings. No controlled study exists to substantiate the relationship of basic skill improvement to improved earning ability. Program reports at local levels sometimes identify numbers of individuals who have found employment and left programs, but no study was identified by me that causally links such employment or improved earning ability to basic skills improvement. Also, no study was found to compare new employment of basic skills students to that of a control group receiving no instruction.

Broadly based correctional studies do identify a clear relationship between basic skills levels and income (Berlin & Sum 1988). Mikulecky and Strange (1986) describe an intensive, integrated basic skills/word processor training program in which 70 percent of the participants moved from receiving state support to earning $20,000+ per year on jobs as word processor operators. Entrance to the program involved passing several screening tests. Program participants were paid to take training for forty hours per week up to twenty-six weeks. They were only released from the program to apply for jobs when they demonstrated basic and technical skills equivalent to the average word processor operator in the local area. This required most of them to improve the equivalent of three grade levels in reading and writing abilities during the six-month period of training. Participants of this intensive program received more training in two weeks than 90 percent of adult basic education students receive per year. They received more training in twenty-six weeks than most basic skills program participants would receive in thirteen years were they to attend that long.

Second-chance basic skills education is not very effective in the U.S. Among the problems of current programs are (a) extremely low enrollment of target populations into programs; (b) significant waiting lists in existing programs; (c) inability to retain the vast majority of learners in programs long enough to make a significant functional difference in skill levels; (d) the uneven quality of instruction (i.e., learners in effective programs learn at double the average rate); and (e) lack of knowledge about several key aspects of basic skills education (i.e., effectiveness of volunteers and technology, impact on productivity and safety, etc.).

Problems and Policy Options

State and federal basic skills education policy options have been effectively outlined in publications by Brizius and Foster (1987) and by Chisman (1989). Following are ideas drawn partly from these two publications.

1. *Incentives.* Several states have already implemented or begun discussion of incentive and mandatory requirement programs of one sort or another. For example, Governor Ashcroft of Missouri has proposed a "Learnfare" program that would require AFDC (aid for dependent children) parents who have not completed high school to enroll in basic education and job-search programs. Virginia has instituted a "no read, no release" program in which reading to a sixth-grade level is an important element in considering probation requests for inmates. North Carolina has considered whether it should refuse to hire dropouts who are not seeking further education. Some states are considering school completion or enrollment in an educational program

as a condition for receiving a driver's license (Brizius & Foster 1987). Recent media reports also suggest that West Virginia's plan to revoke driver's licenses of dropouts below the age of eighteen may have lowered dropout rates by 30 percent.

2. *Enrollment Retention.* Program providers should acknowledge incentives as a way of increasing enrollment and retention of basic skills learners in appropriate programs. Local applicants for state or federal social service funding can be given special consideration if they develop cooperative strategies for agencies to provide transportation, day care, and basic skills education to targeted learners. Decisions for funding can be weighted in favor of programs that involve community groups and other social agencies in identifying and referring learners. Many of these incentives can be developed using existing monies and clearer guidelines for funding applicants.

Tax incentives for businesses and individuals can increase the recruitment and retention of learners in basic skills programs. Industries with a high percentage of displaced workers or other adjustment problems can be targeted with tax support for basic skills programs. Expanding tax credits for on-the-job training to include a wider range of basic skills activities could encourage increased workplace basic skills programs. The overall cost of these efforts would be determined entirely by which industries were targeted and what degree of tax incentives were allowed. These incentives would be linked to guidelines that require significantly more training than the ineffective two to three hours per week now provided in most government-funded programs. Tax incentives could also be developed to enable employers to raise salaries as workers improve in skill levels. Sometimes incentives can be brought about by simply redirecting current taxes. For example, an unemployment insurance program in California allows employers to redirect a portion of unemployment insurance payments to a special fund for retraining current workers.

3. *Increased Direct and Indirect Service.* Few basic skills education services are provided directly by state or federal government. Exceptions are state and federal delivery of service in correctional institutions, some vocational programs, and some military programs. For these programs, increased funding to reduce program waiting lists and to enhance recruitment is in order. In addition, more direct basic skills education service could be provided by existing programs. For example, at the state level, many programs have taken on educational and referral roles with clients. Natural resource agencies in thirty-eight states have included literacy training as an integral component of Civilian Conservation Corps-type programs. In Tennessee, unemployment insurance counselors use special guidelines to diagnose and refer low-literate applicants. In Vermont, unemployment checks are accompanied by cards recruiting basic skills learners. Similar

programs could be instituted by federal agencies or encouraged by federal incentives.

The majority of federal basic skills support is indirect through Adult Basic Education, Adult Vocational Education, and Job Training Partnership Act (JTPA) funding. In addition, the federal government claims indirect literacy support through fourteen federal agencies that have been reported to fund seventy-nine literacy-related programs. The congressional analysis of the government listing suggests the majority of programs cited do not yet offer literacy support, and many program directors are unaware that they are expected to offer basic skills support. Only 36 percent of the budgeted money claimed appears to be actually used for basic skills support. Clearer bureaucratic communication and administration could allocate funds more effectively.

Chisman (1989) suggests the most profitable targets for increased funding and/or clearer guidelines for accountability are JTPA, Carl D. Perkins Vocational Education Act, Adult Education Act, Family Support Act, Even Start Program, and Volunteers in Service to America. In all of these programs, emphasis should be placed upon solutions that provide a significant amount of contact to learners in need of basic skills training and to monitor learner gain. Two to three hours of training per week is not sufficient, in most cases, to make acceptable learner gains. Suggested additional funding levels for the programs previously mentioned are (*a*) additional $100 million to JPTA for large workplace literacy demonstration programs; (*b*) additional $64 million to the Adult Education Act State Grant program to bring funding to the $200 million approved for FY 1989; (*c*) fund Even Start at the $35 million level; and (*d*) add $3 million to VISTA funding for innovative use of voluntary programs. These suggested figures are drawn from the computations compiled to produce *Jump Start* (Chisman 1989).

4. *Increasing the Quality of Knowledge and Instruction.* Adults learn in ways significantly different from children (Valentine 1986). School learning is considerably different from workplace learning (Mikulecky 1982). Little, however, is known about how adults with low basic skills best learn. Also there is very little information on the limits of training with low-literate adults or the impact of improved basic skills on productivity and safety. In terms of learner gain, the best programs are twice as effective as average programs, but there is little evidence on the best ways to move average and below-average programs toward excellence.

5. *Policy Options for Increasing Knowledge.* Policy options for increasing research knowledge about improving adult basic skills include (*a*) earmarking larger amounts of currently allocated Department of Education and Department of Labor research funding

to target adult basic skills issues ($7 million); (*b*) establishing a National Center for Adult Literacy (Chisman 1989) that would conduct basic and applied research, provide technical assistance to professionals and policy makers, and maintain a national data base to monitor the field ($30 million); and (*c*) providing incentives for business to sponsor research about the effectiveness of basic skills training within specific industries.

6. *Policy Options for Improving Quality of Instruction.* Improving the quality of instruction is a more difficult policy issue. Since few basic skills providers are *directly* employed by the federal government, direct intervention is usually not possible. Low-quality instruction is probably related to (*a*) low instructor pay, which is correlated to high turnover rates and low levels of instructor training; (*b*) minimal on-the-job training for instructors; and (*c*) the lack of connection between learner improvement and program funding.

Policy options for improving instructor and program quality include (*a*) developing incentives for learner improvement, which could include merit bonuses for programs with high demonstrated learner improvement and evidence of significant learner improvement as one criterion for refunding programs; (*b*) increasing funding availability to programs who hire full-time reading and basic skills specialists; and (*c*) requiring that 2 to 3 percent of program budget proposals be allocated to state-approved in-service training of instructors. A portion of this could be provided at the state level as part of coordinated efforts for instructor improvement.

Such incentives could be accomplished by adding 10 percent to program funding to be used for incentive bonuses. If no additional funding is available, baseline program funding could be reduced by 10 percent with the remaining funds allocated on the basis of merit and competitive instructor-training proposals.

References

Balmuth, M. 1988. Recruitment and retention in adult basic education: What does the research say? *Journal of Reading* 31:620–23.

Bear, D. R. 1987. *Project TACL: A team approach to community literacy.* Reno, NV: Nevada University, Reno, College of Education.

Berlin, G., and A. Sum. 1988. *Toward a more perfect union: Basic skills, poor families, and our economic future.* NY: Ford Foundation.

Bowker, R. R. 1987. Adult literacy programs: Services, persons served, and volunteers. In F. Simora, M. M. Spier, and D. P. Gray, eds., *Bowker annual of library and book trade information* (32nd ed), 397–410. NY: R. R. Bowker Company.

Brizius, J., and S. Foster. 1987. *Enhancing adult literacy: A policy guide.* Washington, DC: Council of State Policy and Planning Agencies.

Calamai, P. 1987. *Broken words: Why five million Canadians are illiterate.* Toronto, Ontario: Southam Newspaper Group.

Carbone, G. J. 1987. *The 1986 Literacy Tutor Coordination program: A report to the legislature pursuant to chapter 312 laws in 1986.* Olympia, WA: Washington Office of the State Superintendent of Public Instruction.

Chall, J. S., E. Heron, and A. Hilferty, A. 1987. Adult literacy: New and enduring problems. *Phi Delta Kappan* 69:190–96.

Chisman, F. P. 1989. *Jump Start: The federal role in adult literacy.* Southport, CT: The Southport Institute.

Committee reports on reading services offered by businesses. 1989. *Reading Today,* no. 5:4. Newark DE: International Reading Association.

Congress of the United States 1987. *An assessment of the federal initiative in the area of adult literacy.* Staff report of the subcommittee on elementary, secondary, and vocational education of the Committee on Education and Labor, U. S. House of Representatives, 100th Congress. Washington, DC: House Committee on Education and Labor. ERIC Document Reproduction Service no. ED 286–072.

Cook, J. 1986. *Final report: New York City adult literacy initiative.* NY: Literacy Assistance Center.

Darkenwald, G., and T. Valentine. 1985. Outcomes of participation in adult basic skills education. *Lifelong Learning* 8:17–22.

Darling, S. 1984. Illiteracy: An everyday problem for millions. *Appalachia* 18:21–28.

Delker, P. V. 1984. *Ensuring effective adult literacy policies and procedures at the federal and state levels.* Washington, DC: Office of Vocational and Adult Education. ERIC Document Reproduction Service no. ED 260–281.

Denny, V. H. 1988. *Analysis of New York City's 1986–87 data base.* A paper presented at the National Reading Conference, December, Tucson, AZ.

Developmental Associates. 1980. *An assessment of the state administered program of the Adult Education Act.* Final report. Arlington, VA: Developmental Associates.

Diekhoff, G. M. 1988. An appraisal of adult literacy programs: Reading between the lines. *Journal of Reading* 31:624–30.

Diekhoff, G. G., and K. B. Diekhoff. 1984. The adult literacy program attrition problem: Identification at intake. *Adult Literacy and Basic Education* 8:34–37.

Fingeret, A. 1983. Social network: A new perspective on independence and illiterate adults. *Adult Education Quarterly* 33:133–46.

Gaul, P. 1987. *Evaluation of the effectiveness of work study students in extension and expansion of literacy services in Delaware County, Chester, PA.* Harrisburg, PA: Pennsylvania State Department of Education. ERIC Document Reproduction Service no. ED 266–273.

Harman, D. 1985. *Turning literacy around: An agenda for national action.* NY: Business Council for Effective Literacy.

Illinois Community College Board. 1987. *Fiscal year 1987 disadvantaged student grant report.* Springfield, IL.

Jones, P. C. 1988. *The good news about illiteracy.* Toronto, Ontario: Business Task Force on Literacy.

Keefe, D., and V. Meyer. 1988. Profiles of and instructional strategies for adult disabled readers. *Journal of Reading* 31:614–19.

Kirsch, I., and A. Jungeblut. 1986. *Literacy profiles of America's young adults.* Princeton, NJ: National Assessment of Educational Progress at Educational Testing Service.

Lane, M. A. 1984. *California literacy campaign program effectiveness review.* Sacramento, CA: California State Library. ERIC Document Reproduction Service no. ED 263–917.

Mikulecky, L. 1982. Job literacy: The relationship between school preparation and workplace actuality. *Reading Research Quarterly* 17:400–19.

Mikulecky, L. 1987. The status of literacy in our society. In J. Readance and S. Baldwin, eds., *Research in literacy: Merging perspectives,* 211–35. NY: National Reading Conference, 36th Yearbook.

Mikulecky, L., and R. Strange. 1986. Effective literacy training programs for adults in business and municipal employment. In J. Orasanu, ed., *A decade of reading research: Implications for practice.* NJ: Lawrence Erlbaum Associates.

New York State Education Department. 1987. *Adult literacy education program, New York State participant data for 1985–1986.* Albany, NY: New York State Education Department, Division of Adult and Continuing Education. ERIC Document Reproduction Service no. ED 286–004.

Pasch, M., and N. Oakley. 1985. *An evaluation study of project LEARN. Students and tutors 1982–1984.* Paper presented at the 69th Annual Meeting of the American Educational Research Association, Chicago, Illinois.

Pennsylvania Department of Education. 1986. *Adult basic education programs in the commonwealth of Pennsylvania.* Harrisburg, PA: Pennsylvania State Department of Education, Division of Adult Basic Education.

Pugsley, R. S. 1987. *National data update.* A presentation at the Annual Conference, State Directors of Adult Education, Washington, DC, 21 July.

Rogers, J. J. 1984. Maintaining volunteer participation in adult literacy programs. *Lifelong Learning* 9:22–24.

Skagen, A., ed. 1986. *Workplace literacy.* NY: AMA Membership Publications Division.

Sparks, R. 1989. *Workplace literacy.* A paper presented at Functional Literacy: Conceptions and Misconceptions of Competence. University of Toronto, Toronto, Ontario, 24 May.

Sticht, T. G. 1982. *Basic skills for defense.* Alexandria, VA: Human Resources Research Organization.

Valentine, T. 1986. *Issues central to the definition of adult functional literacy.* Contract no. OERI-P-86–3014. Unpublished manuscript presented to the U.S. Department of Education.

Vorst, J. 1988. *Lafayette Adult Reading Academy Newsletter.* Lafayette, IN: Lafayette Adult Reading Academy, Fall.

Woods, G. 1988. *Evaluation of literacy and basic skills initiatives.* Toronto, Ontario: Ministry of Skills Development.

Wright, K. D. 1989. Literacy volunteers of America. *Update: A national newsletter for the adult literacy and the adult learning community.* Washington, DC: U.S. Department of Education, January.

The Private Sector: A Funding Possibility for Adult Literacy Training and Research Projects

William E. Gardner, Jr.

In recent years, a minimum of $10 billion annually of corporate and foundation money has been granted to worthy causes (*Foundation Giving Watch* 1988). Corporate philanthropists and foundations are not awarding grants indiscriminantly, however, and there are many deserving prospective recipients. Competing for the same funds are hundreds of thousands of nonprofit agencies, including hospitals, federated campaigns such as the United Way, libraries, environmental protection groups, drug rehabilitation services, and cultural centers as well as schools (Mirkin 1978; *Foundation Giving Watch* 1988).

By becoming aware of the art of private sector grantsmanship, one can gain an invaluable edge over the competition. Although there is some overlap in the methodology of private sector philanthropy versus governmental-agency giving, there are critical differences. In this chapter I will present those distinctions to you, the reader. I have assumed that you will be attempting to get your project or program funded. So throughout this chapter, I will speak directly to you.

Background

In the public sector, the guidelines for writing proposals tend to be stated in precise, detailed form. The private sector, on the other hand, is quite different because each corporate or foundation giving program is distinct. Therefore, it is important to know as much as possible about the organization from which you are seeking funds. According to Hillman (1980) and Hillman and Abarbanel (1975), there are several areas that you should investigate before approaching the funder. Included among the areas are *why, to whom, what,* and *how* corporations or foundations give. You should also carefully analyze your own needs (Hillman 1980; Hillman & Abarbanel 1975).

Why Corporations and Foundations Give

To approach a corporation or foundation on the assumption that it will fund you simply because you have a good cause is naive. Contrary to what corporate public relations departments or foundation officers would have you believe, these organizations seldom, if ever, give for purely altruistic reasons. The first and foremost rule of corporate giving is that virtually all donations are made in the self-interest of the corporation and/or its decision makers. Foundations tend to have a set of specific reasons that indicate why they give (e.g., to raise the level of literacy in the local community or to improve the quality of life for underprivileged children).

Philanthropy is a useful tool that a corporation can use to project a positive image in the eyes of the general public. To illustrate, if the local utility company lowers prices an average two dollars per month, the customer will probably be happy but will not necessarily think of the company in endearing terms. Consider that same customer's reaction upon hearing that the utility company has donated $500,000 to the school district to improve the literacy levels of certain marginal adults in the city. Foundations frequently use philanthropy to influence public policy. For example, if there is a concern for the homeless or teenage pregnancies, a foundation might direct its grants in these areas to focus attention on the problems.

The grant seeker is well-advised to know the reasons why a corporation or foundation operates a giving program. When a grant seeker misinterprets the true motives of a funder, the request for a donation misses the mark and is unpersuasive. The grant seeker will be off-target when the time comes to develop a match between his or her needs and the interests of the funder.

To Whom the Corporations and Foundations Give

Private funders usually state the categories that they fund in their annual reports. Not only are the categories reported but the percentage of the total amount given in each category is reported. In recent years both corporations and foundations have directed sizable proportions of their giving resources to education. Some are focused toward higher education, and others are open to the entire array of education levels.

It is important to know whom the corporations or foundations are interested in supporting. When a grant seeker fails to identify the groups that the funder has targeted, the request for a grant award is likely not to be given serious consideration.

What Corporations and Foundations Give

Cash is the best-known mode of grant award, whether it comes from government agencies, foundations, or corporations. In virtually all cases, governmental agencies and foundations are limited to this type of award. In addition to cash, corporations also give in-kind (noncash) contributions to charitable causes. This distinguishes corporate philanthropy from that of foundations and most governmental agencies. The various kinds of gifts given by corporations to the grant seeker follow.

Cash

The cash donation can be unrestricted (e.g., used for general operations), or more likely, it can be earmarked for specific purposes such as funding a literacy project for adults or funding a graduate fellowship for reading teachers.

Company Materials

While the most recent U.S. Tax Reform Act severely limited many of the tax advantages previously allowed for donation of materials to charities, the current laws still offer tempting incentives to most corporations. If the recipient has tax-exempt status and the materials have not been fully depreciated on the books, the corporation can take an immediate tax deduction for the undepreciated value of the materials. Materials donated by corporations include:

Artist supplies	Computer software
Athletic equipment	Desks
Audiovisual equipment	Laboratory equipment
Ballpoint pens	Loudspeakers
Blackboards	Musical instruments
Books	Photocopying machines
Bookshelves	Portable buildings
Buses	Tables
Calculators	Television
Clipboards	Typewriters
Computer hardware	Writing paper

Some corporations will sponsor a print or broadcast media advertisement on your behalf. Perhaps you have noticed a local business taking out a full-page newspaper ad or television commercial that appeals for public support of a school for special students. The key question is whether the school would have been better off receiving $1,000 cash rather than receiving the benefits of the ad or commercial. In most cases the answer is no. In the short-term, the advertisement can bring in more than $1,000 worth of contributions, volunteers' time, and other forms of community support. The long-term credibility and financial health of the special school can be improved through the increased public awareness generated by the ad or commercial. From the donor's point of view, the $1,000 gift in the form of an advertisement gives the donation much more visibility and gives the school more of a return than $1,000 cash.

Advertising and Promotion Services

In addition to advertising or public relations promotions, there are other corporation services worth tapping. Some of them include:

Other Corporation Services

Communications	Printing
Data processing	Secretarial services
Personnel management	Transportation
Photocopying	Writing

If the corporation cannot provide the services, inquire if it can get one of its retained agencies to do the work for you free or at cost. This principle is illustrated in the case of an urban school that developed a science literacy project. The project received free hardware from a computer manufacturer, which in turn convinced one of its suppliers to donate the software and the services of its staff to teach youngsters how to use the science materials.

The talent, knowledge, expertise, technical skills, and plain hard exertion of corporate personnel are valuable assets for your project. The pool of personnel consists of individuals from all corporate levels; an example is from clerk to top executive. A few corporations, including IBM and Xerox, have established executive loan programs through which you get the use of the individual's time at company expense. If you cannot get the company to pay for the employee's time, try to get the employee to volunteer on his or

Corporate Personnel

her own. Do not hesitate to ask corporate executives to donate their time, because voluntarism is a firmly entrenched tradition in the U.S.

Corporate Facilities

You can eliminate rental costs charged by hotels and other space renters if you are able to get a corporation to allow you to use its facilities for your workshops, presentations, and other gatherings. You should not be limited in terms of your using corporate facilities; reverse the situation. If you have unscheduled time for your conference room and a corporation plans to rent the same type of hotel space for a seminar, ask the corporation if it will pay you a comparable fee or the equivalent as a donation for use of your facilities.

Matching Funds

This fund-raising mechanism provides incentives for you and excellent public leverage for the corporation. This is the way it works: For every dollar you raise, the corporation will give you one or more dollars according to the agreement. Most matching fund agreements are on a dollar-for-dollar basis, although sometimes the ratio is as high as three to one. You do not always need to raise cash to satisfy your side of the matching fund equation. A few corporations will accept the equivalent value of goods, services, and other gifts in-kind.

Other Forms of Corporate Aid

There are several forms of corporate aid that warrant mention.

- *Bulk Purchasing.* If your project requires large purchases of particular items, such as stationery, envelopes, typewriter or computer printer ribbons, or pencils, you may be able to get a corporation that purchases those items in money-saving bulk quantities to buy extra ones and then sell them to you at the reduced cost. You, thus, get the supplies at the super bulk rate without having to buy in wholesale lots.

- *Loss Insurance.* It is possible to get a corporation to subsidize your fund-raising event by guaranteeing to absorb all or part of any loss you may incur.

- *Underwriting Business Travel Cost.* At times corporations agree to pay all or part of the cost for one or more of your staff to attend an important out-of-town conference, seminar, convention, or workshop.

- *Subcontracting.* A corporation may find it acceptable and even necessary to subcontract to your organization a part of a contract it received from a government agency.

- *Training Programs.* Corporations will frequently agree to give your project participants on-the-job training.

How Corporations and Foundations Give

A number of people are unable to attract corporate and foundation gifts even though they have been successful in governmental or public grantsmanship because they do not know the private side's decision-making process. Those who attract gifts know about the following:

Most major foundations, like government agencies, are staffed by professional money givers. Decisions are, therefore, influenced by traditional philanthropic considerations. Corporate philanthropy, on the other hand, is more likely to be handled as a part-time activity by executives in the public relations or personnel management area. Decisions are influenced by the profit motive or an identifiable benefit to the company.

Staffing

Government agencies tend to be most concerned with standardized guidelines, foundations are next in terms of specific guidelines, and corporations are least concerned with specific guidelines for grants. Corporate giving is usually more informal, in fact, corporate philanthropists respond to person-to-person contact and less-formalized communication with the prospective grant seeker. Frequently, they ask that grant requests are introduced in the form of a short letter.

Proposal Guidelines

The average size of grants varies in terms of source. Government agencies, as a group, tend to give the larger awards. They are followed by foundations, and finally, corporate grants are the smallest in dollar amount. From the perspective of the private sector, a grant application that deviates too much from the funding sources' usual practice will result in little consideration. The larger the corporation or foundation, the bigger its philanthropy budget and the larger average grants are likely to be.

Grant Size

Some corporations and foundations prefer to give a large number of small gifts to a broad selection of recipients in the belief that ''everyone'' will be satisfied. Other corporations and foundations concentrate their philanthropic thrust, believing that their support will be of greater benefit when given to a limited number of donees.

Corporations that are experiencing stagnation and, especially, a decline in profits will generally designate a lower percentage of their pretax income for philanthropy. Similarly, foundations whose incomes are lower will have smaller budgets. In both instances, grants will depend upon the amount of available dollars.

Profit-and-Loss Trend

Each of the considerations listed in this section should be researched and understood before an appeal is made to the corporation or foundation. Successfully completing this step can greatly enhance your chances of getting a project funded.

You now know why, to whom, what, and how corporations and foundations give. But that is not enough; you must also clearly identify your project goal, know your specific needs, know your strengths and weaknesses, and know your chances of success, if you expect to match the priorities of the funding source.

Know Your Needs

Few grant seekers have a vivid perception of exactly what they wish to accomplish. If your goal is ambiguous, the corporation or foundation will have difficulty comprehending it. Odds are that your goal will be misinterpreted and the funder will be unable to determine whether your aim is compatible with its

Identify Your Goal

objective. Just as importantly, an ill-defined goal reveals much about your competence.

A test of the precision of your goal is whether it can be stated in a brief paragraph or two. If not, you are probably groping for the right description. Goals requiring a long exposition usually are still uncrystallized. If you are having trouble articulating your goal, write down on paper what is in your mind, even if your initial thoughts are jumbled. Writing helps clarify your thoughts, as does showing your drafts to colleagues to gain the benefit of their comments and suggestions.

Identify Your Needs

Make an inventory of your needs. List them in order of priority. Corporations and foundations usually find it more advantageous to give to a particular need rather than general support. By emphasizing the more pressing needs, you will bring into focus the real value of your project.

Identify Your Strengths and Weaknesses

Many grant seekers have been frustrated when they ultimately discovered that the abilities, reputations, resolve, and tenacity of certain staff members fell short of expectations. They would have been better off if they had tried at an early stage to answer such questions as: How qualified are the staff members to perform the required tasks? Will enthusiasm wane? How substantial are the staff's contacts with outside individuals and organizations whose cooperation is vital to the project's success?

In determining your strengths, attempt to discover your "marketability." You should know that you are in competition with other worthy fund-raisers for limited corporate and foundation philanthropy.

Identify Your Chances of Success

Private sector fund-raising programs almost always consume considerable preparation time and money. Before thrusting yourself into the required research and proposal-writing tasks, ascertain whether your project stands a chance of being funded. Your fundability decreases if:

- You are an individual or a non-tax-exempt organization. Unless you are a student seeking financial aid or an organization with tax-exempt status, your chances of receiving funds are bleak.

- You are politically oriented. The private sector tends not to support legislation or other political efforts via the route of a charitable donation.

- You appear to be antibusiness or antiestablishment. Few organizations will contribute to what they perceive as their own destruction.

- Your project is potentially controversial. Few members of the private sector want to be associated with projects that may become public relations nightmares.

- Your project is too risky. The private sector loves backing winners, not losers.

- You wish to make a profit. Except in a few cases, such as funding minority enterprises, the private sector does not invest in capitalistic endeavors.

- Your project is not a philanthropic priority. Needless to say, the private sector will not fund projects outside its priorities.

- Your project is located outside geographical boundaries. If the funder limits its support to a specific region and your project is located outside it, you will probably not be funded.

- You seek too big a grant. Most funding organizations in the private sector have grant ranges, beyond which they seldom go (e.g., grants are funded under $25,000).

- Your project is not timely. If your project is passé or premature for the funder, you probably will not receive backing.

- You lack lead time. Eleventh-hour requests that are crisis oriented are seldom successful. You must be prepared to give the funder a reasonable time period for evaluation and decision making.

- You lack the wherewithal. Frequently, funders will not support the entire project. They will fund only a portion of the budget. The fund-raiser must guarantee that the uncovered portion of the budget is available.

- You lack a track record and credentials. If you do not have the proper credentials or your organization does not have a track record (i.e., you cannot demonstrate that you have successfully completed similar projects), funders will hold that against you. One way to get around this dilemma is to emphasize the accomplishments of your staff and board of directors.

Before investing too much time and energy in the development of a private sector grant proposal, you should determine your chances of success.

Know and Select the Proper Funding Prospects

The ability to conduct background research is not enough. Grant seekers must also use resource volumes that identify likely private sector funding prospects. There are a number of excellent publications that help in this process. Examples of these resources follow.

- *Directory of Grants in the Humanities.* The Oryx Press. 1987 edition, 2214 North Central at Encanto, Phoenix, AZ 85004–1483. Its subject listings include English and linguistics. The book has short entries outlining the program, requirements, amounts of grants, and the contact person. It includes all types of funding sources.

- *Directory of Research Grants.* The Oryx Press. 1987 edition, 2214 North Central at Encanto, Phoenix, AZ 85004–1483. Its subject listings include education, elementary education, linguistics, reading, and reading disorders. The book also has short entries outlining the program, requirements, amounts of grants, and the contact person. It includes all types of funding sources.

These two publications are most comprehensive. They include private and corporate foundations.

In addition, there are more specialized resource volumes such as *Sourcebook Profiles, Foundation Directory, Taft Corporate Giving Directory,* and *Taft Foundation Reporter.* Reference libraries and development offices at most colleges and universities usually have copies of these volumes, and they are generally willing to share information on resources they find valuable. With little variation, these volumes list the corporation's or foundation's:

- *Giving programs* that operate in your service area. Proximity strongly influences grant decisions.

- *Types of grants* they typically offer, which include restricted, unrestricted, in-kind, or nonmonetary support.

- *Specific areas of interest,* which include arts and humanities, education, religion, science, and social services.

- *Executives or directors* who can influence grant decisions. The value of this information lies in the fact that although an organization may award the gift, people make the difference. Using your organization's board members or leaders who know the persons who influence grant decisions can be immensely helpful to you.

- *Recent giving level* for each of three recent years. Listed also is the average size of grants, listed by category. These data help the grant seeker determine the organization's potential for giving.

- *Philosophy.* Knowing about a donor helps you to get a bearing on its general outlook and specific interests. Private sector giving is often characterized as being motivated by enlightened self-interest. In this regard, grant requests are evaluated like any other management decision—investments are expected to offer direct or indirect benefits to the donor.

- *Procedure(s)* for submitting grant applications. Corporations and foundations are quite varied in their application procedures. Following their guidelines could mean the difference in being funded or rejected.

- *Contact person.* This person can be very helpful in making sure you are aware of timetables and other requirements of the donor.

To assist you in organizing the information you gather in this section, see the donor research form in Figure 4.1. Appropriate responses to the items in this section will increase a grant seeker's chances for a successful match with a funder.

Figure 4.1 Donor
Research Form

Donor Research Form

1. Name of Organization _____

2. Address _____

   _____

3. Phone _____

4. Current assets: _____

5. Last year's grant total: _____

6. Average size of grant: _____

7. Grant size range: _____

8. Subject area of giving: _____

9. Geographic limitations: _____

10. Other limitations: _____

11. Names, affiliations of funder's board: _____

12. Format for presentations: _____

    a. Program officer _____

    b. Size limitations, format _____

    c. Number of copies _____

13. Timing of solicitations: _____

14. Timing for decisions: _____

15. People associated with you who can act as contacts: _____

16. Your previous history with the funder: _____

Writing the Proposal

The road to the private sector treasury is littered with grant seekers who perished because their written proposal was found wanting. Many of them perished despite their having fundable projects. Perhaps the reason was a lack of proposal-writing expertise. Perhaps it was a lack of care given in the preparation of the proposal. Whatever the reason, the results were the same.

An effective proposal is imperative because it will usually be your only representative when the funders make the grant decisions. What the evaluators deduce will depend, in most cases, on the information presented in the proposal. If the information is hazy, contradictory, incomplete, or otherwise inadequate, your proposal will be weakened, and you will not be there to set the record straight. The proposal must speak for itself.

A standard proposal format for the private sector does not exist, since each donor, grant seeker, and project are different. Therefore, no two proposals should ever be written in the same way. As a grant seeker, your best bet is to ask the funding organization for its suggested guidelines. If these guidelines are nebulous, incomplete, or nonexistent, here are a few suggestions.

Letter Format

Proposals submitted to corporations are generally much shorter and less formalized than those sent to foundations. They are also much shorter and less structured than the ones sent to governmental agencies. If the proposal is to be brief, present it in a letter format, one or two pages long. Letters should almost always be single-spaced with good margins and other white-space-preserving devices to enhance readability. Let neatness be one of your precepts. Your final draft should be professionally typed; no erasure marks, correction fluids, or tape should blemish the pages. If the letter is produced by a word processor or computer, be sure to use a "letter quality" printer (dot matrix print is often difficult to read).

Letter proposals (fig. 4.2), generally the first communication with the funder, should be structured to include the following four elements:

- The project described in the letter should be described as almost an established success. Corporations and foundations like to bet on winners.

- Although successful, the project should not be presented as having run its course. The research should also be presented as not yet completed. These factors suggest two things to the funder: (*a*) a larger gain than usual may be secured through making a grant, and (*b*) it will not be necessary to provide funding beyond a certain point to achieve success.

- It includes a number of references identifying the nature of the project with the interests of the corporation or foundation.

- It mentions other funding organizations who are supporting this project, thus enhancing its creditability (Hillman 1980).

Figure 4.2 Sample
Letter Proposal

March 25, 1989

Mr. John J. Doe
Community Relations Officer
Baytown Telephone Company
Baytown, PA

Dear Mr. Doe:

Thank you so much for meeting with our Board Chairperson, Mrs. Alice Smith, and me to discuss the Westside Adult Education Center and our need for support from the Baytown Telephone Company. Our request was for a $10,000 grant. As you know, our Center has been providing literacy training and other educational programs for adults since 1971. Many of our graduates have gone on to become productive members of the community.

The Westside Adult Education Center recruits, professionally trains, and supervises volunteers who are now working with a large number of undereducated adults. Last year 35 volunteers donated over 3000 hours, serving as one-to-one tutors in reading, writing, math, and other subjects, and helping participants prepare for the GED Examination.

In order to raise a considerable portion of its annual goal of $100,000, the Westside Adult Education Center is seeking financial support from corporations based in our city. This support will enable the Center to expand existing programs, start new tutorial programs in the 15 churches requesting help, and initiate pilot projects working with underemployed adults so they can take over some of the more technical jobs now available in the area.

Among the Westside Adult Education Center's corporate contributors, recent donors of $5,000 or more are the Roadster Automobile Company, Oliveseal Oil Company, New Computers, Inc., Good Foods Inc., AZX Furniture Manufacturers Inc., InterGlobal Communications Ltd., and the Baytown Bank.

In order to carry on our tradition, and to meet the increasing request for the Center's services, we must seek the help and support of local corporations. We are convinced that an investment in the Westside Adult Education Center is an investment in Baytown.

We are grateful for your willingness to consider our request. If you are in need of any additional information, please do not hesitate to contact me. Again, thank you for your consideration of this request.

Sincerely,

Willie S. Brown
Executive Director

Document Format   Frequently, foundations will request that a document format be used in writing the proposal. Some corporations, with formalized foundations, will also request this format after reviewing the initial letter. Document format proposals, which range in length from five to ten pages, depending on the project, should normally be double-spaced to enhance reading ease. Similarly, the proposal should be amply endowed with wide margins and white-space-preserving devices. Another technique for improving readability and visual appeal is the adept use of headings and subheadings. As in the case of the letter format, this proposal should also be professionally typed; make sure that it is not blemished with correction fluid and erasure marks.

Hillman and Abarbanel (1975) suggested that, irrespective of its length, the proposal should flow in the following order:

1. **The Title Page.** In Figure 4.3 a sample title page is presented. It is designed to quickly give the funding officials a sense of the magnitude of the request and an idea of the project's purpose.
2. **The Need.** It is incumbent on you to sharply define the need in terms of its urgency, magnitude, and parameters. A common form of "granticide" is to assume that all people who will be reading your proposal share your awareness of the need.
3. **The Objective.** Do not confuse "objective" with "methods" as do most proposal writers. Your objective is what you want to accomplish, whereas your methods are the means of accomplishing your objective. Your objective should satisfy three criteria: (*a*) it must be attainable (e.g., do you really have the time, abilities, and resources required to conduct the adult literacy program); (*b*) it must be practical (assigning a full-time Ph.D. for each adult student is attainable but not practical; there are better uses for a Ph.D.'s expertise); and (*c*) it must be measurable in quantitative terms (you could specify, for instance, percentile increases in comprehension test scores). Finally, you should try to show that your objective matches that of the funder.
4. **The Methods.** Many private sector executives believe, with some justification, that most nonprofit organizations are poorly managed. To help you overcome this view, present your methods in a step-by-step timetable format that will enable the readers to grasp at a glance your priorities and time frames.
5. **Your Qualifications.** You must convince the funder that you are not only qualified but you are the most qualified individual or organization available. Incorporate into this section your organization's capabilities and biographical sketches of key staff members. List also the names, addresses, and telephone numbers of impartial individuals who can verify your qualifications (secure permission first).
6. **The Evaluation.** More and more, the private sector is requiring nonprofit organizations to show the effects of their gifts. Grantees are required to show in measurable terms how well they have been able to attain their objectives. For credibility's sake, it is a good idea to

Figure 4.3 Sample
Title Page

A Proposal for a

$10,000 Grant

To Support

Adult Literacy Programs
Earmarked for Members of the Westside Community

Submitted to

The Baytown Telephone Company

on
March 31, 1989

By
Willie S. Brown
Executive Director
Westside Adult Education Center
101 Front Street
Baytown, PA

have a third party (the more distinguished, the better) execute your evaluation program.

7. **The Budget.** When estimating your budget, be as realistic as possible. Keep your budget presentation brief—one or two typewritten pages. If the grantor has not provided you with a budget format, use the following:

- *Personnel.* This category will probably consume at least half of your budget. You should divide this category into two sections: "Salary and Wages" and "Fringe Benefits."

- *Outside Services.* Consulting, legal, accounting, and public relations are among the outside services listed in this section. In addition to the services you will purchase, list any donated services along with their estimated value.

- *Rent.* List the rent by annual cost per square foot. If you feel that the funder will consider the rent to be excessive, prepare a justification by obtaining a letter from a local real estate board verifying that rents in your area are higher than the citywide norm.

- *Utilities.* This section should include telephone and other communications costs, and if not included in the rent, gas, water, and electricity fall into this category.

- *Equipment.* If an item exceeds a minimum value, say $250, and if you expect to use it for more than one year, then list it as equipment. Examples of this type of asset include office furnishings (desks, cabinets, carpets) and office/educational equipment (photocopy machines, computers, tape recorders). Equipment does not always have to be purchased. It can be rented, leased, donated, or borrowed. To avoid postproject disputes, be sure to specify in your proposal who will own and take possession of the equipment at the termination of the project.

- *Supplies.* List in this section all items that are below a minimum value, say $250, and will be used for less than a year (printed stationery, typewriter ribbons, postage stamps).

- *Travel and Meetings.* Evaluators are especially suspicious about expenses for out-of-town travel. Do not list your travel cost under a single umbrella such as "Director's Travel" if the total exceeds approximately $100. Rather, individually itemize the expense items such as transportation, hotel, and seminar fees.

- *Miscellaneous Expenses.* This is a catch all category for small expenses that cannot be classified into the other budget categories.

8. **The Program's Future.** Include this section only if your project will extend beyond the funding period of your requested grant. This is designed to allay fear that the donor's investment will be squandered. You should present a realistic plan telling how you will keep the

project afloat financially after you have expended the donor's dollars or gifts in-kind.

Once you have submitted your grant application, whether it is a letter-format or a document-format proposal, you should communicate with the funding organization. Specifically, a week, or so, after submitting the proposal, you should call the corporate or foundation contact person to inquire if the award request has been received. You should also offer to send to the contact person any additional information that the funder might find necessary. Often, it is at this point that the funder will give his or her reaction to your submission. This is also a time when you have an opportunity to elaborate on the nature of your project and to reinforce the fact that you have a match with the funder in terms of priorities and interests.

Follow Through

In an era of declining resources, when there is an increased requirement for literacy research and innovation, the private sector is the most viable funding option, that is, educators will have to turn to the corporate and foundation arenas for financial support of their research and program advances.

Conclusion

By becoming aware of the art of private sector grantsmanship, you can gain an invaluable edge over your competition. Specifically, you must know the resource volumes that are vital in identifying the proper funder from whom to seek grants.

After having conducted the background research, writing a proposal that effectively presents the grant seeker's case is imperative. It is imperative because in almost all situations your only representative, when the funders make grant decisions, is the written proposal. Finally, if you respond properly to the items presented in this chapter you will increase your chances of getting a project funded.

References

Foundation Giving Watch. 1988. *VIII*(3) August.
Hillman, H. 1980. *The art of winning corporate grants.* NY: Vanguard Press.
Hillman, H., and K. Abarbanel. 1975. *The art of winning foundation grants.* NY: Vanguard Press.
Mirkin, H. R. 1978. *The complete fund raising guide.* NY: Public Service Materials Center.

Monetary and Voluntary Contributions to Adult Literacy Programs

Hope B. Richardson

More and more U.S.-based corporations have responded to the literacy crisis by spending hundreds of millions of dollars to increase the literacy levels of their employees, and the literacy of those yet to enter the business world. In the past decade, the price tag for remedial employee training in the basic skills reached $300 million a year (Gorman 1988).

What is the dollar amount businesses and agencies have contributed to adult literacy? There is no one direct answer, according to the Business Council For Effective Literacy (*BCEL* 1988). However, corporate programs in adult literacy have taken a national leadership role, thereby, committing substantial amounts of both money and professional time to their literacy efforts. The Gannett Foundation, B. Dalton Bookseller, Time, Inc., and the Chicago Tribune Charities are notable examples. Their services, collectively, between 1984 and 1987 provided somewhere in the neighborhood of $10 million in new funding and services to the field of adult literacy.

Additionally, dozens of other U.S. companies have given grants and in-kind help to literacy groups in their state and local communities; they have joined or initiated local or state planning activities; funded research; sponsored local, state, or national awareness events; and developed basic skills programs for their own employees. Following are several examples of how foundations and corporations and then agencies and organizations have contributed to adult literacy programs.

Foundations and Corporations

The Gannett Foundation. The Gannett Foundation launched its first adult literacy activities in 1985. Since then, it has awarded 339 grants totaling $4 million to help adults learn to read and write (*BCEL* 1988). Its funds have been given to a variety of organizations in the U.S. as well as Puerto Rico and Canada. It has donated professional staff time and has given help to voluntary and community-based organizations.

The Gannett Foundation has given grants to support and develop state literacy planning and coordination. Additionally, its grants have supported the development of computer-related learning projects, provided salaries for part-time personnel, assisted in the developing and purchasing of books and teaching materials, and assisted in the recruiting of tutors and in the development of English-as-a-second-language (ESL) services. Continuously, the foundation awards grants to the field of adult literacy.

The Barbara Bush Foundation. In March of 1989, the Barbara Bush Foundation for Family Literacy was announced. "The creation of this foundation," noted first lady of the U.S. Barbara Bush, "is just one way to express my commitment to solving the serious problem of illiteracy in our country'' (*BCEL* 1989a). Corporations, foundations, and individual donors have already pledged $1 million in start-up funding. Additional funding will be sought from the private sector to sustain the foundation. Mrs. Bush will be the new foundation's honorary chairperson.

B. Dalton Bookseller. B. Dalton Bookseller plays a leading role among private sector organizations in the fight against illiteracy (*BCEL* 1986). In September 1983, B. Dalton launched a four-year $3 million National Literacy Initiative concentrated in the areas of adult literacy and motivational reading programs for children and youth.

Between 1983 and 1985, B. Dalton awarded 347 grants totaling over $2 million (*BCEL* 1986). In 1985, more than 115,000 adults received literacy services in 400 communities as a result of grants from B. Dalton Bookseller. In 1985, grants ranged from $500 (Oakton Community College in Illinois for volunteer in-service staff training) to $150,000 (ten new programs on the third season of PBS's *Reading Rainbow*). The company has also been very successful in involving its own employees and bookstore managers in the campaign for literacy. Many of Dalton's employees are serving on the boards of local literacy organizations.

Time Incorporated. In *Time*'s sponsored literacy program, magazines are used as textbooks, and specially trained volunteers as tutors. The program was designed to assist adolescents and adults with, at least, a fourth-grade reading level. The students received free subscriptions to *Time* and another magazine of their choice. Instructional techniques included the reading and discussing of real people and events in the program's most popular magazines: *Time, Sports Illustrated,* and *People* (*BCEL,* 1987). *Time* Incorporated has received a U.S. President's Volunteer Award, which was partly sponsored by the White House, for its program "Time to Read."

McGraw-Hill. McGraw-Hill sponsors an employee volunteer literacy program in cooperation with Literacy Volunteers of New York City. It provides classes and tutor training. In fiscal year 1988, it donated approximately $10,000 to Literacy Volunteers of New York City (*Literacy Volunteers of New York City* 1988).

Exxon. The Exxon Corporation granted a total of $225,000 for six adult literacy projects of national scope. Grants had been given to the following literacy projects: Wider Opportunities for Women received $50,000 to help disseminate and replicate its model literacy program for single low-income mothers; grants of $25,000 each went to CONTACT Literacy Center to update and streamline its referred system data base; to Laubach Literacy Action for development and distribution of information through its national clearinghouse, to Literacy Volunteers of America for an evaluation of program effectiveness; to Literacy Volunteers of New York City for its national publications project, and to the Southport Institute for Policy Analysis in partial support of its study on the federal role in adult literacy (*BCEL* 1989b).

United Way. Even though United Way is an agency that provides funds to adult literacy programs in the U.S., in this chapter the reader will find only selected representative funding efforts of programs in three states—New York, New Jersey, and Connecticut. (Additional information can be obtained from individual state United Ways located throughout the U.S.)

United Way of Tri-State and its 37 partner United Ways in New York, New Jersey, and Connecticut help support more than 1,800 health and human care agencies. United Way of Tri-State combines thirty-seven local, autonomous United Ways into a federated fund-raising partnership in New York, New Jersey, and Connecticut (*United Way of Tri-State* 1989). In 1987, this partnership raised $170 million for the 1,800 health and human service agencies (Green 1987).

In New York, several United Way of Tri-State affiliates fund adult literacy programs in diverse areas. The areas in New York City extend from Harlem to Wall Street to Brooklyn, and to suburban Connecticut and New Jersey. Agencies such as Literacy Volunteers and Good Shepherd Services are providing the literacy programs for United Way (Green 1987).

Three examples of literacy programs funded by United Way (*United Way of Tri-State* 1989) are: (*a*) A mother/child program in Westchester County, New York. It provides early intervention for preschool children in predominantly Hispanic American and low-income families with literacy problems. The mothers were given books and other educational materials and were taught how to read to their children. (*b*) In Stanford, Greenwich, Norwalk, Wilton, New Canaan, Wesport-Weston, and Northern County, Connecticut, United Way helps support Literacy Volunteers. Community volunteers tutor teens and adults in reading, writing, and conversational English. (*c*) In Danbury, Connecticut, a special literacy program initiated in conjunction with area businesses offered classes at the work site. Employees were trained as tutors.

Chicago Tribune Charities. In 1984–1985, the Chicago Tribune Charities announced a new grant program in literacy for the Chicago, Illinois, area. Chicago has an estimated 600,000 functionally illiterate adults, a 50 percent school dropout rate, and a growing population of Hispanic Americans and immigrants of various ethnic backgrounds. The Charities believed that their high-illiteracy rate was a key factor in the economic underdevelopment of the city (*BCEL* 1985).

Chicago has received grants of up to $5,000 for special literacy programs. Such programs have used volunteers and students as trained tutors to teach reading, writing, and math skills to school-age youth. Additionally, Chicago has been awarded $70,000 for programs to serve American Indians, Hispanics, refugee and immigrant groups, college-bound adults, out-of-school youth, and others in the city (*BCEL* 1985). In May 1986, the Chicago Tribune Charities took the lead and organized Chicago's first citywide conference of literacy providers. The conference's aim was to improve coordination of literacy services in Chicago.

Public Libraries. Libraries in the U.S. have waged their war against illiteracy. Starting in 1964, when funds became available through the Library Services and Construction Act, libraries made literacy programming for native-born illiterates a priority (Kangisser 1985). Other services by libraries have included the organization of book clubs, story reading, and other literacy development projects for children and adults. Herein, it seems appropriate to mention that since 1973 the American Library Association has maintained an Office of Library Outreach Services. Its purpose was to reach potential clients (school dropouts, the poor, the underemployed, and the disadvantaged racial and ethnic minorities), who are not library users (Kangisser 1985). Overall, libraries are to be applauded for leadership in the fight against illiteracy.

Christian Literacy Programs. There are church-run literacy programs that do effective work in their communities. One such program is the Allegheny County Literacy Council (ACLC) in Pennsylvania. This literacy program is financed through a large grant received from the Lutheran Church. In each given year, donations range from $60,000 to $75,000. (Another chapter in this volume provides a full description of ACLC.)

Community-Based Organizations. Kangisser (1985) reports that community-based organizations have the best track record for reaching illiterates and functionally illiterates. Community-based organizations did not come into existence for the purpose of literacy training. However, in response to community needs, they have taken up this role.

Two well-known voluntary literacy organizations are Laubach Literacy Action and Literacy Volunteers of America. Both have deep roots in the Christian service tradition (Hunter & Harman 1979). They offer a place where it is possible to begin learning basic literacy skills at low-elementary levels (Colvin & Root 1976). Their campaigns to recruit volunteers have continuously reminded the public that there are adults who are unable to read (Hunter & Harman 1979). Laubach Literacy Action, first organized in 1968, is the largest network of volunteer literacy programs in the U.S. Many local affiliates of Laubach Literacy Action are supported by United Ways (United Way of America 1989). Laubach Literacy Action serves 50,000 people. Literacy Volunteers of America serves 20,000 people (Kozol 1985). They do effective work with those they reach.

Laubach Literacy. Laubach Literacy International allocated financial support and technical assistance to developing countries in Latin America, Africa, and Asia. During 1989–1990 their financial commitment to support activities in seven countries were as follows (*Laubach Literacy International:* . . . 1989):

1. Bangladesh—$1,000 to support development of educational materials for fourteen basic literacy centers serving a total of 280 landless rural villagers.
2. Haiti—$2,000 for an experimental project in the jungle community of Tibo providing intensive literacy instruction to 120 young adults who never attended school; $500 for capital supplies for eight adult basic literacy centers in Tibo; $2,000 for materials and training for

postliteracy program facilitators in fifteen centers in Les Cayes, $2,500 for a health worker's literacy instruction program and an intergenerational literacy program in Dondon; $2,000 for capital supplies for twenty-four basic literacy centers in the jungle villages of Bonneau; and $3,000 for a literacy and income-generation project in the city of Carrefour.

3. Kenya—$5,000 for training and support of a program providing basic literacy education and developing literacy materials on animal husbandry and health for the nomadic Gabbra and Samburu tribes.

4. Nepal—$1,000 to support two literacy and postliteracy centers serving landless residents of a resettled area near the Indian border.

5. The Philippines—$2,500 to assist materials development in the Hanunuo Mangyan School Project, and $2,000 to support a postliteracy income-generation project in rural Lanao.

6. Sierra Leone—$3,000 for development and field-testing of thirty manuscripts designed to help people preserve the basic literacy skills they have gained in their tribal language of Temne, Limba, and Mende.

7. Tanzania—$2,000 for production of Swahili-language literacy materials with focus on income generation and development activities, involving 1,500 residents of the rural Moshi region.

Laubach Literacy International's funding for their programs in 1988 came from contributions, trust funds, foundation and corporate grants, bequests, and government grants. Their total public support was $1,747,636. Other revenue that totaled $5,591,295 came from publication sales, Laubach Literacy Action membership dues, investment income, and sales of assets. In summary, total support and total other revenue was $7,338,931 (*Laubach Literacy International: . . .* 1989).

Literacy Volunteers of America. Literacy Volunteers of America (LVA) offers courses (with suggestions about recruiting, publicizing the program, operating and reporting, and training tutors) for those interested in setting up and maintaining local LVA literacy programs (Hunter & Harman 1979).

Literacy Volunteers is partially subsidized by New York State and New York City but is mainly supported by private donors including the Booth Ferris, Vincent Astor, New York Times and New York Life Foundations, the DeWitt Wallace Reader's Digest Fund, the Chase Manhattan Bank, and the Exxon Corporation.

In the summer of 1989, Literacy Volunteers of New York City reported receiving an award of $60,000 from the New York Life Foundation to underwrite an outreach training program and to support its educational services. This program was designed to give technical assistance to existing literacy programs and to community organizations seeking to set up volunteer literacy programs (*Literacy Volunteers of New York City Newsletter: . . .* 1989).

In conclusion, many people in the U.S. seem to be concerned with the fact that far too many citizens are unable to read and write. Corporations and foundations are concerned about this problem and are donating dollars and hours to correct the problem of illiteracy. Voluntary literacy organizations are donating manpower, technical assistance, and dollars to fight illiteracy. Church-related groups are busy trying to bring literacy training to individuals who reside in the U.S. and in other countries. Praise must go to the thousands of volunteer tutors in the U.S. and other countries who are the backbone of the majority of literacy programs. It is heartwarming to know that the first lady of the United States of America has committed herself to help solve the problem of illiteracy in the U.S. In the future, all individuals can expect more attention to problems caused by illiteracy.

Conclusion

BCEL. 1985. Business Council for Effective Literacy. Adult literacy: Programs, planning, & issues. A Newsletter for the Business Community, no. 2 (January):6–7.

BCEL. 1986. Business Council for Effective Literacy. Adult literacy: Programs, planning, & issues. A Newsletter for the Business Community, no. 12 (October):2–3.

BCEL. 1987. Business Council for Effective Literacy. Adult literacy: Programs, planning, & issues. A Newsletter for the Business Community, no. 9 (July):6–7.

BCEL. 1988. Business Council for Effective Literacy. Adult literacy: Programs, planning, & issues. A Newsletter for the Business Community, no. 14 (January):12.

BCEL. 1989a. Business Council for Effective Literacy. Adult literacy: Programs, planning, & issues. A Newsletter for the Business Community, no. 19 (April):2.

BCEL. 1989b. Business Council for Effective Literacy. Adult literacy: Program, planning, & issues. A Newsletter for the Business Community, no. 18 (January):10.

Colvin, R., and J. Root. 1976. *TUTOR, techniques used in the teaching of reading.* Syracuse, NY: Literacy Volunteers of America.

Gorman, C. 1988. The literacy gap. *Time,* 19 December, 56–57.

Green, C. 1987. *United Way at 100—A rich heritage, a bold vision.* NY: The Newcomen Society of the United States.

Hunter, C., and D. Harman. 1979. *Adult literacy in the United States.* NY: McGraw-Hill Book Company.

Illiteracy: A critical issue for United Ways. 1989. Alexandria, VA: United Way of America.

Kangisser, D. 1985. *Pioneers and new frontiers: The role of volunteers in combating adult illiteracy.* NY: The Continuum Publishing Corporation.

Kozol, J. 1985. *Illiterate America.* NJ: Anhor Press.

Laubach Literacy International: 1988 annual report. 1988. Syracuse, NY: Laubach Literacy International.

Literacy Volunteers of New York City. 1988. Annual report.

Literacy Volunteers of New York City Newsletter: The first "R." 1989. Literacy volunteers reach out. Summer: 1, 5.

United Way of America, 1989. 1989. Alexandria, VA: United Way of America.

United Way of Tri-State: The case for giving. 1989. Alexandria, VA: United Way of America.

References

Community Resources for Nonprofit Literacy Programs

Karen R. Norton

Although isolated nonprofit literacy programs have been serving adult students in the U.S. for half a century, it was not until the 1960s that the two largest networks of nonprofit organizations providing direct literacy services—Literacy Volunteers of America and Laubach Literacy Action—were organized and began to expand. Many of these programs depended on private sector support until the emergence of the national literacy movement in the 1980s. Today nonprofit literacy programs receive the largest share of their income from public sources. A Laubach Literacy Action survey of 379 member groups in 1988 showed that 40 percent of their combined income came from the public sector, 17 percent from United Way, 3 percent from service clubs, and 2 percent from churches. The remaining percentages came from individual donations, member dues and volunteer-training fees, special fund-raising events, and sales of instructional materials (*Laubach Literacy Action* 1989).

Older, well-established programs included in the survey often realized 90 percent of their income from one or more of three major sources: United Way, public funding, and corporation and foundation grants. Newer programs tended to rely on corporate support, service clubs, and churches for start-up funding. A much larger share of their income was derived from individual donations, volunteer-training fees, and special events (*Laubach Literacy Action* 1989).

National averages, however, are of little help to local literacy programs. The availability of public funding varies greatly from state to state, and income from other sources depends heavily on local opportunities and the creativity and persistence of local program leaders in cultivating these sources. In addition, because of the significant number of new funders interested in literacy services, the funding outlook for nonprofit literacy programs remained volatile at the end of the 1980s, and whether levels of support from current sources will increase, stabilize, or decrease remains to be seen.

National awareness of the literacy problem, however, is being translated into immediate funding opportunities for local nonprofit literacy programs. Although these opportunities must be investigated locally, the following discussion provides a general outlook for the major private sector forms of support.

Financial Support

United Way. In the mid-1980s, local United Way campaigns raised about $2.5 billion annually, primarily through solicitations of local businesses and their employees. Each local United Way establishes requirements for local agencies that will receive these funds. Much of the funding distributed to United Way member agencies can be used for operating expenses (Aramony 1987). Additionally, local United Ways are eligible to provide training, technical assistance, seed grants, and distribute in-kind donations to member and nonmember agencies.

In 1987 the United Way of America, the national training and service organization for local United Ways, announced a long-term commitment to literacy programming. Also, past participation efforts of local United Ways in supporting local literacy efforts promises to increase. The national organization provides guidance to local United Ways interested in providing technical assistance as well as support for local literacy activities. In 1989 it launched a national literacy grant program for its local units (*Business Council for Effective Literacy* 1989).

Many local United Ways prohibit organizations they support from seeking additional operating funds from corporations that give through the United Way campaign or from conducting fund-raising activities while the yearly United Way campaign is in progress. Given the opportunity, most literacy programs choose to receive United Way funding, but a few do not. For the latter programs, the possibility of raising more money on their own schedule outweighs the advantage of a stable, on-going source of funds from the United Way.

Corporations and Foundations. Foundations are legally organized to distribute funds set aside for philanthropic purposes. In 1987, foundation giving totaled $6.38 billion, or about 7 percent of all charitable dollars given that year (*American Association for Fund-Raising Counsel . . . 1988*). Corporations may make charitable gifts directly, through foundations they have established, or both. Of the 2.3 million American corporations, about 800,000 make philanthropic contributions (Bauer 1988). In 1987 corporate gifts, including gifts made through corporate foundations, totaled $4.5 billion, or less than 5 percent of all charitable dollars (*American Association for Fund-Raising Counsel . . . 1988*).

Beginning in the early 1980s, several U.S. corporations set the pace in providing funding for literacy programs at their local operating sites. Bookstore chains, the print industry, and other businesses whose sales are directly related to literacy have been particularly strong supporters. The Gannett Foundation, for example, earmarked a portion of its funds for literacy, developed application guidelines based on its own analysis of literacy needs, and made funds available through nearly 100 local operating sites.

The need for more literate employees also spurs corporate interest in literacy programs. The Business Council of Effective Literacy (BCEL), which was launched by the McGraw-Hill Foundation, builds on this need to promote corporate involvement, publishes a quarterly newsletter describing corporate participants in the literacy effort, and provides written materials to help local literacy programs that seek corporate support.

Service Clubs. The national offices of several U.S. service clubs have made major commitments to the literacy effort. The Junior League, Altrusa International, General Federated Women's Clubs, Kiwanis, and Rotary have all promoted literacy involvement in publications distributed to their membership.

The Junior League and Altrusa have also made the literacy effort the focus of their national conferences and developed programs to encourage their affiliates to support the literacy effort with funding and volunteer expertise. Although local service clubs do not provide major, on-going funding, some of them have almost single-handedly launched new local literacy efforts and provided major assistance in the expansion of others.

Churches. Individual local churches or citywide councils of churches have played an important role in establishing local literacy programs, which are often spun off as separately organized entities. The Evangelical Lutheran Church of America and the Southern Baptist Convention have their own staffs that promote the literacy effort within their own constituency and train members to organize and conduct local literacy programs. Although local churches are not a major source of funding for literacy programs, many churches provide office and tutoring space, either as an outright donation or for a very low fee.

Donations, Special Events, and Program Fees. In 1987 individual donors accounted for almost 89 percent of all charitable gifts. Even though nearly half of all individual gifts were made to churches, the amount of funding made to other nonprofit organizations by individuals far exceeds corporate and foundation gifts combined (*American Association for Fund-Raising Counsel . . . 1988*).

Some nonprofit literacy organizations receive a modest but reliable share of their income from solicitations of members and friends and special fund-raising events conducted by volunteers. Though not a donation, programs may also realize income from volunteer-training fees, member dues, and sales of instructional materials.

In small or midsized communities where other sources of funding are very limited, individual donations and special events may represent a very significant portion of the program's budget. These forms of support also bring collateral benefits such as increased public visibility and individual commitment to the literacy program. Special fund-raising events, from used book sales to benefit dinners, are also a major opportunity to enlarge the role of adult students and include them as fully participating members of the program.

Fund-Raising

Preparing for Fund-Raising. Any significant fund-raising effort requires a commitment of volunteer and staff time and energy. Federal nonprofit tax-exempt charity status under section 501(c) (3) of the U.S. Internal Revenue Code is required for most kinds of fund-raising. Computerized word-processing and record-keeping systems are also extremely helpful. But the most important fund-raising asset a program can have is a forward-looking but realistic three- to five-year plan that sets forth community literacy needs and describes which of those needs the program is and will be addressing, how they will be addressed, and what the expected results will be. The plan answers why funds are being sought and becomes the heartbeat of all fund-raising activity. Such a plan also motivates volunteers, serves as the backbone of communications tools that support fund-raising activities, and helps identify which funding sources are the best match for the program's needs and fund-raising capacity.

No matter what sources of support the literacy program chooses to cultivate, volunteers are essential to effective fund-raising. A long-range plan gives volunteers a good reason to commit time and energy to fund-raising activities and gives them confidence in selling the plan to others. Recruiting volunteers who are specifically interested in fund-raising may be the first step in building the program's funding base. Most often, literacy programs recruit board members who have some community fund-raising experience or have peers in the business community with whom they can work to develop corporate and foundation support. Some programs also recruit volunteers for separate advisory boards devoted solely to developing corporate and foundation support.

Energized volunteers are also necessary for labor intensive fund-raising efforts from special events to individual solicitations. Volunteers who have allegiance to the program's future as spelled out in the long-range plan are also much more open to committing their own resources, as well as time, to fund-raising efforts. Their financial support, even though modest, impresses institutional donors who like to fund organizations that can demonstrate broad-based support. "Friends of literacy" groups, which are not directly related to the program's board, have also been organized to conduct special events or other forms of fund-raising.

The program's long-range plan is the reservoir of information for the community relations activities that are essential for increasing program funding. The essentials of the plan can be shaped into press releases and brochures and remodeled into direct solicitations, from informal appeals to individual donors to formal proposals for institutional donors.

Finally, the long-range plan pinpoints what the program's priority funding needs are; this is a tremendous advantage in identifying what kinds of donors the program should concentrate on reaching. For example, many programs are most in need of ongoing support for routine operations. Because the trend in corporate and foundation giving is away from providing routine support (*Business Council for Effective Literacy* 1989), a program whose primary need is a steady source of operational income may need to develop its individual donor base or work toward United Way membership. Programs that need funding for start-up expenses, expansion, or new activities are somewhat more likely to find interested corporate and foundation donors.

Corporate and Foundation Fund-Raising. The majority of grants made to local literacy programs from institutional sources are from corporations and corporate foundations. Local foundations created by individuals or families and community foundations, which are often a collection of smaller funds managed by a central staff, are the most likely sources of foundation support. Because decision makers for all of these groups are probably community members, they will be influenced by the program's visibility in the media, by contacts with literacy volunteers and board members, and by other community funders.

Corporate giving, whether conducted through a direct grant program or a corporate foundation, is usually tied to company interests. These interests include visibility in the community, services for its own employees, or general improvement of the community in which its employees live. Knowledge that employees are either volunteering in the literacy program or receiving its services is helpful in successful corporate fund-raising. The national visibility of the literacy issue also helps open the door to the personal contacts that are all important in corporate fund-raising.

Gathering written information about foundation giving is relatively easy because it is, by law, part of the public record. Though corporations are not required to make public a report of their direct grants, some of them volunteer this information to the public either in their own publications or to organizations especially established to gather it. Thus a wealth of printed information is readily available to help grant seekers determine which corporate and foundation donors may be interested in the literacy cause.

The Foundation Center was created to inform the public about foundation activities; it publishes a wide range of information tools and other fund-raising helps. The center's basic materials are available through more than 200 cooperating regional centers and affiliates nationwide; these collections are often located in public libraries. The funding offices of colleges, city governments, and larger nonprofit groups almost always purchase the most basic of these materials and may allow others to inspect them as well.

The Foundation Center's *Foundation Directory* (1987–88) provides a pithy description of the 5,000 foundations with assets in excess of $1 million or annual giving in excess of $100,000. *The Foundation Center Source Book Profiles* (1987–88) provides much more detailed analyses of the giving patterns of the 1,000 largest foundations. *The National Data Book of Foundations* (1989) lists all of the 25,000 grant-making foundations in the U.S.; it provides only the briefest description of each. This book is the easiest way to discover the city, state, amounts of annual giving, and chief officers of the 20,000 foundations that are too small to appear in other materials.

The National Directory of Corporate Charity (1984), also published by the Foundation Center, describes the charitable activities of 1,600 corporations with annual sales in excess of $200 million. The directory includes a description of direct giving activities, employee matching gifts, and in-kind gifts, as well as corporate funds given through foundations. Another source of information about potential corporate sources is the local chamber of commerce. The chamber prepares a directory of corporations arranged by size, and chamber staffs are often aware of which corporations make charitable contributions.

Although directories are a good source of information about funding sources, they are not always up-to-date. Thus getting copies of annual reports, application guidelines, or other written material published by possible funders is very helpful. The Foundation Center's directories indicate which funders provide this information.

Other good sources of information are the state-level funding directories prepared by various organizations as a service to nonprofits within some states. State literacy coalitions or the state organizations of national literacy groups also develop lists of potential sources of support for their member groups. Students or volunteers employed by local corporations may be able to get funding information directly from the corporate giving office.

The first step in grant seeking is to identify funders whose interests match program needs. Grant seekers should approach material that describes grant awards with the following questions in mind:

Grant Seeking

1. Which corporations and foundations will make grants where the program is located? One of the most frequent complaints from grant makers is that proposal writers ignore their geographical and topical limitations.

2. Does the grant maker have specific limitations on what kinds of services and projects they will fund? Funders who underwrite literacy services are now indexed in recent Foundation Center materials, but because literacy education is a factor in meeting many different needs, literacy programs can fit within many topical funding areas. Providing that a case can be made that the funder's interests are being met, literacy programs could submit proposals to funders who support services to underrepresented racial and ethnic groups, women, refugees, the poor, prisoners, mental health patients, and other specific populations that the program serves. Literacy programs may also fit the guidelines for funders interested in voluntarism, improved health care, employment training, voter registration, and other activities for which literacy skills are prerequisite.

   This opportunity to adapt to funder interests poses a danger, especially when the submitted proposal indicates that a large concentration of program resources are peripheral to the program's central purpose. Thus, each opportunity to expand the intent of the program proposal should be scrutinized for its potential to contribute to, and not detract from, the program's long-range plan.

   Foundations and corporations will make clear any restrictions or preferences they have for funding new work or innovative approaches, whether they will provide operating expenses, and other funding preferences.

3. Who is responsible for approving proposals? Larger foundations and corporations have staffed offices for processing and conducting the grants process. Sometimes the funder's staff can be an invaluable source of additional information, but the staff rarely makes the final decisions as to which proposals are funded, with the possible exception of small grants. Usually decisions on corporate proposals are made by the company's chief executive officer and other senior staff. Foundations make grants on the basis of a vote taken by their volunteer

board members. The names of these decision makers should be collected so that any of the literacy program's members who know them can provide their personal endorsement of the program, either through a letter or a direct meeting.

4. What is the average size of the grant? Most corporate grants range between $1,000 and $5,000. Foundation grants may be larger, but first-time grantees with little track record in fund-raising will probably be more successful in applying for grants that are at or below the average amount.

5. What are the guidelines for submitting proposals, and when are they due? Guidelines for proposal submission must be closely followed, but most often proposals to corporate sources need be no longer than two pages and proposals to foundations rarely exceed seven pages. Attachments to the proposal, including a summary of the program's long-range plan, a program brochure, and a letter from a well-known community supporter, if not expressly forbidden, help give the proposal credibility. A list of the program's board members, an audited financial report, verification of the Internal Revenue Service 501(c) (3) status, and other pertinent information are usually required.

Visits to the funder, before or after proposal submission, are highly advisable. If the foundation or corporate giving office is staffed and permits visits, a presubmission visit or telephone call can help refine the proposal. Usually such visits are very brief, and beyond clarifying proposal guidelines, the grant seeker tries to obtain three critical pieces of information. The first is which of several possible projects would be of greater interest to the funder. The second is to determine the appropriate amount of the request. If the funder cannot cover the expenses of an entire project, the proposal must contain a description of how the rest of the needed funding will be obtained. The third piece of information that the corporate and foundation staff can provide is what other funding sources might be interested in the literacy effort. This information can be more valuable than a funded proposal, especially if the staff person recommends another contact, by name, and allows the use of his/her name in making the contact.

Postsubmission contact with decision makers may also be very helpful. The program director, together with a board member or a student, can then discuss the proposal in more detail and attest to the overall accomplishments of the organization.

If the program's first proposal is rejected, successful grant seekers try to find out why and when a second application can be made. Good proposals and programs may be rejected simply because there are far more requests for funding than there are funds; persistence pays off. In addition, grantors are often reluctant to be the first to fund an organization with no track record in corporate and foundation fund-raising, but when one grant is made, other funders tend to follow suit.

If funds are granted, ongoing contact with the funder is vital. Prompt written response to the grant comes first. Quarterly or semiannual reports on the use of funds are sometimes requested, but even if they are not, personal letters describing funded activities or general program progress are important. The funder should be placed on the mailing list for newsletters, annual reports, and other appropriate materials. An invitation to attend funded program events should be extended to the funder. Also, if permission is granted, the funder should be mentioned in press releases that describe the program's work.

Service Clubs and Churches. The key to receiving significant amounts of support from service clubs and churches is involving their constituents in the literacy program. Cultivating these groups begins with a meeting with its leadership, a presentation of the problem and the program needs, and a careful listening as to how the group perceives its role. Often the literacy program director is invited to make a presentation to the organization's general membership. Once general interest is established, service clubs may decide to take on a major, but often distinct and visible, role in literacy program development. Possibilities include fund-raising, board development, publicity, or funding of a special project, such as developing collections of literacy materials.

Noncommercial Funds

Churches or councils of churches can be approached for donations of space and leadership, for recruiting volunteers and students, and for financial support. Churches may provide major leadership and draw on their own volunteer resources to help establish a program or a satellite of an existing program. Most churches or service clubs, however, are not often prepared to provide ongoing financial support.

Literacy programs frequently receive small gifts, usually between several hundred and a thousand dollars, from churches and service clubs that do not participate directly in the program. These gifts often follow presentations to the general membership. The potential of these presentations can be maximized by soliciting specific kinds of volunteer assistance or gifts in-kind from individuals in the group and by asking the program's leadership for membership lists for follow-up solicitations at a later date.

Individual Donations and Special Events. Individual donors are a largely untapped resource for local literacy programs, partly because cultivating individual donors is time-consuming. In addition, literacy programs are pressed for funds to keep up with the rapid growth experienced in the 1980s and are encouraged by a positive fund-raising environment to pursue larger gifts from institutional sources. But building an individual donor base, however slow, is a good way to ensure a steady source of income, and it has many collateral benefits. Making donations to a cause in which the giver believes is not just evidence of commitment, but an increase in commitment is a benefit. Thus individual donors who are capable will be more willing to open doors to corporate and foundation funders and assist in other ways to support "their" program. Some individual donors may be approached for larger gifts or offered the opportunity to participate in deferred giving plans that will benefit local literacy efforts.

Most literacy programs begin building an individual donor base by compiling in-house lists of friends, members and former members, colleagues, vendors, membership lists of service clubs or churches to which individual presentations have been made, and people who call for information. Some programs also give students an opportunity to contribute. The most frequent means of soliciting individual gifts is through a warm, well-written letter from the program's director or a member of the board. These letters, mailed two or three times a year, are more effective than expensive, professional direct mail campaigns that reach cold contacts—people who do not already have some first-hand acquaintance with the program.

There are several other ways to solicit gifts from private individuals. Members may be offered the opportunity for several different levels of membership, part of which is dues, and part a donation. Wealthier friends of the program can be visited by a volunteer or board member and asked for a more sizable donation.

Benefit dinners and other special events, the admission to which includes a donation over and above the cost of the event itself, are another form of individual solicitation. A few literacy programs reap between $10,000 and $40,000 annually from such events. The necessary ingredient for success is to attract individuals capable of more sizable donations. The event's leadership, if only honorary, should be peers of those invited to attend, and the event should include a popular speaker.

Turning the solicitation of individuals into an annual process is the most effective approach to this form of fund-raising. The program's first experience with individual fund-raising will train the volunteers and staff who participate, and repeating a promising campaign in succeeding years becomes easier and more cost-effective.

Conclusion

The proportion of funds received from the previously described sources will depend on their availability within the community and on the program's ability to access them. Ideally the nonprofit literacy program should create as diverse a funding base as possible. The general rule of thumb is to depend on no more than 40 percent of income from any one source. The best strategy for avoiding overdependence on a single source of funding will include developing a core of committed volunteer leaders who are prepared to develop new sources of funding before accustomed sources shrink or disappear. This strategy is especially important for nonprofit literacy programs, which face a promising, but changeable, funding environment for the foreseeable future.

American Association for Fund-Raising Counsel Trust for Philanthropy. 1988. Giving USA: The
Annual Report on Philanthropy for the Year 1987.

Aramony, W. 1987. *The United Way: The next hundred years.* NY: Donald I. Fine, Inc.

Bauer, D. G. 1988. *The "how to" manual.* 2d ed. NY: American Council on Education/Macmillan
Publishing Company.

Business Council for Effective Literacy. 1989. Make it your business: A corporate fund-raising guide
for literacy programs. BCEL Bulletin no. 3 (January).

The foundation center source book profiles. 1987. 2 vols. NY: The Foundation Center.

The foundation directory. 1987–88. 11th ed. NY: The Foundation Center.

Laubach Literacy Action. 1989. 1987–1988 literacy program statistics. Unpublished raw data.

National data book of foundations: A comprehensive guide to grant making foundations. 1989. 13th
ed. 2 vols. NY: The Foundation Center.

The national directory of corporate charity. 1984. The regional young adult project. NY: The
Foundation Center.

Strengthening a Link with Corporations for Adult Education

Cecile M. Springer

> Corporate contributions! That's an oxymoron. A corporation can't just give away its assets. Profits are supposed to go to the stockholder, the investor! If the corporation gives anything away, gives any assets away, it should only be in its own self-interest. (A Stockholder N.d.)

In spite of attitudes similar to those of the previously mentioned stockholder, corporations have taken their place and assured responsibility for participating in the support of the nonprofit sector. Specifically, contributions from corporations have gone to fund religious, educational, and human service programs. The motivation for such funding of programs is complex. My purpose in this chapter will be to examine that complexity through corporations' giving patterns, their purposes for giving, and their priorities. Also, I will present criteria that corporations consider as they review requests for funding, highlight what should be included in a grant proposal, indicate how adult educators might position their request for funding, show what potential grantees should know in order to market themselves, and share tips that have made a difference for past grantees.

Trends

Philanthropy in the U.S. has grown enormously over the last three decades. In 1957, philanthropy in the U.S. totaled $9.26 billion; in 1967, $17 billion; in 1977, $36 billion, and in 1987, close to $94 billion. Over the same period of time, corporate philanthropy increased significantly. In 1957, corporate giving totaled $395 million. By 1987, corporate contributions totaled $4.5 billion.

Corporate giving has surged in recent years. Yet, as a percent of total giving in the U.S., corporations' proportion is about 5 percent. Individuals, through direct giving or through bequests, give close to 90 percent of the philanthropic dollar. Private foundations support total philanthropy annually, around 5 percent (Weber 1988).

The headlines on 1988 charitable donations in the U.S. declared that U.S. citizens gave over $100 billion for the first time! Over $104 billion was given, an increase of 1.8 percent, after adjustment for inflation. Specifically, individuals gave $86.7 billion, bequests contributed $6.8 billion, foundations $6.1 billion, and corporations $4.8 billion. Of the $104.4 billion contributed, religious entities received 46 percent, education and human services 10 percent each, and health 9 percent (*The chronicle of philanthropy* 1989).

While the good news for 1988 charitable giving was the fact that the $1 billion level had been exceeded, there was clear evidence that charitable giving was slowing down nationally. This slowing down of the rate of growth of giving may be due to a number of factors; for example, a slow down in the absolute increase in personal income, the precipitous rise and fall of the stock market over the past two years, and the impact of the 1986 Tax Reform Act. That Tax Reform Act served to cancel charitable deductions from those taxpayers who did not itemize their deductions. Hence, the impact of eliminating nonitemizers' charitable deductions has had a negative impact on their contributions that, in the past, have been used to fund nonprofit organizations' programs.

Companies contribute to worthy causes for three basic reasons. The first is altruism. It is good to give, and giving to appropriate organizations meets the social responsibility of a company in a community where it is located. Giving is part of what it means to be a good corporate citizen. The second is enlightened self-interest. Grants to community organizations are justified on the grounds that what benefits the community overall benefits a company in the long run. And the third reason for corporate giving is community expectation and pressure. The community wants corporate participation in community affairs. By providing visible and measurable financial support, the corporation is assured of community goodwill.

Giving Patterns

Corporations give to communities through a company foundation, direct giving, and noncash contributions. After World War II, the company foundation was the burgeoning approach. Company foundations were formed and funded by corporations in order to perform and financially support their charitable interest. That vehicle makes possible an asset base to meet the charitable goals of the corporation for future years, independent of the level of corporate earnings, which are known to fluctuate over time. Further, the foundation vehicle leads to better management of gift giving by focusing responsibility in specific individuals and trustees. The foundation also offers greater latitude for program development by facilitating long-range planning, by providing tax benefits for the corporation, and by serving as a specific source of goodwill.

Today, corporations are forming foundations at a decreasing rate while at the same time increasingly providing funds through direct giving. The corporation determines annually what proportion of pretax earnings will be set aside for charitable contributions. As a consequence, the actual amount of dollars budgeted for charities reflects the state of company earnings (up in good years and down in bad), which often leads nonprofits to face unpredictable fund-raising environments (*Survey of corporate contributions* 1989).

The Internal Revenue Service oversees these charitable giving activities. Under the Internal Revenue code, a company-sponsored foundation is an independent organization; it must render a report annually that describes the structure, activities, and grant-making outcomes; and similar to private foundations, it must use Form 990–PF, which becomes a public document.

Corporations electing to give grants directly through the corporation need not make their charitable activities public. Hence, it is often more difficult to research direct giving programs than corporate foundations.

A popular approach to giving is noncash gifts. Corporations are donating goods and services to supplement financial support. These contributions take the form of loaned personnel, the use of company facilities and equipment, and gifts of obsolete furnishings or even off-the-shelf nonmarketable products. Other contributions have included used trucks, electrical equipment, transformers, motors, lighting systems, and whole buildings.

Priorities

Corporate giving reflects corporate priorities. In any given year, the budget for corporate contributions and the projects and programs they support will vary. Whereas corporate priorities may be high in one year, they could be reduced in the second year. Currently, corporate giving is leveling off and is not increasing significantly from year to year as demonstrated since 1986. However, support for education remains strong, consuming 40 percent of the total cash contributions. Health and human services continue to slide from a high of close to 40 percent in 1978 to a low of 27 percent in 1987. Civic and community programs receive around 14 percent, while culture and arts receive 10 percent. "Other" category received the remainder. This "other" designation includes gifts of property and products. Industries with relatively large proportions of giving in this category are those in pharmaceutics, paper, food, beverage, and chemicals. These generalized percentages are given here to demonstrate the importance accorded educational support by the corporate community (*Survey of corporate contributions* 1989).

Educational support from corporations, in the past, have been first and foremost for colleges and universities. The disciplines supported reflect the dominant interest of the individual corporations. Pharmaceutical companies, for example, support medical schools, biological research, and graduate studies. Technical and manufacturing corporations target engineering, science, and economics.

Even though corporations overwhelmingly targeted colleges and universities in the past, they have changed. In today's heightened understanding that education is a total process, corporations have begun to expand their educational support base by funding not only higher education programs, but elementary, secondary, and preschool programs as well. Also, education-related organizations and educational research is being funded. The degree to which this expansion occurs in corporations often is a reflection of a corporation's senior management's understanding and sensitivity to community issues. Issues for these managers have gone from total concentration on profit making, productivity improvement, and financial returns to international competitiveness, preschool education, and community economic development among others. Consequently, it is important to know that corporations have acknowledged that educational programs are in need of their cash and noncash assistance.

Criteria

In order to receive a grant, nonprofit organizations are evaluated by corporations to determine if their goals and objectives and/or track record make them a suitable investment. To aid them in determining what organizations to fund, corporations, in the past, have responded to criteria generated by questions such as the following. (*a*) Is the project or program *relevant* to social needs designated by the company as high priority? (*b*) Does the program *concentrate* its energies and finances on a targeted population rather than dilute its resources? (*c*) Is the project or program *innovative* to the extent that it involves a creative and an unusual approach in meeting stated objectives? (*d*) Has the program been structured to achieve *control* and *accountability* for cost and the measurement and evaluation of benefits. (*e*) Will the company's support of the project or program achieve *visibility* with government, opinion leaders, or the general public in appropriate ways? (*f*) Does the project or program have *leadership* potential as a model program? (*g*) What *benefits* exist for maximizing the influence of the project or program by replication, producing institutional changes, making specific impacts? (*h*) Is the project or program likely to engender unacceptable *controversy* or *criticism* from employees or shareholders or any other interested parties? Does it present other *risks*? (*i*) Will *impacts* of the project or program be national or concentrated in cities where the company has operations or large numbers of employees? Through the application of these criteria, corporations have been able to use a more objective approach as the basis for winnowing requests made to them by large numbers of nonprofit organizations. At the same time, the goals and objectives of the corporate giving program has been implemented.

Grant Proposal

The grant proposal opens the door to making the link with a corporation a viable connection. The proposal is an investment document—presenting an opportunity to the corporation to become a partner in an endeavor. As an investment opportunity, a complete picture of the who, what, when, and where of your organization is imperative—presented in a way that the funder wants to read it in detail; able to get all the answers to all the questions needed to make an initial assessment, and strategically positioned so that the funder feels that the partnership is a real win-win relationship for the grantor and the grantee.

The proposal, as an investment document to meet informational and factual needs of the corporate funder, needs to include a cover letter, a table of contents, a project summary, a description of the project, a list of board members, a time schedule, the method of evaluation, a budget, an appendix with a tax-exempt status letter, budget details, an audited financial statement or summary, and a list of funding sources.

The grant proposal presents a picture of one's organization. A well-organized picture along with documentation that demonstrates success, visibility, self-confidence, impact, benefits to society, accountability, and focus that positions the organization to be an investment opportunity for the corporation with the potential of a true win-win relationship (*Corporate 500: The directory of corporate philanthropy* 1986).

Positioning

For the adult and continuing education specialist, the issue is how to position his/her field of interest in order to strengthen the links to corporations.

Strengthened links might increase a corporation's commitment to funding for educational programs. However, one needs to know that corporate funders tend to support specific categories and interests. These interests are defined to meet the corporation's specific needs. These needs are designed to impact in measurable ways the interests of the corporation and to increasingly bring visibility to its charitable actions.

Programs that are funded by a corporation are often measured to determine benefits to the community where it has a major presence and to determine benefits for its business. Therefore, it is necessary to seriously consider these benefits as well as the location of a corporation, its specific business sector, the people in the corporation, the specific program interest, and its funding areas before contacting it for funding.

Potential Grantees

Since corporations selectively fund those programs that promote and support their interest in communities, it behooves the potential grantee to learn as much as possible about the corporation's business interests, geographic areas, officers, contributions committee and trustees, and grants that they have awarded. Such knowledge can be used to assist in the structuring of a program proposal designed for submission to corporations for funding.

The potential grantee should know that the contributions officer in a corporation is the person who receives all requests for funding. She/he is also the most knowledgeable about how and what the individual corporation wants to fund. Other influencers in the process of approving funding of projects are clearly the trustees of the corporate foundation, the members of the contributions committee, the chief executive officer of the corporation, and the members of the top management team. Potential grantees need to know who these decision makers are and, then, get to know them. For example, find out if they are donors to local organizations. Also, find out what specified field of endeavor interests them. Next, actions to initiate personal connections might be established as mentioned in the following paragraphs.

First, program proposals should be positioned to reflect knowledge about the grantor. Specifically, interest in seeking funding for the education program should parallel the corporation's articulated priorities and commitments. Also, a demonstration that their subject area, location interests, targeted population groups, and level of giving is understood by the potential grantee should be evident (*Foundation fundamentals: A guide for grant seekers* 1986).

A second step for those seeking funding is to request a person-to-person interview with a corporate decision maker. Generally, in interviews the following questions will be asked.

1. What is the mission of your organization?
2. What has been your total budget over the past five to ten years? What is your budget for this year? Next year? What are the sources of funding by sector (private foundations, corporations, government)?
3. What successes, impact, and/or accomplishments has your organization achieved in the recent past?

4. What are your specific program projects?
5. What are the strengths and weaknesses of your program?
6. Who is the staff for this project?
7. Who are the customers? What are the products?
8. Do you prepare an annual report and/or an annual audited financial statement?
9. What is your competition?
10. What do you see as the future for your program?
11. Why did you select this corporation to seek funding?
12. Who do you know in this corporation that may serve as an advocate of your organization and recommend funding?
13. How much would you be seeking from this corporation? What other sources of funding would you tap for this project? What would you do if total funding could not be secured?

The purpose of the person-to-person interview and the posing of questions is for both organizations to get to know each other. Potential grantees should be prepared to both answer and ask questions. The outcome from such interviews is better knowledge of both organizations—a potential investment organization for the corporation, a potential grant for the nonprofit, and future relations.

Tips

Corporations hire people with the ability to work efficiently and effectively. The assumption in the recruitment of workers is that they have the skills to be successful workers. As the technological demands of society increase and sophisticated technology takes over the workplace across the employee spectrum, adult and continuing education fields must adopt terminology that the employer wants to hear.

The components of this world of adult and continuing education must be articulated so that the employer in corporations understands what is being taught today—competitive skills, enhanced capabilities to work and meet employers expectations, advanced courses in math and finance, robotic repair technology, government affairs, and so on. The cobwebs of corporate minds hear the words *adult and continuing education* but feel that the emphasis is on high school completion, general education degrees, trade school skills, and introductory programs. What they need to hear is that they can help prepare individuals for the technologies of the future.

I recommend strongly that potential grantees get to know people who are decision makers in corporations; get to know how they think; and use their vocabulary, for example, *bottom line, profitable ventures, measurable outcomes, productivity improvement, total quality.*

Another recommendation is that potential grantees must view their organization's programs strategically and that tactics for operating the program be identified, evaluated, and carried out on a timely basis. A strategic plan developed by organizations that demonstrates marketing ability, understands the environment, structures decision making, and is forward thinking provides some assurance that the organization will endure long enough for the corporation to place an investment in it.

Strengthening the links with corporations is a challenge, particularly if the connections have not been made in the past. The challenge is to forge links that result in partnerships now and for the coming years.

References

The chronicle of philanthropy. 1989. Vol. 1, no. 17. (13 June). Washington, DC.

Corporate 500: The directory of corporate philanthropy. 1986. 5th ed. San Francisco, CA: Public Management Institute.

Foundation fundamentals: A guide for grant seekers. 1986. 3d. ed. NY: The Foundation Center.

Survey of corporate contributions. 1989. Research Report no. 924. NY: The Conference Board.

Weber, N., ed. 1988. *Giving USA: The annual report on philanthropy for the year 1987.* NY: American Association of Fund-Raising Counsel Trust for Philanthropy (AAFRC).

Evaluating Adult Literacy Programs

Dolores M. Harris

A Nation at Risk (The National Commission . . . 1983) indicated that the U.S. was producing students whose achievement was inferior to that of students in other countries. The inferior position in education, it was assumed, would lead to the nation's inability to compete in the world's marketplace. Hence, educators were faced with the responsibility for assuming a new accountability for what they were doing in the schools. There was a new impetus for measuring the progress of students and pressure to show results that indicated that U.S. students were performing on a comparable level with students of other countries, particularly those countries who seemed to be pulling ahead in the competitive world marketplace.

In the late 1950s, Sputnik served to galvanize the U.S. into new places in the knowledge and learning arena. In the 1960s the civil rights movement demanded that previously disenfranchised people be afforded an opportunity to more fully participate in the affairs of the U.S. One of the results of this great movement toward equality for all was the call for new endeavors in education. Head Start was conceived to give children of formerly disenfranchised people the background knowledge and experience that would enable them to participate successfully in school offerings. During that same time period, there was the realization that the adults in the disenfranchised group required educational programs that would help them *catch up* and overcome the effects of early deprivation, if they were to fully participate in the great society.

The efforts to educate adults in the U.S. were not a completely new phenomenon. In previous decades, there had been adult education programs designed and implemented to serve the needs of immigrants who had to develop new skills to cope with the language and customs of their newly adopted homeland. However, in the 1960s, there were some differences in the approach used to evaluate the success of the efforts of adult education programs offered for immigrants and those offered for native U.S. citizens. In general, success for the immigrants was measured in terms of their personal assessment of their ability to speak the new language. The success of native U.S. adult students was measured in quite a different way. Initially, there was a great emphasis upon sheer numbers. The success of a program was measured, in large part, by the size of the enrollment, thereby seeming to assure that the return for the investment reflected an economically defensible cost per student. Then, similar to their counterparts who had the responsibility for educating children, adult educators were asked to demonstrate the effectiveness of their programs in terms of some level of achievement. Specifically they were required to show achievement in relation to grade levels mastered in the basic skills, primarily reading and mathematics. Although there was much discussion about the adult's need to master the life-coping skills, there was little effort to measure progress in any but the basic skills.

While the process of evaluation has been recognized as an imperfect system, little has been achieved, thus far, to remove those imperfections. The concern is critical. As the U.S. moves toward increased educational testing, accountability will continue to be a prominent issue for adult educators. Although educators are held accountable, other unmeasured factors play a role in determining student success. Not the least of these is the amount of time adult students can, or will, devote to their studies. A conflict arises, for example, when other responsibilities take precedence over their academic assignments. The adult student, like the adult educator, is frequently forced to compete with employment, parenting, child care, and/or other life tasks.

Time factors into the accountability formula yet in another way. Educators engaged in literacy efforts may, in fact, have another occupation as their primary responsibility, being employed only in the adult education enterprise on a part-time basis. As in the case of the student, their primary responsibility takes priority over the time they can legitimately devote to the adult student.

Even for those who are engaged in adult education efforts on a full-time basis, the lack of time may be a factor in their lives. Apps (1976) says that adult educators are often so busy *keeping up* with what they have to do that they have little time to consider the foundations for decisions and actions.

In countries that still essentially believe that education is for the young and education should be delivered as cheaply as possible, adult educators are constantly faced with the need to validate their efforts in their search for resources that are often scarce for all educational projects. It is the purpose of this chapter to provide adult educators with suggestions for using the evaluation process to produce results that will effectively defend and validate their programs. The discussion will examine past and present practices in the evaluation of social programs. It will also consider some current trends and present new, or a new way of looking at, methods of educational evaluation that may be useful for all adult educators.

Cronbach and Associates (1980) defined evaluation as the systematic examination of events occurring in, and consequent on, a contemporary program. They also stated that evaluation is an examination conducted to assist in improving the program and other programs having the same general purpose. They defined program as a standing arrangement that provides for a social service. For purposes of this discussion, the definition formulated by Cronbach et al. will be used as the framework for consideration of program evaluation in adult literacy education.

I find it necessary, at this time, to also include a definition for adult literacy. The usual connotations associated with adult literacy speak to the acquisition of basic skills in reading, writing, and arithmetic. I will broaden that definition to include the notion of literacy as a more encompassing term. In this time of rapidly advancing technology, constant change, and a continuing explosion of knowledge, the adult is faced with the task of becoming literate in new areas throughout a lifetime. Terms like *computer literacy, historical literacy,* and *cultural literacy* appear frequently in today's literature and should be included in a definition of adult literacy.

Programs delivering basic skills, funded as they are likely to be from public monies, may be more pressured than other programs to validate the worth of their efforts. Therefore, while this chapter focuses primarily on the evaluation process as it relates to basic skills programs, those readers responsible for a more expanded version of adult education may glean some ideas that will be useful for their programs.

According to Franklin and Thrasher (1976), most writers agree that program **Evaluation Models** evaluation as a specialized function is largely a post-World War II emergence, thereby making its history relatively brief. Also, they stated that the impetus for program evaluation came from the demand for accountability to the public, a public that was no longer willing to accept notions of the "American dream" and "the good life" as sufficient rationale and justification for public programs designed to reach this dream or actualize this life.

Program evaluators have often turned to the private sector, particularly business, and attempted to apply the business model to the evaluation of social programs. However, the transition of this model from business to education was fraught with danger. The criteria for success in business, that is, increased productivity, lower costs of production, higher profits, are not directly transferable to social programs where the products are people and human achievement instead of the production of things.

The attempt to apply the business model often resulted in dissonance between the program managers and the evaluators because the managers felt that the consideration of those measurable variables in isolation produced an inaccurate perception of the real results of the efforts.

Abandoning the business model as inappropriate, some evaluators turned to academia models as a source for the data that managers sought. But this too was unsatisfactory, for the problems associated with the academic approach were many. The academic evaluators were often totally unaware of the reality-based decisions that managers had to make and the nature of the operation of less-than-ideal organizations that often functioned in very untypical ways. Academicians also brought with them the almost arrogant assurance that their methodologies were correct and their techniques were unquestionably powerful and so looked askance at alterations to their modes.

Any evaluation model that will yield the results adult educators seek must consider the dynamic nature of many adult education programs. Often, program managers are forced to assume the role of evaluator. They are required to make on-the-spot decisions about what practices and procedures should be discarded or how best to allocate resources or what results are to be reported in order to assure survival of the organization. Such spontaneous decisions tend to change the nature of the program organization. Variables that are built into a static evaluation plan are either altered, replaced, or even eliminated, a condition that contributes to dissonance between manager and program evaluators.

Adult education managers have yet another concern in evaluating their programs, this from the perspective of politics, namely—how will the results be used? Managers have serious reservations about such issues as who controls the evaluation process; to what use will the results be put; how will the findings impact upon the continued functioning to the organization; and how will the clients or customers be affected.

Practical Applications for Examination

As a graduate student who was involved in the field of adult education as both a program manager and program evaluator, I was guided to a great extent by the views expressed by Weiss (1971). Weiss opined that the purpose of evaluation research is to provide answers to practical questions raised by decision makers. She felt that decision makers wanted to know whether the program should be continued, extended, replicated at other sites, etc. If the program was found to be only partly effective, then the evaluation was expected to identify those aspects that needed to be changed and make recommendations that would lead to improvement. She identified five basic stages of traditional evaluation research: identification of the goals of the program; translation of the goals into measurable indicators of goal achievement; collection of data on the indicators for those who have been exposed to the program; collection of similar data on an equivalent group, known as the control group that had not been exposed to the program; and comparison of the data on program participants and controls of goal criteria.

Weiss indicated that experimental design has long been considered the ideal for evaluation. She described a process in which people in a program were randomly assigned either to the experimental group that received special treatment or to the control group that received a placebo program, standard service, or no program at all. Relevant measures were taken before and after the treatment. The objective was to determine whether the experimental group showed significantly greater positive change than the control group as a result of the program.

There were some major problems with this design into which other program managers, program evaluators, and myself had. The first was the practical problem that arose because it was impossible for us to assign clients to experimental and control groups. Therefore, we often made an extrapolation to groups that were not true control groups to validate claims to effectiveness. For instance, if we were lucky enough to stay in contact with clients for a sufficient period of time to determine that our intervention may have made a change in their lives, we had no true control groups for comparison. Instead, claims of success were "proven" on the basis that the adult student exhibited a higher level of performance than was expected for others in his/her socioeconomic class.

On the political front were the issues of locus of control, what was to be evaluated, and how the evaluation results were to be used. In adult literacy programs, the funders often set the tenor of evaluation designs. While programs strove for lofty aims such as helping adults learn coping or life skills, become better parents, become more productive citizens, etc., the actual indicators of program success were apt to be very different. The number of students enrolled in the program was often the measurement for success because of the need to prove cost-effectiveness. Cost-benefit analysis consisted of dividing the cost of the program by the number of students and consequently basing claims to success on the number of students served through the expenditure of the funding agency.

Assessment then evolved into attempts to assess the actual progress that adult students had made while enrolled in the program. Many adult educators made a valiant effort to design and implement programs that addressed those lofty goals expressed in the preceding paragraph. However, because the locus of control was with the funding agency, the only results that were considered in many cases were the scores achieved on standardized tests. To exacerbate the problem, the test results chosen for reporting were often restricted to reading and arithmetic.

Consequently, many adult educators were unable to avoid the goal trap discussed by Deutsch (1976). Deutsch cites a number of sources to make his point that organizations are rarely what they pretend to be. He says that:

> The distinction between the formal and informal or the stated and the real is made in various ways, but it is always made. Organizational theory suggests that the structure, the processes, and the goals of any organization must be assumed to vary in fact from their descriptions. (Pp. 249–50)

Deutsch stated that the likelihood of discrepancy between formal goals and actual goals is central to a discussion of program evaluation. Accountability demands that for a proposed program to be funded, it must state clearly what it intends to do, how it will do it, and what resources are needed. In adult literacy programs, program managers often express the goals that funding agencies require and state that they will achieve the goals with the allocated resources. One of the major problems that confronts the program managers lies in the fact that resource allocation is often dictated on the basis of some formula and not a true consideration of what actual resources are needed to attain the goals demanded by the funder. Consequently, the program managers may truly hope to accomplish the stated goals but find that they have overestimated what can be achieved.

At other times, the adult educator becomes disenchanted because the rhetoric of the agency is not reflected in the goals that the program is forced to set in order to get a proposal funded. Then there is the trap that becomes evident when the adult educator is unable to articulate achievement of success in terms that the funding agency can accept. For example, if the funder demands that success be validated on the basis of test scores only, how can the educator prove that when an illiterate adult learns such skills as counting the correct change in a shopping situation or reading well enough to order food from a menu; but earn low test scores due to test anxiety, that the skills were learned in an adult literacy program.

Deutsch also states that both programmer and evaluator can become victims of the goal trap. Evaluators as well as agencies are frequently so insistent that goals be measurable that they force the program director into stating goals that are not the true goals of the program. The stated and actual goals of the program may be totally different so that, in the words of Weiss (1971, 138), ". . . it is possible that the evaluation is attributing the effects (or 'no effects') to a phantom program."

Weiss (1973) states that the reason evaluations are often disregarded is that they only address official goals. It might be useful to assess other kinds of goals if the results are to be taken seriously by decision makers. I concur with Weiss who points out that adult educators need to be able to influence decision makers so that evaluation efforts can be made more viable.

Considerations for Future Evaluation

Smith (1981), in the introduction to a series of works on evaluation, states that as the need and concern for evaluation continue to grow in education and other areas of social programming, questions about evaluation's quality and usefulness will continue to be raised. Under Smith's direction, a project at Northwest Regional Educational Laboratory attempted to develop new methods or alternatives of educational evaluation through the adaptation of metaphorical paradigms and techniques from other disciplines.

Smith uses the literature to support his contentions that both traditionalists and revisionists acknowledge the need for exploring new alternatives in evaluation. He further states that there is evidence to suggest that evaluation practitioners are also looking for other ways to approach their work. Of particular interest to the adult literacy educator is Smith's report on the findings of studies conducted to determine the attitudes toward, use of, and expressed needs for changing evaluation among various educational settings. Among others, he cited Caulley and Smith who asked twenty-five state departments of education about the adequacy of their evaluation methods. Virtually half of the respondents indicated that there were evaluations for which they had inadequate methods. Sixty percent reported that there were information needs of decision makers for which they did not have sufficient methods. It should be noted that eleven of the twenty-five states reported that they were occasionally required to use methods that they deemed to be unsuitable, and 72 percent indicated that they would like to try new evaluation methods. Methods suggested were goal-free and self-evaluation procedures.

Other cited studies, in Smith's presentation, helped develop the conclusion that many practitioners at state and local educational levels have indicated a need for alternative evaluation methods, but research that demonstrates the effectiveness of these methods must accompany the program's design.

In a discussion of one plan, Guba and Lincoln (1981) offer investigative journalism as a metaphoric paradigm. They point to the fact that there are certain similarities between investigative journalism and educational evaluation, which suggest that it may be useful to use the former discipline as a metaphor for the latter. Further, both are processes of inquiry; they utilize many standard data collection and analysis techniques, that is, interview, observation, records analysis; they take place in a naturalistic setting, that is, the context in which the entity is being evaluated on the one hand or being investigated, on the other hand; and they depend heavily on the interaction of an inquirer-evaluator or reporter with people so that the nature of the outcome is heavily influenced by the nature of that interaction.

Guba and Lincoln speak to salient points of difference between the two disciplines. They include a difference in purpose—the evaluator seeks to establish the worth or merit of some entity while the investigative reporter wishes to expose a situation or condition inimical to the public interest; a difference in the degree of secrecy—the evaluator is nearly always a public figure while the reporter maintains an environment of secrecy; differences in assumptions one can make about cooperation or conflict with the person with whom one deals; differences in the degree to which they rely on available versus newly generated information—the reporter relies heavily on traces of events or activities that are past while the evaluator is more likely to use de novo information as the basis for his inquiry; differences in criteria by which they will judge their work—the investigative reporter uses criteria such as warrantability and defensibility while the evaluator is concerned with reliability and validity and practical considerations such as timeliness and relevance.

Even when differences are considered, there are areas of similarities. Although they differ in purpose, both purposes have a consumer advocacy flavor. While criteria for judging their work may be different, both entities are concerned about the factualness of their reports and about the cost-effectiveness of their operation.

In further explication of their rationale for using investigative journalism disciplines to develop a metaphor for educational evaluation, Guba and Lincoln stated that there should be sufficient ground (elements in common) and sufficient tension (differences in elements between principal subject and metaphoric term) to make the metaphor useful for providing new perspectives and insights.

Presented in the following paragraphs are some other parallels between evaluation and investigation and investigative journalism, which Guba and Lincoln judged to be worthy of exploration.

Investigative Parallels. While the evaluator does not confront such extreme cases as the reporter may encounter in a conflict situation with respect to the target of the investigation, it would be naive of the evaluator to believe that the cooperation of all who are involved in an evaluation can be counted upon. If the investigative reporter seeks the reform of conditions so that the public interest is better served, then the investigative evaluator may also seek the reform of conditions so that the adult literacy student and society are better served. The evaluator may find an investigative posture more realistic and useful than a cooperative one.

Legal Parallels. The evaluator, as well as the investigative reporter, needs to show that what was printed or said is true. Accountability judgments are often based on information called by the evaluator. If decisions are made that are perceived by some as personal or programmatically harmful or if a program is approved by an evaluator and subsequently fails, can the evaluator be held accountable? Students at various levels are already bringing suit to seek restitution for some perceived or real damages suffered in the educational arena. It is not too unrealistic to think that evaluators could be sued for damages to a participant in the evaluation process.

With a few exceptions, freedom of information laws are intended to guarantee citizen access to information collected as part of any public process. On the one hand, the evaluator may access the information he needs because it was produced as part of an activity paid for with public funds. On the other hand, the evaluator's information may also be accessed by others under the same laws. Both evaluators and investigative reporters need to maintain files that could be subject to scrutiny under suit.

The U.S. Supreme Court has upheld some lower court decisions requiring reporters to disclose their sources. Although evaluators' information is usually considered to be public, it should be noted that evaluators often promise anonymity to a respondent in a questionnaire or interview situation. Can the evaluator really guarantee the maintenance of that anonymity any more than some investigative reporters have been able to protect the guarantee?

Objectivity/Fairness Parallels. Objectivity assumes a single reality to which the story or the evaluation must be isomorphic. It is also assumed that a person can deal with an object (or another person) in a nonreactive and noninteractive way. Journalists are coming to realize that objectivity cannot really be attained. If fairness is substituted for objectivity, it permits the reporter to deal with multiple truths; it provides for consideration of a criterion that is adversarial in nature, that is, both sides of the case can be reported; it assumes that the subject's reaction to the reporter and the interaction between them affects the determination of what the reporter perceives; and it is a relative criterion measured by balance rather than by isomorphism in enduring truth. Evaluators may be well advised to begin admitting that complete objectivity is unattainable and begin working out their own standards of fairness.

Operational Parallels—The Key Interview. Both the investigative reporter and the educational evaluator are often faced with the uncooperative subject. Both may also need to test a report, an allegation, or a claim with the person(s) it most directly affects. Therefore, the evaluator will need to test his report with various subjects for reasons similar to those of the reporter, that is, to check on credibility, solicit reactions, and obtain further details that may clarify and extenuate. The evaluator might be wise to learn the techniques that the reporter uses in the key interview.

Operational Files—Indexes, Chronologies, and Summaries. The investigative reporter develops files for his/her cases that become an important permanent record, serve as the basis for the story that is written, and may serve as invaluable backup in case of legal action. The filing system includes the development of chronologies, cross-referencing, and summaries of subjects' characteristics and life-styles. The process of keeping careful files is obviously useful for the evaluator, especially if the evaluation process is intended to monitor or to track program transactions.

Operational Parallels—Reporting. Guba and Lincoln (1981) indicate that in order for investigative reporters to have a good story, they must, of course, possess the qualities of good writing. They must also provide answers to some central questions: What am I trying to prove? Who is the primary audience for the story? Why will my primary audience care? Seemingly, most evaluators do not ask themselves the questions that the reporters ask of themselves. Written reports of evaluators, then, seem to fit some kind of reconstructed logic of what the process entails, or the reports try to emulate the model of scientific reporting rather than to communicate to some audience a description and judgment of an entity in which they have a stake.

This abbreviated discussion provides some information on the comparison between the role of the investigative reporter and that of the adult literacy educator. It is important to note that Smith (1981) explored eight disciplines to use as metaphors for evaluation of adult education programs. Readers interested in studying the topic further are directed to Smith's work, in which other such comparisons are developed.

Recommendations

The literature that identifies metaphor paradigms for education evaluation must be investigated by adult literacy educators as a source for new approaches to evaluation. Old approaches that sought to fit adult educators into a mold dictated by an imperfect system of evaluation (supposedly built upon a scientific model) must be reexamined to determine what must be discarded and what new approaches need to be considered.

Adult educators should not adopt what seems to be new practices that are just as inappropriate as the old. The National Assessment of Educational Progress (NAEP) might seem to hold some promise, but adult educators must remember that the NAEP was designed for students in traditional school settings and that it was designed to measure trends, a measurement that might not be useful for adult literacy programs. In addition, Psacharopoulos (1987) states there are two problems with trend studies such as NAEP.

> First, there are the problems of meaningfulness where the curriculum of the schools is changing and new curricular emphases are evolving . . . . A second set of problems is concerned with the statistical procedures that are employed to scale a constantly changing sample of test items to obtain a reliable measurement of educational achievement. (P. 372)

For persons working in adult literacy programs, the need to establish new paradigms and new perspectives in evaluation is urgent. Many traditional approaches do not work for the adult student enrolled in basic education classes. Therefore, it is particularly appropriate for adult educators to provide the leadership for looking at evaluation in a different way. The bugaboos attendant upon the use of the traditional approaches have only served, in many cases, to validate the notion that basic skills is not an efficient expenditure of resources. Actual student progress must be validated in order to acquire a fair share of the resources available.

Adult educators must become familiar with evaluation practices and provide input into the process instead of just accepting the evaluation standards imposed by funding sources. They must acquire the skills to determine the approach, or approaches, to be used. Then they must be sure that the results of evaluations are disseminated in a manner that impacts on the decision makers. Anderson and Ball (1978) suggested that evaluations of educational and human service programs are like seed sown in thin soil or among thorns. When evaluation results are undisseminated or confined to a select few, such is of little value. Adult educators must assure that evaluation results influence program decisions and win support from funding agencies and the public.

Numerous examples of persons who could not be accurately and adequately judged by the traditional and experimental design approaches to evaluation can be found in the experiences of adult literacy educators. As long as people live in a society that Kushner (1990) says values the making of money more than the shaping of souls and working with numbers is more valuable than working with human beings, the adult literacy educator is faced with an awesome task, that of proving his/her worth to educate illiterate adults.

References

Anderson, S. B., and S. Ball. 1978. *The profession and practice of program evaluation.* San Francisco: Jossey-Bass Publishers.

Apps, J. W. 1976. A foundation for action. In C. Klevins, ed., *Materials and methods in adult and continuing education.* NY: Klevins Publications, Inc.

Cronbach, L. J., and Associates. 1980. *Toward reform of program evaluation.* San Francisco: Jossey-Bass Publishers, Inc.

Deutsch, I. 1976. Toward avoiding the goal-trap in evaluation research. In C. C. Abt, ed., *The evaluation of social programs,* 249–65. Beverly Hills: Sage Publication, Inc.

Franklin, J. L., and J. H. Thrasher. 1976. *An introduction to program evaluation.* NY: John Wiley & Sons.

Guba, E. G., and Y. S. Lincoln. 1981. *Effective evaluation.* San Francisco: Jossey-Bass Publishers, Inc.

Kushner, H. S. 1990. Make more family time. *Redbook,* 92–93.

Psacharopoulos, G. 1987. *Economics of education research and studies.* Oxford, England: Pergamon Press.

Smith, N. L., ed. 1981. *Metaphors for evaluation: Sources of new methods.* Beverly Hills: Sage Publications, Inc.

The National Commission of Excellence in Education. 1983. *A nation at risk: The imperative for educational reform.* Sixty-five page report. Washington, DC: Government Printing Office.

Weiss, C. H. 1971. Utilization of evaluation: Toward comparative study. In F. Caro., ed., *Readings in evaluation research,* 136–42. NY: Russell Sage Foundation.

Weiss, C. H. 1973. Where politics and evaluation research meet. *Evaluation* 1:37–45.